Human Sexuality

THIRD BRIEF EDITION

Human Sexuality

THIRD BRIEF EDITION

Stephen P. McCary
Private Practice, Houston, Texas
University of Houston

James Leslie McCary
(1919–1978)

Wadsworth Publishing Company
Belmont, California
A Division of Wadsworth, Inc.

Health Editor: Bob Podstepny
Production Editor: Deborah M. Oren
Managing Designer: Cynthia Bassett
Designer: Louis Neiheisel
Copy Editor: Joan Pendleton
Cover: Stephen Rapley

Chapter-Opening Photo Credits
Chapter 1 United Press International, Inc.
Chapter 2 Erika Stone
Chapter 3 Norwegian Information Service
Chapter 4 German Information Center
Chapter 5 Erika Stone
Chapter 6 Erika Stone
Chapter 7 Edward Lettau/Photo Researchers, Inc.
Chapter 8 Charles Gatewood Photography
Chapter 9 Richard Frieman/Photo Researchers, Inc.
Chapter 10 Ginger Chih
Chapter 11 Randy Matusow
Chapter 12 Charles Gatewood Photography
Chapter 13 Michael Hanulak/Photo Researchers, Inc.
Chapter 14 Robert Levin/Black Star
Chapter 15 Monkmeyer Press Photo Service

Printed in the United States of America

9 10

ISBN 0-534-02980-9

Library of Congress Cataloging in Publication Data

McCary, Stephen P.
   Human sexuality.

   Rev. ed. of: Human sexuality / James Leslie McCary.
   Bibliography: p.
   Includes index.
   1. Sex. 2. Hygiene, Sexual. 3. Sexual intercourse.
4. Human reproduction. I. McCary, James Leslie.
II. McCary, James Leslie. Human sexuality. III. Title.
HQ12.M4 1984   613.9'5   83-14779
ISBN 0-534-02980-9

BRIEF CONTENTS

CHAPTER 1 Sex and Today's Society _____ 2

CHAPTER 2 The Biochemistry of Sex _____ 20

CHAPTER 3 The Male Sexual System _____ 34

CHAPTER 4 The Female Sexual System _____ 48

CHAPTER 5 The Creation of New Life _____ 68

CHAPTER 6 Birth Control _____ 90

CHAPTER 7 Intimacy and Love _____ 114

CHAPTER 8 Sexual Expression _____ 132

CHAPTER 9 Orgasm _____ 158

CHAPTER 10 Sexuality throughout
the Life Cycle _____ 174

CHAPTER 11 Sexual Attitudes and Behavior 192

CHAPTER 12 Sexual Variance _____ 216

CHAPTER 13 Homosexuality _____ 244

CHAPTER 14 Sexual Dysfunctions _____ 262

CHAPTER 15 Sexual Diseases and Disorders 286

GLOSSARY _____ 312
REFERENCES _____ 322
INDEX _____ 336

CONTENTS

Preface   xiii

CHAPTER 1 Sex and Today's Society ————2
TRUE OR FALSE?   2
A Heritage of Confusion   5
"Protecting" Children from Sex   5
Religion, Sex, and Marriage   7
Breaking the Bonds of Sexual Fascism   9
Facts—And Arguments—About Sex Education   9
BOX: *What I Would Tell My Daughter and Son about Premarital Sex*   12
BOX: *What My Father Told Me about Sex*   14
A Suggested Approach to Sex Education   16
Making Responsible Sexual Decisions   17
Summary   18
TRUE OR FALSE: THE FACTS   18
Suggested Reading   19

CHAPTER 2 The Biochemistry of Sex ————20
TRUE OR FALSE?   20
Early Development of the Male and Female Genitalia   22
Development of the Internal Genitalia   23
Development of the External Genitalia   23
The Physical Changes of Pubescence   27
Sexual Development in Pubescent Girls   27
Sexual Development in Pubescent Boys   29
Glands and Hormones   30
BOX: *The Quest for Sexual Vitality*   32
Summary   32
TRUE OR FALSE: THE FACTS   33
Suggested Reading   33

∅ CHAPTER 3   The Male Sexual System _____ 34
TRUE OR FALSE?   34
The Male Genitalia   36
BOX: *How Much Does Size Matter?*   40
BOX: *The Myth of* Penis Captivus   41
Erection   42
Ejaculation   44
Physiosexual Changes in the Aging Man   44
Summary   45
TRUE OR FALSE: THE FACTS   46
Suggested Reading   46

∅ CHAPTER 4   The Female Sexual System _____ 48
TRUE OR FALSE?   48
The Female Genitalia   50
BOX: *The G Spot: Fact or Fiction?*   54
Menstruation   58
BOX: *Menstruation Myths*   62
Physiosexual Changes in the Aging Woman   62
The Climacteric or Menopause   63
Summary   64
TRUE OR FALSE: THE FACTS   65
Suggested Reading   65

∅ CHAPTER 5   The Creation of New Life _____ 68
TRUE OR FALSE?   68
The Genetics of Conception   70
BOX: *Genetic Technology*   71
Factors Affecting Fertility   72
BOX: *Artificial Insemination—Old and New*   73
Signs of and Tests for Pregnancy   73
The Pregnant Woman   74
Activities during Pregnancy   74
Consumption of Drugs during Pregnancy   75
Exposure to Infectious Disease during Pregnancy   76
Disorders and Disease States of Pregnancy   76
Prenatal Development   77
Birth   80
Lactation   83
The New Childbirth   83
Myths about Conception and Childbirth   84
Summary   86
TRUE OR FALSE: THE FACTS   87
Suggested Reading   88

CHAPTER 6 Birth Control _____ 90

TRUE OR FALSE?   90
BOX: *A Historical Perspective on Birth Control*   93
Abstinence   94
Sterilization   94
Methods of Sterilization in Women   94
Methods of Sterilization in Men   96
Abortion   98
BOX: *Viewpoints on Abortion*   99
Methods of Inducing Abortion   100
Contraception   102
Contraceptives Available Only with a Doctor's Prescription   103
Contraceptives Available without a Doctor's Prescription   107
Other Methods of Birth Prevention   108
Birth Control in the Future   109
Summary   110
TRUE OR FALSE: THE FACTS   111
Suggested Reading   112

CHAPTER 7 Intimacy and Love _____ 114

TRUE OR FALSE?   114
What Is Intimacy?   116
Avoidance of Intimacy   118
The Game Called Courtship   119
What Is Love?   120
Falling in Love   121
Kinds of Love   122
Romantic Love   123
Maintaining Love and Intimacy   124
BOX: *Building Marital Communication Skills*   125
Love and Sex   127
Summary   128
TRUE OR FALSE: THE FACTS   129
Suggested Reading   130

CHAPTER 8 Sexual Expression _____ 132
TRUE OR FALSE?   132
BOX: *Sexual Complaints*   135
Techniques of Sexual Arousal   135
Pace and Style   137
The Value of Fantasy   137
BOX: *Fantasies*   138
The Erogenous Zones   139
Developing One's Sexuality   139
BOX: *Sexuality's "Dark Ages"*   140
Forms of Heterosexual Arousal   141
Oral Sex   143
Anal Sex   144
Positions in Sexual Intercourse   144
Sexuality and Disability   150
Aphrodisiacs and Anaphrodisiacs   150
Summary   155
TRUE OR FALSE: THE FACTS   156
Suggested Reading   157

CHAPTER 9 Orgasm _____ 158
TRUE OR FALSE?   158
BOX: *What Does an Orgasm Feel Like?*   161
BOX: *The Difference between Vaginal and Clitoral Orgasms*   162
The Excitement Phase   162
The Plateau Phase   166
The Orgasmic Phase   168
The Resolution Phase   169
The Question of Simultaneous Orgasms   170
Summary   172
TRUE OR FALSE: THE FACTS   172
Suggested Reading   173

CHAPTER 10 Sexuality throughout the Life Cycle _____ 174

TRUE OR FALSE?   174
Infancy and Early Childhood (Birth to Five Years)   176
Forms of Sexual and Sensual Expression   177
Awareness of Roles Based on Gender   177
BOX: *The Seeds of Androgyny*   179
Latency: Myth or Fact? (Six to Twelve Years)   180
Sexual Behavior   180
Growing Heterosocial Interests   181
Adolescence (Thirteen to Nineteen Years)   181
The Adolescent: Child or Adult?   181
Sexual Behavior   183
BOX: *Remembering First Sexual Experiences*   184
Adult Development   184
Young Adulthood   185
Marital and Sexual Adjustment   185
Transitions in Middle Age   186
Late Adulthood   187
Summary   189
TRUE OR FALSE: THE FACTS   190
Suggested Reading   191

CHAPTER 11 Sexual Attitudes and Behavior   192

TRUE OR FALSE?   192
A Climate of Attitudinal Conflict and Change   195
BOX: *The Sexual Revolution*   196
Religious and Racial Influences on Sexual Attitudes   199
Attitudinal Formation in Young People   200
BOX: *Is There Moral Decadence among Our Youth?*   201
Forms of Sexual Expression   202
Masturbation   203
Nocturnal Orgasm   204
Heterosexual Petting   204
Heterosexual Intercourse   205
Premarital Heterosexual Intercourse   205
Marital Heterosexual Intercourse   207
Extramarital Sexual Behavior   208
Postmarital Sexual Activity   210
Summary   211
TRUE OR FALSE: THE FACTS   213
Suggested Reading   213

CHAPTER 12 Sexual Variance_____216
TRUE OR FALSE?   216
Variance in Methods of Sexual Functioning and Quality of Sexual Striving   219
Sadism   219
Masochism   219
Exhibitionism   220
Scopophilia and Voyeurism   221
Troilism   221
Transvestism   222
Transsexualism   223
Gender Identity Disorders of Childhood   224
Variance in Choice of Sexual Partner or Object   225
Pedophilia   225
Bestiality   227
Pornography and Obscenity   227
Fetishism   231
Incest   232
Mate-Swapping   233
Variance in Strength of Sexual Drive   234
Nymphomania and Satyriasis   234
BOX: *Nymphomania: A Case Study*   235
Promiscuity   236
Prostitution   236
Rape   238
BOX: *Rape Prevention*   239
Summary   240
TRUE OR FALSE: THE FACTS   242
Suggested Reading   243

CHAPTER 13 Homosexuality_____244
TRUE OR FALSE?   244
Incidence   246
Suggested Causes   249
Hereditary Theory   249
Environmental Theory   250
BOX: *The Status of Homosexuality in Ancient Times*   251
Hormonal Imbalance   251
Homosexual Patterns and Practices   252
Attitudes toward Homosexuality   254
BOX: *The Status of Homosexuality in Modern Times*   256
Homosexuality and Children   257
Bisexuality   258
Summary   259
TRUE OR FALSE: THE FACTS   260
Suggested Reading   261

CHAPTER 14 Sexual Dysfunctions _____ 262

TRUE OR FALSE?   262
BOX: *What Happens in Sex Therapy?*   265
The Nature of Sexual Dysfunction   267
Male Sexual Dysfunction   268
Erectile Dysfunction (Impotence)   268
Ejaculatory Dysfunction   271
Female Sexual Dysfunction   273
BOX: *Sex Therapy for the Handicapped: A Case Study*   274
Female Sexual Unresponsiveness   275
Orgasmic Dysfunction   276
Vaginismus   277
Dyspareunia   278
Inhibitions of Sexual Desire   279
Seeking Professional Counseling   280
Summary   280
BOX: *The Use of Surrogate Partners in Sex Therapy*   281
TRUE OR FALSE: THE FACTS   283
Suggested Reading   283

CHAPTER 15 Sexual Diseases and Disorders 286

TRUE OR FALSE?   286
Sexually Transmitted Diseases   288
Gonorrhea   290
Syphilis   291
Genital Herpes   294
BOX: *If You Get Herpes . . .*   295
Acquired Immune Deficiency Syndrome   296
Nonvenereal Diseases   297
Nonvenereal Syphilis   297
Leukorrhea   297
Trichomoniasis   298
Candidiases or Moniliasis   298
Carcinoma   299
Dermatoses   302
Inflammation of Internal and External Genitalia   302
Sexual Disorders   304
Chromosomal Anomalies   306
Hermaphroditism   306
Summary   308
TRUE OR FALSE: THE FACTS   310
Suggested Reading   311

GLOSSARY _____ 312
REFERENCES _____ 322
INDEX _____ 336

PREFACE

H uman Sexuality: Third Brief Edition is the product of an evolutionary process. This book, derived from the landmark 1967 college text Human Sexuality, by James Leslie McCary, endeavors to bring together the essential facts and perspectives of sexuality as understood by modern sexologists. From its first through fourth editions, McCary's Human Sexuality has examined many cogent points and details of human sexuality. The previous two editions of Human Sexuality: A Brief Edition and the present third brief edition give a broader survey of the salient issues of the field. This brief edition has the advantage of allowing instructors to use another text dealing with marital and family issues. For many instructors, the brief edition has served as the main text for their courses, especially since a thorough review of the pertinent facts of human sexuality can be accomplished with supplementary selected readings or with the instructor's lectures.

New Focus

Previous editions of McCary's Human Sexuality and Human Sexuality: A Brief Edition emphasized biological and clinical aspects involved in human sexuality, because those were the aspects that guided research into the developing field of sexuality. More recent trends explore the psychosocial and cultural facets of the human sexual experience. Human Sexuality: Third Brief Edition incorporates these new concerns in its coverage of prominent social and developmental issues. Chapters on sexuality across the life span and on homosexuality exemplify this book's consideration of social issues important in the 1980s.

Human Sexuality: Third Brief Edition also has more specific coverage of topics being studied by modern sexologists. Topics such as disease states of pregnancy, the effects of drugs on sexual functioning, new understandings of human sexual response, the emotional impact of rape, intrafamilial sexual experiences, the effects of erotica and violent pornography, disorders of sexual desire, and newly researched sexually transmitted diseases, such as AIDS and herpes, have been included in this book. Other topics dealing with abortion, marital communication skills, and sexual expression among the disabled have also been highlighted.

Furthermore, the present edition is more than a sourcebook for technical information. An attempt has been made to respond to the reader's need for personal relevance, which is found to be lacking in many of the lengthier, more technical volumes. The reader is encouraged to examine the information presented and to consider it in light of personal values and concerns about sexual life-style decisions. From the outset, in Chapter 1, the reader is asked to reflect upon his or her sexual options, choices, values, and responsibilities.

Features

In trying to impart such a wealth of information to the reader in a way that it can be assimilated and understood, it is important that a book be clearly written and accessible to the student. Boxed materials, improved illustrations, and a pronunciation guide in the glossary are new to this edition. In addition, pedagogical aides, such as chapter outlines, thought-provoking true-false items, chapter summaries, and annotated suggested readings, have been provided so that the reader can better assimilate the text material.

With the new focus and clear presentation, the instructor can emphasize and/or integrate the material in a manner that is most useful for his or her course. Some instructors may wish to emphasize biological information, and they will find Chapters 2–5 most useful. Others may wish to emphasize sociological information, and they will find Chapters 7 and 8, 10 and 11 best suited for their purposes. Psychological information is concentrated in Chapters 9 and 12–14. Health educators may be particularly interested in Chapters 5, 6, and 15. Many instructors will, of course, wish to integrate all the information, and they can follow the book from Chapters 1 through 15 or assign the chapters in the order they find most effective. Learning objectives, discussion questions, suggested readings, and media resources are included in the instructor's manual that accompanies *Human Sexuality: Third Brief Edition.*

Acknowledgments

Many people have made important contributions to this volume. My thanks go to the reviewers who have added their creative ideas and insights to enhance the quality of the book. With much appreciation, I extend my gratitude to Roseann Cappella, East Stroudsburg State College; Frederic H. Chino, Portland State University; Michael S. Davidson, Montclair State College; V. Galin-Galler, Laney College; Donald E. Herrlein, Northeastern Oklahoma State University; Thomas M. Kelly, Lake Superior State College; Kay R. Murphy, Oklahoma State University; Martin E. Rand, Ithaca College; Judy Rollins, Kansas State University; Carol Schramm, University of Tennessee; and A. B. Silver, Bakersfield College.

I am also indebted to the editorial staff at Wadsworth for their help in organizing, editing, and overseeing the production of the book. In particular, I am grateful to Marshall Aronson, Bob Podstepny, and Debbie Oren for their professional assistance, as well as their personal dedication, toward making this edition as good as possible.

To my friend, colleague, and personal editor, Larry Hanselka, I extend my sincerest appreciation and thanks. Larry added his creative touches and tender loving care to the manuscript in many thoughtful ways. I respect and admire his professionalism, and I value our friendship most of all.

I am also grateful to Barbara Hanselka for her help in typing and collating the manuscript. She gave up her husband on numerous weekends and evenings so that he could work on the book, and her support has been appreciated. My thanks also go to my friend, Cathie Robinson, for her editorial assistance.

To my mother, LaVirle P. McCary, go my thanks for her emotional support and encouragement to keep me going to complete this revision. Following the death of my father, James Leslie McCary, she stood firm in her commitment to seeing that a revision of this book be accomplished.

Finally, to my wife, Sandra, and my children, Kevin and Kirstin, I express my love and appreciation because you accepted my long hours and hectic schedule so well. In addition, Sandra put in many hard hours in helping correct, type, and polish the manuscript. For your love, care, and patience I am thankful, and I count myself fortunate indeed to have you in my life.

Stephen P. McCary
July 1983

Human Sexuality

THIRD BRIEF EDITION

TRUE OR FALSE?

Young children must be protected from sexual knowledge because they are not emotionally equipped to deal with the subject.

❦

There are no absolute "right" or correct standards of sexual conduct.

❦

Most Americans do not favor sex education in the public schools.

❦

Sex education has no place in our schools because it leads to: (1) sexual acting out, (2) a rise in promiscuity, (3) an increase in premarital pregnancy, and so forth.

Sex and Today's Society

CHAPTER 1

A Heritage of Confusion
"Protecting" Children from Sex
Religion, Sex, and Marriage
Breaking the Bonds of Sexual Fascism
Facts—And Arguments—About Sex Education
A Suggested Approach to Sex Education
Making Responsible Sexual Decisions
Summary
Suggested Reading

In the past ten or fifteen years the subject of sex has emerged (or has been pushed) from its Victorian closet into broad daylight. There it has been examined and talked about as perhaps never before in history. Many behaviorists claim that a sexual revolution has occurred. But can one really accept the idea that sexual ignorance and anxiety have appreciably lessened because of the modern environment of sexual frankness?

Without doubt great strides have been made toward more formalized, adequate sex education programs for the young and the reeducation of those not so young. A reflection of these changes is a more wholesome attitude toward sex education in many schools, colleges, and universities throughout the country. Educators are finally beginning to think realistically and to acknowledge that their students are vitally interested in sex, that they are going to engage in some form of sexual activity, and that they need and deserve as much accurate sex information as possible. Have we achieved, however, the final goal of a guilt-free, sufficiently broad understanding of sexuality that will ensure a greater fullness to our lives? Probably not, at least not yet. Too much sexual conflict and doubt persist, and many people are still searching for answers to sex-related problems. When accurate information is not available, they accept misinformation as truth.

Sexual ignorance can breed sexual anxiety, and the primary cause of both is simple. Adults in a position to instruct the young are all too often filled with sexual guilt. Further, they may be painfully uncertain about what they truly believe to be acceptable sexual behavior. In addition to this ignorance and conflict, they may be reluctant to admit to these shortcomings.

When young people are given rigid proscriptions in sexual matters that are not counterbalanced with a rationale for sexual morality, then guilt must be used to control their sexual behavior. Young people incorporate these rules into their emotional makeup, so that if and when the rules are broken, emotional stress often results.

Human sexuality encompasses a broad spectrum of human behavior and includes the biological systems that determine patterns of sexual responsiveness and sexual functioning, the psychological factors that are of vital importance to adequate sexual adjustment, and the sociological implications of individual sexual behavior. No doubt an understanding of these several factors and their interrelationships contributes to healthy attitudes about human relationships in general and better sexual adjustment in particular.

Few authorities in human behavior would deny that sexual adjustment is essential to maturity and successful adaptation to one's environment. Scientific investigations and clinical observations confirm that sexual adjustment is positively correlated with well-timed, ongoing, accurate sex education presented in a wholesome manner (Malcolm, 1971; Thornburg, 1970). If given this information, today's young adults will be in a position to educate their own children adequately in sexual matters. Only in this way can the cycle of sexual ignorance and anxiety be broken.

A Heritage of Confusion

In the past, inadequate sex information was passed around partly because there were too few sources of accurate information. Unlike other areas of research, sex was not considered an appropriate topic for investigation. With the work of Dr. Alfred Kinsey in the 1940s and 1950s, and, more recently, the highly informative studies by other scientists, notably William H. Masters and Virginia E. Johnson, much has been added to our knowledge of human sexual attitudes and behavior. Nevertheless, today ordinary people and scientists alike are often reluctant to consider new scientific findings. When current research appears to lend support to long-held prejudices, it is quickly accepted as being scientifically accurate. But when it threatens cherished personal theories, the results tend to be discounted as suspect, and its conclusions judged as being distorted by sample and examiner bias. Many people are simply unable to change their old notions about this very sensitive and morally loaded subject.

The consequences of our society's tenacious clinging to traditional myths and prejudices about human sexuality are apparent in the unrealistic expectations many couples have about marriage and intimacy, our number of illegitimate births, and our soaring incidence of sexually transmitted disease. If one examines the advertisements, books, magazines, newspapers, movies, and other products of the mass communication media of our culture, one sees how American attitudes on sex, love, marriage, and family relations have been distorted by our woefully inadequate knowledge of sex. The growing sales of "nudie" magazines, the use of attractive males and females as seductive hucksters to sell everything from cigarettes to shoe polish to salad dressing, the suggestive ads for many films—all are examples of how sex drives can be misdirected. The mass communication media do not control our sexual behavior; they merely mirror our sexual anxieties. Confusion begets confusion, and there is a disturbing conflict in our social order. Our culture condemns many sexual relationships, but it also depicts them as desirable and exciting.

"Protecting" Children from Sex   *Misconception*

Parents often suppose that if their children do not know about sex they will avoid it. For example, parents will frequently withhold information on contraception and sexually transmitted diseases (STD) altogether, or will recount only the dangers and shame of illegitimate pregnancy and STD, expecting thereby to keep their children from engaging in premarital coitus (sexual intercourse).

The facts, however, do not support this assumption. One study compared the sexual habits of women students at a large state university with the accuracy of their knowledge about sexual matters. The study revealed that of the sexually active women, over 25 percent failed to answer *any* question about sex correctly; only 59 percent answered half the questions correctly, and none

DOONESBURY   by Garry Trudeau

Sex education. *Copyright 1971, G. B. Trudeau. Reprinted with permission of Universal Press Syndicate.*

answered all of them correctly. Of the less sexually active women, 80 percent correctly answered half the questions and 9 percent correctly answered all of them. This study suggests that the more a woman knows about sexual matters, the more discriminating she is in her sexual behavior.

Although knowledge of contraception may not ensure that a young woman will protect herself in premarital coitus, the evidence is that sexually active teenagers are becoming more aware of contraception's importance and are using it more often. Zelnik and Kantner (1977) have shown that in 1971 only 45 percent of sexually active young women aged fifteen to nineteen used any method of contraception the last time they had intercourse. In 1976, by contrast, 63 percent of coitally active young women in this age group were using contraceptives, with 33 percent using the Pill or an intrauterine device (IUD).

Studies of the relationship between sexually transmitted disease and sexual knowledge have found that the incidence of STD is drastically reduced by adequate knowledge. In a public school where a course including factual knowledge about sexually transmitted disease was introduced, for example, the cases of gonorrhea, one of the most common sexually transmitted diseases, decreased by 50 percent in two school years. In another school in the same area that did not include such a course, the number of gonorrhea cases increased during the same time period; when a similar course was offered there, the incidence of gonorrhea also decreased by approximately 50 percent (Levine, 1970).

Some parents try to keep their children from engaging in premarital sexual activity by instilling fear of illegitimate pregnancy or STD in them. This approach to sex education has been found to be quite ineffective. Studies have shown clearly that neither fear of pregnancy nor fear of STD is an effective deterrent to premarital sexual intercourse. Before the modern effective cures for sexually transmitted disease or reliable birth control methods were available, people had sexual relations with little regard to the possibility of either becoming pregnant or contracting a sexually transmitted disease.

Results of investigations around the world have demonstrated that ignorance, not knowledge, of sexual matters causes sexual misadventure. This fact has been confirmed by psychotherapists and marriage counselors who deal with the subsequent strife and heartbreak experienced by parents and their children who become the victims of such misadventure.

Adequate sex information has a significant impact not only on the general mental health of an individual, but also on marital adjustment. Research evidence indicates that a high degree of sexual knowledge is positively associated with marital satisfaction (Sarver & Murry, 1981). Other surveys indicate that of the leading ten factors found essential to a successful marriage, an adequate sex education in childhood is ranked third. The happiness of the parents' marriages and an adequate length of acquaintanceship, courtship, and engagement rank first and second.

Religion, Sex, and Marriage

Few people in a position to judge would deny that one of the greatest menaces to psychosexual health is a guilt-instilling religion. Leaders of such religions have succeeded remarkably well in training their followers to believe that sex is dirty and animalistic and is to be looked upon only as a necessary evil—with the emphasis on evil. This attitude is best seen in the prudery of the Victorian era, when "decent" women, not daring to expect pleasure from the sexual act, endured it only because of their "duty" to their husbands.

Changes in attitudes toward sex and marriage, reflecting changing needs but often lagging behind them, have occurred throughout history. Early Israelite tribes permitted **polygynous** marriage (marriage with more than one wife at a time), for example, and women were regarded as little more than property; marriages were primarily of legal rather than of religious concern. Some men were left without female partners as a result of polygyny, and a more fair distribution of women became necessary. Thus **monogamy** (marriage with only one person at a time) evolved.

Much of the ancient interpretation of Mosaic laws—upon which our prevailing Judeo-Christian morality is founded—was based on the need for larger and stronger tribes. From these laws evolved a single justification for sexual expression—*procreation* (the production of offspring). By extension, sexual activity for any other purpose became an act of perversion, a "wasting of seed."

Our culture has derived its sexual mores not only from Judeo-Christian teaching, but also from the early Greeks. With the Spartan overthrow of Athens in the fifth century B.C. came a change in the sexual practices of the Greeks. From a philosophy that had accepted sex as a pleasurable and natural function, the Greeks turned to one that emphasized denial of pleasure and a rigorous self-control in all matters. **Celibacy** (abstention from sexual activity) and other denials of sexual pleasure thus became exercises in self-discipline. In addition, when Alexander the Great, in his world conquest during the third century B.C., opened up many new avenues of cultural exchange, some Eastern spiritual attitudes were brought to the West and became influential. In some of these, sexual desire was considered an evil to be overcome by self-denial in order to attain salvation of the soul, and thus celibacy was glorified.

Jesus said surprisingly little about sex. The vast majority of sexual restrictions associated with Christianity are actually outgrowths of the philosophies of later Christian theologians; most restrictions were not formulated until long after Christ's death. Paul was probably the first Christian to speak out specifically on sexual morality. He emphasized the need for marriage as a means of avoiding **fornication** (sexual intercourse between two unmarried persons), although he apparently considered sexual abstinence a more admirable goal in life.

Virginity has long been associated with purity in religious teachings. The virgin birth of Jesus and the springing of Athena full grown from Zeus's forehead illustrate that the Christians and Greeks were in accord with other religions of the world whose teachings also included nonsexual origin of deities. It is therefore not difficult to understand why sex and the concept of sin (impurity) are so closely associated, or how sexual experiences and thoughts, in marriage or out, can easily produce feelings of guilt and emotional stress.

With the development of Judaic and Christian theology came the evolution of an ethical code governing marriage. Morally acceptable sexual activity was henceforth limited to the marriage bed, and any deviation was considered sinful. But a marriage ceremony does not necessarily serve as a magician's wand to correct the "thou-shalt-not" attitudes handed down by parents and society. Believing that sex equals sin, many brides and grooms eventually suffer from such unfortunate reactions as guilt, pain, frigidity, impotence, and premature ejaculation. It is too much to expect that the mere recitation of marriage vows can change sex from something evil into something good.

Although remnants of sexual rigidity are still evident in certain religions, these doctrines are, fortunately, being gradually analyzed with respect to their relevance to Our Town, U.S.A. In a good example of self-analysis, the United Methodists issued a policy statement in 1973 (Smith, 1975), which stated in part:

> We support the development of school systems and innovative methods of education designed to assist each child toward full humanity. All children have the right to full sexual education, appropriate to their stage of development, that utilizes the best educational techniques and insights.

Further, the United Methodists engaged one hundred sex educators from among their membership to teach six thousand young people and their parents during the initial two years of a sex education program, which is expanding and strengthening yearly.

An individual would do well to examine the ramifications of any moral code that includes rules about sexual expression and arrive at his or her own conclusions regarding the probable effects on oneself and others. If this is done, it is more likely that sexuality will be managed in a manner that is normal, healthy, and anxiety-free. When we as a society mature to the point that we no longer feel compelled to impose our personal biases on others, we will encounter and engender fewer emotional difficulties, including sexual ones.

Breaking the Bonds of Sexual Fascism

Some people arbitrarily evaluate certain sexual attitudes, values, and behaviors—their own, of course—as being right and superior to those of other people, and they will go to great lengths to impose their views on others. Anyone who fails to comply with these arbitrary standards is considered to be perverted, sexually inferior, or immoral. Those who hold such rigid standards could be called "sexual fascists." They neither understand nor care, for instance, that women's response to sex relations is different from men's. They simply expect women to employ and respond to the same sexual techniques that are successful with men. They accept uncritically the traditional double standard of morality for men and women: women must be virgins until marriage while men are allowed, even expected, to have many premarital experiences. Women are considered much more to blame for having children out of wedlock than are the men who father the babies.

A reasonable degree of flexibility in the major aspects of one's life is crucial for emotional health and normal adjustment. We do not expect all people to eat or even like asparagus; and indeed we do not expect those who do eat asparagus to want to eat it all the time. Students of human behavior generally recognize the extreme difficulty of trying to define precisely what is and what is not sexual deviation. For instance, such noncoital activities as masturbation and oral-genital contact are sometimes viewed in Western cultures as perversions. Yet masturbation is commonly practiced by most men and women, and oral-genital contact occurs in most relationships among people at middle- and upper-class levels. Most women respond intensely to noncoital methods of stimulation and may actually prefer them to intercourse. Further, evidence suggests that most women first experience oral-genital stimulation at a younger age than do men (Cowart & Pollack, 1979; Hite, 1976; Kinsey et al., 1948, 1953; Masters & Johnson, 1966).

Significant differences in acceptable norms of sexual behavior are found in various cultures. For example, the man-above coital position is not widely assumed anywhere except in a few Western countries; among young men of Arab countries, masturbation is less acceptable than homosexuality. Remember that individual and cultural differences will continue to exist and that practices in one culture are not more proper than those of another. A good sex education program, therefore, would take these individual differences in sexual tastes and pleasures into account. No person or group has the moral (nor should it have the legal) right to force its ethical views on others.

Facts—And Arguments—About Sex Education

Professionals who have the most intimate knowledge of troubled people—psychologists, psychiatrists, marriage counselors, and ministers—have long realized that guilt feelings aroused by inadequate sex knowledge interfere with happy, effective living. Scientific investigations have confirmed that people who receive an appropriate sex education are less anxious and more able to adjust well to life's stresses than those without one, since the latter tend to repress their anxiety by avoidance and denial.

People who are highly knowledgeable in sexual matters are more capable of enjoying their sexual feelings and of deriving pleasure from all forms of sexual activity than are the less knowledgeable (Wright & McCary, 1969). Anxiety has been found to lead to restraint of normal sexual impulses, and the greater the amount of accurate sex information an individual has, the less his or her anxiety.

The sexually mature individual is one who can cope effectively with sexual feelings and needs. Sexual maturity is fostered when a person is able to learn the basic facts about sex as a child in a manner that helps him or her feel natural and comfortable about it. The child needs to be able to hear the subject of sex presented without embarrassment by at least one trustworthy adult, and to be able to participate in sexual discussions with other children in a healthy and wholesome manner. Parents who wish to help their children grow up to be sexually mature individuals with adequate general psychological adjustment, therefore, should not make the common error of feeling that they should "protect" their children from sexuality. Research and clinical findings have shown that such an idea is fallacious.

Those who insist that providing the young with sex education is tantamount to giving license to sexual promiscuity frequently cite distorted statistics as proof of their position. Opponents of sex education insist that teaching sex without a moral or religious context can lead to casual, superficial, or warped attitudes toward sexuality. Such attitudes, opponents suggest, ultimately might lead to greater marital instability, higher divorce rates, and higher incidences of sexually transmitted disease and teenage pregnancy (Sarver & Murry, 1981). However, most studies clearly show that adequate information about sex encourages sexually responsible behavior. In a recent study of the effects of a sex education course on the attitudes of eighth-graders, Luffman and Parcel (1979) found that the student sample developed more permissive and accepting attitudes toward sexual behavior in committed relationships. At the same time they developed less tolerant attitudes toward sexual behavior in casual relationships. Stephen McCary's study (1976) shows that college students who received their sex education in the classroom and from other factual sources remain more conventional in their sexual behavior than do students whose information comes from nonacademic sources.

Despite the arguments of a vocal minority, surveys indicate that the majority of American parents and young people are in favor of including sex education in the public schools. Those individuals who are aware of the benefits to individuals and to society of adequate sex education are faced with the problem of how best to provide for it. They should pay attention to the concern of some parents that sex education might be presented in too dehumanized a fashion in the classroom or that "too much too soon" might be introduced, particularly for primary-school children. Others are concerned that sexually irresponsible persons will be given the task of teaching sex education.

These concerns are valid, but they can be dealt with by instituting specific criteria for the selection, training, and evaluation of instructors and by research-based guidelines to dictate at which age students will best benefit from specific blocks of sex information. Studies by Stephen McCary (1976, 1978) of the ages when college students first learned about or experienced sexual concepts suggest that a prudent approach would be to present sex information in a formal sex education program a year or so earlier than the students ordinarily learn it from their peers. This approach would allow young people to learn about sex accurately and in a wholesome atmosphere.

Of all the arguments against school sex education, perhaps the most valid concerns the professional qualifications of those who teach it. Few institutions train people specifically to teach this sensitive subject. Indeed, many of those teaching sex education courses receive no special training beforehand. Consequently, they have obtained much of their material from nonprofessional sources. Because of personal embarrassment, some teachers conduct their courses in a strained, mechanical manner, or perhaps they avoid material that might be really meaningful to their students. Certainly the attitudes, values, and behaviors of teachers toward their students and the subject matter can be as important as the content of the material taught (Francoeur & Hendrixson, 1980). Some teachers inject religious prejudice and personal guilt into sex instruction, which probably does the student more harm than good. Once again, better education and training would alleviate the problem.

Ideally, sex education should be presented in the home, but in reality most youngsters obtain sex information from peers, from books and magazines, and from pornographic materials. A small minority receive explicit sex instruction from parents, their church, or professionals. Studies have indicated that those with the most positive attitudes and the most factual knowledge learned about sex in formal classroom instruction. The same studies found little difference in the accuracy of sex information received from peers and that received from clergy and parents; all these sources provided inaccurate and insufficient information. When parents do provide sex instruction for their children, it is frequently limited to the facts of menstruation and pregnancy. Details (frequently distorted) about other aspects of sex are much more frequently learned from peers than from any other source (S. P. McCary, 1976, 1978).

Schools have assumed an increasingly important role in sex education during the past several years. A recent study (Bennett & Dickinson, 1980) found that a sampling of college students preferred that parents be the primary source of sex education. However, most of the students reported that the bulk of their sex information came from teachers and peers and not from their parents.

Mandatory sex education programs have been implemented or planned in several states. The emphasis of these programs has been on the junior high and senior high age groups, because opposition from certain political and religious groups has led to a dilution or elimination of the curriculum in the elementary

What I Would Tell My Daughter and Son about Premarital Sex

Psychologists who deal with problems of sexuality are often asked what they would tell their own children about premarital sex. Most often the question is meant to embarrass the psychologists, the questioners assuming that the psychologists will talk out of both sides of their mouths. That is, they might make certain liberal statements about sexual matters to the public, but when it comes to their own offspring, they will forget their academic views and become as rigid adherents of a double standard as any other parents.

Traditionally, the double standard of sexual ethics, long rampant in our society, has meant that people have not applied the same rules of human behavior and human decency equally to both sexes. Young adult males are expected to try every maneuver, trick, and "line" at their disposal to seduce young females. Young females, on the other hand, must use every method and technique known in order to sexually attract young males, yet they are expected to stop short of sexual intercourse. Such games are obviously immature and foolish. Equally unwise and illogical is a tendency on the part of parents to apply one standard to their own children but another to other people's children.

The question of what I would tell my children about sex is one that cannot be answered in one short statement because a whole lifetime sets the stage for the answer. Basically, there must be a healthy attitude toward sex in the home. If the parents are well adjusted in the area of sex, if they have a healthy attitude toward sex, then the children, also, are likely to have healthy sexual attitudes. Since sexual attitudes are formed in the home, I would want consistency in sexual matters there, both within each parent and between the parents. Each parent should feel at ease with his or her own ideas in order to present the same ideas day in and day out, and one parent should not make certain demands and present one set of ideas while the other makes different demands and presents a different set of ideas. Inconsistency can only produce confusion and insecurity within the children.

In addition to internal consistency within each parent and within the marriage, I would want my children to understand what is expected and demanded of them by society, and I would want our home to be somewhat consistent with the outside world. My children should know, however, that there will be some inconsistencies between society's expectations and what they are taught in our home. They must understand the attitudes of bigots, the sexual fascists who are ready to condemn and even persecute anyone who does not conform to their way of thinking.

I'd want my son and daughter to understand the views of various religions and to know that unwise adherence to some religious ideas and ideals can produce guilt and repression. I'd also want them to understand guilt and repression; if they avoid any aspect of sex, I'd want them to do so because of rational factors and not because of guilt. For guilt in this area, as in others, leads to many problems; and sexual conflicts resulting from guilt can be devastating.

I would want my children to know the physiological and psychological makeup of both sexes, and to understand the differences between men and women. I would want my children to be well versed in all aspects of sex, including techniques, in order for them to give their partners as much pleasure and satisfaction as possible in whatever form of sexual relationship they might enter. They should place their partners' needs and satisfaction on a plane equal to their own in order to give and to receive the maximum pleasure and fulfillment in sexual exchange.

I'd also want my children to know that young men between the ages of seventeen and twenty-one have reached the height of their sex drive and that there is a sound biological basis for their great interest in sex at this time. Women, however, do not have such a strong physical drive until they are about thirty years old. If a young woman *does* become sexually involved with a man, therefore, she usually does so because of emotional rather than sexual needs. I would want my children to realize that the responsibility in these matters is largely their own and that they should take into careful consideration possible outcomes of premarital sex, including feelings of guilt and pregnancy.

I would want both my children to have a kind and fair attitude toward other human beings. I'd want them to be ethical in all relationships, including sexual ones. There should be no cheating, no lying, no taking advantage of others. I'd want each of them to understand that when their behavior in any way harms other persons or themselves, that behavior should be reconsidered.

Each of my children should understand that the seductive behavior of others may be motivated by feelings other than affection. Men who feel sexually inferior, for instance, find an ego boost in seduction. When my daughter finds men behaving in such a manner, she must understand that it is their problem and not a personal thing directed toward her, and she must deal with it accordingly. Similarly, my son should realize that an immature and maladjusted woman may try to "prove" her desirability and worth as a person through sex; or she may use sex to snare some man who appeals to her; or she may attempt to shore up a faltering relationship through sex. He should be aware of these possibilities and avoid entering into sexual relationships that he thinks are motivated by emotional disturbances.

I'd want both my daughter and my son to know methods and techniques of sexual outlet other than sexual intercourse, and I'd want them to know the values of these methods. I would want them to know that masturbation and petting are perfectly normal modes of behavior—that they can and will satisfy sexual urges, yet do not cause some of the problems that can result from premarital sexual intercourse.

The elements basic to all successful human relationships, and perhaps most especially to sexual relationships, are honesty, fairness, decency, kindness, respect, understanding, and love. If these qualities are present and maintained, no relationship is likely to be harmful to the people involved. Neither party, in my opinion, is likely to be damaged by premarital sexual intercourse—*if* they are believers in decency and fair play; *if* they have a mature, guilt-free attitude toward sex; *if* they have decided that they wish to go ahead only after a rational discussion and not when they are caught up in the passion of sex play; and *if* they are mature enough to accept the responsibilities that go along with intercourse.

If, with all this information, together with the attitudes and background of our home, my son or daughter still decided to engage in premarital sexual intercourse, then I would certainly want them to know about and have access to contraceptive devices. I'd also want them both to be informed about pregnancy and sexually transmitted diseases.

If either of them decided to have sexual intercourse before marriage, furthermore, I would want them to know that so long as they hurt neither themselves nor others, my respect and love for them would not change. And I would hope—and I believe it would follow—that if either of them ever needed a friend, they would turn first to their parents and know that we would support them. These are the principles in which my wife and I believe and the ones by which we have reared our daughter and son, both of whom are now happily married. I do not know whether or not either of them had premarital sexual intercourse—and frankly, I couldn't care less. I respect and love both of them too much to pry, although I could ask and they could answer without embarrassment to any of us.

Neither my son nor my daughter has the guilt, shame, or fear that causes sexual repression. Their attitudes and behavior toward others are honorable and decent. Because of their ethical and sexual philosophies, among other things, both of them are likely to remain emotionally stable and healthy.

James L. McCary (January 1973)

What My Father Told Me about Sex

Many years have passed since my formative years, and my memory is clouded as to specific discussions my father and I had regarding sex. Rather, I remember my sex education as being a continual, ongoing process and not the product of a series of isolated occurrences or specific discussions about the subject. What I remember most clearly is that my father was a sympathetic listener, that he was warm and loving and kind, and that he cared about me in all respects. My father was concerned about my overall development as a person, and he was concerned that I would treat others with respect, honesty, and sensitivity.

I honestly recall only one specific lecture about sex, and that one took place when I was about nine or ten years of age. On that occasion he told me about basic male and female sexual anatomy, about how men have penises and women have vaginas, and so forth, and I responded to these revelations with only lukewarm interest at best. A more emphatic reaction resulted when he informed me that my sister, with whom I had engaged in many sibling battles, also had a vagina. To this my response was, "It can't be *that* good, then!" I might add that my view of female sexuality took a more positive turn by the time I reached age twelve or thirteen.

I recall feeling free to ask my father questions about sex (or about any other subject for that matter) whenever I chose. I remember on one occasion a teenage boy who was a neighbor was taunting me with his knowledge (and my ignorance) of sexual slang. He suggested, probably in hopes of causing me trouble or embarrassment, that I go home and ask my father what the slang words meant. So, I promptly went home and asked my father what the slang words meant. Without hesitation, and without any further questions, he calmly and directly explained to me the meanings of the slang words. Undoubtedly, the neighborhood teenager was disappointed when he did not hear screams of remorse coming from my house.

I recall that factual, informative books and magazines about sex were always available to me; and, around the age of twelve, I spent a great deal of time taking advantage of their availability. I remember thinking about sex as being a very natural subject to read and learn about—as natural as math, history, or English.

As I reached my mid- and late-teen grades. Despite such setbacks, important strides have been made in recent years in providing objective, appropriately timed sex education programs for our youth (Francoeur & Hendrixson, 1980).

If a person is to achieve sexual maturity, the information obtained about sex (from whatever source) needs to be integrated into the individual's personal ethical code. If one assumes that the moral climate a child lives in is the greatest determinant of his or her ethical values, then personal philosophies are largely molded by the home and by the attitudes of parents. It is within the context of the morality that comes from the family and society, then, that the schools can impart the factual and objective knowledge the child needs to develop a mature sexual ethic. Parents do not abdicate their responsibilities toward the sex education of their children when they encourage teaching it in schools.

years, I recall hearing my father tell occasional stories of a sexual nature. I remember the anecdotes as being tasteful as well as humorous, and I recall the pleasure and warmth that he felt in sharing these stories with me as well as with others. These humorous stories partly demonstrated my father's human side and added immensely to our father-son bond.

I remember that my father was the main person in our family who imparted sex information to me, but my mother also took part in some of our discussions and interactions. I think both my parents valued the importance of a good sex education for me, perhaps because they had been exposed to faulty or limited sex education while they were growing up. The intimacy and love that my mother and father shared served to reinforce my perception of what is involved in mature, caring man-woman relationships.

In sum, my sex education was interwoven naturally with all the other aspects of day-to-day family living. My father showed awareness of and sensitivity to the various aspects of my sexual development; and, through the many supportive comments, insights, and loving gestures that he made, he attempted to impart his knowledge about sexual matters to me.

I think that my father's attitudes about sex are reflected in the attitudes that I convey to my own children. Not long ago, my son was playing with some Star Wars figures while involved in a school function. Suddenly he remarked in childhood innocence how he was going to engage the figures in the act of "making love." His remark fell on somewhat startled ears as his teacher heard his comment. This presented a momentarily awkward situation, but the outcome was my getting to know my son's teacher just a little bit better!

Perhaps to some degree my father was able to develop a greater sense of the developing sexual concerns of all young people by observing some of the growing pains that my sister and I experienced. I do not know specifically what my sister's comments would be regarding her sex education, and I would not attempt to speak for her. However, I know she enjoyed her own special relationship with my father, and I believe they shared a mutual love and respect that greatly enhanced their emotional lives. I can only attest to the depth and richness of my relationship with my father, and I was fortunate to be reared in a home environment that allowed me to flourish.

Stephen P. McCary (12 June 1983)

How do parents, having developed their personal code of sexual behavior, present this ethic in the sex education of children—an instructional process that begins at a far earlier age than many suspect? The evidence is clear that sex education begins long before nursery school. It begins, in fact, with the first intimate mother-infant contact after birth.

Many factors significantly affect children's emerging sexual attitudes and conduct: the way their mothers and fathers love, fondle, and hold them (as well as each other); the soothing or harsh sound of parents' voices, which comes to be associated with love or with rejection and hostility; the feel of their skin; the smell of their bodies. Whether they realize it or intend to do so, parents begin a child's sexual training in the earliest days of life. Even when parents avoid discussing sex altogether, the child nevertheless detects their attitudes—

stressful or happy—through nonverbal communications. Further sexual inter-action or sex rehearsal play among children and adolescents may help them learn about and establish healthy relationships in adult life (Money, 1980a).

A Suggested Approach to Sex Education

Van Emde Boas (1980) has provided a list of "ten commandments" for those parents who strive to provide sex education for their children. While this list may not be definitive, it provides a framework to consider issues pertinent to the sex education process. A reworded version of Van Emde Boas's list follows:

1. Do not isolate sex education from other educational experiences. Realize that sex education begins in infancy.
2. Realize that our skin and our hands are perhaps our most important sensual and sexual organs.
3. Do not inhibit or negate open, spontaneous sex expressions in children.
4. Answer truthfully all questions posed by children, but do not answer in such detail as to go beyond their comprehension or understanding.
5. Realize that children learn through modeling and from real-life examples better than they do from written or spoken words.
6. Realize that sex education in the schools can only be an extension of the sex education provided in the home.
7. Realize that teaching the appropriate relational and emotional components of sexuality is as important as teaching the biological components.
8. Teach your children that sexual exploitation and manipulation of others is as reprehensible as other forms of manipulation and exploitation.
9. Teach your children that intimate and caring relationships are more meaningful and satisfying than casual and superficial sexual encounters.
10. Do not underestimate the importance of having discussions with your children about birth control matters.

We hope the material in this book will assist readers toward a better understanding of themselves and their sexuality, and will encourage them to work toward changes in society that will better prepare their children for healthy, well-adjusted sex lives. There is considerable evidence to show that the only way our society is going to achieve proper sexual stability and mental health, which are undisputed requirements for maturity, is to instigate and persevere with sound sex education for everyone. Such a sex education course must include dispassionate, accurate information about the physiological and psychological aspects of sex and must be presented with sensibility in the framework of present-day Judeo-Christian society. The criteria for such sex education programs have been set forth by the American Association of Sex Educators, Counselors and Therapists (AASECT). Application forms and details of qualification standards for sex educators and therapists who are candidates aspiring to certification are available from the organization (2000 N St., NW, Suite 110, Washington, D.C. 20036).

Making Responsible Sexual Decisions

Sexuality is an important dimension in all our lives. Sexual expression is not simply a matter of responding to biological urges or of impressing others with our sexual or romantic prowess. Increasingly, we are recognizing that making responsible sexual decisions is a vital aspect of the human sexual experience.

A personal examination of our own individual values is an essential component of this decision-making process. Further, an understanding of societal restrictions and limitations on the indiscriminate expression of sexual urges is necessary in order to determine how we as individuals are to fit into society. Certainly we cannot be isolated from the rest of society in formulating the values our sexual decisions are based upon.

Perhaps, as you read the pages that follow, you will begin to examine your personal values in light of the information we present. We hope you will gain some insight into how society's attitudes, values, and perspectives regarding sexuality have evolved. As a result, you will perhaps be able to formulate your own ideas about how you can express your sexuality more fully and comfortably and in a responsible manner.

As you continue the process of developing sexual awareness, you might consider the following questions:

- What are the biological similarities and differences between men and women?
- How can I appropriately express feelings of love and intimacy toward persons of either sex whom I deem significant?
- What is the difference between love and friendship?
- How do the values of society conflict with those that I hold? How can I begin to appropriately resolve this conflict?
- How do I begin to resolve some of the significant differences that exist between my attitudes and those of persons of other generations?
- What role do religion and moral decisions play in my life?
- How can I best deal with individuals whose behaviors and values may differ from my own?
- How do my sexual values affect the choices that I make with respect to family planning and birth control?
- What sexual values do I want to be fostered in my children by me, by teachers, by legal authorities, and by the clergy?
- How can I go about gaining the fullest measure of sexual satisfaction? How do I resolve sexual problems and emotional issues when they arise?
- Is it better to avoid or ignore certain sexual issues, or is it better to face them and resolve them?

You, the reader, no doubt will formulate many other questions to consider. If we can challenge you to examine freely and honestly these and other important issues and, by doing so, to arrive at a clearer perspective of effective sexual decision making, then we will have accomplished a major goal of this book.

Summary

Sexuality is part of our heritage from birth. Yet human beings do not know about sexuality from instinct; they must *learn* about the three main aspects of sexuality—the emotional, the physiological, and the psychological. At present, however, much of this sex education is picked up at random from parents and peers, from what they say or don't say. Misinformation leads to confusion, ignorance, and guilt. A proper sex education can aid in adjusting to life and in breaking this cycle of ignorance and guilt.

Many of our sexual beliefs are based in the teachings we receive early in life. These teachings, particularly those in history and religion, reflect concepts thousands of years old that may need to be reexamined in light of present circumstances. Sexual fascists, those with rigid views and inflexible attitudes, perpetuate the ignorance-guilt cycle, adding to the anxiety that exists for many people. An open, understanding, and sensitive approach is needed to overcome the biases and bigotry that surround human sexuality.

Sex must be guilt-free in order to be truly satisfying. Formal sex education programs are important ways to help people relieve their sexual anxieties and sexual guilt. Such programs, when presented by qualified and emotionally aware individuals in a thorough, objective manner, can help establish healthy attitudes and values. It falls upon such programs to carry the responsibility because other sources of sex information are frequently inadequate, wrong, or too late. This chapter presented a few ideas for such a program, which would include some pertinent physiological and psychological information. We also examined emotional, cultural, and religious influences on sexual adjustment.

TRUE OR FALSE: THE FACTS

Young children must be protected from sexual knowledge because they are not emotionally equipped to deal with the subject.
False. Young children who hear the facts about sex presented without embarrassment from a trustworthy adult feel natural and comfortable with those facts: sexual maturity is fostered in such children. (*10*)

There are no absolute "right" or correct standards of sexual conduct.
True. Those standards advocated by many in our Judeo-Christian culture have evolved from ancient Mosaic law, from Greek (Spartan) and Eastern influences, and from Christian theologians—not from Jesus nor from any "absolute" right. (*7–8*)

Most Americans do not favor sex education in the public schools.
False. Surveys indicate that the majority of American parents and young people are in favor of including sex education in the public schools. (*10*)

Sex education has no place in our schools because it leads to: (1) sexual acting out, (2) a rise in promiscuity, (3) an increase in premarital pregnancy, and so forth.
False. One study of college women showed that the more they knew about sexual matters, the more discriminating they were in their sexual behavior. (5–6)

SUGGESTED READING

Calderone, Mary S., and Johnson, Eric W. *The family book about sexuality.* New York: Harper & Row, 1981.
This creatively written sex education text for the family covers all significant topics related to human sexuality and relationships. Important features include a bibliography of additional family readings and a listing of family planning and counseling services.

Dolgin, Janet L., and Dolgin, Barbara L. Sex and the law. In B. Wolman and J. Money (Eds.), *Handbook of human sexuality.* Englewood Cliffs, N.J.: Prentice-Hall, 1980.
This article studies the application of law to sexual activity and the interrelationship between law and sex. Citing relevant court decisions, the authors consider such matters as sex discrimination, contraception, homosexuality, obscenity, abortion, prostitution, consensual sodomy, and rape.

Kaplan, Helen Singer. *Making sense of sex.* New York: Simon & Schuster, 1979.
Free of technical jargon, this book presents up-to-date, honest treatment of human sexuality for young people. Topics include sexual biology, sexual development, forms of sexual response, sexual problems, reproduction, birth control, sexually transmitted diseases, and love and sex.

McCary, James Leslie, and McCary, Stephen P. *McCary's human sexuality* (4th ed.). Belmont, Calif.: Wadsworth, 1982.
This book is the unabridged hardcover edition of the present volume and includes a more detailed and technical discussion of all the topics in the brief edition. Chapter 1 is especially pertinent to sex and today's society.

Otto, Herbert A. (Ed.). *The new sex education.* Chicago: Follett, 1978.
This source volume for educators is a comprehensive survey of the field of sex education by twenty-eight leading authorities. The book examines current approaches to sex education, professional issues, and programs in schools, clinics, and churches.

Tannahill, Reay. *Sex in history.* New York: Stein & Day, 1980.
This fascinating book examines sexual attitudes, customs, and practices in the world's major civilizations from ancient times until the present.

COLLEGE OF

TRUE OR FALSE?

The sexual systems of men and women are markedly similar both in structure and in function.

A girl has reached puberty when her first menstruation occurs.

Hormones produced in the ovaries play a major role in regulating the sex drive of most women.

A man whose body is functioning normally produces male and female sex hormones; a woman whose body is functioning normally produces male and female sex hormones.

CHAPTER 2

Early Development of the Male and Female Genitalia
Development of the Internal Genitalia
Development of the External Genitalia

The Physical Changes of Pubescence
Sexual Development in Pubescent Girls
Sexual Development in Pubescent Boys

Glands and Hormones

Summary

Suggested Reading

exual maturation and reproduction, as well as sexual desire and function, are chiefly under the control of the **endocrine glands**, also called the ductless glands or glands of internal secretion. These are the pituitary, thyroid, parathyroid, pancreas, and adrenal glands; in addition to these five glands, the hypothalamus of the brain acts as a gland, and so do the **gonads** (testes in male and ovaries in female). Their products, the **hormones**, are not secreted at the body's surface through ducts, as saliva and sweat are; they enter directly into the bloodstream. Hormones are chemical messengers, sending information to specific body organs sensitive to their actions. The quantities of hormone concentrations present in the bloodstream at any one time are minute, but their effect is profound: hormones as well as other blood serum elements are excreted in the urine, and so their concentration in the bloodstream can be quite variable within normal limits and subject to rapid change (Schwartz et al., 1980).

In addition to the influence of hormonal activity on human emotions and sexual behavior, the brain also plays a vital role in coordination (or dysfunction) of emotions and behavior in humans and other higher species. The cortex controls cognitive functions, such as thought and memory. It also controls voluntary behavior. The **hypothalamus**, lying within the mesencephalon or midbrain, appears to serve as a form of biological timing device. Interacting with the endocrine glands, it controls the onset of puberty, fertility cycles, and sexual arousal. Stimulation of the hypothalamus dramatically influences emotional reaction, including sexual responses. In addition to hormonal influence, then, a satisfying sex life is dependent on the interplay of cortical and hypothalamic functions as well (Barclay, 1971).

Early Development of the Male and Female Genitalia

In very early prenatal life, the presence of certain hormones brings about the changes, or differentiation, of the embryonic sex-cell mass into female or male **genitalia** (internal and external sexual or reproductive organs). At puberty, other hormones are responsible for the sexual maturation of the individual.

Despite what many people think, men and women are not vastly different creatures. Even the sexual systems, where the primary differences between male and female lie, are quite similar. From early embryonic through mature stages of human development, there are marked likenesses both in structure and function of the two sexual systems. The completely developed genitalia of the adult man and woman maintain **homologous** (similar in embryologic origin) but modified structures and have complementary functions.

The genitalia of both sexes originate from the same anatomical structure. In the first eight weeks after conception, the reproductive system appears as an undifferentiated genital thickening on the epithelium (posterior outer layer) of the embryonic body cavity. The differentiation into male or female results from hormonal signals initiated by the special chromosomal pattern established in the embryo at conception.

Although every **ovum** or egg cell produced in the female bears only an **X** chromosome, each male **sperm** contains either one X (female) or one **Y** (male) chromosome. Sperm containing X- and Y-bearing chromosomes are produced in equal numbers. The sperm is the sex-determinant of the offspring: of the approximately two hundred million sperm contained in an average ejaculate, only one will penetrate and fertilize the female ovum or egg. If an X-bearing sperm fertilizes the ovum, an XX, or female, child is conceived; a Y-bearing sperm will produce an XY, or male, child.

Development of the Internal Genitalia

In their early formative periods, the internal organs (gonads and ducts) of both sexes follow an identical course of development and are sexually indistinguishable (Figure 2.1). Most of the structures in the embryonic reproductive system either disappear, degenerate, or are replaced by new structures long before the end of fetal life. During the undifferentiated period, a gonad originates from a genital ridge, which develops from the early epithelial cell mass. Two systems of ducts, the **Wolffian** and **Müllerian**, develop from the gonad of each embryo before the true sex is established. These primitive genital ducts are the forerunners of specific sexual structures. Human embryos, like those of other mammals, have, at the very beginning, the potential to be either male or female. Under hormonal influence, the Wolffian ducts will evolve into the male genitalia, and the Müllerian, into the female.

The embryo's internal sexual transformation, first observable about six weeks after conception, starts with the differentiation of the gonad into male **testes** or female **ovaries**. Later in life these gonads produce procreative **germ cells** (the male sperm and the female ova) and are also involved in the hormonal interplay of the body. After maleness or femaleness has been established by gonadal development, the ducts of the opposite sex for each embryo remain undeveloped or degenerate.

Development of the External Genitalia

The growth, development, and differentiation of the external genitalia of both sexes are similar to what has been described for the internal genitalia. The external genitalia arise at a common site, located between the umbilical cord and the tail of the embryo (Figure 2.2). This site becomes the genital tubercle. It is at first an undifferentiated area, then becomes a phalluslike projection that eventually develops into the male or female external sexual organs. In about the fourth week of prenatal life, the front area of the genital tubercle begins to form a vertical groove. In the male, the developing **penis** with its penile urethra parallels the development in the female of **vagina** (muscular tube that receives penis during coitus), uterus, and intrauterine formations. The external genitalia are first recognizable at about the sixth week of embryonic formation, and for a period of some weeks they remain indifferent in appearance.

Two folds or swellings (labioscrotal swellings) develop on the elevated edges (lateral and parallel) of the urethral groove and differentiate into the female labia majora or into the male scrotal pouch. Once begun, genital develop-

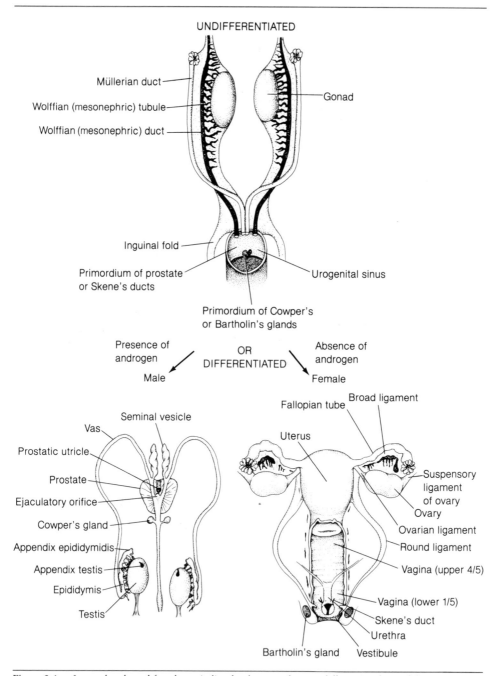

Figure 2.1   Internal male and female genitalia: development from undifferentiated into differentiated stage.

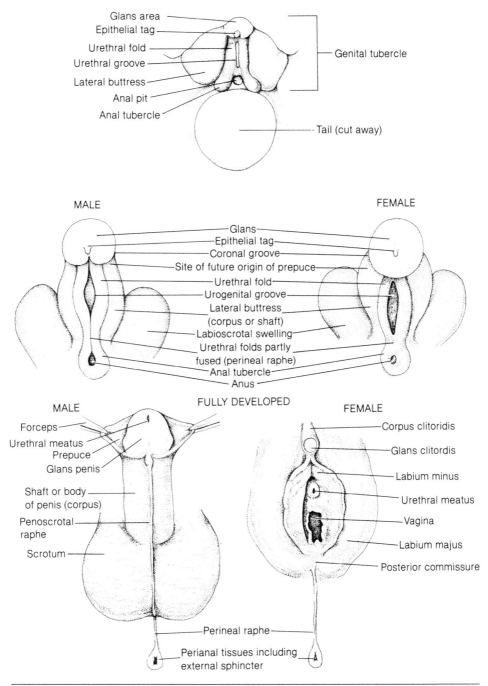

Figure 2.2   External male and female genitalia: development from undifferentiated into differentiated stage.

ment is rapid, and by the fourth month of gestation the sex of the fetus is easily recognizable.

The male embryo reaches a definitive stage about the tenth week when the edges of the urethral groove fold and grow together. By the end of the third month the male urethra is fully formed. The **prepuce** (foreskin) develops over the glans of the penis simultaneously with the formation of the urethra. The outside opening of the urethra at the end of the penis is called the penile meatus.

The female external genitalia are slower to develop than those of the male. A phalluslike projection slowly develops into the body and glans of the **clitoris**, the most sexually sensitive organ in the female sexual system. The developing **labia majora** (major lips), the outer protective lips of the vaginal region, continue upward to terminate in the **mons veneris**, or **mons pubis**, the fatty tissue on the upper exterior of the female genitalia.

In its early stages, the female urethral groove follows the same pattern of formation as the male's. However, the groove never closes to form a tube. Instead, part of it deepens to fashion the **vestibule**, the area surrounding and including the opening of the vagina. The urethral folds do not unite in the female, and they gradually develop into the **labia minora** (minor lips), the inner protective—and highly erogenous—lips of the vagina.

The female **urethra**, or bladder outlet, is similar to the prostatic portion of the male urethra. It is just above the vagina and, as does the vagina, opens into the vestibule. A prepuce or foreskin, often referred to as the hood, also develops over the glans of the clitoris. **Vulva** is a collective name used for the whole of the external female genitalia.

There is an interesting contrast in the differentiation process of the male and female embryo. Although genetic sex is fixed at the instant of fertilization, the sex-related genes do not exert their influence until the fifth or sixth week of prenatal life. Prior to that time, all embryos appear to be structurally bipotential—that is, they could become either male or female in structure. At the fifth or sixth week, however, the contrast between the sexes begins. In the genetically male embryo, normal development of the masculine sex tissue depends upon the presence of the hormone **androgen**. If for any reason the male embryo is deprived of or fails to metabolize androgen, then the male sexual structures fail to develop; and the result is an incomplete or ambiguous appearance of the external genitals. While androgen is necessary for the differentiation of the male sex organs, no such hormonal addition is necessary for the development of the female sexual structures.

In those rare cases where the male embryo is deprived of androgen, the external genitalia cannot differentiate into penis, foreskin, and scrotum (although the testes and the male accessory organs are present internally). Instead they form homologous (parallel) female sex organs: clitoris, clitoral hood, and the labia minora and majora. At birth, these rare males appear to be completely female and are usually reared as such. The error may not be discovered until they reach adolescence, when the development of the male secondary sexual characteristics (facial hair, voice change, and so on) begins. The analogue to this irregularity in the male is the female embryo that becomes masculinized under the influence of excessive androgen, usually from a malfunctioning adrenal cortex.

The condition where a person is genetically a male or female but has ambiguous external genitalia or the outward appearance of the opposite sex is called male or female **hermaphroditism**. If discovered soon enough in the child's life, the situation can be corrected with surgery and hormonal therapy.

The Physical Changes of Pubescence

The second period of major hormonal influence on the development of the male and female sexual systems occurs during **puberty**. Puberty is that stage of life when **secondary sexual characteristics** (those sexual ornaments that biologically signal the opposite sex) begin to develop and reproduction becomes possible. It is directly preceded by a period of rapid maturational change known as pubescence (also called the pubic growth cycle). Pubescence is a transitional period during which the sexual glands mature, and physiological differences between the sexes become more marked. Pubescence also is a period of "sexual awakening." Although younger children have sexual desires and interests, the pubescent boy or girl experiences a heightening of interest and focusing of attention on sexual matters. Attitudes, interests, and emotions change; and sexual experimentation increases in frequency.

There is no "typical" pubescence. Every boy and girl has his or her own style, and the range of individual differences is broad, although, generally speaking, a boy's physiological maturation moves more slowly and continues longer than a girl's. A positive attitude toward oneself and an understanding of society's expectations contribute to the emotional well-being of both sexes at this time.

Sexual Development in Pubescent Girls

Pubescence usually begins in a girl when the breasts begin to increase in size and the nipples begin to project forward. At about age thirteen, soft, downy, rather colorless pubic hair appears, together with some axillary (underarm) hair growth. Gradually, the pubic hair thickens and coarsens, becoming curly and dark in color as it grows downward to the pubic area in a typical inverted triangular shape. With these bodily changes and the unfolding of the classic feminine form, **menstruation** (the monthly discharge of blood and other material from the uterus through the vagina) is imminent.

The onset of menstruation (also called the **menarche**) occurs about two years after the breasts begin budding, and about one year after pubic hair appears. However, **ovulation** (the release of a mature egg) usually does not begin until a year or so after menstruation first occurs. Puberty is reached at about age fourteen, when a girl's ovaries produce their first mature eggs.

There is considerable variation in the age of puberty because of individual differences in general health, developmental maturation, and heredity. Evidence also shows that puberty occasionally occurs at a very early age. For in-

Puberty: Girl or woman? *Jean Shapiro.*

stance, in 1939, a normal, healthy son was born to a Peruvian girl five years of age. The baby had been fathered by a mentally retarded teenage stepbrother and was delivered by caesarean section. The five-year-old mother was sexually mature, and physicians confirmed that she had menstruated since approximately the age of one month. Although menstruation ordinarily precedes ovulation, there are exceptional cases on record of pregnancy and childbirth having occurred before the onset of menstruation. The apparent explanation is that the girl released a mature ovum just before she would have begun menstruating, so that the resulting pregnancy delayed menstruation until after delivery. In the last few centuries, the age at which the menarche occurs has been dropping about four months per decade (Tanner, 1969). The downward trend seems now to be leveling off (W. Sullivan, 1971), and in the United States the average age at which menstruation begins is 12.76 years (National Center for Health Statistics, 1974). Approximately one-half of American girls are believed to begin ovulation between the ages of 12.5 and 14.5 years.

Female genital changes continue on into adolescence. The mons pubis becomes prominent, and the labia majora develop and become more fleshy, hiding the rest of the external genitalia, which are ordinarily visible during childhood. The labia minora also develop and grow. At this time, the clitoris rapidly

Puberty: Boy or man? *Dean Hollyman/Photo Researchers, Inc.*

develops its extensive system of blood vessels and the vagina turns a deeper red color. The mucous lining of the vagina becomes thicker, remaining so until the **menopause** (the cessation of menstruation), when it reverts to the thinness of childhood. Vaginal secretions now become acid. At physical maturity, around age eighteen, the average American female is 5 feet 4 inches tall and weighs 123 pounds.

Sexual Development in Pubescent Boys

A boy's pubic growth curve lasts from four to seven years and parallels that of a girl's but, as we have noted, lags behind her's by a year or two. Progress to and through puberty varies considerably from boy to boy. The greatest variability in physical size and physiological development is observable at the age of twelve or thirteen, and growth continues until about age eighteen. The average eighteen-year-old American male today is 5 feet 9 inches tall and weighs 150 pounds. He can expect to grow another quarter to half inch in the next four years.

At the age of eleven, a boy shows few outward signs of pubertal change. He may first blossom into a "fat period," often a forerunner of male pubescence. Penile erections occur spontaneously at this early age, from various sources of stimulation, not all being sexual. By the age of twelve, his penis and scrotum begin to increase in size, one of the earliest indicators of approaching puberty. Erections occur more often, but still spontaneously. While he might know about ejaculation, he probably has not yet experienced it.

A boy's pubic hair commonly appears at the age of thirteen or fourteen, following the spurt of genital growth by a year or so, although it is sometimes observed as early as the twelfth year. For the average boy of thirteen or fourteen, ejaculation is now possible. Secretion of sperm begins—a process parallel to ovulation in a girl, although neither sperm nor ova are yet necessarily mature. Growth of underarm and facial hair follows that of the pubic hair. **Nocturnal emissions** (wet dreams) are now probable if a sexual outlet of another nature is not utilized. A change of voice occurs about the fourteenth or fifteenth year, due to hormonal effects on the larynx, so that the voice of a mature man is about an octave lower than that of a mature woman.

Glands and Hormones

The growth, development, and sexual activity of both males and females is greatly influenced by the **pituitary gland,** which can have a harmonizing or disturbing effect on the other endocrine glands. Lying at the base of the brain, the pituitary is divided into an anterior (front) lobe, an intermediary lobe, and a posterior (back) lobe.

The anterior pituitary lobe, under the control of the "releasing hormones" of the hypothalamus, secretes at least six hormones, three of which are **gonadotropic,** or directly related to gonadal function. These three hormones are concerned with the production of sperm and ova and with the secretion of milk by the mammary glands following childbirth.

The sex glands or gonads (ovaries and testes), in addition to other functions, produce three groups of sex hormones. Two of these hormone groups are female and one is male. Each is a natural substance that is a basic component of living cells. Once used by the body, the sex hormones are broken down and eliminated, usually in the urine.

Estrogen, one of the two female hormones, is essentially a growth hormone highly important in the development of the body structure, the genital organs, and the secondary sexual characteristics. It also influences the menstrual cycle. In lower female animals, the presence of hormones stimulates receptivity to copulation; but, in women, the ovarian hormones do not appear to play a major role in regulating sex drive. A recent study found that no correlation exists between sexual receptivity and estrogen cycles in women. This finding points up a major difference between female humans and other mammals. Further, a study of women who had experienced bilateral ovariectomies (surgical removal of the ovaries) showed that 90 percent of such women experienced no change in sexual desire or in functioning. In contrast, 84 percent of women whose pituitary and adrenal glands (a pair of endocrine glands located near the kidneys) had been removed reported a complete loss of sex drive. The hormones produced by the pituitary and the adrenal glands therefore appear to be much more important in the level of a woman's sex drive than are the estrogenic hormones. Assuming her glands are intact and functioning normally, a woman's sexual responsiveness is more influenced by emotional and physical factors than by hormonal conditions (Luttge, 1971).

Progesterone is the second female hormone. It is of primary importance in preparing the lining of the uterus for implantation of fertilized ova and in maintaining pregnancy. As we shall discuss in some detail in the section of Chapter 4 that deals with menstruation, progesterone is gradually withdrawn if impregnation does not occur, resulting in a breakdown of the uterine lining and the onset of the monthly menstrual flow. If an ovum is fertilized, on the other hand, progesterone is produced for the duration of the pregnancy.

Progesterone stimulates the secretion capacity of a pregnant woman's mammary glands, causing her breasts to enlarge. It also acts to prevent premature uterine contractions. For this reason, physicians often prescribe progesterone when there is danger of a spontaneous abortion, especially during the tenth to sixteenth week of pregnancy when the threat of miscarriage is greatest. In a woman who is not pregnant, abnormally high levels of progesterone may produce **dysmenorrhea** (painful menstruation) and other gynecological problems.

Testosterone, the male sex hormone, is produced in the testicles beginning in pubescence, when a boy's testicles begin to grow and develop rapidly. During pubescence various gonadotropic hormones manufactured by the pituitary gland stimulate the maturation of sperm and the production of testosterone in the testes. Testosterone controls the development and preservation of masculine secondary sexual characteristics, including facial and body hair, change of voice, muscular and skeletal development, and sexual desire. (Testosterone does not influence whether a man's sexual attraction will be directed toward same-sex or opposite-sex partners, but it does help stimulate libido.) It controls as well the development, size, and function of accessory male sex organs (seminal vesicles, prostate, penis, and scrotum).

Healthy males produce more than an ample supply of sex hormones for adequate sexual functioning. Men who have only one testicle, for example, show no evidence of hormonal deficiency. Even men whose ejaculate contains as little as 60 percent of the usual hormonal content lead normal, satisfactory sex lives (Raboch, 1970; Weaver, 1970).

Androgen and estrogen are produced in the gonads and adrenal glands of both sexes—that is, a small amount of estrogen is found in the male, and a small amount of androgen in the female. Thus, normal men and women excrete traces of both types of hormones in their urine. In adulthood, an excessive amount of androgen in a woman and too much estrogen in a man can produce marked changes in secondary sexual characteristics. For example, excess estrogen in a man may lead to certain feminizing effects, such as enlarged breasts and fatty tissue deposits, though gender itself, of course, does not change. Too much androgen in a woman may enhance her sex drive and may cause her to become hirsute, or abnormally hairy (Money & Ehrhardt, 1972).

An imbalance in the natural hormonal state in an infant or growing child can produce abnormalities in primary sexual characteristics, as well as changes in the secondary characteristics. Hormonal therapy is often successful in ad-

The Quest for Sexual Vitality

Through the ages, men have long tried to increase their sexual prowess by eating testicles—sometimes of a defeated enemy, sometimes of animals. As late as 1889, the renowned French physiologist Charles E. Brown-Sequard was, at the age of 72, apparently dissatisfied with his sexual vigor. He tried to outwit nature by injecting himself with extracts from the testicles of dogs. But despite his reports of spectacular rejuvenation, any benefits he actually derived must surely have been the result of the strength of his belief, because one would need to inject the extract from approximately five hundred pounds of bull testicles to furnish what is considered an average dose of male sex hormones! However, Brown-Sequard did stimulate a considerable amount of research in this area. Since his time, well-controlled experiments with hormones have shown that we are physically, mentally, and emotionally influenced by the action of our endocrine glands and that our physical and emotional states may, in turn, affect the function of these glands.

justing the imbalance and, in turn, correcting or preventing associated problems. The endocrine system is complex, and only those hormones that more or less directly affect the sexual systems have been discussed here. As we have seen, sexual development, growth, and functioning depend upon these sex hormones. Released into the bloodstream in small, measured doses, they have a tremendous impact on the physiology and psychology of the individual.

Summary

The endocrine system plays a vital role in sexual maturation and reproduction, as well as in regulating sexual desire and function. The endocrine system and the brain have an important combined effect upon the coordination of human emotions and sexual behavior.

This chapter emphasized the many ways in which male and female sexual systems are similar in structure and in function. The gonads, first recognizable about six weeks after conception, later differentiate into the male testes or the female ovaries. The external genitalia, observable initially in an undifferentiated state at the sixth week of embryonic formation, later develop into the male penis and scrotum or the female clitoris, labia majora, labia minora, and vestibule. The presence or absence of the hormone androgen significantly affects the direction sexual development takes.

Final maturation of the male and female sexual systems occurs during puberty. Genital growth and the development of secondary sexual characteristics occur in both sexes, together with menstruation and ovulation in girls and ejaculation and voice changes in boys. Generally, physiological maturation and development takes place earlier in girls than it does in boys.

Hormones play a great role in sexual maturation and development. In women, estrogen is primarily a growth hormone that also affects the functioning of the menstrual cycle. Progesterone is the reproduction hormone that prepares the uterine lining for implantation of the fertilized egg. In men, testosterone induces and maintains the male secondary sexual characteristics. Hormonal imbalances sometimes occur, resulting in deviations in secondary sexual characteristics. Hormone therapy can be employed to correct hormone imbalances through the appropriate use of androgen and estrogen.

TRUE OR FALSE:
THE FACTS

The sexual systems of men and women are markedly similar both in structure and in function.
True. Throughout all stages of human development, there are marked likenesses in both structure and function of the two sexual systems. *(22)*

A girl has reached puberty when her first menstruation occurs.
False. A girl reaches puberty when her ovaries produce their first mature eggs, a year or so after menstruation first occurs. *(27)*

Hormones produced in the ovaries play a major role in regulating the sex drive of most women.
False. In general, women without ovaries do not report a diminished sex drive; but, in one study, 84 percent of women without adrenal and pituitary glands reported a complete loss of sex drive. *(30)*

A man whose body is functioning normally produces male and female sex hormones; a woman whose body is functioning normally produces male and female sex hormones.
True. Androgen and estrogen are produced in the gonads and adrenal glands of both sexes so that a small amount of estrogen is found in the male, and a small amount of androgen in the female. *(31)*

SUGGESTED READING

Mazur, Tom, and Money, John. Prenatal influences and subsequent sexuality. In B. Wolman and J. Money (Eds.), *Handbook of human sexuality.* Englewood Cliffs, N.J.: Prentice-Hall, 1980.
This brief yet informative article discusses genetic and endocrinological influences in prenatal sexual development. Emphasis is placed on prenatal influences as they affect subsequent gender identity/role differentiation and development.

McCary, James Leslie, and McCary, Stephen P. *McCary's human sexuality* (4th ed.). Belmont, Calif.: Wadsworth, 1982.
Chapter 3 is related to the biochemistry of sex.

Money, John, and Ehrhardt, Anke. *Man and woman, boy and girl: The differentiation and dimorphism of gender identity from conception to maturity.* Baltimore: Johns Hopkins University Press, 1972.
Drawing upon the findings of many disciplines, this book provides comprehensive treatment of sexual differentiation and development and contributes to understanding of homosexuality, transsexualism, transvestism, and sexual anomalies.

TRUE OR FALSE?

Muscular men have the largest penises and make the best lovers.

A large penis is not of great importance to a woman's sexual gratification.

A man with a large penis is no more sexually potent than a man with a small penis.

Because of its calorie content, semen, if swallowed during oral sex, is fattening.

Humans can get "hung up" (that is, experience *penis captivus*) during sexual intercourse.

The Male Sexual System

CHAPTER 3

The Male Genitalia
Erection
Ejaculation
Physiosexual Changes in the Aging Man
Summary
Suggested Reading

Centuries of observation and experimentation have demonstrated that living organisms are produced exclusively by other similar living organisms. In higher orders of life—specifically, humans—the genetic continuation of the species depends ultimately upon some form of cooperative function and utilization of the reproductive glands and organs of the two sexes. At least these facts hold true today, even though there is some evidence that in the distant future scientists may be able to modify genetic and reproductive processes significantly. In this chapter and the next one, the physiology and functions of the human reproductive organs as we know them today are explained in detail.

The Male Genitalia

In the male, the **testicles** (also called **gonads** or **testes**) are the first sexual structures to be formed (Figure 3.1). They develop as a pair in the abdominal cavity and descend shortly before or just after birth into the **scrotum**, a loose pouch of skin that is an outpocket of the abdominal cavity. In about 3 percent of male infants, the testicles have not descended into the scrotum at the time of birth, in which case endocrine or surgical assistance is needed. This should be done by the time the child is four or five years of age (Vaughan & McKay, 1975).

The testicles are egg-shaped bodies that vary in size but in the adult are usually about 4 centimeters long and about 2.5 centimeters in diameter (Figure 3.2). The scrotum where they are housed is supported by special muscles and tissues that regulate the temperature of the gonads. Ordinarily the scrotal temperature is slightly lower than that of the body itself. This lower temperature is necessary for sperm production. The supporting muscles and tissues act to contract the scrotum when the outside temperature is low, thus bringing the testicles closer to the warm body. They relax when the temperature is high, lowering the testicles away from the body. Long hot baths, prolonged use of athletic supporters, high fever, and the like have for centuries been thought to cause infertility, especially in men with a low sperm count to start with. A 2° to 3°C increase in temperature does in fact occasionally result in temporary sterility in men, but fertility returns after a short time. There is little evidence that taking prolonged hot baths is a successful contraceptive technique, although it is considered in some countries to achieve that purpose.

Sperm are produced within each testis in tubules (called the **seminiferous tubules**), which are lined with germinal tissue. The process is known as **spermatogenesis**. As a boy grows older and hormonal function increases, the inner surface of the seminiferous tubules yields an increasing number of cells known as primitive spermatogonia. These make up the first stage of spermatogenesis. Spermatogenesis begins when a boy is about eleven, although the age varies considerably, as can be judged by the different times at which puberty is reached.

Through the process of **mitosis**, or ordinary cell division, each spermato-

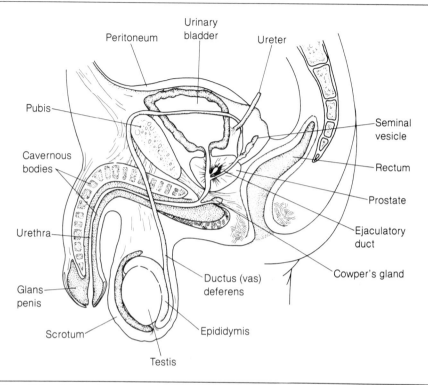

Figure 3.1   Schematic representation of the male pelvic region, showing organs of reproduction.

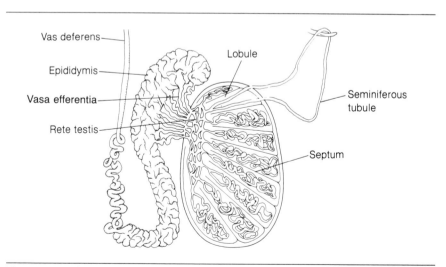

Figure 3.2   Schematic representation of the testicle.

gonium divides and produces two cells, both containing the full component of forty-six chromosomes. One cell is another spermatogonium, which remains at the surface of the tubule ready to split again, thus perpetuating formation of future spermatogonia. The other is a primary spermatocyte, which constitutes the next stage of spermatogenesis. The primary spermatocyte is a large cell that moves toward the center opening of the tubule. It undergoes **meiosis** or reduction division, producing two smaller secondary spermatocytes. In meiosis, the number of chromosomes in each cell is reduced to twenty-three: twenty-two autosomal chromosomes (nonsex chromosomes) plus an X (female) chromosome in one secondary spermatocyte, and twenty-two similar nonsex chromosomes plus a Y (male) in the other. X and Y sperm are thus produced in equal numbers.

The secondary spermatocytes immediately split by mitotic division to form the last primitive male germinal cells, the spermatids. Spermatids develop without cell division into the mature **spermatozoa**, or fully formed sperm cells, each having only twenty-three chromosomes. Spermatogenesis proceeds to the spermatid stage after a boy is approximately twelve years old. The testes then grow rapidly because of marked enlargement of the seminiferous tubules, this germinal activity increasing as the boy advances to his mid-teens. At about age fifteen or sixteen, he is usually capable of full spermatogenesis.

After the sperm are produced in the testes, they travel to the **epididymis**, a swelling attached to each testicle, where they mature or ripen for as long as six weeks. They are then transported in the **vas deferens**, a small tube about 45 centimeters in length that serves as a passage to one of the two **seminal vesicles**, pouches near the top of the **prostate gland** behind the bladder. The mature sperm have little motility until they mix with **prostatic fluid** to form **semen** or ejaculate (Figure 3.3). That part of the prostatic secretion that constitutes the larger portion of the semen is a highly alkaline, thin, milky fluid containing many substances, including proteins, calcium, citric acid, cholesterol, and various enzymes and acids. The alkalinity of the secretion apparently helps the sperm move through acid areas at a rapid pace, since, for example, acid in the vaginal fluid will easily destroy them if left in contact even for a short time.

The consistency of seminal fluid varies from man to man, and variations are to be expected in the same man from time to time. Sometimes the fluid is thick and almost gelatinlike, while another time it will be thin and somewhat watery. Frequent ejaculations generally result in a thinner fluid.

The average amount of semen ejaculated at any one time is 4 cubic centimeters, which weighs about 4 grams. Given the protein and fat contained in semen, the average ejaculate probably represents less than thirty-six calories. There is no convincing evidence, therefore, that a normal discharge of semen in any way "weakens" a man (Clark, 1969). Furthermore, it is a myth that a woman who swallows seminal fluid during oral sex will become inordinately fat or that she will become pregnant from thus ingesting the semen.

Along with the seminal vesicles and the prostate, the **Cowper's glands** make up a man's accessory reproductive glands. During sexual excitement, the Cowper's glands secrete an alkaline fluid that lubricates and neutralizes the

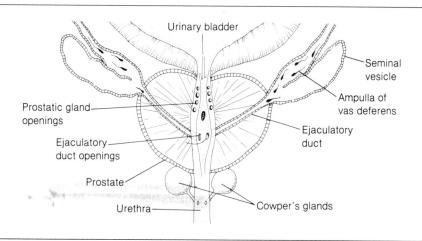

Figure 3.3   Schematic representation of the prostate gland, showing ejaculatory duct openings joining the urethra.

acidity of the **urethra** (the duct through which urine and seminal fluid pass out of the body) for easy and safe passage of the semen. This fluid from the Cowper's glands can be observed at the opening of the head of the penis during sexual excitement and before ejaculation. The fluid does not ordinarily contain sperm, but some sperm do occasionally make their way into the fluid. It is therefore possible for a woman to be made pregnant by penetration even if the man does not ejaculate.

Situated just below the Cowper's glands is the base of the **penis**, a cylindrical organ composed mostly of erectile tissue. During sexual excitation, this tissue becomes enlarged with blood, causing the penis to become erect and hard. In the adult male, the observable part of the average penis is from 2.5 to 4 inches long when flaccid (limp), slightly over 1 inch in diameter, and about 3.5 inches in circumference. The size, of course, varies considerably from man to man. When in a state of **tumescence** (**erection**), the average penis extends 5.5 to 6.5 inches in length and becomes 1.5 inches in diameter and about 4.5 inches in circumference. Again, the size of the erect penis shows considerable variation from man to man.

If a hormonal malfunction occurs during childhood, the size of a man's penis may be adversely affected. However, when no hormonal deficiencies occur, the size of the penis is fixed by heredity. In rare instances surgical procedures have been employed to enlarge abnormally small penises (Dailey, 1980a).

There is little relationship between the size of a flaccid penis and its size when erect, and there is even less relationship between penile size and general body size than exists between the dimensions of other organs and the body (Masters & Johnson, 1966). The measurement of a perfectly functioning erect penis can vary from 2 inches (5 centimeters) in one man to 10 inches (25 centimeters) in another, with one no less capable of coital performance than the

How Much Does Size Matter?

Scientists at the Sexological Institute of Prague, Czechoslovakia, have investigated the relationship between penile size, male hormone functioning, and potency. Their sampling consisted of thirty-four adult male subjects, most aged twenty-five to thirty-five. Their hormonal secretions had been deficient during the critical adolescent years of sexual development, and their flaccid penile length was consequently under 2.2 inches (5.6 centimeters). Through hormonal treatment, size was increased within a few months to the normal 2.5 to 4 inches (6.5 to 10 centimeters) (Raboch, 1970). Of the subject population in this study, potency disturbances rarely affected those men whose flaccid penises were shorter than 2.4 inches (6.1 centimeters) and narrower than 0.8 inches (2 centimeters), evidence that male impotence has very little to do with a small penis.

other. Comfort (1980) notes that, although men believe that penis size is a matter of special importance, women tend to report that other physical attributes, such as men's legs or buttocks, are more attractive to them.

Men are often concerned about the dimensions of their penises because childhood experiences have conditioned them to associate an adult's larger penis with strength and masculinity. When a boy conditioned in this way grows up, he may well think that to be a man of sexual prowess he must have an inordinately large penis. Yet, as will be discussed, most researchers argue that a woman's vagina has few nerve endings. Aside from psychological influences, therefore, the size of a man's penis has little to do with the pleasure experienced by either partner, unless there is some physical or hormonal dysfunction (Masters & Johnson, 1966). Some recent evidence, however, suggests that with similar coital techniques and positions, and based on both physical and fantasy factors, the larger penis may provide a woman with greater sexual enjoyment. One reason appears to be that many women mistakenly equate the larger penis with greater masculinity. Another is that the larger penile circumference places greater pressure on the vaginal-ring muscles and is more likely to cause a pleasurable tugging of the labia minora. Further, the longer penis sometimes heightens pleasurable sensations with its thrusting against the cervix (Keller, 1976). In some cases, of course, these same above-average penile dimensions can prove uncomfortable for a woman and detract from her sensual enjoyment.

By far the most sexually sensitive and excitable part of man's body is the **glans**, the smooth, conelike head of the penis (Figure 3.4). Its surface is filled with nerve endings, especially at the **corona**, the ridge at the back edge of the glans at the juncture of the glans and penile shaft. When stimulated, the corona is a primary source of sexual pleasure and excitement. The most highly sensitive area is the **frenulum** (also called the **frenum**), the thin tissue on the underside of the glans which is also attached to the skin at the top of the penile shaft.

The Myth of Penis Captivus

A surprisingly persistent myth in human sexuality is that of **penis captivus**—that humans can get "hung up" in sexual intercourse. This notion may result from observing the behavior of animals and attributing the same possibility to humans. Further, most people have heard stories of couples who became locked together while copulating, the services of a physician being required before the penis could be re-leased. The story is characteristically sworn to be true and to have happened to a friend (or to a friend of a friend), although no one has ever witnessed the phenomenon or experienced it. It is, of course, possible for a woman to experience sudden strong muscle spasms of the vagina (vaginismus) during intercourse, and the vagina may momentarily tighten around her partner's penis. But even in these circumstances, the pain or fear that a man would experience would cause loss of erection, permitting easy withdrawal of the penis. There are no scientifically verified cases of *penis captivus* in modern medical literature.

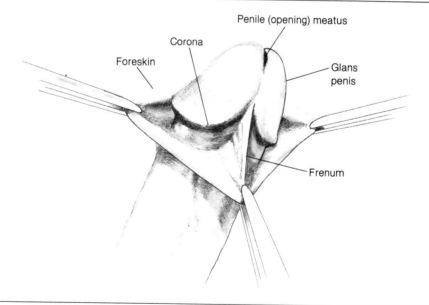

Figure 3.4   Glans penis and foreskin, showing position of the frenum.

The **shaft** of the penis is covered by loose skin that allows free movement and full erection when the penis becomes engorged with blood and elongates and enlarges. Near the tip of the penis, the skin is no longer attached to the organ directly. Encompassing the glans, it usually hangs loosely, and the flap of overhanging skin is known as the **prepuce** or **foreskin** (Figure 3.5). For hygienic, functional, and, in certain instances, religious reasons, a portion of the

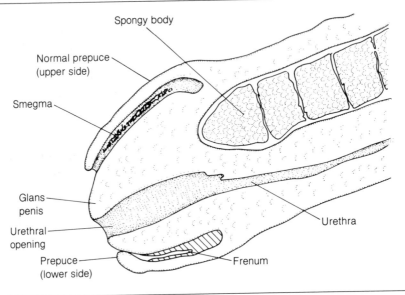

Figure 3.5   Representation of the penis, showing a collection of smegma.

prepuce covering the glans is frequently removed surgically in the well-known procedure called **circumcision.**

Just behind the glans are the Tyson's glands. These are modified sebaceous glands, which secrete a fatty lubricant material. These secretions, together with cells shed from the glans and the corona, form a smelly, cheeselike substance known as **smegma.** If the prepuce is tight over the glans, smegma can collect and emit an unpleasant odor. The area may also act as a breeding ground for irritants and disease. Prevention of the collection of smegma is one of the main purposes of circumcision. Some research has indicated that the accumulation of smegma may encourage penile cancer, in which case circumcision would be recommended. However, the evidence is inconclusive, and the American Academy of Pediatrics has formally stated that there are no valid medical grounds for routinely circumcising the newborn.

Erection

The penis is composed of three bodies of spongy tissue that become erect when filled with blood (Figure 3.6). The erection is lost when blood leaves the penis through the veins faster than it flows in through the arteries.

Although the penis is ordinarily erect at the time of ejaculation, it is not necessary for it to be so. The penis, however, must be at least partially erect if it is to penetrate the vagina and thus be capable of impregnating. Of course, a woman can become pregnant without penetration—for example, through artificial insemination—but in the present discussion only the usual method of impregnation is implied.

Erection of the penis, which is controlled by nerves in the spinal cord at the lower end of the central nervous system, involves the synchronization of several reactions. These reactions are brought about by several forces working separately or together: friction at the surface of the penis and/or surrounding areas, which sends impulses to the sacral area of the spinal cord; sexual thoughts, dreams, erotic odors, and so on, which cause impulses to be sent from the brain to the spinal area; stimulation of the sexual system by sex hormones; and impulses from full ejaculatory ducts. Unlike the ejaculatory reflex, erection is not under voluntary control. However, as long as there is proper and sufficient stimulation from the nerve endings of the penis and proper and sufficient impulses from the brain, a man will maintain his erection. Inappropriate impulses—for example, such severe stimulation of the penis that excessive pain results, or a disturbed emotional state, such as fear, anger, guilt, anxiety, or shame—can cause an erection to collapse or can prevent its occurrence in the first place. Interestingly, however, Wolchik et al. (1980) have presented preliminary evidence suggesting that emotional states such as mild anxiety or anger may actually lead to increased sexual arousal.

Nevertheless, emotional difficulties are the most frequent cause of loss of erection, and of impotence as well. It is understandable that a man who fails to have a satisfying erection, then worries over his "failure" and about his abilities the next time he attempts intercourse, may be establishing a vicious circle of failure in his sexual behavior.

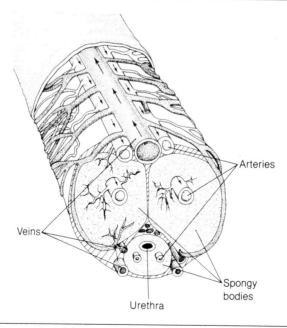

Figure 3.6   Representation of the penis showing the flow of blood. The spongy bodies, composed of erectile tissue, fill with blood to bring about an erection.

Ejaculation

Ordinarily, erection sets the stage for **ejaculation**, the spurting discharge of semen through the penis. This physical reaction is accompanied by a distinct and highly pleasurable sensation known as **orgasm**, discussed in Chapter 9. The strength of the ejaculation varies from man to man. Some men ejaculate with such force that the discharged semen may go three feet or more beyond the penis, while the semen of others may travel only a few inches or simply ooze out the urethra. The extent of the force usually depends upon such factors as general health, age, degree of sexual stimulation, and the condition of the prostate. Most men report that semen is ejaculated with little force, although they sometimes tend to correlate the subjective pleasures of orgasm with the force of ejaculation.

It is perhaps coincidental that ejaculation and orgasm occur together. Ejaculation can occur in paraplegics and quadriplegics, for example, if the spinal injury is high enough not to have damaged the nerve area directly responsible for the emission of the semen. But ejaculation in men who have had spinal cord transections is not accompanied by the usual subjective sensation of orgasm unless the transection is incomplete. Paraplegic men may have sensuous thoughts and also may have dreams of vivid orgasmic imagery despite their inability to experience the subjective sensation of orgasm (Pepmiller, 1980). Some individuals with spinal-cord injuries may experience increased sexual tension that may culminate in a "para-orgasm" (Kenan & Crist, 1981).

Both erection and ejaculation may occur without any physical stimulation. The best example is nocturnal emission, which is primarily the result of an erotic dream. In many instances nocturnal emissions occur to sexually active people who, despite a recent orgasm, may become so sexually aroused by some new erotic stimuli that they experience another orgasm during sleep. These nocturnal responses can occur quite frequently—especially among better-educated young men, who appear more responsive than others to erotic stimuli of a psychological nature. Furthermore, both men and women have been known to have orgasms from erotic thoughts alone or from stimulation of nongenital areas, such as the lips and breasts (Masters & Johnson, 1966).

Ordinarily each ejaculation contains millions of sperm, although the sperm count per ejaculate tends to diminish as frequency of intercourse increases. Although the reason is not known, the higher the sperm count is, the greater the proportion of male sperm; conversely, the lower the sperm count, the greater the proportion of female sperm. (See Chapter 5 for a discussion of the role of sperm in sex determination.)

Physiosexual Changes in the Aging Man

As a man grows older, certain physical changes become evident. The size and firmness of the testicles diminish. They do not elevate to the same degree that they did when he was younger. The seminiferous tubules thicken and begin a degenerative process that, to an ever-increasing degree, inhibits the production of sperm. The prostate gland often enlarges, and its contractions during orgasm are weaker. The force of ejaculation often weakens, and the seminal fluid is thinner and more scant. Orgasm is slower in coming and may not last as long as it once did. The intensity and duration of the **sex flush** (a rashlike condition on the skin) during sexual excitation abate; and the involuntary muscular spasms accompanying orgasm decrease (Belliveau & Richter, 1970; Corbett, 1981; Masters & Johnson, 1966). Even by age forty, the quality of a man's sexual pleasure may have begun changing noticeably. The shift is from the intense sensations localized in the genitals, as is common to the young, to a more generalized sensation diffused throughout the body (Kaplan, 1974).

When he was young, a man may have required only a few seconds of stimulation to achieve erection; as an older man he may require several minutes. His erections are less vigorous and frequent. Objective investigations of male erectile responsiveness have shown that the response of men aged nineteen to thirty years is 5.8 times faster than that of men aged forty-eight to sixty-five (Solnick & Birren, 1977).

Despite these changes, however, the older man has certain advantages over the younger one because his ejaculatory control is much greater. He is able to maintain an erection for a considerably longer time without the ejaculatory urgency that plagues the younger man (J. L. McCary, 1973). Furthermore, a young man who experiences problems with premature ejaculation in his younger years may find he is better able to control his ejaculation after reaching middle age. This greater control in turn may help him become a more adept lover (Laury, 1980).

Some men undergo a **climacteric** (physiological and hormonal changes of middle age), referred to in women as the **menopause**, but usually not until they are about fifty-five years old. When it does occur, it is typically part of the fear, common to these middle years, of aging and death—of time's running out (Ramey, 1972). The climacteric may cause men some reduction in sexual vigor and interest because of the depressive or other negative emotional conditions it can produce, but it appears to be less traumatic for them than for women.

Summary

The main components of the male sexual system are the testes, the scrotum, and the penis. The testes, housed internally within the scrotum, contain seminiferous tubules in which spermatogenesis takes place. Sperm then move from the testes to the epididymis and from the epididymis to the vas deferens. The vas deferens connects with the seminal vesicles, the prostate gland, and the Cowper's glands. These organs produce fluids that combine with sperm to make semen. Below the Cowper's glands is the penis, an organ composed primarily of erectile tissue. The glans, or smooth acornlike head of the penis, is the highly sensitive area that is covered by the foreskin or prepuce. The prepuce is frequently removed at birth in a surgical operation known as circumcision.

Erection of the penis, which ordinarily occurs prior to ejaculation, is controlled by nerves in the lower spinal cord. Emotional factors also influence whether a man maintains or loses his erection. Ejaculation, the spurting discharge of semen through the penis, usually occurs with the sensation known as orgasm. However, erection, ejaculation, and orgasm need not occur together, as shown in cases of physical injury or disease, or in cases involving erotic thoughts and nocturnal emissions.

Certain physiological changes occur in older men. Men might experience changes in the size and firmness of their testicles; degeneration of seminiferous tubules might occur, and sperm production might be inhibited. There can be enlargement of the prostate gland, a diminished force and consistency to ejaculation, less vigorous and less frequent erections, and an overall decrease in orgasmic response. Men can also experience emotional changes as they grow older.

TRUE OR FALSE:
THE FACTS

Muscular men have the largest penises and make the best lovers.
False. There is even less relationship between penile size and general body size than exists between the dimensions of other organs and the body. (39)

A large penis is not of great importance to a woman's sexual gratification.
True. Women report that they find other physical attributes more attractive; penile size might have a psychological influence on sexual satisfaction, and some evidence suggests that a large penis *sometimes* provides a woman with greater enjoyment—but not necessarily. (39−40)

A man with a large penis is no more sexually potent than a man with a small penis.
True. Measurements of perfectly functioning erect penises vary from 2 inches to 10 inches, and all are capable of coital performance. (39)

Because of its calorie content, semen, if swallowed during oral sex, is fattening.
False. The calorie count of an average ejaculate is thirty-six calories or less. (38)

Humans can get "hung up" (that is, experience penis captivus) during sexual intercourse.
False. Even if a woman's vagina momentarily tightens around the penis during intercourse, pain or fear would cause a man to lose his erection. (41)

SUGGESTED READING

Chesterman, John, and Marten, Michael. *Man to man.* New York: Paddington Press, 1980.
Clear, straightforward, and free of medical jargon, this book answers many questions men ask concerning health and sexuality. Topics such as sexual variance,

homosexuality, and sexually transmitted diseases are discussed frankly and honestly.

The Diagram Group. *Man's body: An owner's manual.* New York: Bantam Books, 1976.
This easy-to-read reference book for men provides comprehensive treatment of the male sexual system.

McCarthy, Barry. *What you still don't known about male sexuality.* New York: Thomas Y. Crowell, 1977.
This book presents factual information related to the various aspects of male sexuality, dispelling misconceptions surrounding male sexual attitudes, feelings, and relationships. The author stresses the need for deeper understanding of male sexuality among both men and women.

McCary, James Leslie, and McCary, Stephen P. *McCary's human sexuality* (4th ed.). Belmont, Calif.: Wadsworth, 1982.
Chapter 4 is specifically related to the male sexual system. Chapter 14 discusses sex in the later years.

Zilbergeld, Bernie. *Male sexuality: A guide to sexual fulfillment.* Boston: Little, Brown, 1978.
Honest and forthright, this book deals with many of the physical and emotional aspects of sex for men of all ages.

TRUE OR FALSE?

The absence of the hymen proves that a girl is not a virgin.

The presence of the hymen is not positive evidence that a girl is a virgin.

Sexual intercourse during the menstrual flow will cause physical distress.

A woman's cycle includes a "safe period" when she cannot become pregnant.

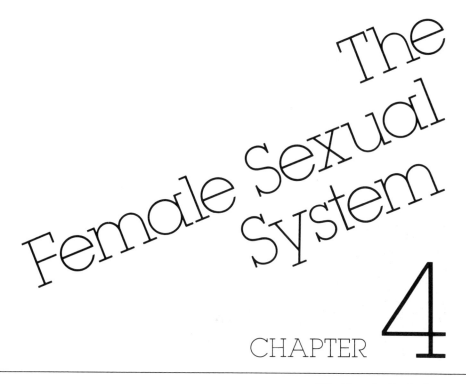

The Female Sexual System

CHAPTER 4

The Female Genitalia

Menstruation

Physiosexual Changes in the Aging Woman

The Climacteric or Menopause

Summary

Suggested Reading

T
he internal female genital organs consist of two ovaries, two uterine or fallopian tubes, the uterus (or womb), and the inner two-thirds of the vagina (Figure 4.1).

The Female Genitalia

The **ovaries** produce **ova**, or eggs, and are homologous to the testes of the male. Located on either side of the uterus, the ovaries are pinkish-gray bodies roughly the size, shape, and weight of an unshelled almond. **Oogenesis**, the development of ova, corresponds to the male function of spermatogenesis. Although smaller than the period at the end of this sentence, the human ovum is a relatively large cell, one of the largest of mammalian eggs (Eastman & Hellman, 1961). Oogenesis consists of four developmental stages: oogonium, primary oocyte, secondary oocyte, and mature ovum. In the first phase of development, the oogonium, or basic cell of the ovum, is enclosed in an ovarian follicle. It then develops into a primary oocyte, which is somewhat larger than the original cell. Just prior to ovulation, the primary oocyte undergoes a process known as reduction division, or **meiosis**. The paired chromosomes within the oocyte divide, with one of each pair going to each of the two cells created by the division. The number of chromosomes in each cell is therefore twenty-three rather than the usual forty-six.

One cell, called the secondary oocyte, is much larger than the other because it retains practically all the cytoplasm, the material that maintains the life of the cell's nucleus, of the original cell. It is the secondary oocyte that unites with the male sperm, each thus contributing twenty-three chromosomes to make up the forty-six common to humans. The second cell, which is referred to as a polar body, has little function and ultimately degenerates.

Within each ovary are a number of round vesicles called **follicles** (Figure 4.2). Each follicle houses an oocyte (an ovum in an early stage of development). Each month, about midway through the menstrual cycle of the physically mature female, one follicle ruptures, discharging the ovum into the peritoneal cavity in the process known as **ovulation**. (Perhaps twenty follicles ripen to the point of readiness for ovulation. Because of circulating gonadotropic hormones, however, only one of these follicles usually ruptures; the others degenerate.) Since the average woman is fertile for approximately thirty-five years and ovulates about thirteen times every year, you can see that only four hundred to five hundred of the many thousands of oocytes are discharged. The numerous primitive follicles that reach only a certain stage of development and then disintegrate serve a purpose, however, because before degenerating, they are an important source of female hormones. Although ovarian hormones (estrogen and progesterone) contribute to a woman's sexual desire, their primary function is to prepare and maintain the uterus for implantation of the fertilized ovum. By measuring these hormones and using other clinical diagnostic procedures, doctors can help determine the time of ovulation (Eddy, 1979). Such procedures may aid women who have had difficulty in becoming pregnant.

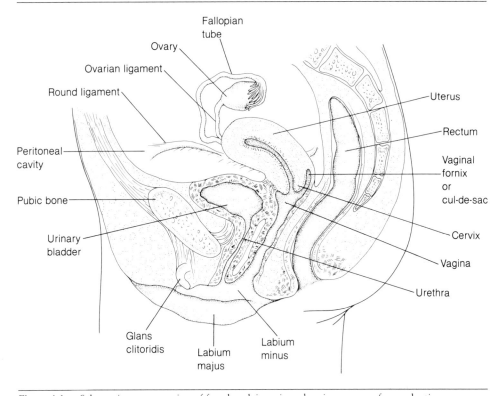

Figure 4.1   Schematic representation of female pelvic region, showing organs of reproduction.

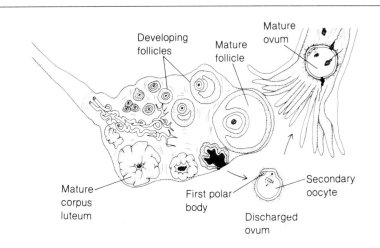

Figure 4.2   Schematic representation of the ovary, showing developing follicles, mature follicle, and corpus luteum.

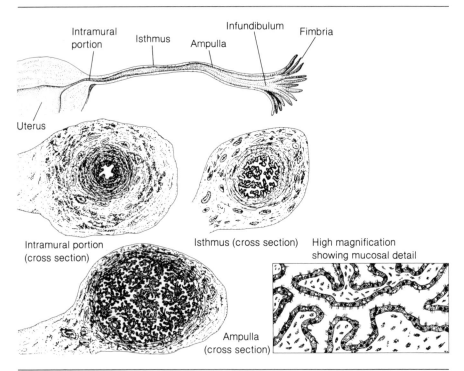

Figure 4.3   Schematic representation of fallopian tube, showing its gross and microscopic structure.

In the course of ovulation, the secondary oocyte moves from the follicle into the **fallopian tube**, where fertilization, if it is to take place, usually occurs (Figure 4.3). The ovum is not considered to have reached full maturity, the fourth stage of oogenesis, until it is fertilized, for the developmental processes of the nucleus are not complete until then. In the physically mature female, ovulation is generally assumed to occur alternately in each ovary, but one ovary may in fact discharge several times in succession. A single egg is usually released at the time of ovulation, but two or more ova may be discharged. Although women are generally assumed to ovulate once a month, an additional egg may be discharged during the month, especially during a peak of sexual excitement. This eventually may contribute to the high incidence of impregnation occurring during the so-called "safe" period—the time of the menstrual month at which conception is thought least likely to occur (Neubardt, 1968).

Fertilization usually occurs in the ampulla portion of the fallopian tube, which cups over the ovary and picks up each ovum as it is discharged. The **conceptus** (fertilized ovum) is then swept by tiny, hairlike projections called cilia toward the **uterus**, a hollow, thick-walled muscular organ shaped somewhat like a pear (Figure 4.4). The uterine walls contain longitudinal and circu-

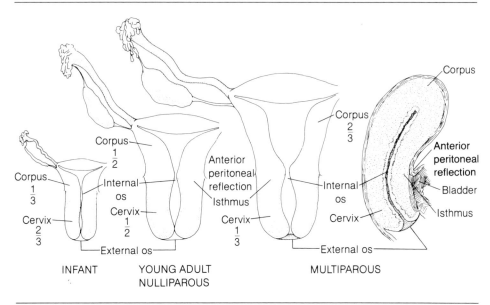

Figure 4.4   Schematic representation of normal uterus (front view) and appendages, showing comparative size of infantile, adult nonparous (not having been pregnant), and multiparous (having been pregnant) uteri. Side view of multiparous uterus is also shown.

lar muscle fibers that spiral and run through the walls in both clockwise and counterclockwise directions. The basketlike interweaving of the muscles allows the uterus to stretch to gigantic proportions during pregnancy and to exert tremendous pressure by contracting in a downward manner at the time of labor. Contraction of these muscles also takes place in the orgasmic phase of a woman's sexual response cycle and at certain times during menstruation, causing cramping in some women.

The fallopian tubes enter the uterus at the upper, larger portion of the organ, known as the corpus or body. The cavity of the uterus is a flattened space that is little more than a slit, its total length being about 2.5 inches (6 or 7 centimeters). The flattened cavity narrows to a tiny opening near the center of the organ, then continues through the **cervix** (the lower end of the uterus) as an opening smaller than a soda straw. The cervix is smaller than the body of the uterus, the size ratio in mature women being about one to two. In the newborn female, this ratio is reversed, the cervix being about twice as large as the corpus. The cervix is more fibrous than the body of the uterus, and its foldlike lining contains glands that produce a mucous secretion, once erroneously thought to attract sperm cells. About one-third to one-half inch (0.8 to 1.3 centimeters) of the cervix extends into the vagina, thus producing a connection for the passage of sperm into the place where they may meet the ovum. During

The G Spot: Fact or Fiction?

While it is generally recognized that women do not ejaculate as men do, researchers have reported cases where women have experienced ejaculatory expulsion of a prostaticlike fluid through the urethra during orgasm. Such responses occur most frequently from stimulation of the Grafenberg spot or "G spot," an area located on the anterior wall of the vagina. Research supports the contention that a "G spot" exists (Ladas, Whipple, & Perry, 1982). Some interesting points established by this research are the following:

1. There is an area on the anterior wall of the vagina approximately 2 inches (5 centimeters) from the introitus that is responsive to deep pressure. This area has been named the "Grafenberg spot" in recognition of Dr. Ernst Grafenberg, the first contemporary physician to have described it.

2. When stimulated adequately, the G spot swells and orgasm can result in many women.

3. During orgasm some women may ejaculate a fluid through the urethra that is similar in biochemical composition to the male ejaculate, except that it contains no sperm. Further, this fluid is expelled through an ejaculatory process and not as the result of uncontrolled urination.

4. The G spot can be stimulated manually or by the penis during sexual intercourse. The woman-above coital position usually affords more effective stimulation of the G spot than the man-above or "missionary" position.

5. Use of a diaphragm for birth control protection can interfere with effective stimulation of the G spot in many women. For women who are so affected, other forms of birth control, such as the cervical cap, may remove this hindrance.

6. Women may enhance their ability to reach orgasm through coitus if they learn to strengthen their pubococcygeus muscle. Men also can learn to strengthen their pubococcygeus muscle and thereby learn to experience multiple orgasms and to separate orgasm from ejaculation.

7. Women and men experience several kinds of orgasm. Women can experience a vulval orgasm triggered by clitoral stimulation, a uterine orgasm triggered by coitus, and a "blended" orgasm, a combination of vulval and uterine orgasms. Men can experience orgasm triggered by penile stimulation and orgasm triggered by stimulation of the prostate.

Certainly this research contradicts the view that orgasm in women results mainly from direct or indirect stimulation of the clitoris and that orgasm in men results mainly from penile stimulation. Research does not suggest that there is a "right" or "wrong" or "better" or "worse" way to experience orgasm. It does indicate that women and men may be capable of a greater variety of sexual responses than heretofore believed.

pregnancy the cervix is typically closed by a mucous plug that prevents bacteria and other undesirable matter from entering the uterus, thereby reducing the possibility of infection.

The **vagina** is a muscular tube, capable of considerable dilation, that extends from just behind the cervix to an external opening in the vestibule of the vulva. About 3 inches (7.6 centimeters) long on the front wall, and about 3.5 inches (8.9 centimeters) on the back wall, the vagina extends upward in an approximately vertical manner in a standing woman, roughly at right angles to the uterus. It is the organ that receives the penis during the act of sexual intercourse. The vaginal tube elongates somewhat during sexual excitation. The walls of the vagina are in contact with each other under ordinary conditions. They have a wrinkled appearance and contain an intricate network of erectile tissue which helps to dilate and close the vaginal canal.

Vaginal lubrication, present during sexual excitement, is brought about by the vagina itself. It secretes a fluid through a process similar to sweating that remains something of a puzzle (Masters & Johnson, 1966). As sexual excitement builds and continues, small beads of "sweat" appear on the vaginal surface. This fluid serves as a lubricant to aid in penile penetration, making sexual intercourse easier to perform.

Although many women claim that the sex act is incomplete and unsatisfying to them without penetration, the vagina contains very few nerve endings that give sexual pleasure. Thus, many professionals have held that psychological reasons underlie women's claims of coital satisfaction. Recent research, however, suggests that the basis of coital enjoyment for women may be physiological as well as psychological (Ladas et al., 1982).

The birth of children and aging are factors that may lead to vaginal muscles too relaxed to afford maximum coital satisfaction. A woman whose vaginal muscles are overly relaxed can strengthen them with proper exercise (Witkin, 1980). One such exercise (the Kegel exercise) involves a series of alternating voluntary contractions and relaxations of the vaginal muscles. This and similar exercises also can be employed by men to tone their pubococcygeal muscles and hence to maximize their orgasmic pleasure (Powell, 1981). Women may supplement vaginal-muscle exercises by the use of a battery-operated, hand-held device called the Vagette (Dailey, 1980b).

The **hymen,** or **maidenhead,** is the fold of connective tissue that partially closes the external opening of the vagina (Figure 4.5). This tissue may prevent full penetration of the penis and, if intact, is usually ruptured by the first act of sexual intercourse. More often, however, the tissue is broken by accidents to the pubic area or by experimentation. A ruptured hymen, therefore, is certainly not in itself evidence that a female is not a virgin. On the other hand, rare cases exist where the hymen is so flexible or pliable that coitus can take place repeatedly without rupturing the tissue. An intact hymen at the time of marriage is extremely important to some women. Some cultures, for example, expect—even demand—that women be virginal at marriage, so their gynecologists frequently perform surgery to create an artificial hymen.

Pain accompanying first intercourse—frequently assumed to be a cause of frigidity—is often the result of hymenal rupture. If the hymen is intact, it would be wise to have a physician cut or remove it rather than risking the tissue's being torn by forceful penile penetration. In the case of an annular (ring-shaped) hymen, a doctor may suggest inserting and rotating the fingertips or using a small dilator, either of which will stretch the tissue and permit penile penetration without pain or difficulty. Obviously the hymenal tissue does not close off the vagina completely, since the menstrual flow is discharged

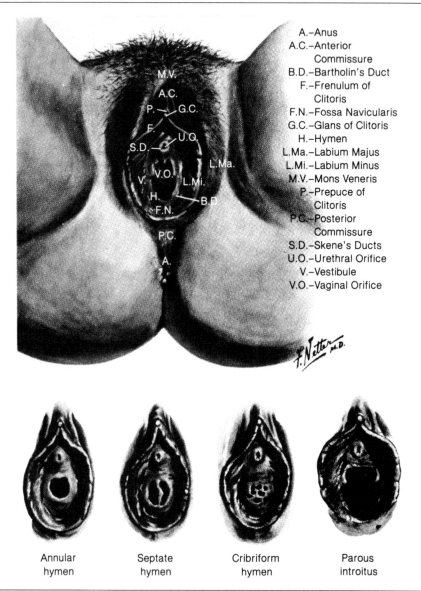

A.–Anus
A.C.–Anterior
      Commissure
B.D.–Bartholin's Duct
F.–Frenulum of
      Clitoris
F.N.–Fossa Navicularis
G.C.–Glans of Clitoris
H.–Hymen
L.Ma.–Labium Majus
L.Mi.–Labium Minus
M.V.–Mons Veneris
P.–Prepuce of
      Clitoris
P.C.–Posterior
      Commissure
S.D.–Skene's Ducts
U.O.–Urethral Orifice
V.–Vestibule
V.O.–Vaginal Orifice

Annular	Septate	Cribriform	Parous
hymen	hymen	hymen	introitus

Figure 4.5   External female genitalia with comparison of four types of hymens. © Copyright 1954 and 1965 CIBA Pharmaceutical Co., Division of CIBA-GEIGY Corp. Reproduced with permission from THE CIBA COLLECTION OF MEDICAL ILLUSTRATIONS by Frank H. Netter, M.D. All rights reserved.

as easily from virgins as from nonvirgins. The tissue is usually annular or perforated, or in some other way only partially covers the opening. In those rare cases in which the vagina is completely sealed over, a minor operation before the onset of menstruation will solve the problem (Capraro et al., 1981).

In addition to the pain of tearing the hymenal tissue, there is sometimes pain during early, and especially first, sexual intercourse because of powerful contractions of the vaginal muscles—usually the result of fear and ignorance of the facts of coitus. If a woman is relaxed and unafraid, there is little reason why she cannot comfortably and pleasurably accommodate a very large penis, even though she has not had sexual intercourse before. Women under emotional stress, however, even though they might be highly experienced sexually, can experience these vaginal muscle spasms (**vaginismus**), making forced penetration extremely painful or even impossible.

The external genital apparatus of a woman, known as the **vulva**, consists of the following visible parts or areas: the mons veneris (also called mons pubis), the labia majora (major or large outer lips), the labia minora (small inner lips), the clitoris, and the vestibule.

The **mons veneris** or **mons pubis** is composed of pads of fatty tissue lying below the skin over the pubic bone. It is covered with springy, curly hair. This area houses certain nerve endings that when stimulated by weight, pressure, or similar conditions can produce sexual excitement. From this prominent mound, two longitudinal folds of skin bearing pubic hair serve laterally to form the outer borders of the vulva.

The **labia majora** are the two folds of skin that enclose the vulval cleft (indentation). The lips are quite fatty; their inner sides contain sebaceous follicles and sweat glands but no hair. The **labia minora** are also two longitudinal folds and are located within the major lips. Rich in blood vessels, nerve endings, and small sebaceous glands, they contain no hair or fat cells. These small lips form the lateral and lower borders of the vestibule. They fuse at the top to form the prepuce and to enclose the clitoris.

The **clitoris** is a small cylindrical erectile structure that terminates in the glans, or head, and is situated at the top of the vestibule. The entire clitoris, except the glans, is underneath the upper part of the labia minora where its two lips join to form the clitoral prepuce. Unlike the penis, the clitoris does not hang free, only its glans is exposed. Like the penis, the clitoris is composed of spongy erectile bodies that become engorged with blood, and erect, when stimulated. Ordinarily, the clitoris is less than 1.2 inches (3 centimeters) in length, although there are striking individual variations in its measurements. When sexually stimulated, it may enlarge to twice its flaccid size or more. The diameter of the clitoral shaft becomes especially enlarged.

The glans of the flaccid clitoris has a diameter less than one-fourth inch (4 to 5 millimeters). Like the glans of the penis, it contains an abundance of nerve endings and is the most sexually excitable area of a woman's body. Direct contact with the glans—such as the man's pubic bone rubbing against it—and indirect stimulation through the pulling and tugging of the minor lips as the penis moves in and out of the vagina are coital methods of bringing a woman to orgasm. Masters and Johnson have pointed out that, in self-manipulation of the clitoris, many women stimulate to the side of it rather than stimulating it directly.

It is possible to remove the clitoris completely without destroying a woman's erotic sensations or even her orgasmic capability. The nerve supply to the vulval area is so great that large amounts of erogenous tissue may be surgically removed without significantly decreasing sexual gratification. In fact, women may remain orgasmic after the entire vulval region has been removed by surgery. It appears, therefore, that frequency and intensity of sexual activity, including orgasm, are related less to anatomical size or the amount of tissue than to other factors, including psychological ones (Money, 1970). Paralyzed women generally lose their capacity to respond orgasmically, although some cord-injured women may achieve orgasm through stimulation of body areas, such as the breasts, above the point of injury (Kenan & Crist, 1981). Regardless of whether orgasm is possible, emotionally gratifying sexual experiences may be enjoyed by handicapped women (Pepmiller, 1980).

Smegma, an accumulation of genital secretions, can collect under the prepuce covering the clitoris, resulting in abrasions and adhesions between it and the glans. Some specialists believe that this condition can cause severe pain when the clitoris enlarges during sexual excitement. The present-day medical practice is to rid the area of the ragged lumps by means of a probe.

The **vestibule** is the cleft region enclosed by the labia minora. It houses the openings of the vagina and the urethra. This area is rich in nerve endings and blood vessels, and is highly responsive to stimulation. The **Bartholin's glands** are situated on each side of the vaginal orifice. Each gland secretes a drop or so of lubricating fluid during sexual excitement. Although this fluid was once thought to aid in penile penetration, recent research has shown that the secretion is too slight to be of significant benefit in vaginal lubrication (Masters & Johnson, 1966).

Menstruation

As noted previously, most girls begin puberty between the ages of eleven and fifteen. Accompanying the development of breasts, reproductive organs, and secondary sexual characteristics is the **menarche**, which is that point during puberty when a monthly uterine "bleeding" begins. This monthly discharge of blood and other fluids and debris from the uterine wall is called **menstruation**. Between the menarche and the climacteric, the average woman menstruates from three to five hundred times. The menstrual cycle is measured from the onset of one menstrual flow to the day before the next flow and varies considerably in women. While the average length is from twenty-four to thirty-two days, younger women, especially teenagers, tend to have longer cycles than do older women, and young women also tend to have greater variation in the length of their cycles. Actually, the length of the menstrual cycle can vary from

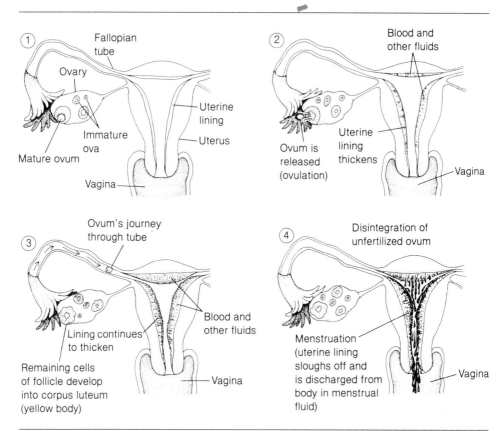

Figure 4.6   The menstrual cycle: (1) During early part of cycle, ovum matures in ovary; endometrium begins to thicken. (2) About fourteen days after onset of last menstruation, mature ovum is released; endometrium is thick and spongy. (3) Ovum travels through fallopian tube; ruptured follicle develops into a glandular structure, the corpus luteum; blood and other fluids engorge uterine lining. (4) If ovum is not fertilized, endometrium breaks down and sloughs off in a form of bleeding (menstruation).

twenty-one to ninety days and still be considered physiologically normal (Worley, 1980).

Menstruation can occur without ovulation having taken place (Worley, 1980). However, the menstrual flow typically commences when progesterone, the hormone that has prepared and maintained the walls of the uterus for the implantation of a fertilized ovum, is withdrawn because no egg has been fertilized. Withdrawal of the hormone causes the uterine lining (the endometrium) to break down, slough off, and be discharged from the body in the form of bleeding. This phase of a woman's cycle is called the destructive phase. The approximate time required for the discharge of the uterine fluids and debris is from three to seven days, and at the end of that time the uterine wall is very thin (Figure 4.6). The amount of fluid discharged varies widely from woman to woman and sometimes from cycle to cycle in the same individual, but the average amount is approximately one cupful. However, the amount of actual blood loss on even the heaviest day of menstruation is rarely more than one tablespoonful.

There are a few physical and psychological signals of the beginning of the menstrual flow. Some are due to the condition of the body at this time as well as to an imbalance between progesterone and estrogen. Others may be due to negative attitudes toward sexuality in general and menstruation in particular. Almost every woman has suffered some menstrual problems. Fortunately, many women are able to achieve symptomatic relief from their menstrual problems with appropriate medical attention (Dingfelder, 1980).

Discomfort or pain occurring before menstruation is called the **premenstrual syndrome**, and that experienced during menstruation itself, **dysmenorrhea**. Fatigue, headaches, and irritability are sometimes experienced in the premenstrual period, and other symptoms occurring before and during menstruation include an increase in the size and firmness of breasts, frequency of urination, dull pain in the lower abdomen (cramps), water retention, and acne. The body's toxicity increases as the uterine tissue dies and sloughs off. The bloodstream then picks up some of this toxic material and circulates it through the body, sometimes producing malaise and fatigue. Further, the marked decrease of progesterone in the body just before menstruation produces an imbalance between it and estrogen. This hormonal imbalance is believed to cause the physical and emotional reactions just described.

The degree of premenstrual tension that a woman experiences correlates with her general response to stress. The better she handles stress, the less upset she becomes just before menstruation, and the more easily she recovers from whatever stress occurs. Some women, however, suffer almost unbearable premenstrual tension which appears to be associated with sodium imbalance and the resulting water retention. Dramatic relief has been reported when treatment is instituted to rid the body of excess fluid (Neu & DiMascio, 1974).

Recently, a disease called **toxic shock syndrome** (TSS) has come to the attention of health officials. TSS, although rare, is thought to be associated with the continuous use of tampons throughout the menstrual cycle. The disease is sudden in onset and is characterized by symptoms such as vomiting, fever, diarrhea, a sunburn-like rash, and a quick drop in blood pressure. Although the cause of TSS is yet unknown, health officials suspect that tampons may favor the growth of a certain bacterium in the vaginal canal. The toxin secreted by the bacterium may be absorbed into the bloodstream from the uterus or vagina. The further study of toxic shock syndrome should lead to a better understanding of its causes and insights into its cure ("Toxic Shock," 1980).

After the menstrual flow stops, the uterine wall is very thin. At this time, as well, the breasts have decreased in size and have become somewhat soft, permitting easy examination by touch. Women are therefore encouraged to examine themselves during this time for the presence of lumps or other abnormal masses (Reyniak, 1976). Following menstruation, the follicular phase begins.

Under the stimulation of estrogen, which is secreted by follicles located in the ovaries, the uterus begins a process of growth that lasts about nine days. Many follicles contain developing ova (hence the name of this phase), most of which cease to grow. Only one usually reaches maturity in a single cycle. Called the **graafian follicle**, it can at full growth occupy as much as one-fourth of the ovary. Approaching the fourteenth day of the menstrual cycle, the follicle ruptures and a mature ovum is discharged. This event is called ovulation.

During the follicular phase the secretion of estrogen increases gradually. Estrogen concentration in the blood is at its maximum at the moment of ovulation. Following ovulation, the remaining follicular cells multiply rapidly and fill the cavity of the follicle just ruptured. The new cell growth is yellow in color and is known as the **corpus luteum**, or yellow body. The corpus luteum begins to secrete progesterone, marking the luteal phase.

Estrogen concentration decreases as progesterone begins preparing the uterus for the fertilized egg. The mucous membrane of the uterus becomes thicker and more vascular as small "lakes" of blood, called lacunae, are formed within the uterine endometrium. The lacunae provide nourishment for the ovum if it becomes fertilized and implants itself in the endometrium. If conception does not occur during the menstrual cycle, the corpus luteum degenerates and the concentration both of estrogen and progesterone decreases immensely. This sudden decrease in the amounts of both hormones is believed to bring about the destructive phase of menstruation, and the entire cyclic process then starts all over again.

There are rare instances in which extragenital bleeding occurs during the menstrual flow. Called "vicarious menstruation," such bleeding is usually from the nose, although it has been known to occur from the lungs, the retina of the eye, and so forth. This phenomenon is brought about by an endometrial vasospasm (sudden decrease in the size of the blood vessels) approximately forty-eight hours before the menstrual flow begins. There is disagreement over the cause of this phenomenon. Some relate it to **endometriosis**, an ectopic (misplaced) growth of the endometrial tissue lining the uterus. Others maintain that its causes are psychological. In 30 percent of the cases uterine bleeding is totally displaced, while in the rest the two flows occur simultaneously.

The general agreement among physicians is that women should carry on their usual activities during the menstrual period. Participating in sports, taking a bath or shower, or shampooing the hair at this time will not harm the reproductive organs. It is a myth that sexual intercourse during the menstrual flow will cause physical distress. To the contrary, research has clearly indicated that sexual activity may provide relief from pain or discomfort connected with menstruation (Masters & Johnson, 1966). Women who have experienced orgasm shortly after the onset of menstruation have reported reduced pelvic cramping and backache, possibly due to the sudden expulsion of menstrual fluid by orgasmic contractions of the uterine muscles.

Studies indicate wide variations in the effect of the menstrual cycle on women's sex drive. Some women experience the peak of their sexual desire just before menstruation. Others experience it just after the flow begins or midway

Menstruation Myths

An expert in the field of folklore, F. M. Paulsen of George Peabody College, has collected a list of myths about menstruation. Incredible as it may seem, the following myths were gathered primarily from present-day college students in various parts of the United States.

1. If a soiled menstrual pad is picked up or handled by a man, from that time onward the woman who wore the pad will be an easy victim of sexual advances.
2. If an impotent man performs oral sex on a menstruating woman, his potency will be restored.
3. A frigid woman can be brought to numerous orgasms if she has sexual intercourse during her period.
4. Well-trained domestic animals will not respond to directions from a woman who is menstruating.
5. Dogs fed by a menstruating woman will develop worms.
6. Plucking pubic hair at night will assure the woman a painless menstrual period.
7. Shaving armpits or legs during menstruation will cause the woman to become weak and listless and will result in a difficult menstruation.
8. A menstruating woman's hair will not "take" a permanent wave, and kinky hair cannot be straightened during the menstrual period.
9. A soiled menstrual pad placed under a woman's pillow each time she has intercourse will prevent her from becoming pregnant. An unused pad under the pillow will assist a woman in becoming pregnant.
10. If menstrual cramps disappear while a woman is petting, the pain is likely to be transmitted to her lover.

in the menstrual cycle (Cavanagh, 1969). There is evidence that men, as well as women, have cyclic changes in hormone production and consequently in emotional responses. Several studies have shown there is a pronounced rhythm during thirty-day cycles in the amount of hormones found in the urine of males (Ramey, 1972). Moreover, men's emotions seem to vary predictably within these cycles. That men and women function within rhythmic cycles should not be difficult to understand. Any traveler weary from transoceanic flight and time change can attest to the discomfort and mood changes that occur when his or her circadian rhythm (internal clock) is disturbed. Why should we not be equally affected by other changes in rhythm?

Physiosexual Changes in the Aging Woman

Certain physiological changes occur with the menopause, to be sure, and some of them can make coitus unpleasant. Thinning vaginal walls and diminished lubrication during sexual excitation make the vaginal vault less elastic and more liable to injury or pain, and uterine contractions during orgasm cause some women severe pain. But these problems are merely signs of postmenopausal hormone deficiency and can be circumvented by hormone replacement, administered either orally or by suppository. Although a cancer scare arose during the mid-1970s, recent studies show that hormonal replacement, when used at a low-dosage level with judicious follow-up for about a year, has not been shown to increase the risk of cancer (Greenblatt & Stoddard, 1978; Landau, 1979).

After about the age of forty, women may begin to experience a sharp decrease in the secretion of estrogen, a decrease that continues gradually for the remainder of their lives (Corbett, 1981). In the past, physicians reasoned that, since the ovaries dwindle in their production of estrogen at and after the menopause, a woman's sex drive would accordingly diminish. It is now known that a woman's sex drive often does not diminish even when the ovaries are surgically removed. A woman's sex drive ordinarily continues undiminished until she is sixty years of age or older, after which its decline is very slow, if she remains sexually active (Kinsey et al., 1953; Masters & Johnson, 1966).

The Climacteric or Menopause

When the woman is about forty-five or fifty years of age, ovulation begins to taper off, usually stopping altogether within about two years. The time interval during which the woman's ovulation and menstrual cycles gradually cease to exist is known as the **climacteric** or **menopause**. Ovulation and the menstrual flow are erratic at this time, sometimes causing the woman to believe that there is no longer a possibility of pregnancy. As long as any menstrual periods occur at all, however, the possibility of pregnancy remains. The woman cannot be reasonably sure that ovulation has ceased completely until she has gone a year without a menstrual period. While reports of childbirth by women over age fifty are publicized occasionally by the news media, there have been in the last one hundred years fewer than thirty authenticated cases of women past the age of fifty giving birth.

The climacteric can be disturbing, sometimes filled with considerable emotional upset. The most serious mental symptoms which sometimes accompany the physical changes of the climacteric are depression and paranoia. Because of greatly improved techniques of hormonal therapy and other medication, however, most of these reactions can be alleviated. Tranquilizers and psychotherapy can also be used in treatment, so that menopausal difficulties are not nearly so troublesome as they have been in the past. Only about 25 percent of all menopausal women have any sort of distressful emotional symptoms. Generally speaking, the better the health of the woman before the climacteric, the fewer unpleasant symptoms she will have when it occurs (Coleman, 1972). The hormonal imbalance occurring in menopause causes instability in the vasomotor system and occasional changes in the diameter of the blood vessels. These changes permit more blood to flow at one time—inducing hot flashes—and less at another. Hot flashes last from a second or so to several minutes, and can occur several times a day. Hot flashes of short duration may occur because of sudden changes in temperature or excessive alcohol consumption or because of the effects of anger or anxiety. Hot flashes of longer duration probably result from problems related to estrogen secretion (Labrum, 1980).

The median age for the onset of menopause has advanced in the last hundred years from 46.6 to 50.1 years. Those who start menstruating earlier in life tend to continue to menstruate longer. Similar patterns occur in other spheres of sexual life: people who begin erotic activity at an earlier age tend to maintain their sexual vigor longer, for example, and those who engage in frequent sexual activity tend to continue sexual activity later in life than those whose activity is less frequent (Kinsey et al., 1948, 1953).

Summary

The main components of the female sexual system are the ovaries, the fallopian tubes, the uterus, and the vagina. In a mature woman, the ovaries produce ova, or eggs, in a process known as oogenesis. An ovum is discharged monthly in a process known as ovulation. Fertilization of an ovum by the male sperm, if it occurs, takes place in one of the fallopian tubes. The ovum moves down toward the uterus, a pear-shaped, muscular organ divided into a corpus and a cervix. If fertilized, the ovum implants itself in the endometrial lining of the uterus; the unfertilized ovum is discharged from the body of the uterus along with the menstrual flow.

The vagina, or birth canal, extends from the cervix to an external opening and is also the organ that receives the penis during sexual intercourse. Vaginal muscles that may have become too relaxed from aging or giving birth can be strengthened through proper exercise. Young women may have a hymen, a fold of connective tissue partially closing the vaginal entrance. If necessary, the hymen can be surgically broken, or dilated, by a doctor in order to facilitate sexual intercourse.

The external genitalia, or vulva, consists of the mons veneris, the labia majora, the labia minora, the clitoris, and the vestibule. The mons veneris is most often covered with springy, curly hair; the labia majora extend from the mons veneris to enclose the vulval cleft. The labia minora, located within the labia majora, fuse at the top to enclose the clitoris. The clitoris is the most sexually excitable area of a woman's body and is at the upper end of the vestibule, the area of the vaginal and urethral openings enclosed by the labia minora.

Menstruation usually begins when a young woman is in her early teens. The purpose of the menstrual cycle is to help prepare and maintain the uterus for implantation of the fertilized egg. The menstrual cycle can be divided into three phases: the destructive phase, the follicular phase, and the luteal phase. Withdrawal of progesterone causes the uterine lining to break down and be discharged through menstruation. Menstrual difficulties, including premenstrual tension, toxic shock syndrome, and dysmenorrhea, may occur because of problems associated with this phase. During the follicular phase, the secretion of estrogen increases until its highest concentration is reached at ovulation. During the luteal phase, the corpus luteum begins to secrete progesterone, and this hormone prepares the uterus to receive the fertilized egg. If conception does not occur, then estrogen and progesterone decrease and the cycle starts anew. These changes in hormone production are sometimes cited as having effects upon a woman's sex drive and emotional responses.

Women are encouraged to carry on their usual activities—including sex—

during menstruation. Women appear to fare better when they continue with vigorous activity rather than succumb to the usual mild physical discomfort or to the emotional effects of the mythology surrounding menstruation.

Certain physiological changes occur in older women. Women may experience thinning of the vaginal walls, diminished vaginal lubrication, and decreases in estrogen secretion; but these problems often can be circumvented by hormonal replacement.

The cessation of the menstrual cycle happens to most women between the ages of forty-five and fifty and signals the climacteric or menopause. At this time ovulation (and the possibility of conception) ends. During menopause, usually lasting a few years, some women experience distressful emotional and physical symptoms. Generally, the better the mental health of the woman, the better she is able to adjust when the climacteric occurs.

TRUE OR FALSE: THE FACTS

The absence of the hymen proves that a girl is not a virgin.
False. Often the tissue is ruptured by accidents to the pubic area or by experimentation. (55)

The presence of the hymen is not positive evidence that a girl is a virgin.
True. In rare cases, the hymen is so flexible that it is not ruptured during intercourse; in addition, surgery can create an artificial hymen. (55)

Sexual intercourse during the menstrual flow will cause physical distress.
False. Sexual activity during menstruation might actually provide some relief from pain or discomfort. (61)

A woman's cycle includes a "safe period" when she cannot become pregnant.
False. Although women generally ovulate once a month, an additional egg may be discharged during the month, especially during a peak of sexual excitement—even during the "safe" period that includes menstruation. (52)

SUGGESTED READING

Barbach, Lonnie Garfield. *For yourself: The fulfillment of female sexuality.* New York: Doubleday, 1976.
   This book is an excellent practical guide for women who have orgasmic difficulties or other sexual concerns. Topics include female sexual anatomy and physiology, masturbation, orgasm, sexual exercises, sex and pregnancy, menopause and aging, and childhood sexuality.

Boston Women's Health Collective. *Our bodies, our selves.* New York: Simon & Schuster, 1979.
   This easy-to-read reference for women describes female sexual anatomy and women's feelings about their sexuality.

Ladas, Alice K., Whipple, Beverly, and Perry, John D. *The G spot and other recent discoveries about human sexuality.* New York: Holt, Rinehart & Winston, 1982. Written in nontechnical language for the general reader, this book offers a thorough description and discussion of the Grafenberg spot, an anatomical structure located on the anterior wall of the vagina that, when stimulated, enhances sexual pleasure for many women. The authors also discuss the phenomenon of female ejaculation, kinds of female orgasm, and similarities in sexual functioning between men and women.

Lanson, Lucienne. *From woman to woman.* New York: Alfred A. Knopf, 1981. Written by a gynecologist for the general public, this book answers frequent questions concerning female sexual physiology, menstruation, sexual intercourse, pregnancy, contraceptives, menopause, gynecological problems, and other areas. Language is straightforward and nontechnical.

McCary, James Leslie, and McCary, Stephen P. *McCary's human sexuality* (4th ed.). Belmont, Calif.: Wadsworth, 1982. Chapter 5 is specifically related to the female sexual system. Chapter 6 discusses menstruation and the climacteric. Chapter 14 discusses sex in the later years.

TRUE OR FALSE?

An unborn child can be marked.

🍒

"Virgin birth" (parthenogenesis) occurs in humans or animals.

🍒

Humans and infrahuman animals can crossbreed.

🍒

The woman determines the sex of the child.

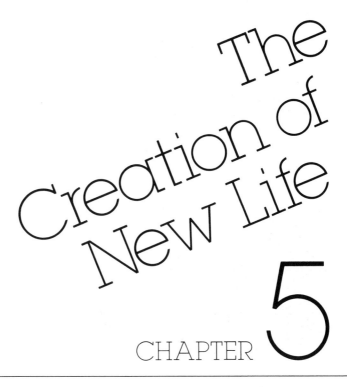

The Creation of New Life

CHAPTER 5

The Genetics of Conception
Factors Affecting Fertility

Signs of and Tests for Pregnancy

The Pregnant Woman
Activities during Pregnancy
Consumption of Drugs during Pregnancy
Exposure to Infectious Disease during Pregnancy
Disorders and Disease States of Pregnancy

Prenatal Development

Birth
Lactation

The New Childbirth

Myths about Conception and Childbirth

Summary

Suggested Reading

The union of the male and female germ cells or **gametes**—the sperm and the ovum—is referred to as **conception** or **fertilization**, and the result of this union is a single cell from which a new being develops. The two microscopic germ cells carry the basic units of heredity, the **genes**, which hold a complex and detailed design for building all the parts of the human body. An equal number of genes from the father and the mother are combined in the union of the sperm and the ovum, so that the new person is a unique combination of his or her parents. Thus is the fundamental material of life passed on from one generation to the next.

The Genetics of Conception

The cell is the basic unit of life. Within the nucleus of the human cell are forty-six **chromosomes**, arranged in twenty-three pairs, which contain the genes. (The word *chromosome* comes from the Latin words *chromo*, meaning color, and *soma*, meaning body. The structures are so named because they become visible if put in special dyes.) The human body has millions of different kinds of cells, all of which develop from a single cell (the combined sperm and ovum) by a process called **mitosis** in which a single cell divides into two new cells, each with a full set of forty-six chromosomes. These two cells divide into four, and so on. This same cell division process is also responsible for body growth and repair.

There are two kinds of cells in the human body: germ cells (gametes) and somatic cells. The gametes function to reproduce the organism; all other body cells are somatic.

The gametes begin their development with a full component of forty-six chromosomes. However, when they are fully developed, each gamete (either a mature ovum or a mature sperm) contains only twenty-three chromosomes. Of these, twenty-two are single, nonsex chromosomes (autosomes). Each autosome has a different genetic content and is usually different in appearance from the others. The twenty-third chromosome is either an **X** or a **Y sex chromosome** and is the one that determines the sex of the new individual (Figure 5.1).

When a mature sperm fertilizes a mature ovum, each parent contributes twenty-three chromosomes to the genetic makeup of the new individual: twenty-two autosomes and one sex chromosome. All normal, mature ova contain one X chromosome. Normal, mature sperm contain either an X (female-producing) or a Y (male-producing) chromosome, and sperm containing X-bearing and Y-bearing chromosomes are produced in precisely equal numbers. Should the ovum be fertilized by an X-bearing sperm, an XX (female) child is conceived. Should the ovum be fertilized by a Y-bearing sperm, an XY (male) child is conceived. Thus it is that both parents contribute equally to the genetic characteristics of the newly conceived individual, and the sex of the individual is determined by the kind of sperm that fertilizes the egg.

When an ovum is penetrated by a sperm, an immediate change occurs in the

Genetic Technology

Gene transplantation is now a reality, at least in simple organisms like bacteria. But it has caused one of most vehement controversies in all of science. On the one hand, the ability to transfer genetic material from one cell to another of an entirely different species will permit biochemists to broaden their understanding of how cells (for example, cancer cells) reproduce. Perhaps the procedure will supply genetic particles that will cure such diseases as diabetes. Already through a procedure called recombinant DNA, a bacterium has been created experimentally that one day may be able to absorb oil spills and then die without leaving pollution. However, gene transplantation also poses serious dangers. It artificially creates a mutation, and mutations go on to reproduce themselves in the normal way. Critics foresee the creation of organisms never intended by nature, over which we will have no control. Many see a need for some form of federal control of genetic experimentation. Others see such a prospect as invasion into scientific investigation and progress.

Genetic technology has advanced so rapidly that many scientists think that cloning, or exact duplication of a human being, is in the foreseeable future. Although no one has yet cloned mammals, much less humans, a frog was cloned in 1966 by Oxford University cell biologist J. B. Gurdon. He replaced the nucleus of a frog ovum, having twenty-three chromosomes, with the nucleus of a body cell from a donor frog. The body cell nucleus, which had forty-six chromosomes, then directed the growth of the cell into an embryo and finally into a frog having the identical characteristics of the donor. Dr. Gurdon was able to replicate this ten more times, although the eleven successful clones resulted from over seven hundred attempts. As yet, gene transplantation offers more problems than solutions.

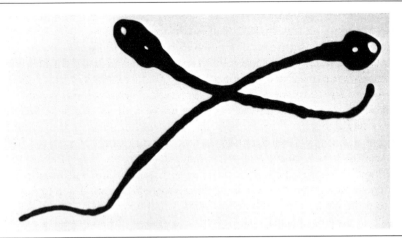

Figure 5.1 Microscopic view, showing the difference between X-bearing sperm (with larger, oval-shaped head) and Y-bearing sperm (with smaller head, longer tail). *Photograph courtesy of Landrum B. Shettles, M.D.*

egg that prevents other sperm from penetrating it. The gene-carrying portions of the nuclei of the sperm and ovum join, resulting in a fertilized egg that contains the full component of forty-six chromosomes common to all human cells.

Factors Affecting Fertility

The age of the woman has a significant bearing on her ability to conceive. Generally speaking, younger women have higher rates of **fertility**, with fertility progressively decreasing from the early twenties onward. No such age differences appear to exist in the fertility rates of men.

There are many reasons why a couple is, or seems to be, unable to conceive a child. One-third of all couples in the United States have difficulty in conceiving. Some couples are infertile and simply cannot conceive; many others can conceive, but the woman is physiologically unable to carry a baby to term. Approximately one couple in ten is never able to have children—although adoption allows a couple to have a family.

Various diseases, notably sexually transmitted infections and illnesses such as mumps, can leave one permanently or temporarily sterile. But when no disease exists, any of several other factors, such as alcohol or drug usage, injury, exposure to radiation, and hormonal imbalance, may be responsible. Personality factors, sexual attitudes, and emotional stress also may underlie the fertility problems experienced by some couples (Mudd, 1980). Prolonged use of marijuana may affect fertility in men and women. Heavy marijuana use in males may lead to significantly reduced production of testosterone and sperm (Kolodny et al., 1974). Recent evidence suggests that marijuana smoking may also affect female hormone levels (Smith, 1980).

The difficulty in 30 percent of the cases lies with the male. And the man is responsible in an important contributory way in another 20 percent. Men often possess a low sperm count and sometimes have no active sperm at all, even though they are quite capable of having frequent and pleasurable intercourse. Too much or too little sexual activity can negatively affect a man's fertility (Masters & Johnson, 1967); generally speaking, the optimal time interval between ejaculations to insure maximum fertility is about forty-eight hours. Recent experience indicates that, following the use of antidepressant drugs, sperm production is accelerated and fertility heightened. On the other hand, exposure to excessive heat, such as that experienced when a man has a high fever or takes hot baths, can temporarily adversely affect sperm production and sperm motility (Poulson, 1980).

Women may have any of several congenital defects or obstructions in their reproductive organs (caused sometimes by disease or infection). They can develop, as well, antibodies that eventually appear in the vagina and produce an immunity to sperm, making conception impossible (Masters & Johnson, 1966). This immunity may be built up against the sperm of any man. But in some cases the immunity may exist against one man's sperm but not another's.

The possibility of conceiving a test tube baby holds hope for some infertile couples. Cambridge University physiologist Dr. R. G. Edwards and obstetrician Dr. Patrick Steptoe have developed a process whereby an ovum can be

Artificial Insemination— Old and New

One method of solving the problem of infertility is **artificial insemination** (AI). This method has proved successful in many cases for couples who have experienced difficulties in conceiving a child: sperm of the husband (AIH) are artificially placed in his wife's vagina or uterus when conception is most likely to take place. Should the difficulty in conceiving be the result of a low sperm count, the sperm of a donor (AID), rather than those of the husband, are inserted.

Artificial insemination has been practiced for years. As early as the fourteenth century, Arabic tribes are said to have secretly used semen from an inferior breed of stallions to impregnate the thoroughbred mares of their enemies. Today, AI is regularly used to build up the bloodlines of various species of animals. Artificial insemination of humans has been performed in this country since the turn of the century.

In 1955, the Society for the Study of Sterility passed almost unanimously a resolution approving AID, with the stipulation that the procedure must be in harmony with the medical opinion of the physician and the ethics of both partners. Undoubtedly this resolution has contributed significantly to the increase in AI pregnancies in the United States. One investigator estimates that about 10,000 children are born every year as the result of AID. An unknown number of children, though probably fewer, are born every year through AIH.

In recent years, the practice of using donor surrogate mothers has received more attention. In the typical case, a couple wants a child that is genetically the man's, even though the woman is unable to conceive. Another woman volunteers to be anonymously impregnated by AID (usually for a fee and coverage of medical expenses). The practice has received much national media coverage and raises several questions: What if the genetic mother decides she wants to keep the child? What if the genetic father refuses to accept the child? Some issues are legal; others must be considered ethical.

extracted from a woman and fertilized in a sterilized dish with sperm from her husband. After fertilization the ovum can be reimplanted in the woman's uterus where it can continue to develop. Pregnancy then continues to term just as if the ovum had been fertilized inside the woman's body. On July 25, 1978, Louise Joy Brown or "Baby Louise" was born, making her the world's first "test tube" baby. Since 1978, other test tube babies have been born, among them a sister for Louise and several sets of twins. Moral, legal, and ethical issues underlying the medical technology of test tube babies have yet to be completely resolved.

Signs of and Tests for Pregnancy

Surely one of the most dramatic and important changes in the relationship of any couple occurs when their first child is born. Yet the child's conception cannot be perceived when it occurs, and **pregnancy** may not be suspected for several weeks—or even months—after conception.

When a woman becomes pregnant, the first signs she notices are a cessation of menstruation; nausea, which often occurs on rising in the morning and is called "morning sickness"; changes in the size and fullness of the breasts; dark coloration of the **areolae** (the brown pigmented area) around the nipples; fatigue; and frequency of urination.

More objective indications of pregnancy are discernible by pelvic examination by a physician and include an increase in the size of the uterus and a considerable softening of the cervix. By the third month, the enlarged uterus can be felt through the abdominal wall and the abdomen is enlarged. By this time, too, there are slight, intermittent contractions of the uterus. Signs that positively confirm pregnancy are fetal heartbeats, active fetal movements, and X-ray detection of the fetal skeleton.

Women do not ordinarily wish to wait for confirming signs of pregnancy and depend instead on their physician or a laboratory technician to determine their pregnancy. Endocrine tests can give accurate proof of pregnancy approximately three weeks after implantation of the fertilized ovum, which is about six weeks after the last menstrual period. In the agglutination test, a sample of the woman's urine is mixed with certain chemicals. A hormone found in the urine of pregnant women will prevent agglutination, or clotting; if agglutination occurs, she is not pregnant. There have very recently been developed new tests involving the radioactive detection of specific proteins in the maternal system that can detect pregnancy within a few days of a missed period.

If there is concern that an unborn child might have a certain defect, **amniocentesis** can be performed, usually during the fifteenth or sixteenth week of pregnancy. In this procedure, most frequently performed when the expectant mother is over age thirty-five, an amount of amniotic fluid is drawn off via a needle inserted into the pregnant woman's abdomen. The fluid will contain cells sloughed off by the fetus, which can be analyzed for such diseases as, say, sickle-cell trait, thought to exist in 10 percent of American blacks, and cystic fibrosis, a genetic disease afflicting chiefly white people.

Despite certain risks for the mother and the fetus, the diagnostic benefits usually outweigh the risks. Additionally, the sex of the expected child can be determined (S. Elias, 1980). Prenatal testing will also reveal Down's syndrome (mongolism). The most widely used genetic test, required by law in forty-three states, is for PKU (phenylketonuria), done in very early infancy. PKU is treatable (by strict diet), but without treatment the child is doomed to irreversible mental retardation.

The Pregnant Woman

Activities during Pregnancy

Much has been written about the dangers of travel, exercise, sexual intercourse, and driving a car during pregnancy. These are, however, not dangerous for the healthy woman when done moderately and sensibly; on the contrary, they are often beneficial. During wars, pregnant women have traveled for hun-

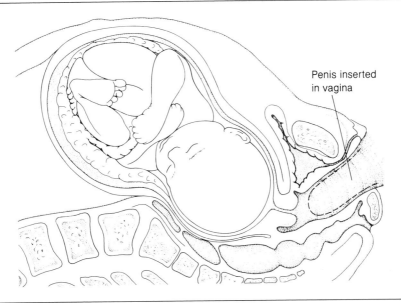

Penis inserted
in vagina

Figure 5.2   Diagram showing practicality of intercourse even in advanced pregnancy. Dotted line demonstrates angle at which penis may be introduced into vagina.

dreds of miles by all modes of transportation, much of it uncomfortable, in order to be with their husbands. Interestingly enough, they had a lower miscarriage rate than those women who stayed home. Coitus is ordinarily permitted and encouraged by obstetricians until the final six weeks. After this time, sexual relief through noncoital means such as mutual masturbation is now recognized as valuable to both the husband and wife as well as to the marriage itself (Figure 5.2). While most couples limit their sexual activity as pregnancy progresses, some women experience an increase in sexual desire during pregnancy (L. R. Rosen, 1980).

Consumption of Drugs during Pregnancy

The long-suspected damaging effects of smoking on a fetus have recently been made more clear (Fielding, 1978). Tobacco smoke contains many harmful substances, such as nicotine and carbon monoxide. Carbon monoxide, when ingested by the expectant mother, interferes with the transport of oxygen to the fetus, resulting in increased risk to the unborn child of low birth weight, premature delivery, and stillbirth. Smoking may damage the small arteries in the uterus, leading to permanent changes that may affect future pregnancies.

While the effects of alcohol on the unborn are not definitely known, researchers (Clarren & Smith, 1978; Hanson et al., 1978) have presented data indicating that alcohol may adversely affect the developing baby as early as the time of conception. The fetal alcohol syndrome (FAS), a predictable syndrome of abnormalities including central nervous system deficiencies and facial disfigurements, can occur in the babies of mothers who drink even limited amounts of alcohol on a regular basis during pregnancy. FAS is a frequent cause of retardation in the Western world, and caution is advised when even one ounce of alcohol is consumed daily. Other drugs, such as aspirin and caffeine, also have been indicated as potentially dangerous to the developing fetus, although their precise effects are unclear.

Exposure to Infectious Disease during Pregnancy

A number of diseases can affect the pregnant mother and her developing child. Toxoplasmosis, a disease with symptoms similar to mononucleosis, can be contracted by people who eat poorly cooked meat or by people who are exposed to cat feces. Toxoplasmosis may have serious consequences for the unborn children of pregnant mothers who contract the disease. The disease may cause intrauterine death of the fetus, or the child who survives the pregnancy may have central nervous system damage and mental deficiency. Proper attention to dietary issues and personal hygiene are important in avoiding exposure to toxoplasmosis (Ledger, 1980).

Sexually transmitted diseases such as gonorrhea, syphilis, and genital herpesvirus present significant problems for pregnant women and their unborn children. Without medical care, fetal morbidity and fatality rates increase, and maternal health problems often become more severe. Physicians and their pregnant patients should explore whether the woman may have been exposed to a sexually transmitted disease so that appropriate treatment can be begun (Gregg & Ismach, 1980; Knox et al., 1980).

Babies born to mothers exposed to rubella (German measles) run a grave risk of defects such as blindness, deafness, heart defects, and mental retardation. The risk of defect is particularly great if the exposure occurs during the first three months of pregnancy. Women susceptible to rubella may become inoculated with rubella vaccine. However, women are advised not to become pregnant for three months after receiving the vaccine.

Disorders and Disease States of Pregnancy

Several disorders and diseases have special implications for fetal development. One disorder that can adversely affect fetal development involves an incompatibility in parents' Rh blood factors. About 85 percent of all people have the Rh factor in their blood. When the mother lacks the Rh factor in her blood, and the father has the Rh factor in his blood, a type of anemia may result that can be fatal to an expected child. When maternal and fetal blood mix at the time of the first childbirth, maternal antibodies develop that can pose serious risk in a second pregnancy; there is no risk involved in the first pregnancy, as excess maternal antibodies are not yet present. A drug known as RhoGam can be effective in controlling problems associated with Rh blood incompatibility; RhoGam is administered subsequent to the delivery of the first child.

Toxemia is a disease that can affect the mother as well as the developing fetus. Symptoms of toxemia include increased blood pressure, body fluid retention, and protein loss. Without proper medical attention, the disease may progress to eclampsia, a stage of the disease characterized by a dramatic increase in blood pressure. In eclampsia, coma, convulsions, and even death may occur (Cefalo, 1979; Diamond & Karlen, 1980).

Diabetes and thyroid problems are health concerns that deserve special concern during pregnancy. Diabetic mothers are more likely than nondiabetic mothers to experience stillbirths or to give birth to infants with respiratory problems, malformations, and other complications (Gabbe, 1979; Goldstein, 1980). While thyroid problems may not mean any special threat to the pregnant mother, the risk of untreated thyroid problems to the unborn child may be premature birth (Mestman, 1980).

Prenatal Development

Prenatal life can be divided into three periods. The first, the period of the ovum, encompasses the conceptus as **blastocyst** and zygote and lasts one week from fertilization. The second is the period of the embryo, the second through eighth week. This period is characterized by the conceptus's placental attachment to the mother and by the appearance in primitive form of external bodily features and principal organs. The third, the period of the fetus, extends from the third month to birth, during which time tissues and organs continue their differentiation and attain the ability to perform their specialized functions.

From the time of fertilization until the second week, the developing cell mass is referred to as a **zygote**. The zygote undergoes mitotic cell division, forming a spherical cell mass, which moves through the uterine tubes into the uterus. In rare cases, the zygote implants and grows not in the uterine wall, but in the wall of the fallopian tube itself. This results in a tubal or ectopic pregnancy and requires immediate surgical removal of that portion of the tube, for an ectopic pregnancy cannot proceed to term. However, tubal pregnancies are very rare; in the vast majority of cases, the zygote passes into the uterine cavity and implants there. This cell mass forms three internal cellular layers: the ectoderm, or outermost layer; the mesoderm, or middle layer; and the endoderm, or innermost layer. These three layers constitute the embryonic disc, from which the embryo develops.

From the second to the eighth week, the developing conceptus is referred to as an **embryo** (Figure 5.3). It implants itself in the wall of the uterus, and the ectoderm, mesoderm, and endoderm become differentiated. The nervous system, sense organs, mouth cavity, and skin eventually come from the ectoderm; the muscular, skeletal, circulatory, excretory, and sexual systems develop from the mesoderm; and the digestive and respiratory systems come from the endoderm (Arey, 1974).

After the eighth week, the developing conceptus is referred to as a **fetus**. At this time, the rudimentary systems of the body have all appeared, and initial development has begun (Figure 5.4). The fetal stage consists of further growth and elaboration of the existing rudimentary systems. From approximately 1

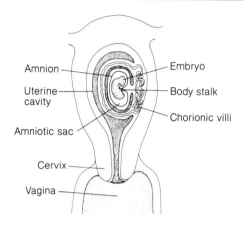

Figure 5.3   Schematic representation of implanted embryo.

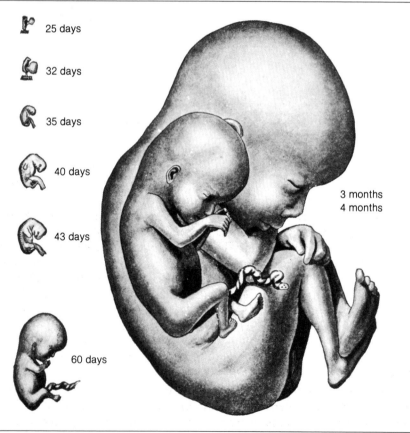

25 days

32 days

35 days

40 days

43 days

3 months
4 months

60 days

Figure 5.4   Human embryos aged twenty-five days to four months. Actual size. *From Arey, Developmental Anatomy, 7th ed. Philadelphia: W. B. Saunders Co., 1974.*

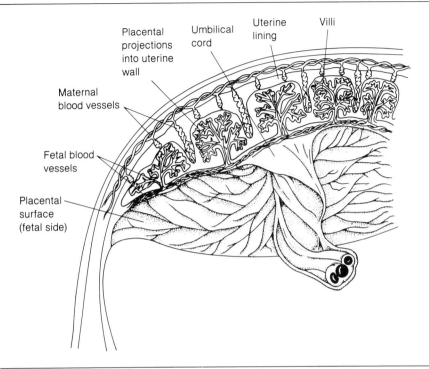

Placental projections into uterine wall

Umbilical cord

Uterine lining

Villi

Maternal blood vessels

Fetal blood vessels

Placental surface (fetal side)

Figure 5.5   Schematic representation of placenta's attachment to uterine wall, showing interchange between maternal and fetal blood vessels through the tiny chorionic villi.

inch (2.5 centimeters) in length and one-thirtieth of an ounce (1 gram) in weight, the fetus develops until birth, when the average infant is 20 inches (50 centimeters) long and 7 pounds (3 kilograms) in weight.

Before the body of the embryo has taken a definite shape, the **amnion**, a thin, transparent, tough membrane, forms. Within its hollow cavity is a clear, watery fluid called the **amniotic fluid**. The amniotic fluid equalizes the pressure around the embryo, preventing jolts and injuries, and also prevents the embryo from forming adhesions to the amnion. In addition, it allows for changes in position of the developing conceptus and facilitates childbirth by helping to dilate the neck of the uterus. The fetus usually begins to swallow some of the amniotic fluid at about the fifth month of pregnancy, and the first bowel movements are a discharge of this liquid. At birth, the baby's respiratory passages may have to be cleared of some of the fluid so that normal respiration can begin.

An organ of interchange between the embryo and the mother is the **placenta**, composed of uterine tissue and interwoven villi (Figure 5.5). The villi (fingerlike protrusions that enter the maternal tissue) of the placenta are kept steeped in fresh maternal blood, which enters the placental spaces about the villi by means of small blood vessels. As the blood drains back into the veins of the uterus, it is replaced by fresh blood from the uterine arteries.

At no time during any stage of normal pregnancy do maternal and fetal blood intermingle. Both the maternal and fetal blood circulate within the placenta, but they are kept separated by the walls of the umbilical blood vessels. The interchange between the two systems, which is by diffusion and absorption, provides for the nourishment of the fetus and for elimination of fetal waste products.

Fetal blood absorbs food and oxygen. It also eliminates carbon dioxide and other metabolic waste products. These are taken into the mother's blood and expelled along with her own wastes. Although the cellular barrier between the two blood systems generally prevents the passage of bacteria and other disease germs, some substances, such as antibiotics and certain viruses and disease germs, are capable of crossing the barrier. During the fifth week of pregnancy, the **umbilical cord** is formed, by which the embryo is suspended in the amniotic fluid. The fully developed cord is about 20 inches (50 centimeters) long.

The expected birth date of a child can be estimated by adding 280 days to the date on which the mother's last menstruation started. To be more precise, one would have to know the exact date of conception. The period of **gestation** (pregnancy) varies among women and according to the sex of the child. Women who engage in strenuous physical exercise usually have their babies twenty days earlier than less athletic women, and brunette women deliver slightly sooner than blondes. Furthermore, girls are often born five to nine days earlier than boys. Although about 3 percent of pregnancies last three hundred days or more, placental withering may occur after an overlong gestation, increasing the possibility of infant death. Most **obstetricians** induce labor if they suspect placental shrinkage when the pregnancy is prolonged.

Birth

The process of childbirth, or **parturition**, takes place in three stages. The first stage begins when contractions of the uterus commence, usually at fifteen- to twenty-minute intervals. Initially, each contraction lasts about thirty seconds, and they increase steadily in frequency, intensity, and duration until they finally occur every three to four minutes, at which time the fetus is well on its way. Toward the end of labor, each contraction lasts a minute or more. During the first stage, the cervix dilates from its normal size of less than 1 centimeter to approximately 10 centimeters (4 inches). Full **dilation** of the cervix marks the beginning of the second stage of parturition.

Another event that most often occurs during the first stage is the rupture of the amniotic membrane with a resulting flow of clear, waterlike fluid from the vagina. This "breaking of the bag" is a result of continuing cervical dilation and accompanying uterine pressure and, together with the increased strength and duration of uterine contractions, is an indication that the time to notify the obstetrician has arrived.

The second phase of parturition extends from the time the cervix is completely dilated until the fetus is expelled. When the infant's head emerges from the vagina, it turns spontaneously either to the right or left, depending upon the way the shoulders are turned. After expulsion of the head and shoulders, delivery of the rest of the infant is a simple matter because the trunk and limbs are quite small in comparison with the head and shoulders (Figure 5.6).

Over 99 percent of all infants are born in a longitudinal position (with the body's trunk presented vertically), usually with their heads first. Because of the great pressure exerted on a baby during delivery, the head may be oddly molded in the birth process, or the facial features may be bruised and swollen. While this may be distressing to the new parents, the irregularities correct themselves within a few days and there is rarely permanent damage.

In 4 percent of longitudinal births, the buttocks are presented first (the so-called **breech birth**), resulting in temporary swelling and discoloration of the infant's buttocks and genital area. Almost 50 percent of infants assume the breech presentation prior to the seventh month of fetal life, then make a 180° turn before the ninth month. A fetus that does not make the turn can often be manipulated by the obstetrician into the head-first position during the later stages of pregnancy.

Once in every two hundred births, the fetus lies crosswise with a shoulder, arm, or hand entering the birth canal first. In these cases either the fetus must be turned during labor or a **caesarean section**, in which the child is delivered through a surgical incision in the abdominal and uterine walls, must be performed.

About fifteen minutes after the baby's birth, the placenta is delivered, marking the third stage of parturition. Muscular contractions shrink the uterus and the area of placental attachment, detaching the placenta from the uterine wall and expelling it into the vagina. The obstetrician sometimes presses the uterus downward to facilitate expulsion.

Now that the infant is breathing oxygen from the outside world, it no longer needs the placenta or the umbilical cord. Once the cord stops pulsating and the baby is breathing regularly, the cord is clamped and cut about three inches from the infant's abdomen. The clamp is left in place until the stub dries up and separates.

If the birth has been uncomplicated, the new mother and her infant usually leave the hospital within two or three days after the delivery. The birth of a child is traditionally the cause of celebration for the new parents and their families; however, the first few weeks at home can be difficult for the mother. She must deal simultaneously with the many needs of her infant, who is totally dependent, and also with her own feelings about the changes in her life that the child creates.

Many women experience feelings of sadness and periods of crying sometime during the first ten days after delivery. These "**postpartum** (after birth) blues" are attributed partly to psychological factors and partly to the drastic hormonal changes that occur at this time.

1. Head floating, before engagement

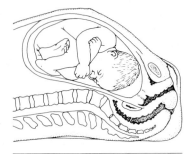

2. Engagement, flexion, descent

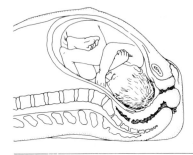

3. Further descent, internal rotation

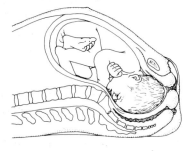

4. Complete rotation, beginning extension

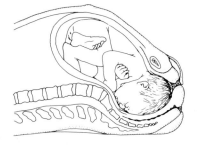

5. Complete extension

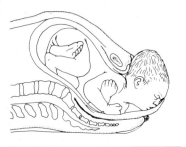

6. Restitution, external rotation

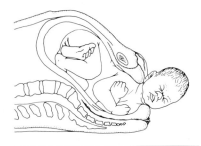

7. Delivery of anterior shoulder

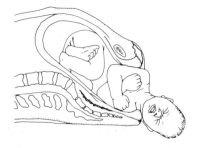

8. Delivery of posterior shoulder

Figure 5.6   Principal movements of the fetus in process of labor and delivery.

Lactation

Lactation is the process of milk secretion from the mother's breasts following childbirth. After the placenta has been expelled in the last stages of childbirth, its inhibiting hormones are no longer produced, and the mother's pituitary gland begins to produce **prolactin,** the hormone that induces lactation. The first secretion the baby receives from the breast is **colostrum,** a substance present in the breast immediately after birth. Colostrum is of high protein content and is believed to aid in giving the infant immunity to many infectious diseases during the early months of life. True milk replaces colostrum within two or three days after delivery.

The infant's sucking prompts contractions in the mother's uterus that help reduce it to its normal size. Breast-feeding also provides certain psychological satisfactions to the mother and can lead to a greater feeling of closeness to the baby. Some advocates of breast-feeding suggest that breast-fed infants have fewer problems with obesity, hypertension, and allergies than do infants fed with formula (Robertson, 1980). Other advantages of breast-feeding are that the milk is free, always at the right temperature, and always immediately available.

Although breast-feeding prolongs the absence of menstruation following childbirth, it is possible for a woman to ovulate before her first postpartum mentrual flow. Some women (Tietze, 1970) become pregnant again without having menstruated after childbirth.

As many as 90 percent of all babies were breast-fed in the not-too-distant past. Although the practice declined for a time, there are indications that young mothers of today are returning to the practice of breast-feeding. Many mothers are apprehensive that nursing will cause their breasts to sag, making the figure less attractive. Such concern over the size and shape of the breasts reflects our cultural emphasis on breasts as a symbol of ultimate sexuality.

The New Childbirth

For those expectant parents who wish to share the experiences of pregnancy and childbirth more actively, new approaches to childbirth education have been developed that seek to increase the understanding and involvement of both husband and wife. Termed "natural childbirth" by its originator, Dr. Grantly Dick-Read, this training is now also called "prepared," "controlled," or "cooperative" childbirth.

Several methods of preparation for childbirth, ranging from physical training to hypnosis, are now prevalent. The approach most favored in this country is the psychophysical one, typified by the Lamaze method, which originated in Russia and was introduced to the Western world in 1951 by Dr. Fernand Lamaze.

Advocates of natural childbirth feel that childbirth should be a rewarding experience for both parents. Consequently they are critical of the routine use of heavy sedation during labor and delivery, since a heavily sedated woman is hardly aware of what is happening and cannot participate actively. Although none of the approaches insists on a woman's doing without light medication during labor or without some form of anesthetics during the actual birth if she wishes it, these approaches also encourage parents to consider the possible ill effects of anesthetic drugs on the newborn. They criticize depersonalized obstetrical care and the arbitrary separation of mother, father, and baby practiced in many hospitals. Those who believe in natural childbirth also favor the presence of the husband in the labor room and in the delivery room; "rooming-in" privileges, where the mother and her baby are in the same room during their hospital stay; and breast-feeding.

In the Lamaze method, classes are held where both the expectant mother and the father are given detailed accounts of what they may expect during pregnancy, labor, and delivery. Training in muscle-control exercises and breathing techniques to be used during labor is provided, and the man is taught how to assist the woman in her practice sessions at home and during delivery. The primary goal is to help the woman participate actively in the birth of her baby with a minimum of fear and pain. Presence of the man gives both a sense of sharing and contributes to the well-being of the mother. The Leboyer method, a newer concept of delivery, centers on the infant's immediate emergence into the world. Instead of being born into a confusion of bright lights, movement, cold metal scales, and harsh fabrics, the infant is introduced into a quiet, dimly lit room and placed immediately on its mother's belly to recapture contact with her. It is then given a warm soothing bath, thus further muting the shock of the journey from the dark, silent womb to the outside world (Leboyer, 1975).

Myths about Conception and Childbirth

Myths and folklore concerning fertility, pregnancy, and childbirth abound in every society.

One widespread myth concerning pregnancy is that an unborn fetus can be "marked" by some experience of the mother. This notion, of course, is completely false, since there is no direct connection between the nervous systems or blood systems of mother and fetus. What usually happens is that when a child is born with an unusual birthmark, the parents attempt to explain the mark by "remembering" some incident during the mother's pregnancy when she was in some way unsettled by something bearing that general shape. It is true, of course, that the mother supplies nourishment for the fetus. Her diet and chemical intake can have a direct effect on certain physiological reactions of the child, both before and after birth, but these effects are not what is usually meant by "marking" a baby.

Many people mistakenly believe that handicapped women are unable to bear children. With medical advice, care, and attention, however, many handicapped women, like their physically normal sisters, can give birth to healthy children (Pepmiller, 1980).

Another myth that has been prevalent for centuries is that human beings and lower animals can interbreed. This myth continues to have some believers. However, not only is it impossible for humans to crossbreed with infrahuman animals, but interbreeding among the various genera of lower animals is equally impossible, although members of different species of the same genus may produce crossbred offspring. For example, a man and an ape cannot interbreed, nor can an ape and a tiger. But two members of different species—in the cat family, for example—can crossbreed. Undoubtedly knowledge of the wondrous creatures of Greek and Roman mythology—the centaurs, sphinxes, mermaids, and satyrs—has given credibility over the centuries to the myth that humans and lower animals can interbreed.

There are three interesting phenomena concerning pregnancy that are rare but known to actually occur. One of these is **pseudocyesis**, or false pregnancy. This occurs in both animals and humans, and the symptoms are remarkably similar to those of true pregnancy. In some cases a woman will actually go into labor only to deliver an accumulation of air and fluids. This condition is due to a strong desire on the part of the woman to have a child, and psychotherapy is sometimes required to dispel the notion that she is indeed pregnant.

A second, and somewhat related, phenomenon is the practice in primitive cultures of **couvade**, wherein the husband experiences labor in much the same manner as his wife. In our own society the husband sometimes shows symptoms related to his wife's pregnancy. The expectant father may become nauseated, vomit, and suffer abdominal pains, all such symptoms disappearing after his wife has delivered their infant.

The third phenomenon, **parthenogenesis** or "virgin birth," is known to exist in animals and is the sole method of reproduction among certain insects. In parthenogenesis, a female egg is "fertilized" without contact with a spermatozoon. Animal experiments have indicated that various stimuli may induce development just as if the egg had been fertilized in the usual manner. For example, cooling the fallopian tubes of rabbits, heating the eggs of certain moths, and even applying saliva of human males to carp eggs have sufficiently stimulated the eggs to prompt their development.

An obvious question arises: Is this phenomenon possible in human beings? Investigators, past and present, disagree widely on the subject. One thing is certain, however; if parthenogenesis were to occur, the offspring would always be female. Since women have only one type of sex-related chromosome (X), only the X chromosome could be passed on. Furthermore, a child born of parthenogenesis would be a replication of her mother (except for the role of recessive genes), since her heredity would be based solely on the mother's genes.

The phrase "**virgin birth**" usually denotes a human pregnancy and subsequent birth without union of ovum and sperm. In this context, the possibility of a true virgin birth has never been scientifically established. However, "virgin birth" also suggests pregnancy and subsequent birth without sexual intercourse, the connotation being that the woman who delivers as a virgin is more "pure" than ordinary mothers. It is possible for a woman to become pregnant without experiencing sexual intercourse. Sperm make their way toward ova with complete disregard for the manner in which they are deposited in the vagina, and an ovum fertilized without intercourse develops in the same manner as an ovum fertilized as a result of coitus.

Presence or absence of a hymen is incidental in such cases, since an intact hymen does not prevent migration of sperm to the uterus any more than it prevents the menstrual flow from the uterus. During sex play, for example, a man may have his penis near or on a woman's vulva. If he ejaculates, semen can enter the vaginal opening and make its way through the vagina into the uterus. Sperm can also be introduced into the vaginal canal by way of manual manipulation of the woman's genitals after a man's hands have come into contact with his ejaculate. This is a particular possibility if he should insert a semen-covered finger into the vagina. If pregnancy were to result in either of these instances, the subsequent childbirth might accurately be called a "virgin birth." It can certainly be recognized that a virgin woman may become pregnant through artificial insemination. Since no penis enters her vagina, the resulting conception and delivery could be classified as a "virgin birth."

Summary

Fertilization occurs when one of the male germ cells, or sperm, unites with the female germ cell, or ovum. The twenty-two autosomes, or non-sex chromosomes, and one sex chromosome that are within the sperm combine with the twenty-two autosomes and one sex chromosome that are in the egg, resulting in a fertilized egg containing forty-six chromosomes, the number common to all human cells.

When genetic defects are thought to exist in the developing child, amniocentesis can be performed to determine whether or not there is a problem. Another genetic test, to rule out the presence of PKU, is done in early infancy. Cloning and other forms of genetic experimentation offer intriguing possibilities for the future.

As many as one-third of couples experience difficulties in conceiving, and one in ten couples is never able to have children. Disease states, alcohol or drug use, hormonal imbalances, and emotional distress are factors that may contribute to fertility problems. The possibility of conceiving a "test tube baby" may offer hope for some infertile couples.

The first signs of pregnancy include cessation of menstruation, morning sickness, and changes in the breasts. More objective signs are a softening of the cervix and an increase in size of the uterus. Signs that confirm pregnancy include fetal heartbeat and fetal movements. Tests for pregnancy, including the agglutination test, can give accurate proof of pregnancy soon after implantation occurs.

When women become pregnant, they can continue to engage in normal activities, including travel, exercise, sexual intercourse, and driving. Smoking and alcohol and drug use by a pregnant woman may adversely affect the developing baby.

Women who are exposed to diseases or disorders such as toxoplasmosis, gonorrhea, syphilis, herpesvirus, rubella, and Rh blood incompatibilities may be endangering their health as well as the health and development of their unborn children. Women who experience noninfectious disease states such as toxemia, diabetes, and thyroid problems also are advised to seek appropriate medical care.

Prenatal life can be divided into three periods: (1) the period of the ovum, which lasts one week from fertilization; (2) the period of the embryo, which lasts from the second to eighth week of gestation; and (3) the period of the fetus, which lasts from the third month until birth. The fertilized egg, or zygote, undergoes mitotic cell division and forms a cell mass that implants itself in the wall of the uterus. Three germ layers—the ectoderm, the endoderm, and the mesoderm—combine to form the embryonic disc from which all bodily components develop. The amnion, a tough membrane filled with amniotic fluid, protects the developing embryo from injuries. The placenta, a special organ of interchange between embryo and mother, provides for the nourishment of the embryo and the elimination of wastes.

The process of childbirth, or parturition, takes place in three stages. The first stage can be recognized by the beginning of labor pains or rupture of the amniotic membrane. The second stage of labor extends from complete cervical dilation until the baby is born. The third stage includes delivery of the placenta. Most babies are born in cephalic or head presentations; breech presentations are rare. When prebirth difficulties occur, a surgical procedure known as caesarean section can be performed to deliver the child.

Following childbirth, milk is produced in the mother's breasts in a process known as lactation. Prolactin is the hormone that induces lactation. At first, colostrum is secreted by the breasts and received by the nursing baby; but, two or three days after delivery, true milk is secreted.

Several programs of childbirth preparation, such as the Lamaze method, have been developed that emphasize the use of educational methods and relaxation techniques. The Leboyer method of childbirth emphasizes a natural delivery in a quiet, warm, dimly lit room.

Pregnancy is a human condition shrouded in mythology and by unusual, interesting phenomena. One myth is that a child can be "marked" as the result of some physical or emotional trauma experienced by the mother. Another myth is that humans and lower animals can crossbreed. Pseudocyesis and couvade are interesting phenomena of pregnancy that have been observed occasionally in humans.

TRUE OR FALSE: THE FACTS

An unborn child can be marked.
False. There is no direct connection between the nervous systems or blood systems of mother and fetus. *(84)*

"Virgin birth" (parthenogenesis) occurs in humans or animals.
True. Parthenogenesis does exist in animals, but not in humans. *(85–86)*

❦

Humans and infrahuman animals can crossbreed.
False. Humans and infrahuman animals cannot crossbreed, nor can different
genuses of lower animals crossbreed. *(84–85)*

❦

The woman determines the sex of the child.
False. Although both parents contribute equally to the genetic characteristics,
the man determines the sex of the child by contributing either an
X or a Y chromosome, whereas the woman always contributes an X
chromosome. *(70)*

SUGGESTED READING

Kitzinger, Sheila. *The complete book of pregnancy and childbirth.* New York: Alfred A. Knopf, 1980.
This well-illustrated, comprehensive guide for the expectant mother delivers a wealth of information on pregnancy and childbirth. Topics of special interest include the effects of drugs and cigarettes during pregnancy, the changing marital relationship, sex during pregnancy, breast-feeding, and postpartum exercises.

McCary, James Leslie, and McCary, Stephen P. *McCary's human sexuality* (4th ed.). Belmont, Calif.: Wadsworth, 1982.
Chapter 7 contains an abundance of information related to fertilization, prenatal development, and birth.

Neilson, Lennart. *A child is born.* New York: Seymour-Laurence, 1965.
This brief book presents spectacular color photographs of fetal development.

Pritchard, J. A., and MacDonald, P. C. *William's obstetrics* (16th ed.). New York: Appleton-Century-Crofts, 1980.
This highly technical medical textbook is a valuable source of accurate and detailed information on obstetrics and gynecology.

Silber, Sherman J. *How to get pregnant.* New York: Charles Scribner's, 1980.
This book discusses in simple terms a wide range of topics related to conception and contraception. Some subject areas include male and female reproductive physiology, tests of fertility, treatment of conditions causing infertility, artificial insemination and sperm banking, test-tube babies and cloning, and birth regulation and sterilization.

TRUE OR FALSE?

Birth control methods involving sterilization procedures will cause
impairment of the sex drive in both men and women.

❦

Douching after intercourse is a safe, effective contraceptive technique.

❦

Thanks to modern medicine, pregnancy and childbirth offer no risk to a
woman.

Birth Control

CHAPTER 6

Abstinence

Sterilization
Methods of Sterilization in Women
Methods of Sterilization in Men

Abortion
Methods of Inducing Abortion

Contraception
Contraceptives Available Only with a Doctor's Prescription
Contraceptives Available without a Doctor's Prescription
Other Methods of Birth Prevention

Birth Control in the Future

Summary

Suggested Reading

For nearly thirty centuries of recorded history, and almost certainly long before that time, human beings have attempted to control reproduction. Today the attempt assumes greater importance than ever before; the world's population has increased to the point that its resources, limited in the capacity to sustain a population, are being depleted. While some individuals minimize the importance of and necessity for birth control, most experts who have studied the problem extensively maintain that, in order to have a population that can be adequately fed and housed and that is psychologically healthy, every couple should limit the number of children they produce to two.

The term **birth control** was coined by Margaret Sanger, founder of the movement in the United States, in her efforts to popularize the concept of contraception. A nurse working among the very poor in New York, Sanger witnessed the coexistence of poverty and uncontrolled childbearing, as well as high rates of infant and maternal mortality. As a feminist and a sensitive human being, she strongly supported a woman's right to determine the size of her family and devoted herself to removing legal barriers to the distribution of birth control information.

In the United States, as well as in other countries, birth control passed through successive periods of active opposition, permissiveness, and open support, as governments came to recognize the severe hindrance to social and economic progress posed by uncurbed population growth. But while the birth rate has declined in the United States and in many other nations—with credit for the decline due to the wider availability of birth control devices—the world's population-growth rate continues to increase. If allowed to continue at the present rate, the number of the world's people will double by the year 2007.

In terms of individual emotional well-being, the matter of population control becomes much more than an academic exercise or public debate over world resources; it becomes a matter of personal importance. Millions of unwanted children are born every year. These children grow up with emotional difficulties directly related to their being unwanted, regardless of how conscientiously the parents may try to disguise their feelings. Many of the emotional ills that plague our population would be alleviated if every child born were truly wanted. In addition to the need to ensure that every child born is a wanted child, there is often a need for couples to postpone a first pregnancy and to control the spacing of subsequent pregnancies for their own sake. Young married couples need time to adjust to each other and to marriage before they add the complicating presence of a baby; the birth of a child or even the fear of pregnancy can interfere with both sexual and marital adjustment. Couples need to know that they are physically, emotionally, and financially capable of providing a loving home for children. In some cases, there is a need to halt the perpetuation of inherited diseases, and a couple may elect to adopt the children they want rather than risk inflicting a natural child with a disability such as Huntington's chorea, a genetically carried disease characterized by irregular movements, disturbance of speech, and gradually increasing loss of intellectual faculties. For all these reasons, birth control is of vital importance to

A Historical Perspective on Birth Control

In the long search for effective forms of birth control other than abortion and infanticide, primitive people evolved some curious contraceptive techniques. In the attempt to cope with imperfectly understood biological processes, these people often brought religious beliefs, superstition, and magic into their efforts to control fertility.

An ancient Chinese belief, for example, was that a woman would not become pregnant if she remained completely passive during coitus. The philosophy underlying this belief was that a woman's enjoyment of intercourse was evil and merited punishment, pregnancy apparently being a form of it. Even today some women persist in the belief that if they do not have an orgasm simultaneously with their partner, they will not become pregnant.

The oldest medical prescription for a contraceptive (about 1850 B.C.) is found in the Egyptian Petri Papyrus. Women were advised to use a vaginal suppository concocted of crocodile dung and honey. The pastelike substance was apparently expected to prevent the sperm from entering the cervix. Over the centuries some incredible substances and techniques have been tried—mouse dung, amulets, and induced sneezing, as examples. Some methods were at least partially effective; and, when they were, a refinement of them occasionally led to a reasonably efficient contraceptive. The ancient Greeks, for instance, wrote that certain materials permeated with oil might constitute a workable contraceptive because oil slows down the movement of sperm. Therafter, oil-saturated papers were inserted in the vagina to cover the cervix—a crude forerunner, perhaps, to today's diaphragm.

The eighteenth-century adventurer Casanova is alleged to have placed a gold ball in the vagina to block the sperm's passage. He is also credited with using a hollowed-out lemon as a diaphragm to cover the cervix. Perhaps the lemon shell did serve as an effective contraceptive, for citric acid can immobilize sperm. But if Casanova's reputation for sexual activity was deserved; and, if in fact he managed not to impregnate any of his ladies (as he claimed), the most logical explanation is that his frequent ejaculations maintained his sperm count at such a low level that he was in effect sterile.

Some writers say that the condom has been used for centuries, perhaps even by the ancient Romans. The history of condoms includes the questionable story that a Dr. Condom in the court of England's King Charles II devised the contraceptive to help limit the number of the monarch's illegitimate offspring (Charles acknowledged fourteen such children). Or the word may come from the Latin word *kondus*, meaning receptacle, or the Persian *kendu* or *kondu*, meaning vessels for grain storage made from animal intestines. The sixteenth-century Italian anatomist Fallopius, who identified the female uterine tubes, recommended the use of linen condoms to prevent the spread of sexually transmitted diseases. Whatever its early history, the sheath was originally used more as a protection against STD than as a contraceptive.

married couples. The decision they make regarding the number, spacing, and timing of pregnancies affects not only their immediate family circle but also their community and, eventually, the world. Married couples, however, are not the only people who are concerned with birth control. The personal distress and numerous sociological problems created by an unwanted nonmarital pregnancy can be avoided if adequate birth control measures are taken.

Although birth control and contraception are often discussed as if they were synonymous, they are not. **Contraception** is any means or device that prevents conception when two fertile partners have sexual intercourse. As such, contraception is only one method of birth control. Others are abstinence and sterilization. Although in our culture abortion is not a method of birth control to be regularly "practiced" (like contraception), we do include it in this chapter.

Abstinence

Dictionaries define **abstinence** as "self-denial; an abstaining from the gratification of appetite." As a means of birth control, sexual abstinence in marriage should be mutually agreeable. There are, of course, occasions when temporary abstinence is sensible—for example, during an illness, to avoid contracting or spreading sexually transmitted diseases, during late pregnancy, or immediately after childbirth. In these cases, other sexual outlets may be enjoyed, such as mutual oral or manual stimulation. In the general context of human sexuality, not much can really be said for abstinence except that it is profoundly successful as a birth control technique.

Sterilization

Sterilization is a surgical procedure that renders a person incapable of reproduction. It may be sought by men and women who wish to ensure against the possibility of their having more children. By 1970, it ranked second only to the pill as the birth control method of choice among married couples. Since 1973, it has become the leading means when the wife is over thirty (Brody, 1976), and the U.S. Agency for International Development (AID) estimates that it has become the world's leading birth control technique. During 1980 over one million Americans chose to be sterilized. About thirteen million Americans now rely on the protection of this permanent birth control procedure ("One Million Americans Chose," 1981). Aside from family limitation, sterilization is of value in some cases involving inheritable diseases. But forced sterilization of the habitual criminal or so-called moral pervert is virtually uncalled for because there is little scientific evidence that heredity plays any part in criminal or other amoral acts.

Young to middle-aged couples who voluntarily seek sterilization are advised to consider other methods of birth control if they have any serious doubts about becoming sterile. About 20 percent of sterilized persons express regret that they became sterilized. The best candidates for voluntary sterilization are persons over thirty years of age who have at least two children, who are emotionally stable, and who have carefully considered their options (I. C. Bernstein, 1980).

Methods of Sterilization in Women

In **tubal ligation** or partial **salpingectomy** the fallopian tubes are cut, a small section of the tube is removed, and the ends are tied to prevent them from

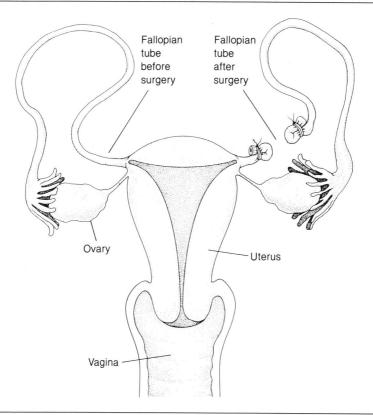

Fallopian tube before surgery

Fallopian tube after surgery

Ovary

Uterus

Vagina

Figure 6.1   Schematic representation of female reproductive system, showing effect of a tubal ligation. Note that in sterilization, surgery is performed on both sides of the body.

meeting (Figure 6.1). The sperm and the ova are thus kept from coming into contact. The operation may be accomplished by abdominal incision or through the vagina. Reconnecting the fallopian tubes after surgery is about 50 percent successful, but thereafter the risk of tubal pregnancy rises.

Laparoscopic sterilization is a technique that has recently captured considerable attention in this country. Performed under general anesthesia, this operation involves two small incisions, which are made in a woman's abdomen. The fallopian tubes are severed, and the ends are cauterized (sealed) by an electrical instrument. Only Band-Aids are needed to cover the incisions, hence the name "Band-Aid operation," and the patient need remain in the hospital only until she is fully awake (Pritchard & MacDonald, 1980). The procedure is inexpensive and leaves no unsightly scars. Attempts to rejoin the tubes after this operation have been only 25 percent successful.

Oophorectomy, the surgical removal of the ovaries, brings the process of ovulation permanently to a halt. **Hysterectomy**, the surgical removal of the uterus, may or may not include the removal of the uterine tubes and the ovaries. Estrogen replacement therapy may be helpful if a woman's hormonal bal-

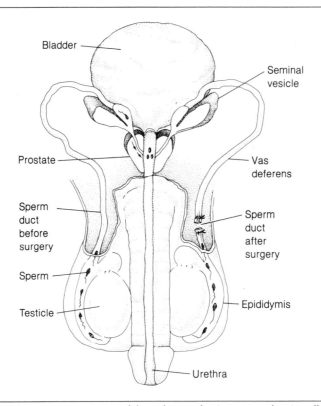

Figure 6.2   Schematic representation of the male reproductive system, showing effect of vasectomy. Note that in sterilization, surgery is performed on both sides of the body.

ance is affected by such procedures (Martin, 1980). Total **salpingectomy** is the surgical removal of the fallopian tubes. These last three procedures result in permanent sterility and are usually performed for the purpose of correcting certain abnormalities rather than for sterilization alone.

None of these procedures will impair a woman's **sex drive**. On the contrary, there may be an increase in drive because of the sense of freedom a woman has when she is no longer threatened by an unwanted pregnancy.

Methods of Sterilization in Men

Vasectomy, by far the most desirable of the two surgical procedures available to men, consists of cutting and tying the vas deferens, thus preventing the passage of sperm to the ejaculatory ducts (Figure 6.2). The site of the incision is in the scrotum, well above the testicles, and the operation is a simple one that can be performed in a doctor's office with a local anesthetic (Pritchard & MacDonald, 1980). Since sperm will already have been stored in the seminal vesicles and ejaculatory ducts prior to surgery, the man's first few ejaculations after a vasectomy will contain sperm. Although the seminal fluid will probably be sperm-free after ten to twenty ejaculations, it is wise to have two laboratory evaluations before the man can assume he is sterile (Pritchard & MacDonald, 1980; Zinsser, 1976). Despite the fact that they know rationally a vasectomy does not decrease sex drive or the ability to satisfy it, some men are nevertheless reluctant to have the operation. As many as two-thirds of men who undergo vasectomies actually might experience enhanced sexual enjoyment during coitus (Lewis & Lewis, 1980b). The increase in sex drive might result from the psychological effect of removed fear of pregnancy.

Vasectomy is now a commonly performed procedure. Current estimates indicate that 1 million men undergo this form of sterilization every year (Lewis & Lewis, 1980b). Although studies have indicated that very few men ever ask for a reversal of a vasectomy (researchers estimate that as many as one out of 2,000 vasectomized men seek reversal surgery [Lewis & Lewis, 1980b], the effects can be undone surgically by rejoining the severed ends of the vas deferens. Reversibility success has been reported as high as 70 percent, but a more realistic figure when conventional surgical techniques are used might be as low as 5 percent (Hatcher et al., 1980). Willscher (1980) reports that use of microscopic surgical techniques helps to achieve a more precise connection of the previously severed vas; reversibility success with this method rises to near 50 percent.

A promising new nonsurgical alternative to vasectomy is a process of male sterilization called **vas sclerosing**. In this procedure, the wall of the vas deferens is injected with a small amount of material that causes scarring, thus blocking the passageway of the vas. The technique greatly reduces the risks inherent in any surgical process, as well as overcoming the psychological objections that many men have to any cutting in the genital area.

For men who would like to retain the option of fathering a child without undergoing reversal surgery, there are at least four centers in the United States where a man's sperm may be frozen and stored for future insertion into the vagina or uterus of a woman in a process called artificial insemination.

Castration, the second surgical procedure of sterilization available to men, involves the removal of both testicles. This operation does not necessarily mean **impotence** (the inability to achieve an erection sufficient for satisfactory sexual intercourse) if performed on an adult, although there is a gradual loss of sexual desire because of the loss of male hormones produced by the testicles. The hormonal deficiency may also cause the man's voice to become higher, his beard may become sparse, and he may acquire excess fat. Hormone therapy can correct these undesirable changes in secondary sexual characteristics.

A nonsurgical alternative to castration involves the use of an antiandrogenic hormone, medroxy-progesterone acetate (MPA). This hormone can be effective in lessening libido, and yet it can be eliminated from a treatment program at any time without any known permanent, negative, or residual effects. MPA has been used with promising results in treatment programs with sex offenders (Money, 1981; Money & Bennett, 1981).

Abortion

Spontaneous **abortion** is the term applied to an unintentional expulsion of the fetus from the uterus before the third month of pregnancy. It is not a form of purposeful birth control. Induced **abortion**, on the other hand, is the term used to describe the intentional termination of pregnancy.

Spontaneous abortions, also called **miscarriages,** occur at a much higher rate than many people realize. It has been estimated that about 33 percent of all fertilized eggs abort before the next menstrual period is overdue. In these cases, most women never realize that they are—or were—pregnant. An additional 25 percent of all pregnancies miscarry between the time of fertilization and labor, meaning that almost 60 percent of all pregnancies end before a viable birth occurs.

The subject of induced or elective abortion appears throughout history in social, economic, political, and particularly religious contexts. The Chinese are said to possess the oldest method of abortion, the procedure having been described in a manuscript over four thousand years ago. One of abortion's strongest opponents is the Roman Catholic Church. Yet the Church's position in the matter has shifted several times over the centuries, the present attitude having been established only a hundred years ago. In 1869, Pope Pius XI condemned all abortion, regardless of circumstance and length of pregnancy. The 1973 landmark Supreme Court decisions that permitted women legally to have abortions on demand led to the formation of many anti-abortion groups, the most prominent of which is the National Right to Life Committee. During the late 1970s and early 1980s, a more politically conservative trend developed in this country, allowing anti-abortion groups to make headway in curbing the availability of abortion. Anti-abortion legislation, including a proposed amendment to the Constitution, has been promoted by certain politicians and anti-abortion groups that could eventually lead to a restriction or prohibition of abortion ("Abortion Amendment," 1981). Despite their efforts, however, in 1983 the Supreme Court rejected as unconstitutional many attempts on the part of certain states and localities to place limits on a woman's obtaining an abortion (Epstein, 1983).

Authorities differ on the incidence of "criminal" abortion prior to the easing of American law, but a reasonable estimate was 1 million per year (Hatcher et al., 1976). It is now estimated that there are 1.5 million abortions per year in this country ("Abortion Amendment," 1981). While married women seeking abortions were once said to outnumber single women four to one, the ratio between married and single women dropped to about fifty-fifty immediately after legalization of abortion. In 1976, the single women outnumbered the married women four to one.

While there is some risk involved in almost all birth control techniques, the incidence of death relative to the major nonsterilization forms of birth control is very low in comparison with pregnancy and childbirth mortalities. Investigations into the medical and legal problems related to abortion reveal that abortion is a safe, simple procedure that seldom involves serious psychiatric

Viewpoints on Abortion

In a landmark 1973 decision, the U.S. Supreme Court affirmed the constitutional right of a woman to terminate an unwanted pregnancy, ruling that the decision to abort a fetus may be made by the pregnant woman during the first trimester of pregnancy upon the advice of her physician. Since this Supreme Court ruling, opponents of legalized abortion have joined in an organized effort to bring about the repeal of existing legal statutes allowing abortion. Anti-abortion groups, such as the Right to Life Committee and the National Committee for a Human Life Amendment, have spoken out in an effort to influence anti-abortion legislation by making their viewpoint heard through Congress and other legislative bodies.

The pro-abortion forces, including such organizations as the Planned Parenthood Federation of America and the National Abortion Rights Action League, have continued to rally public support to protect the right of a woman to have a legal, medically safe abortion. Following are some of the ideas that anti-abortionist and pro-abortionist groups present in support of their respective points of view.

The anti-abortion forces contend that:

- Human life begins at conception; therefore, abortion is murder of a person.
- The fetus is not actually "part" of the mother; rather, the fetus is a separate person.
- The unborn fetus has the right to live, and the unborn fetus's right to live takes precedence over the woman's right to "control her body."
- Abortion is immoral, and legalized abortion is an indication of the moral decay of a country.
- Abortion is never necessary because alternatives are available—for example, giving up a child for adoption by foster parents.
- Abortion is destructive to the family unit.
- The availability of abortion as well as contraception encourages sexual acting-out behavior in teenagers.

The prochoice position with regard to legalized abortion holds that:

- The time when human life begins has not been established by the scientific community; thus abortion is not murder of a person.
- The fetus depends entirely on the mother's life-support systems and cannot be termed a "separate" person.
- A woman should have the constitutional right to terminate her pregnancy; the fetus is not a person and should not be considered a person with constitutional rights.
- Whether abortion is immoral is a matter for the individual to decide; many people believe forcing a woman to choose between an unwanted child and an illegal abortion is immoral.
- Adoption is not a perfect solution to an unwanted pregnancy; pregnancy involves much psychological and physiological stress that adoption in no way solves.
- Abortion is not as harmful to the family as a child born unwanted who may cause emotional and financial pressures that can be harmful to the family unit.
- Society must deal with the reality that many teenage girls get pregnant regardless of available birth control measures; formal sex education programs in the schools would encourage responsible sexual behavior among teenagers.

effects, except when there are medical or legal obstacles. Then it can become an emotionally traumatic experience. There are, to be sure, more legal abortions performed now than in the recent past. Even so, far too many women are still denied the right to have a legal abortion when they want one.

Generally speaking, the higher a woman's educational level, the more receptive she is to the idea of abortion. White women tend to be more in favor of abortion than black women at all levels of education. White Catholic college graduates are least favorable to abortion for any reason, while white non-Catholics with the same level of education are the most favorable (Westoff & Westoff, 1971).

Methods of Inducing Abortion

Abortion, one of the oldest forms of folk medicine known, has been attempted through an incredible range of methods. Primitive methods include jumping on the abdomen; probing the uterus with sticks; using potions made from animal secretions, dung, herbs, or seawater; and relying on magic and mystical incantations. Self-induced abortion has been attempted through medications such as pills and injections, spraying the uterus with chemicals, and violent physical exercise. And, where abortion is not legal, there remains the illegal abortionist, who more often than not is a dangerous amateur. The most common procedure is a form of dilatation and curettage of the womb; this is most often done by the woman's partner or an abortionist, who inserts some sort of instrument into the uterus and scrapes away the embryo. Such are the indignities, dangers, and stresses women must undergo to obtain an abortion if one is not legally and safely available. No law prohibiting abortion has kept a woman from getting one—no matter how unsafe—if she really wants one. A 1980 Supreme Court decision banning federal financing of abortions has changed the incidence of legal abortions for low- and middle-income persons ("Supreme Court," 1980).

An important aspect of liberalized abortion laws is that a woman can obtain an abortion quickly. Under restrictive laws, she is often forced to delay the abortion because of not knowing quite what to do, the effort to find someone to perform it, the problem of raising the necessary money, and so on (Tietze & Lewit, 1972). Research has indicated that the optimum time to perform an abortion is between the eighth and tenth weeks of pregnancy. Abortions taking place after the thirteenth week of pregnancy are three to four times more risky than those performed earlier. The greatest risk of all is to women who wait until the fifteenth week or later to seek an abortion.

Therapeutic abortions are recommended when certain pathological conditions exist, such as serious heart disease, some kidney diseases, or German measles during the first three months of pregnancy. Since the recent annulment of laws against abortion, therapeutic abortions may also be performed for nonphysical reasons. Therapeutic or elective abortions are performed in several ways. The most common are as follows.

Menstrual extraction can be used when menstruation is only a few weeks

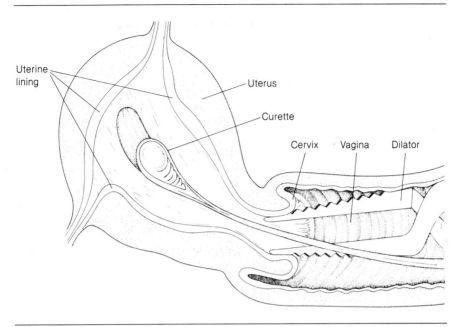

Figure 6.3   Lateral view of female reproductive system, showing dilatation and curettage. Dilator opens cervix through which curette is inserted to scrape uterine lining.

late. It is a suction technique in which a thin, flexible plastic tube is inserted into the uterus without the necessity of cervical dilation. Parts of the uterine lining and menstrual fluids that have been building up during the month are extracted, including a fertilized ovum if one happens to be present. The process requires a minimum of medication, takes only a few minutes to perform, can be done on an outpatient basis at relatively low cost, and has no troublesome aftereffects. The menstrual extraction suction technique is performed within the first two weeks of a missed period.

Vacuum curettage, another suction method, can be used until the twelfth week of pregnancy, when the woman knows she is pregnant. After that, the uterus is too soft and the fetus too large. In this procedure, a tube is inserted into the uterus and a vacuum pump is used to suck out the embryo and other uterine content. The technique is safe, is easier and faster to perform than dilatation and curettage, and causes the patient less trauma.

The procedure of dilatation and curettage (D&C, as it is called) is frequently performed if pregnancy has not progressed beyond the twelfth or thirteenth week. This procedure is performed in a hospital with the patient under anesthesia. The cervix is dilated by inserting graduated sizes of instruments to stretch the opening, the largest dilator being about the size and shape of a small cigar (Figure 6.3). Or a seaweed (*laminaria*) plug is inserted, which in eight to twenty-four hours will have swollen sufficiently to dilate the cervix, permitting an easy D&C after its removal (Pritchard & MacDonald, 1980). Once dilation is accomplished, a spoonlike instrument, a curette, is used to scrape the implanted embryo or early fetus from the uterus.

Hysterotomy is a method used after pregnancy has reached twelve weeks (Pritchard & MacDonald, 1980). One technique, actually a minor caesarean section, is resorted to because the fetus is too large for the usual vaginal methods of removal. Another technique entails a vaginal incision near the cervix; a slit is then made in the lower part of the uterus through which the fetus is removed.

Saline abortion, widely used in Japan after World War II but now abandoned because of maternal postabortion complications and death, has gained popularity in the United States in cases of pregnancy advanced beyond the fourteenth week (Pritchard & MacDonald, 1980). A needle is used to withdraw slightly less than a cup (about 200 cubic centimeters) of amniotic fluid through the wall of the woman's abdomen. The fluid is then replaced with an equal amount of salt solution of a specified strength. Abortion occurs spontaneously, usually within twenty-four hours. Besides salt solutions, compounds such as urea and prostaglandins have been injected to induce abortion (Hatcher et al., 1980).

Contraception

Despite the great technological advances of recent decades, the failproof contraceptive does not yet exist. And of all birth control means, only two provide absolute safety from pregnancy: celibacy and the removal of the male or female gonads or the uterus. A contraceptive pill combining estrogen and progestin is not far behind in effectiveness. But despite a birth control technique's effectiveness rating, user error and inconsistency of use contribute far more to failure than does faultiness in the method itself (Sandberg, 1976).

Different investigators and organizations accord slightly different success-failure ratings to various birth control methods, and they use different means to arrive at their totals. One system uses the term *woman-years* and is calculated on the thirteen menstrual cycles per year that a woman normally has. Fifteen failures of a particular technique per 100 woman-years means that fifteen pregnancies occurred in 1,300 cycles despite its use. Planned Parenthood Federation further defines success and failure according to *user* and *method*. User failure implies that a mistake, accident, or carelessness on the part of the user is involved. Method failure implies that the method was used correctly and was used each time that coitus took place, yet pregnancy occurred anyway.

The educational level of couples is directly related to whether or not they use contraceptives: the higher the education, the more likely they are to use them. Furthermore, one of the most important considerations in an individual's or couple's consistent use of a birth control technique is their motivation to do so, motivation that is closely related to the technique's acceptability to them.

It is important to recognize that today the responsibility for contraceptive use as well as for other forms of birth control is not so readily viewed as belonging to the woman exclusively. Traditionally, women have been expected to assume responsibility for the prevention of unwanted pregnancies. This attitude appears to be changing as more men are willing to share this form of sexual responsibility with their mates. For instance, men today may not be so quick to assume that their partner is taking birth control pills. Instead, men may take responsibility for delaying intercourse or modifying sexual activity, especially if the woman is in the middle of her cycle. Or they may share in the decision as to which form of birth control is most appropriate. A fortunate by-product of this emerging attitude is that it furthers the cause of equality between the sexes. Moreover, it encourages responsible sexual decision making for both partners in the relationship.

Contraceptives Available Only with a Doctor's Prescription

A **diaphragm** is a thin rubber dome-shaped cup stretched over a collapsible metal ring, designed to cover the mouth of the uterus (the cervix). The diaphragm must be fitted by a physician because of individual physiological differences in women. Having the correct size and shape in a diaphragm is important for both the wearer's comfort and its effectiveness as a contraceptive. A virgin cannot be fitted with one until her hymen has been broken or incised by the physician. The device need not interfere with the conduct or pleasure of intercourse for either partner.

Used with contraceptive cream or jelly, the diaphragm seals off the cervix and prevents sperm from entering the uterus (Figure 6.4). The cream or jelly is toxic to sperm and provides lubrication as well. The diaphragm may be inserted several hours before coitus or immediately before. It must not be removed until six hours after intercourse and should not be left in place longer than twenty-four hours, lest it encourage the growth of bacteria and infection. Douching is unnecessary, since the natural processes of a healthy woman keep her vaginal tract clean. But if a woman prefers to douche, especially if several applications of spermicide have been used, she must wait at least six hours following coitus to allow ample time for the spermicide to be fully effective.

A unique advantage of the diaphragm is that it can be used to hold the menstrual flow internally for twenty-four hours, which makes for tidier coitus during menses (Hatcher et al., 1976). But diaphragms are considered by some to be inconvenient, uncomfortable, and difficult to use. For some couples, the advance preparation necessary interferes with spontaneity, which may detract from sexual pleasure. Another objection is that they can become dislodged in intercourse, especially in the woman-atop position (Hatcher et al., 1976). Method failure is recorded at two to four per 100 woman-years; user failure, ten to twenty per 100 woman-years.

The *cervical cap* is a miniature diaphragm of soft rubber or impermeable plastic that fits over the cervix and is kept in place by suction. Past estimates indicate the failure rate at eight per 100 woman-years. However, studies of the effectiveness of new cervical caps are presently being done (Hatcher et al., 1980).

Oral contraceptives or birth control pills, popularly called "the Pill," are a

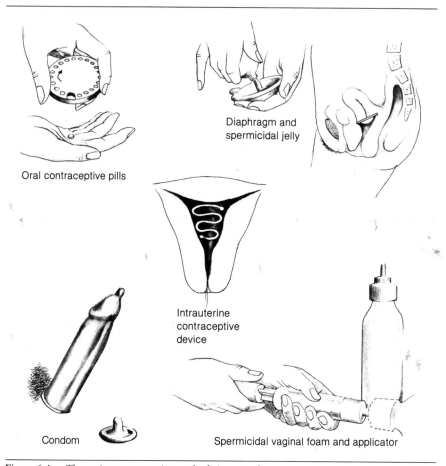

Figure 6.4   The major contraceptive methods in use today.

combination of synthetic hormones (progesterone and estrogen) that prevents ovulation by mimicking the hormonal state of the body during pregnancy. Since no ovum is released, pregnancy cannot occur.

With most brands of pills (approximately thirty are on the market [Hatcher et al., 1980]), one pill is taken daily for twenty days, beginning on the fifth day after the beginning of a menstrual period. The pills are preferably taken at the same hour each day. Menstruation will commence within two to five days after the last pill is taken, although in about 3 percent of the cases it may fail to occur altogether. In the latter event, a physician usually advises his patient to take another round of twenty pills, beginning seven days after the last pill was taken.

If one pill is missed, there is a remote chance of pregnancy, and a woman is usually advised to take the missed pill as soon as she realizes she has omitted it. If taken as prescribed, oral contraceptives are virtually 100 percent effective—

a success that is unequalled by any other means of contraception. Method failure with combination pills is less than one per 100 woman-years; user failure, two to four.

Should a woman become pregnant while taking the Pill, some physicians recommend that she seek an abortion. Other physicians are not as concerned because the associated risk of having a malformed infant is only slightly increased when the Pill is taken during the first or second months of pregnancy (Hatcher et al., 1980).

Negative side effects of the Pill may occur in about 40 percent of women (Hatcher et al., 1980). The danger of the Pill for women over forty has been confirmed by the Population Council (Tietze et al., 1976). The risk of death is twenty times greater for them than for younger women. It has also been suggested that the Pill should not be used by girls who have not reached physical maturity—between thirteen and eighteen years, with the average being sixteen years—because it can interfere with completion of normal growth and maturation. Further, since the Pill suppresses milk production, its use is not recommended during the period just after childbirth when a mother is nursing her baby. There is also evidence that if a mother takes the Pill while nursing a male child, the unusual combination of hormones in her body can enter the baby's bloodstream and have a feminizing effect on him.

The Pill's grave complications include pulmonary embolism, cerebral thrombosis, stroke, clotting disorders, and heart attack (DeLora & Warren, 1977). A major study showed that Pill users of all ages incur a fourfold risk over nonusers of strokes involving arterial blockage by blood clots (Collaborative Group, 1975).

One investigation has suggested that dangers concerning the Pill are exaggerated ("Reassessing the Pill's Risks," 1980). Although many of the negative effects of the Pill have been eliminated, occasional discomfort or unpleasantness, such as mild gastrointestinal disturbances, nausea, weight gain, a bloated feeling, and irregular bleeding, may be experienced by some women, especially in the first few months. These symptoms usually are temporary, however, and disappear as the cycles of pills are repeated. The continued presence of side effects may dictate a switch to one of the minipills.

Minipills have been in use since 1973. They are taken throughout the month, even during menses, thereby eliminating the chore of counting pills and of stopping and restarting a series. Their use is indicated for those who have developed adverse estrogen-related symptoms, or might do so, from the combination pill. The estrogenic component causes most of the pill-associated complications. Containing progestin alone, minipills do not necessarily inhibit ovulation, nor do they interfere with menstruation. Instead, they make the reproductive system resistant to sperm transport, ovum transport, or blastocyst implantation should fertilization take place. Their effectiveness is slightly less than that of the combination pill, failure being highest during the first six months of use (Hatcher et al., 1980; Pritchard & MacDonald, 1980). Method failure has been set at two to three per 100 woman-years; user failure, two to four.

All cautions about the Pill should be weighed against the hazards of unwanted or dangerous pregnancies that the Pill might have prevented. In one study, it was estimated that the risk of dying was 3.5 times greater without the Pill than with it, thromboembolic and other disorders notwithstanding, because of the complications arising from pregnancy, childbirth, and the postpartum period—complications that may result from using less effective contraception. Among women using no method of birth control, incidentally, the risk of maternal death is 7.5 times greater than it is among women taking the Pill (Hardin, 1970). Even with the favorable reports concerning the safety of using the Pill, the wise woman will have regular consultations with her gynecologist on the advisability of continuing its use.

Some women have expressed concern that taking the Pill will adversely affect their sex drive. Indeed, some authorities warn women to expect a reduction in sex drive after taking the Pill for eighteen to thirty-six months, and women are advised to substitute other methods of contraception after about eighteen months of continual use in order to restore the original hormonal balance of the body. It is not always true, however, that there is a reduction in sex drive with oral contraceptives. One study (Bragonier, 1976) shows that women on the Pill have sexual intercourse more frequently than other women of the same age, race, religion, and education, and their coital rate increases with time.

In addition to its contraceptive effect, the Pill is also used to treat certain discomforts and disorders of the menstrual cycle, such as irregularity, overly copious flow of blood, and discomfort before or during menstruation.

Intrauterine contraceptive devices (IUDs) are small plastic devices of various sizes and shapes that are designed to fit into the womb. It is thought that the IUD in some way acts as an irritant to prevent the implantation of the fertilized ovum in the uterine wall. Technically, therefore, this method is more correctly called *contraimplantation* than contraception.

The device must be placed in the uterus by a physician, who can remove it at any time that the woman wishes to become pregnant. After the birth of a child, it may be repositioned in the uterus until another pregnancy is desired. The device in no way affects the fertility of the woman or the health of children who are born after the removal of the IUD.

The shapes and materials of IUDs are many. Perhaps the most widely known are the Lippes Loop, the Copper 7 (small, made of plastic, and wound around with 0.03 ounce of copper wire), the Copper T, and the Saf-T Coil (Pritchard & MacDonald, 1980). Another T-shaped device, called Progestasert, is an important recent addition to the IUD family. A small, flexible unit, it is the first hormone-enhanced IUD on the market. It releases small continuous doses of the natural female hormone progesterone and thus combines the effects of an IUD and hormonal inhibition of blastocyst implantation (not ovulation). It also acts to thicken cervical mucus, which impedes sperm passage (Connell, 1975). An additional plus is that Progestasert seems less likely than most IUDs to cause cramping. It must be replaced every year, however, because it loses its hormonal effectiveness. The Copper T and Copper 7 must be replaced every two to four years for similar reasons (Brody, 1980). Others may remain in place indefinitely, until a pregnancy is desired.

Tiny plastic threads attached to the IUD should extend an inch or so into the vagina. If the threads cannot be felt by testing with the fingers, it can be assumed that the IUD has been rejected and is not in place. If it is protruding from the cervix, it is also ineffective. In both instances the woman must see her doctor and, in the meantime, use another form of birth control.

There are certain disadvantages to using IUDs. Some women experience pain on insertion and cramping for several days afterward. Some have heavy menstrual bleeding and spotting, especially in the early months of emplacement. Uterine perforation and pelvic inflammatory disease sometimes occur (Sandberg, 1976). Another bothersome problem with the IUD is undetected expulsion. It is estimated that spontaneous expulsion is experienced by 8 to 10 percent of women, especially by those who have never been pregnant (Boston Women's Health Book Collective, 1973). After menses, the woman or her partner should check for the tiny threads, a check that should be made once a week between periods. Failure rate is estimated at two to four per 100 woman-years. When pregnancy does occur, the spontaneous abortion rate is 25 percent if the device is removed, about 50 percent if it is not (DeLora & Warren, 1977; Pritchard & MacDonald, 1980).

Contraceptives Available without a Doctor's Prescription

The **condom**, one of the most widely used contraceptives in the United States, is cheap, easy to obtain and use, and disposable. Designed to fit the erect penis, the condom is made of thin rubber or of sheep's intestine and measures about 7 inches (19 centimeters) in length.

Unless the condom breaks during intercourse or slips off after ejaculation, it offers almost total effectiveness. To lessen the possibility of accidental pregnancies, the man should blow air into it before use to make sure there are no tears or breaks. After intercourse, he should carefully hold it while he withdraws his penis from his partner's vagina in order to prevent semen from spilling into the vaginal opening. He can then fill the used condom with water in another test to make sure that no breakage has occurred. If a condom should prove to be broken, the woman should immediately insert a contraceptive cream or jelly into her vagina. If neither of these is available, a douche, even if with plain water, is the next best course of action. Once a condom has been used, it is best to throw it away and not try to reuse it.

Short of abstinence, the condom is one of only three effective male birth control techniques demonstrated to date (the others are withdrawal and sterilization). The method failure of condoms is two to four per 100 woman-years; user failure is ten to twenty. These figures are no doubt reduced when the condom is used along with contraceptive foam. In addition to its use as a contraceptive, the condom is the best method, after total abstinence, of preventing the spread of STD.

Chemical contraceptive methods include creams, jellies, and foams that block the entrance to the uterus and that are toxic to sperm. They must be inserted into the vagina no later than fifteen to thirty minutes before intercourse, and they must be reapplied if intercourse is repeated. Method failure is two to four per 100 woman-years; user failure is ten to twenty per 100.

There are various other insertable **spermicides**—jellies, suppositories, tablets—but their effectiveness varies widely. Generally speaking, aerosol foams have been the most successful of the chemical contraceptive agents (Hatcher et al., 1980).

Douching should not be considered a means of birth control; there is no medical support for its effectiveness. Its purpose is to flush seminal fluid from the vagina before it has a chance to enter the mouth of the womb. Actually, however, sperm move so quickly that the douche often fails to reach them—or it can push sperm more quickly toward the cervix than they might otherwise travel (DeLora & Warren, 1977). Since viable sperm can be detected in a woman's fallopian tubes ninety seconds after her partner ejaculates, we can conclude that douching is not an effective method for preventing pregnancy (Connell, 1982).

Other Methods of Birth Prevention

Coitus interruptus or withdrawal, the oldest known form of contraception, requires that the male withdraw his penis from the vagina of the female before he ejaculates. Many couples use this method exclusively and find it satisfactory, while other couples find the technique highly undesirable, both because of its effect on the enjoyment of intercourse and because of its undependability. The man must withdraw just at the crucial moment and must wait a considerable period of time before having intercourse again because of the possibility of sperm remaining in his urethra. In the absence of any other birth control, coitus interruptus is certainly better than nothing. The failure rate is nine to fifteen per 100 woman-years in consistent users, and its overall failure is twenty to twenty-five (Hatcher et al., 1980).

The **rhythm method** requires that a couple abstain from sexual intercourse during that period of a woman's menstrual cycle when she is capable of conception—just before, during, and just after ovulation. The major problem with the rhythm method is that only about 30 percent of women have sufficiently regular menstrual cycles that they can correctly pinpoint their "safe" period. The *temperature method* is a variation of the rhythm method and is based on the belief that a woman's temperature changes according to the changes in her menstrual cycle. One problem with this method is that many women have no marked or consistent temperature changes. Another difficulty is that many women ovulate more than one time during a menstrual cycle, with the possibility existing that sexual excitement itself can trigger ovulation. A form of "natural" birth control called the Billings method relies on monitoring changes that occur in the cervical mucus in order to determine when a woman is in her fertile period. While this method allows for a more accurate identification of when a woman is in her fertile period, it requires sophistication on the woman's part to monitor changes in the cervical mucus (Klein, 1982). Method failure in the periodic abstinence techniques is five to ten per 100 woman-years, and user failure is twenty to thirty.

A "morning-after pill"—diethystilbestrol (DES)—can be used when un-protected coitus has occurred. However, the possibility exists of severe side effects—not only for the woman but also for the infant, if one is already con-ceived. Because of these risks, the FDA has given approval for DES as an emer-gency measure only. It is not to be considered a primary method of birth control.

Regardless of the contraceptive technique used, its effectiveness depends on how well the user follows prescribed directions and how consistently the method is used. Carelessness in the use of even the most effective contraceptive increases the chances of pregnancy.

Birth Control in the Future

There is considerable evidence that people need a much better method of fer-tility control than is now available. The side effects of the Pill, and fear of it, have caused many women to abandon its use. Other facts pointing to the need for more effective methods of birth control include the discomfort, expulsion rate, and occasional failure of IUDs; the high failure rate of most other con-traceptives; and the consequent number of abortions and unwanted babies. About 75 percent of all American women are sterile, pregnant, or trying to become pregnant; or, they are using a birth control technique that is relatively ineffective, inconvenient, messy, or incompatible with the natural, spontane-ous enjoyment of intercourse (Westoff & Westoff, 1971). Realizing these facts, scientists are turning their attention to new techniques and methods of birth control.

A technique involving a low dosage of progestin is currently being devel-oped. An inch-long spaghetti-like capsule containing progestin is inserted into the woman's leg, arm, or groin by means of a hypodermic needle. The capsule releases just enough progestin at a constant rate to keep her from becoming pregnant. If she then decides to have a baby, the capsule is removed. Capsules capable of releasing progestin for as long as one, three, or ten years—or even a lifetime—may be used.

Biochemists continue to work on a hormonal birth control technique for men designed to suppress production of sperm manufactured by a man in his reproductive life. In the view of most researchers, a workable technique is still several years away (Hatcher, et al., 1980). To date, inhibition of spermato-genesis, by testosterone or progesterone, has caused complications serious enough to call into question its advisability—such as its effects on the sex drive, the slow return of fertility upon discontinuing its use, its incompatibility with alcohol, and its possible linkage with cancer. A pill that acts to prevent sperm from maturing may be more of a possibility, but one has not yet been perfected.

Other possible future birth control techniques may involve the development of vaccines to immunize a woman against her partner's sperm; use of contraceptive beverages such as teas; and biosynthesis of a substance to block removal of the decapacitation factor (DF), which protects the surface of the sperm cell (when DF is removed, the sperm can enter the egg cell).

Nothing in history matched the contraceptive revolution of the 1960s, sparked primarily by the introduction of the Pill, which demonstrated that improved technology can play a crucial role in combating unwanted pregnancy. Yet contraceptive failure has continued in epidemic proportions. One survey in the United States of persons with low income revealed that less than half possessed sufficient knowledge to use a contraceptive effectively. This ignorance was particularly apparent among young people aged fifteen to eighteen years (Speidel, 1970). The problem is even more acute in underdeveloped countries.

Today, in many cultures, procreation and recreation are recognized as two separate goals in sexual activity, neither of which need be subordinated to the other. The remaining problem relates to worldwide, out-of-hand population growth. Research in future contraceptive technology apparently needs therefore to concentrate on the unsolved mysteries of human reproduction.

Summary

Birth control has been an important topic in this country since the time of Margaret Sanger and the founding of the planned parenthood movement. Birth control methods have been used increasingly as people have recognized the severe hindrance to social and economic development created by uncurbed population growth. Other purposes of fertility limitation have been to: (1) further certain physical and socioeconomic objectives; (2) aid early sexual and marital adjustment; (3) prevent unwanted pregnancies among the unmarried; and (4) curb inherited diseases. Methods of birth control include abstinence, sterilization, abortion, and contraception.

Abstinence, though successful as a birth control technique, is seldom preferred by couples. Sterilization methods, or surgical procedures to render a person incapable of reproduction, have been employed to aid in limiting family size. The two principal methods of female sterilization are tubal ligation, or cutting or tying the fallopian tubes, and laparoscopic sterilization, or "Band-Aid sterilization." Surgical procedures including oophorectomy (removal of the ovaries), hysterectomy (removal of the uterus), and total salpingectomy (removal of the fallopian tubes), may be performed. The two major types of male sterilization are vasectomy, or cutting and tying of the sperm-carrying ducts, and castration, removal of the testicles. Vas sclerosing, a method of scarring the walls of the vas deferens to produce sterilization, may provide an alternative to vasectomy.

Abortion, or premature expulsion from the uterus of an embryo, can be a form of birth control. Spontaneous abortion, or miscarriage, is unintentional and thus is not considered a form of birth control. Menstrual extraction, suction abortion, vacuum curettage, and dilatation and curettage (D&C) are methods of induced abortion that may be performed within the first trimester of pregnancy. Saline abortion and hysterotomy are methods used when pregnancy has advanced beyond twelve or thirteen weeks.

Effective contraceptive techniques have been developed, although the failproof contraceptive does not exist. Contraceptives can fail because the *user* does not properly use them or because the *method* does not work for some reason. Contraceptives that are available only with a doctor's prescription include: (1) the diaphragm, a dome-shaped cup that covers the entrance to the uterus; (2) the cervical cap, a miniature diaphragm that fits over the cervix; (3) birth control pills, containing a combination of synthetic hormones that prevents ovulation; (4) minipills, containing progestin alone, which help make the reproductive system resistant to sperm transport, ovum transport, or blastocyst implantation; and (5) IUDs, or intrauterine devices, small devices designed for insertion in the womb.

Contraceptives that are available without a doctor's prescription include: (1) the condom, a cylindrical sheath that is rolled onto the penis before intercourse, and (2) foams, jellies, and creams, substances introduced into the vagina that keep sperm from entering the cervix or are toxic to sperm. Douching, sometimes used for birth control purposes, is not effective. Other methods of birth prevention are these: (1) coitus interruptus, which requires the man to withdraw his penis from his partner's vagina before he climaxes; and (2) the rhythm or calendar method and its variations, which rely upon timing coitus so that it occurs during the woman's "safe" or infertile period.

A possible after-the-fact measure is diethystilbestrol (DES), a "morning-after pill." Insertion of a progestin capsule into a woman's body, birth control pills for men, and the development of contraceptive teas are among the birth control techniques of the future.

TRUE OR FALSE:
THE FACTS

Birth control methods involving sterilization procedures will cause impairment of the sex drive in both men and women.
False. Neither men nor women experience impaired sex drive after sterilization; indeed, they often experience an increase in sex drive when the fear of pregnancy is removed. *(96–97)*

Douching after intercourse is a safe, effective contraceptive technique.
False. Viable sperm can be found in a woman's fallopian tubes ninety seconds after her partner ejaculates, making douching ineffective. *(108)*

Thanks to modern medicine, pregnancy and childbirth offer no risk to a woman.
False. Even with the risks of the Pill, a woman is 3.5 times more likely to die of possible complications arising from pregnancy, childbirth, and the postpartum period. *(106)*

SUGGESTED READING

The Alan Guttmacher Institute. *Teenage pregnancy: The problem that hasn't gone away.* New York: Planned Parenthood Federation of America, 1981.
This valuable report summarizes studies related to teenage contraception and abortion, providing important insights into teenage contraceptive behavior.

Guillebaud, John. *The Pill.* New York: Oxford University Press, 1980.
Written for the general consumer, this book attempts to dispel myths and fears concerning the use of oral contraceptives. The book answers many often-asked questions related to safety and effectiveness of birth control pills.

Hatcher, Robert A., Stewart, Gary K., Stewart, Felicia, Guest, Felicia, Schwartz, David W., and Jones, Stephanie A. *Contraceptive technology, 1980–1981.* New York: Irvington Publishers, 1980.
This book offers thorough, up-to-date information on various contraceptive techniques and issues related to contraception. This valuable general reference contains useful charts and tables and additional information on medical concerns and family planning services.

McCary, James Leslie, and McCary, Stephen P. *McCary's human sexuality* (4th ed.). Belmont, Calif.: Wadsworth, 1982.
Chapter 13 gives detailed information on all forms of birth control, past, present, and future.

Tietze, Christopher. *Induced abortion: A world view.* New York: The Population Council, 1981.
This book offers a comprehensive examination of abortion and related issues.

TRUE OR FALSE?

Psychologists are in agreement that a couple "fall in love" when their relationship has matured to the point where intimacy is possible.

❦

Romantic love is the ultimate expression of sexual and emotional intimacy that a couple may experience.

❦

The ability to communicate effectively with one's partner is part of the "magic" of the love relationship and thus is not a skill that one can learn.

❦

Sexual intercourse alone can be equated with total and complete intimacy in a relationship.

Intimacy
and Love

CHAPTER 7

What Is Intimacy?
Avoidance of Intimacy
The Game Called Courtship

What Is Love?
Falling in Love
Kinds of Love
Romantic Love
Maintaining Love and Intimacy

Love and Sex

Summary

Suggested Reading

Since the beginning of civilization, the terror of loneliness has been one of humankind's great threats. People will go to incredible lengths to avoid loneliness and will pay an unbelievable price in terms of money, property, time, and personal rights to prevent it. The most obvious and meaningful way to avoid loneliness is to establish and maintain intimate, constructive relationships with others. But the solution is far more complex than it would seem. For the road to intimacy is cluttered with many barriers arising from the individual's cultural background, personal needs, and private fears. Growth and survival of intimacy is a bleak prospect when either or both partners in a relationship have through the years internalized feelings of distrust, isolation, and rejection, or have developed the unfortunate protective mechanisms of withdrawal and withholding of self. These traits of alienation have become signs of our times.

Present-day feelings of distrust and isolation come from several sources: eroding social structures; blurring of male and female roles, once well defined; confusion over personal identity and goals; geographic changes forced by job transfers (the "average American" moves seven times in his or her lifetime and changes professions three times), necessitating the difficult, often painful process of forming new friendships; political unrest; and disillusionment over the integrity of governments. All have taken a heavy toll in personal security and confidence.

The ease of travel has expanded lists of acquaintances but has done little to improve the quality of friendship. The mass (and muddle) of communication has thrust a confusing assortment of voices and views into our lives without appreciably increasing the quality of our understanding of either ourselves or others. Far too many people feel, at least at times, that they stand on a curbstone, lonely bystanders watching the rest of the world pass by without a nod. Even in the midst of a crowd, they feel miserably alone. They stand in paralyzing fear of rejection should they dare reveal themselves to others because they cannot believe that anyone could like or love their real selves. Yet they desperately need an intimate relationship and realize that personal revelation is essential to its evolution. They therefore compromise by substituting masks and role-playing for self-revelation. The typical result is a shallow, unrewarding acquaintanceship with another person, not an honest, close bond.

Deeply satisfying intimate relationships among friends add immeasurably to human contentment, and it is important that the concepts of intimacy and love be examined in a book basically concerned with sexuality. For intimacy is the backbone of love, and with intimacy in a loving relationship, the potentials of sexual gratification are extraordinary. Intimacy is what it's all about.

What Is Intimacy?

Perhaps this discussion should focus initially on what intimacy is *not*, for one of the barriers to achieving intimacy is accepting counterfeits for the real thing. Intimacy is not mere "togetherness." One can be with another person in the sense of closeness of bodies, yet live emotionally and mentally on separate planets. People can pass their entire lives very much in one another's physical presence, but never overcome the gap of spiritual separation. Nonintimate togetherness is railroad tracks running endlessly parallel but never touching. The missing part in parallel existence is not that the two persons are doing different things or even thinking separate thoughts or experiencing different responses; it is that they are simply not *sharing* experiences, thoughts, or feelings. For body, mind, and emotions are all crucially involved in intimacy. An intimate relationship involves a special kind of emotional bond, in which there is mutual caring, responsibility, trust, open communication, and a nondefensive sharing of feelings (Kaplan, 1979).

Many consider intimacy much more realistic than love in meaningful human relationships; certainly it is fundamental to love. Two basic requirements for the evolution of intimacy are time and privacy, because they provide the opportunity for development of its five primary components. In order of development, these components are *choice, mutuality, reciprocity, trust,* and *delight* (Calderone, 1972).

Two people meet; they like each other; they make overtures toward establishing a closer relationship by exchanging small confidences. The two have made a *choice*. The fact that each has made the same choice makes the act *mutual*. The choice must be a mutual one, since a unilateral choice would obviously exclude intimacy; in a truly intimate relationship, one cannot be more intimate than the other. More and more is revealed as the two grow in the confidence that they are understood by each other without having to apologize or defend. Each confides, understands, and gives equally to the other; thus *reciprocity* develops. Greater depths of feelings are then shared as each recognizes that the other's responses are consistent, nonjudgmental, and nondestructive. More and more is revealed as the two grow in confidence. With these revelations and acceptance, *trust* grows. Intimacy can then expand to its limits: an unconditional acceptance of the other, exactly as he or she is, creating a relationship in which both partners can flourish and thus experience *delight* (Coutts, 1973).

Individual ranges of sensitivity, awareness, and emotionality vary enormously. The closer two people match in these respects, the greater are the chances that true intimacy will evolve. If needs are similar they can be met more easily, and there is little necessity to be apologetic about them. Intensity and marks of affection or tenderness are vastly important to a beginning relationship. But one must allow intimacy to develop subtly; "coming on too strong" can be as defeating as an attitude of distance and coldness (Coutts, 1973). Many long-standing relationships (especially marriage) become stunted because sharing and self-revelation, the supports of intimacy, cease. Although confidences were shared at the beginning of the relationship, the habit of sharing tends to become selective, weakens, and is lost in the course of years. It becomes easier and easier for a couple to ignore disturbing feelings by refusing to admit that they exist or to avoid any unpleasantness by not talking about them. This is especially true when other troublesome aspects of living—jobs, children, community obligations—demand immediate attention.

One must also remember that one cannot develop intimacy with everyone.

Some people simply are not on the same wavelength, so we should not become upset when initial reaching out is met with a blank stare. Because of the self-revelation involved, good judgment must be exercised when one seeks intimacy. One must feel justified in trusting the other, for there are those whom one truly cannot trust. They may be hostile and unforgiving by nature; or merely curious, not compassionate; or interested only in making themselves important to others by passing on newly learned confidences as gossipy tidbits. Disclosing oneself to someone whom one threatens is equally dangerous. And it is fruitless to disclose oneself to someone who is very insecure and finds one's honesty in disclosing fears and failures a terrifying reminder of his or her own weaknesses. An honest interchange of feelings would be impossible because the feedback would be warped.

The partners in intimate relationships are assured of acceptance and do not have to defend their failures; self-worth remains intact (although sometimes a little battered). The total acceptance by another person generates greater ego strength, leaving the individual more flexible and less demanding in other personal relationships. He or she becomes warmer, more tolerant, and more respectful toward others, as well as more assertive and honest. There is no necessity to screen thoughts or weigh words. Such a person is "less anxious, less defensive, and better able to throw off reactions that are inappropriate" (J. L. McCary, 1975, 1980). Those who are intimate tell each other the truth, and all of it. Each has the capacity to forgive—a fund that must be drawn upon periodically in an intimate relationship. The ability to laugh at one's own and the other's imperfections, but never to ridicule, must exist. Those who find it difficult to laugh often find it difficult to forgive as well.

Avoidance of Intimacy

With so much to be gained, why is intimacy deliberately avoided? Why is it so hard to achieve? Society is at fault, first of all, in that it conditions us to deny feelings, play roles, and please others even to the detriment of ourselves. A premium is placed on always being in control of emotions. By expressing no feelings, we leave the impression of having none. Second, we as individuals often miss out on engaging in intimate interactions because we fail to take active participatory roles in our interpersonal endeavors. Rather, we often find it easier to take less rewarding, passive spectator roles than to immerse ourselves in emotionally rewarding, intimate relationships (Kaplan, 1979).

Another barrier to intimacy is anger. It is an unacceptable emotion, we are told, so we go to great lengths to suppress, deny, and disguise it. But these efforts only mask anger; it lingers, and it destroys intimacy. The most successful means of getting rid of anger is, first, to admit to oneself that it exists. Next, one should express it directly to the person who aroused it, although in an acceptable manner lest one generate yet another set of problems (J. L. McCary, 1975, 1980). Constant bickering and attempts to bring up old grievances can lead to the demise of the love relationship. Attempts to emphasize the positive aspects of the relationship and well-chosen words are more likely to defuse destructive anger and reestablish communication (Mace, 1980). Once anger is defused, the door to intimacy can be opened again.

Courtship: An emergence of sensual and emotional awareness. *Kenneth Karp*.

The most formidable of all barriers to intimacy is fear, notably fear of rejection. In revealing ourselves we dread the possible humiliation of appearing stupid, weak, unworthy. We too often assume that we stand as uniquely inferior creatures in a world almost wholly populated with exceptionally talented, intelligent, sophisticated, and beautiful people. We are curiously blind to the fact that the desirable others are also frightened, because they, too, have suffered failure.

The Game Called Courtship

Inappropriate efforts to establish intimacy are perhaps best exemplified in traditional courtship, American style. An unfolding male-female relationship can and should be an apprenticeship in intimacy, but more commonly only a superficial togetherness develops.

To ensure acceptance—to avoid the misery of rejection—the lover usually presents his or her better self (as he or she sees it) by going to some pains to hide flaws. In such cases, real or total feelings are only minimally revealed or are suppressed entirely. Role-playing becomes a burden, loneliness deepens, and resentment at having to maintain a facade is often projected toward the loved one. Further, the lover's presentation of the image of perfection and, it follows, the expectation of it, arouse feelings of inadequacy in the partner. Fearing to look bad by comparison, the partner likewise begins role-playing.

So what emerges is two actors playing parts in which they are extremely uncomfortable. Each grows increasingly tense trying to outguess the other in what he or she finds lovable, then twists himself or herself into that image (Van

Den Haag, 1973). Both no doubt fervently wish that they could start from the beginning and be their genuine selves, however imperfect.

A healthy substitute for the superficialities of traditional courtship is what might be called "the pairing system"—a getting-to-know-you period in which openness and honesty predominate in the couple's relationship. Fears and self-doubts, often very painful, are trotted out and examined. Each finds wonderful relief in recognizing that the other is undergoing the same small agonies in the search for identity and the establishment of self-worth. A bond develops as each demonstrates a feeling of responsibility for the other. Neither will violate the confidences and personal integrity of the other. This interaction creates trust, and once trust is established true intimacy is possible (Bach & Deutsch, 1973).

What Is Love?

Endless observations on the nature and quality of love have been made by poets, philosophers, behaviorists, and simpler folk. Yet despite the outpouring of ink, words, tears, and even venom on the subject, a precise definition of love remains as elusive today as it was (no doubt) at the dawn of history. Because love has a tremendous range of meanings, and the need is enormous both to give and to receive it from birth until the day we die, it is one of the most complex, poorly understood facets of human existence. Love in our culture tends to be defined according to intensity of feeling and how one should act when one believes oneself to be in love. Some use the word "love" so freely that it has little meaning; others invest the word with such enormous meaning that they may never be able to say honestly "I love." Still others consider the word such an irreversible commitment to another person that they become frightened by the enormity of the commitment and responsibilities involved. They therefore not only avoid *saying* the word, but avoid as well any but the shallowest of feelings.

To love implies the ability to be alone without feeling lonely. To need another merely for company signifies dependency, not love. Meeting the legitimate emotional needs of another person is quite a different matter from trying to solve his or her emotional problems. In fact, neurotic mutual dependency is a basic marital problem (Fromm, 1956; Lederer & Jackson, 1968). Filling one's voids through another person rather than developing one's own resources places the other (and in the long haul, oneself) in bondage. This sort of dependency is as addictive as drugs. Love, by contrast, shares, yet it frees. Unselfishness is essential to a deep love, but only when it is mutual and neither partner sacrifices his or her integrity in the service of the other.

Because it is a goal that must be worked for, mature and lasting love requires total commitment. Commitment arises from two kinds of feelings—responsiveness to the other, which is involuntary, and being responsible for him or her, which is a conscious, acknowledged obligation. The interaction of two people in these circumstances "creates an overpowering sense of involvement and identification, of oneness, which some people call love, and it is the original source of commitment" (Masters & Johnson, 1975). The ultimate success or failure of the relationship depends upon whether there is more pleasure than displeasure in the commitment, for certainly there will be both.

Falling in Love

Much is heard of "falling in love," a concept that most psychologists reject. They contend that we do not fall in love; rather, we grow in love and love grows in us, beginning in infancy. Children first love their parents, then their playmates, then their teachers, and then other adults. It might be said that we grow in love as we grow in intimacy with another person, both processes requiring work, time, the willingness to risk pain, and the ability to be there when we are needed.

How does acquaintanceship progress to liking and thence to love? The evolution is much the same as that of intimacy. When two people first meet, they typically present themselves to each other with what they consider an acceptable mixture of conventional and personal ideals or opinions. That tentative step taken, they next express certain personal needs, which either clash with the other person's or prove to be mutual. If too many views are in conflict, the relationship settles at the acquaintanceship level. But when personal needs are mutual and aspirations similar, a friendship can be launched. Even though there is initial satisfaction in the relationship, however, the couple tend to proceed cautiously, still concealing many of their real feelings. As they become better acquainted and learn to trust one another, they disclose more and more of their deeper selves. They come to know the best and worst about each other. They like and accept one another either because or in spite of these revelations. The next step is profound identification or empathy with the other. The Menningers commented, as early as 1959, that friendship merges into love at the point of this identification.

What is the particular attraction that draws a couple together in what they call love? A particular magic? Fate? Not really, because the choice on either side could have been made from an endless number of people with similar sociocultural characteristics. In addition to sufficient mutual physical attraction to permit them to start the relationship in the first place, their backgrounds are sufficiently alike that communication is possible. They recognize feelings of rapport, which are then followed by more and more self-revelation. Each now has someone to confide in, joke with, share feelings with. Finally they recognize that they fill each other's emotional needs—needs for affection, understanding of moods, respect, stimulation of ambition. They love each other. Some would say that they are "in love."

The distinction is often made between "loving" someone and "being in love" with someone, the first usually interpreted to mean a deep concern over the welfare of a person, the second a more intense romantic or sexual feeling for him or her. The two emotions are not necessarily exclusive. They coexist in courtship, in the early part of many marriages, and, fortunately, in some marriages of long duration. It is when the romance, excitement, and "magic" disappear from the relationship, or significantly abate, that marriage counselors most often hear "I still love him [or her], but I'm just not 'in love' with him anymore." Disillusion over the loss of romantic love can threaten any long-standing relationship. It is particularly dangerous when the partners are immature or hold unreasonable expectations for the relationship, especially marriage. For, feeling that they are no longer "in love" with their partners, many married people grant themselves the license to seek romance with another person—only to find the illusion-disillusion pattern repeated. Few people who have experienced intimacy with its full delight would deny that perhaps intimacy is the force that binds "loving" someone and being "in love" with someone.

Kinds of Love

To help sort out the many emotions clustered under the banner called love, many observers have broken the word down into categories or classifications. Murstein (1974), as an example, lists three kinds of love. The first, *romantic love*, is identified as a "strong emotional attachment to the opposite sex, a tendency toward idealization, and a marked physical attraction." The second is *conjugal love*, described as affection between couples who have been together some years. In this love, passion has evolved into deeper feelings of spirituality, respect, and contentment. *Agape*, the third kind of love, is described as a spontaneous, selfless giving, working toward developing the maximum potential of another or others.

Fromm (1956) has characterized love as a giving, expressive act performed by persons who have developed the capacity to love. A person who has not acquired the ability to give of self cannot attain the capacity to love. Beyond the giving character of love, Fromm has identified four elements common to all kinds of love. First is the element of caring. Care is the active concern for the growth and well-being of another or others. It is the element of care that usually is the most evident in the love relationship.

The second element is responsibility, or the ability or readiness of a person to respond to the needs of another. As an element of love, responsibility does not mean a sense of duty or obligation to another that may be imposed from the outside. Rather, responsibility is voluntary; it involves a willingness to respond in the interests of another.

The third element of love is respect. Respect involves awareness and acceptance of another as a unique individual. When there is respect for another, there is concern that the loved person will "grow and unfold for his own sake." When a couple who share love are independent as individuals, there is no need for one to exploit the other or use the other to satisfy selfish needs.

Care, responsibility, and respect depend on knowledge, the fourth element of love. To know another does not imply merely to understand some superficial aspects of the person. Knowledge as an element of love involves the attempt to understand the individual at a deeper level, to fully appreciate the humanness of the individual.

It is important to recognize that the elements of love are not entirely distinct or separate qualities. They are interdependent and are found in the mature, loving person—a person who has developed his or her personality to the fullest extent possible (Fromm, 1956).

Romantic Love

Classical descriptions of love in terms of agony and ecstasy usually refer to romantic love. Despite all that has been said and written on the subject, it is small wonder that young people (and older ones too, for that matter) are perplexed about what romantic love is really like and whether or not it can last. Their confusion grows when they look at the comfortable day-in-day-out non-passionate relationship of their parents and compare it with the passionate and romantic love found in great works of literature. Both affectionate marital love and passionate romantic love exist, and both are valid. But can the second really endure over a long period of time? It cannot. The commonest attack on the concept of romantic love concerns its unreality, however enthralling, and the bitter disillusion that usually follows when couples marry in the attempt to perpetuate it.

"Love and marriage . . ." the song goes. But *do* they go together like a horse and carriage? Van Den Haag (1973) doubts it, commenting that love is a "very unruly horse, far more apt to run away and overturn the carriage than to draw it." Romantic love was certainly not viewed historically as a rational ground for marriage and social stability. Except for a few societies—notably our own and those of northwest Europe in this century—marriage has traditionally been regarded primarily as the means of perpetuating the family, not the means of perpetuating romantic love. Certainly women hoped for a kindly man, a hard worker, and men for a good housekeeper and conscientious mother. No doubt both hoped for affection. But to them romantic love was a remote concept. When most of us marry, the enchanted ideal is swiftly brought into focus as an imperfect reality. We must then either abandon the longing for romantic love or shift the longing to another person. Because romantic love is so intensely pleasurable, many people understandably feel a great loss when it dissipates. Memory of the excitement and pleasure frequently propels a married person into an affair with another person, usually under highly favorable circumstances. The series of new, intensely pleasurable events—the rewards— outweigh the rather stale, predictable routine of home life. Romantic love has blossomed anew. If the involved partner obtains a divorce and quickly marries the new love, he or she will quite likely find, with dismay, romantic love slipping away once more. And the whole process will have to start over again— and again. If he or she does not divorce and remarry, time and daily living will dissolve the romantic ideal. Over time, degrees of sexual gratification and quality of love in a stable relationship change. The longing typical of romantic love may be replaced by tenderness, gratitude, or affectionate companionship, or by indifference or hostility. But inevitably in long-term relationships, romantic love will be replaced by other emotions.

People may become involved in romantic love because they have irrational thoughts, beliefs, and "self-talk" about what love is (Zastrow, 1979). In romantic love there is the tendency to idealize, through one's self-talk or thinking, the attributes of one's lover. In contrast, rational love involves a realistic appraisal of the loved one's qualities.

Although cynics say that marriage is the only game at which both players can lose, it still appears to hold the greatest potential (until something better comes along) for personal fulfillment, for protection against the aloneness that threatens all of us. Indeed, statistics show that, for whatever reasons, the married enjoy greater health and longer life than the unmarried. Cynics also point to the spiraling divorce rates (1 million divorces versus 2 million marriages in 1975) as evidence that marriage as an institution has failed. But in truth marriage has not failed; rather, our expectations of it are unrealistic, thereby making it unworkable. Since romantic love depends upon the couple's not knowing very much that is real about the other, the types of early and ongoing relationships shared by an increasing number of young people today suggest that romantic love may be on its way out. Unlike their parents, young adults today often know each other too well to be caught by great surprises after setting up housekeeping together. However, merely "living together" is a far cry from marriage or a true marriagelike relationship. The solidity of love cannot be proved until it has been tested in such ongoing responsibilities as car payments, housekeeping, and coping with illness.

Maintaining Love and Intimacy

"Love is appealing, but its practice is appallingly difficult." The most important tool in its practice is *communication,* however overworked the word has become in recent years. When communication is blocked, the ground is fertile for misunderstanding, and the constructive energy of love can turn into resentment and hostility. A recent survey found that women most missed open and honest communication of intimate thoughts and feelings in their relationships with their husbands. The respondents claimed that empathy and understanding were missing ingredients in their relationships (Gittelson, 1980).

Even if the individuals in a relationship are open to discussing their feelings, empathy, understanding, and communication may not follow. The words one chooses and the context in which one uses the words potentially can affect the love relationship. In some contexts, for instance, men appear to be more inclined to use slang or colloquial expressions in their sexual vocabularies, while women tend to use more formal language or euphemisms (such as "making love") in their sexual vocabularies. A breakdown in communication may occur when men and women use different sexual expressions or language in talking with one another. In other words, perceptions of and attitudes or behaviors toward one's partner may be influenced by the way one's partner uses language to express his or her thoughts and feelings (Simkins & Rinck, 1982).

Of course, communication means not only speaking words, but also listening attentively, using the other's name, watching closely the other's eyes, paying close attention to facial expression, helping the other to express accurately what he or she is trying to say. In sum, maintaining love presupposes that the intimacy discussed earlier exists and is nourished throughout the relationship with ready communication.

Building Marital Communication Skills

Couples occasionally seek marriage counseling because of difficulties they have in communicating effectively. The task of the marriage counselor often is to help provide the couple with insights into how they are communicating inappropriately as well as to suggest techniques they can use to improve their communication skills. Some therapeutic suggestions that might be offered couples are these:

- Learn to communicate concerns in the form of "I" statements rather than "you" statements. For example, instead of saying "*You* hurt me" or "*You* made me angry," one would more effectively say "*I* feel hurt" or "*I* feel angry." This form of communication reduces the tendency for one to blame one's partner and thus accept greater responsibility for one's own feelings.
- Try to identify specific behaviors as the object of concern rather than blame the entire person for his or her actions. For example, instead of angrily saying "You stupid idiot," one would communicate more effectively by assertively saying "I think you behaved foolishly in this instance." The latter statement emphasizes wrong or mistaken actions; the former statement blamefully attacks the worth of the entire individual.
- Learn to recognize and point out the positive aspects of the relationship rather than always emphasize or dwell on the negative. For example, try to say "I think we work well together as parents even though we have disagreements" instead of "All we have in common is the children." Such an approach attempts to build upon a couple's assets rather than focus on their limitations and failures.
- Learn to compromise and seek mutually agreeable solutions in working out differences rather than always rigidly adhere to a fixed position. For example, try to say "I disagree with you, but I'm willing to discuss the matter further" instead of "I'm right and you know it." The former approach is likely to encourage mutual respect and a give-and-take attitude in a relationship; the latter, an attitude of rigidity and stubbornness.

There are, of course, other important techniques, including the appropriate use of humor, nonverbal communication or "body language," active listening skills, and so on, that can be applied in improving marital communication. Patience, persistence, and hard work at improving communication usually will help keep the marital bond strong. However, couples who continue to experience difficulty communicating or those who desire help in resolving their problems may elect to seek marriage counseling.

Communication is a skill, one that is not learned overnight. To listen does not mean merely to hear words, then to wait till the other has finished so that one can get on with one's own monologue. To speak, to make oneself understood, requires effort and practice. The process may be discouraging at first, but the rewards are enormous. Furthermore, the alternative is to leave the other second-guessing, and the likelihood is that the deductions will be wrong.

The development of communication skills is important not only in maintaining the love relationship but also in developing and maintaining satisfying sexual relationships. Women are especially apt to express a desire for more verbal interactions with their sex partner. Women in particular often do not like to be rushed into sex, and they like their relationships to unfold gradually. A leisurely stroll around the block, a picnic in the park, an opportunity to share light conversation, and so on, can often be effective stimulants for women and allow sexual interaction to more easily follow.

Men are often more readily responsive to patently sexual stimuli. They may tend to "push" or to encourage sexual activity more quickly than women, and they may not easily understand their partner's lack of spontaneous arousal and responsiveness. Sometimes women will express favorable attitudes toward forming relationships with middle-aged or older men, because such men are not as "edgy" or rushed in pursuing the sexual encounter.

Men and women also may have different desires and expectations in their sexual relationships. Women may tend to emphasize touching, warmth, and emotional closeness, whereas men may focus on direct genital stimulation. Certainly women can be as responsive and as interested in sex as men, but the routes that men and women take in pursuing sexual fulfillment often are different.

Becoming sensitive to the differing desires and expectations of one's partner is an important key to overcoming communication gaps that may exist. A man, for example, might attempt to respond to his partner's more romantic nature by arranging a candlelight dinner, by sending her a card or telegram expressing his affection, or by surprising her with flowers. A woman might respond to her partner's overtly sexual interest by reading sex novels with him, by accompanying him to an erotic movie, or by arranging to meet him at a hotel for a weekend of sexual adventure. In brief, one can expend creative energy in attempting to think of novel ways to interest, arouse, or titillate one's sexual partner.

Perhaps most important, it is crucial that men and women keep the lines of communication open. Instead of pointing an accusing finger, sulking, or withdrawing when something goes awry in a relationship, it is critical that the couple confront and share their emotional and sexual concerns. Assuming that one's partner "should" already know one's desires and needs is likely to lead to further misperceptions, misunderstandings, and misinterpretations. Reacting with hurt, anger, or rejection is likely to beget further emotional and sexual distress. Open and honest communication—direct statements presented in an assertive yet calm and sensitive manner—is most likely to lead to resolution of conflicts or problems in a relationship.

Even under the best of circumstances, embarrassing moments or sexual concerns occasionally arise between a man and a woman. For example, lack of sexual interest, even when all the "right" moves have been made, or experiences of sexual impotency or orgasmic dysfunction can occur even in the best of relationships. However, if the man and woman share a relationship based on mutual understanding, respect, and acceptance, then they are likely to resolve such distressing issues. Failures, mistakes, and embarrassing instances only become intensified and magnified when effective communication is lacking in a relationship.

Love and Sex

Cultural conditioning often makes it very difficult for many people, especially men, to enter into any close, loving relationship, including the sexual, with others. Little boys are often taught that to be tender and compassionate is to show characteristics of a "sissy"; little girls are admonished that it is "forward" to be warmly responsive. Growing up in an environment that restricts positive emotional responses makes it likely that the individual will learn to express only negative ones, such as anger and hostility. Nonetheless, these people grow into adulthood with the abstract knowledge that some warm emotional exchanges are vital and expected in successful sexual interaction. But because they learn in their formative years to express only negative responses, such people will actually instigate quarrels or fights with their sexual partner in order to express the only type of emotionality they understand.

Men who have never learned how to express tenderness, or who are afraid to do so, will often ignore the woman with whom they are sexually involved or make belittling remarks to her. These men *want* to demonstrate their commitment but, not knowing how to use the appropriate positive emotions, use the only emotional expressions they are familiar with—the negative ones. Married women often accuse their husbands of showing affection only when they have intercourse in mind; husbands deny this. What often happens is that the husband commences simply to show affection to his wife with no ulterior motive in mind; but in the process of expressing affection, especially if his wife responds warmly, he becomes sexually excited. The wife then judges only in terms of the final outcome.

Fortunately, both men and women can be taught to be receptive of close, warm, and loving relationships. If they have not acquired this knowledge through normal maturational processes and are too fearful of forming intimacies, help is available in several forms. (However, it is important to remember that complete agreement does not exist among behavioral scientists on how best to handle the complex of human problems.) When men and women recognize that free expression of affection is certainly nothing to fear, nor a barometer of weakness, all their relationships, including the sexual ones, will be much fuller and happier.

Rollo May (1969) points out that humans are the only creatures who copulate face-to-face, looking at their partners and baring their most tender and vulnerable parts. The intense scrutiny of the other's eyes; the sharing of the other's body, delight, and passion; the touching; the participation as a dual being, and the eventual separation into two individual selves—these elements constitute one of the most powerful acts in human experience. Touching is vitally important in human relationships, although it is typically thought of merely as a means to an end (sexual intimacy). But it is increasingly apparent that the need to touch and be touched is an essential form of communication. It is an end in itself. Babies need it and will sicken and die without it. Older children express the need through rough-and-tumble playing; adolescents, through kissing, necking, and petting (Masters & Johnson, 1975). Further, touching may be important in helping eliminate general stress or depression.

When there is a deprivation of touching or physical contact, *marasmus*, or a sense of "wasting away," may negatively affect us (Kirkendall, 1980).

> Coitus cannot of itself be equated with total intimacy, although, unfortunately, it is the only form of intimacy that many ever achieve or even recognize. A dependence on copulation to express feelings overburdens sex with the task of supporting a relationship emotionally, a task that should, for success, be aided by many other aspects of living. Good sex means more than the number and quality of climaxes, frequency of coitus, positions assumed, or techniques used. The best sex is not merely a physical response but a mature affirmation of love.
>
> Sexuality in a concerned relationship takes three forms. First, each partner confirms that the other is admired, desired, and appreciated as a sexual being. Second, each confirms that the partner is not a sexual freak in his or her sexual desires and performance, that each shares in the universality of sex. Third, they are assured that what they share sexually is special and unique. (Masters & Johnson, 1975)

The maturity, freedom, interdependence, and fulfillment to be found in a committed love relationship have not been better described than by Kahlil Gibran: *

> . . . let there be space in your togetherness,
> And let the winds of the heavens dance between you.
> Love one another, but make not a bond of love:
> Let it rather be a moving sea between the shores of your souls.
> Fill each other's cup but drink not from one cup.
> Give one another of your bread but eat not from the same loaf.
> Sing and dance together and be joyous, but let each one of you be alone,
> Even as the strings of a lute are alone though they quiver with the same
>   music.
>
> Give your hearts, but not into each other's keeping.
> For only the hand of Life can contain your hearts.
> And stand together yet not too near together:
> For the pillars of the temple stand apart,
> And the oak tree and the cypress grow not in each other's shadow.

Summary

In order to overcome feelings of alienation and loneliness, men and women strive to establish and maintain intimate relationships. Intimacy is the backbone of love. The primary components of intimacy are choice, mutuality, reciprocity, trust, and delight.

* Reprinted from *The Prophet* by Kahlil Gibran with permission of the publisher, Alfred A. Knopf, Inc. Copyright 1923 by Kahlil Gibran; renewal copyright 1951 by Administrators C.T.A. of Kahlil Gibran Estate and Mary C. Gibran.

Unfortunately, many people avoid intimacy by denying feelings, playing roles, and constantly trying to please others. Too often people take passive, spectator roles rather than active, participatory roles in interpersonal endeavors and miss engaging in intimate relationships. Destructive anger and hostility destroy communication and interfere with the development of intimacy. Fear, notably fear of rejection, causes people to avoid potentially fulfilling intimate relationships.

Traditional courtship patterns have frequently led to superficial togetherness between men and women. Too often these patterns lead to stereotyped interpersonal interaction and thus create barriers to intimacy. The pairing system—a getting-to-know-you period when openness and honesty predominate—provides a healthy alternative to the superficiality of traditional courtship.

Most psychologists reject the idea that people "fall in love." Rather, people grow in love and love grows in them. Ideally, people love their partner and also have a sense of "being in love" with that partner. Intimacy is the force that links "loving" someone with "being in love" with someone.

One observer has described three kinds of love: romantic love, conjugal love, and *agape*. Another observer has identified four basic elements of love: care, responsibility, respect, and knowledge.

Romantic love is based on idealism, perfection, and passion. Ultimately, romantic love dissipates or fades away. Rational love is based on reality, acceptance of imperfection, and affection. Rational love is most likely to lead to fulfilling, long-lasting relationships. Mature love and intimacy are maintained through open and honest communication.

Love involves tenderness and compassion as well as cuddling, stroking, and touching. When there is deprivation of touching, "marasmus," or a sense of wasting away, may overcome us. Sexual intimacy, at its highest level, is probably expressed best when physical sensations and emotions are fused with empathy and sensitivity toward the partner.

TRUE OR FALSE: THE FACTS

Psychologists are in agreement that a couple "fall in love" when their relationship has matured to the point where intimacy is possible.
False. Most psychologists reject the concept of "falling in love," contending instead that we grow in love as we grow in intimacy with another person. *(121)*

❦

Romantic love is the ultimate expression of sexual and emotional intimacy that a couple may experience.
False. Although pleasurable and enthralling, romantic love is based on unreality, on idealized imaginings, and therefore precludes true intimacy. *(123)*

❦

The ability to communicate effectively with one's partner is part of the "magic" of the love relationship and thus is not a skill that one can learn.
False. Communication skills require effort and practice. *(125–126)*

❣

Sexual intercourse alone can be equated with total and complete intimacy in a relationship.
False. Sexual intercourse alone cannot be equated with true intimacy because it cannot support all the emotional needs in a relationship or allow expression of all the feelings that are part of intimacy. *(128)*

SUGGESTED READING

Fromm, Erich. *The art of loving.* New York: Harper & Row, 1956.
This brief book is a classic work on the subject of love and loving.

McCary, James Leslie. *Freedom and growth in marriage* (2nd ed.). New York: Wiley, 1980.
This book for the student and general reader considers various aspects of marriage, dating, and mate selection, focusing on implications for individual growth and freedom within the marriage relationship.

McCary, James Leslie, and McCary, Stephen P. *McCary's human sexuality* (4th ed.). Belmont, Calif.: Wadsworth, 1982.
Chapter 8 presents a comprehensive discussion of love and intimacy.

Murstein, Bernard (Ed.). *Exploring intimate lifestyles.* New York: Springer, 1978.
This outstanding volume examines intimate life-styles in contemporary society, including open marriage, communal living and group marriage, cohabitation, singlehood, and homosexual and other life-styles that extend beyond traditional conceptions of marriage and family.

Tennov, Dorothy. *Love and limerence: The experience of being in love.* New York: Stein & Day, 1979.
The author coins the term "limerence" to describe the powerful form of romantic love that is experienced as overwhelming and beyond rational control. Many interesting viewpoints on love are presented.

Wells, J. Gipson (Ed.). *Current issues in marriage and the family* (3rd ed.). New York: Macmillan, 1983.
This informative book presents articles by leading authorities examining various issues related to marriage and family, including gender roles, whether to marry or have children, abortion, marital fidelity, and divorce.

TRUE OR FALSE?

Oral-genital sex is perverted and animalistic.

❦

Masturbation is practiced by most men and women.

❦

Alcohol is a sexual stimulant.

❦

Vaginal-penile intercourse is only one normal method of having sex relations.

Sexual Expression

Techniques of Sexual Arousal
Pace and Style
The Value of Fantasy
The Erogenous Zones
Developing One's Sexuality

Forms of Heterosexual Arousal
Oral Sex
Anal Sex

Positions in Sexual Intercourse

Sexuality and Disability

Aphrodisiacs and Anaphrodisiacs

Summary

Suggested Reading

Although some fundamental male-female differences certainly exist with regard to sexual response patterns, there is probably considerably less dissimilarity between the sexes than there is individual variation among members of the same sex (Kronhausen & Kronhausen, 1965). For example, some recent research confirms that women like erotica, that their fantasies are as clear and self-arousing as men's, and that they are turned on by sexual descriptions just as men are (Heiman, 1975).

Basically, the sex drive of women is as powerful as that of men. But men and women may respond to different types of both psychological and physiological stimulation, and they respond to the same stimuli in a slightly different manner. Heiman's study (1975) also indicated that women may have greater difficulty than do men in recognizing sexual arousal. This may be because physiological changes in women are not as readily detected. Heiman also found that women become as sexually aroused as men, but they may not be quite as ready to admit their arousal. Women have been conditioned for generations to inhibit their sexuality, if not deny it altogether, and to stifle their normal response to sexual stimuli. These culturally imposed inhibitions no doubt account for the popular misconception that women are less responsive than men. Fortunately, women today have been able to participate more freely and actively in their sexual relationships and thus overcome the influences of the past (James, 1980).

Often, a young couple who sincerely wish to give each other an enjoyable sexual experience are hampered by their mutual ignorance and inexperience. Young men are expected somehow to possess skill and finesse and to be able to take the lead in sexual encounters with smooth confidence. Young women, on the other hand, frequently feel that naiveté and femininity go hand in hand, and they therefore may place unrealistic demands on their partners to teach them "all about sex." Acquiring information about effective techniques of sexual stimulation will lead to confidence in both partners and to a more equal responsibility for the enjoyment of sex.

In time, a couple usually builds up their own private store of verbal endearments, which are then used advantageously to set the stage for satisfying sexual interplay. Making the sexual partner aware that one enjoys his or her appearance, abilities, intellect, strengths, and the like is only half of a successful preliminary sexual interaction. The partner must also be made to know that he or she is enjoyed and appreciated as a lover. Of the many suggestions that might be helpful in molding a good sexual relationship, three are particularly important. A couple will usually do well to avoid sexual acts that are dangerous or unfulfilling to either of them. Once they have experimented sufficiently—perhaps with the help of good books on sexual techniques or even under the direction of a sex therapist—they should reject any activity they truly do not enjoy. And they should take great care to learn each other's preferences and do everything reasonable to incorporate them in their sexual technique (Comfort, 1972). But whatever form a technique takes, freedom of response and expression is the key.

Sexual Complaints

Here Hite (1976, 1981), in her widely publicized national surveys of the sexual attitudes and behavior of men and women, has revealed many of the frustrations and criticisms that men and women have of each other's lovemaking. Among the complaints of the women are the following:

- "Most of the men I've slept with have had absolutely no idea of what I want or need and no interest in finding out."
- "They jumped on and rode."
- "A little kiss, a little feel, a finger for arousal, a touch of breast, and he's on top, wham it's over."
- "Most didn't seem to be aware that what brought them to climax was not what brought me to climax. That about sums it up."
- "Foreplay, always too short, then penetration."

Among the complaints of the men are the following:

- "More. I just want more."
- "I do not like to always have to be the one who gets things rolling."
- "I have a great feeling of pressure on me to ask the girl for a date, to kiss her, to start a romantic conversation, to be the aggressor in sex, and to dominate it, all because I feel it is expected of me to behave like this."
- "I have felt that my wife was too passive."
- "I'd love to be a sex object at least for a while."

Techniques of Sexual Arousal

Much of the enjoyment of sexual activity, for most men and women, is in the initial stage when each partner contributes to the sexual arousal of the other. The act of arousal, in fact, is a rewarding and pleasurable experience in itself and should not be looked upon as a series of "preliminaries" preceding the "real thing."

Some of the elementary requirements for sexual arousal are patently obvious, but they are overlooked with distressing frequency. The most important of these is personal grooming. Sexual happiness is not reserved only for the "beautiful people"; visual stimulation is important in a sexual relationship. Clean, shiny hair, a clean body that is supple and healthy, neatly trimmed nails, and clean, appropriate clothing are the first steps in being desirable to the opposite sex.

The sense of smell is also very important in sexual activity. The man whose sexual technique is absolutely flawless will fail to excite the most receptive woman if he has bad breath, offensive body odor, or unclean hair. Even if he has a session with shower, toothbrush, and razor later in the evening, his partner's memories of his earlier unattractiveness will detract from her pleasure in the sexual encounter. Further, if a woman considers her sexual partner untrustworthy, crude, physically threatening, or just plain stupid, she may be so repelled by these characteristics that she has difficulty in responding to him sexually, no matter how physically attractive he is or how skillful a sexual technician. A woman who allows herself to become significantly over- or under-

The expression of tenderness and sensitivity is an important part of lovemaking. *Charles Gatewood.*

weight or permits urine, vaginal, or underarm odors to become detectable should recognize that she risks repelling her lover and damaging their sex life if these matters offend him. And the woman who is consistently caustic and belittling toward her sex partner cannot expect him to be freely responsive to her. It is, of course, expecting too much of a wife who holds an exacting job or has sole responsibility for highly active children to be rested, seductive, and glamorous every night. It is equally unreasonable to expect a tense, harassed husband always to act, or look, like a film or TV idol. But, unfortunately, after marriage too many people stop making even minimal efforts to keep themselves interesting in the eyes of their partner. Disenchanted, they find their sex life growing stale, and one or both may begin to look elsewhere for the glamor they feel is missing in the marital relationship.

On another level, the qualities of courtesy, kindness, and sensitivity to the needs and desires of others, which are so fundamental to all successful human interaction, are particularly vital to sexual relationships. For example, to most women, a particularly meaningful part of lovemaking is being talked to during the act. Men may not appreciate this need—a need for tenderness, essentially—or may fail to meet it, despite the woman's asking her lover to "talk to me." Some couples find their sexual encounters enhanced when the woman feels free enough to express her desires and to initiate the sexual interaction at least some of the time (James, 1980).

Pace and Style

Pace and duration, as well as style, are matters of individual taste. Generally speaking, however, an unhurried pace is most likely to bring the greatest satisfaction to both partners. Women are more likely to enjoy sex—and therefore to make it more enjoyable for their partners—if there is ample time (at least fifteen or twenty minutes) for them to reach a peak of excitement before intercourse. A woman's orgasmic capacity and enjoyment are further heightened if her partner is able to continue intercourse for an extended period of time.

A man usually achieves orgasm within about four minutes after **intromission** (the insertion of the penis into the vagina), while the average woman requires over ten minutes of sexual intercourse before she attains an orgasmic response. With manual, electric vibrator, or oral-genital stimulation, however, a woman can usually reach orgasm in less than four minutes (Kinsey et al., 1953). The muscle control necessary for a man to engage in lengthy acts of **coitus** is developed through training and exercise, just as any other muscle control is developed. A man can often condition himself, during masturbation, to delay ejaculation for longer and longer periods of time. If premature or early ejaculation persists in sexual intercourse, training in methods of ejaculatory control can overcome the problem in almost all cases. The rewards to his partner—present or future—and to himself will be well worth the effort expended in such training.

The Value of Fantasy

Playing soft music, using mirrors to observe the intimacies of the sex act, and perusing sensuous literature and art are other devices that help keep boredom out of the bedroom (Ellis, 1960). The value of fantasy in augmenting sexual arousal should never be overlooked. It is superior to such commonly accepted techniques as erotic writings and photographs. In a recent study, Harris, Yulis, and LaCoste (1980) found that the ability to form clear and vivid images in fantasy was associated with self-reports of higher sexual arousability in both sexes. Another study (Baron & Byrne, 1977) revealed that couples experienced greater sexual excitement when they relied on their own imaginings rather than on erotic books or pictures. Furthermore, the uninhibited couple share their sexual fantasies with one another (Comfort, 1972). Caution must be used in such disclosures, however, because certain fantasies can be disturbing to some who are insecure (and jealous) or are nervous about the form of sexual activity the partner might be fantasizing.

For people who are not threatened by them, fantasies can provide an acceptable outlet for thoughts or feelings that one may be hesitant to act upon in reality. Fantasies are creative expressions and, as such, are the product of an imaginative, active mind. Repression of one's sexual fantasies may make life dull or boring as well as make sex humdrum or mechanical. People are encour-

Fantasies

Two hundred fifty university students enrolled in a marriage, family, and sex education course were asked to anonymously describe their favorite sensual or sexual fantasy. Some of the responses given by the women were these:

- ". . . to be pursued and seduced by a handsome prince in the forest."
- ". . . having sex on the 50-yard-line of a football field late at night."
- ". . . teasing and tantalizing my lover until he's really aroused but delaying sex until neither of us can stand it any longer."
- ". . . having my boyfriend tied up and making him watch while I make love to another man."
- ". . . taking a bubble bath with my husband, having gentle conversation, sipping champagne. . . ."

Some of the responses given by the men were these:

- ". . . having sex with three beautiful women all at the same time."
- "I come upon a castle filled with gorgeous women, and there's no other man to satisfy them."
- ". . . to have wild, uninhibited sex with a stranger, knowing that I'll never see her again."
- ". . . to make love in front of a fireplace on a very cold night with a woman I really care about."
- ". . . to have sex outdoors in a garden or a park. We can hear others nearby, but we get it on fully clothed, except for my fly unzipped and her panties taken off."

aged to formulate constructive thoughts or fantasies about careers, life goals, and anticipated achievements. Why, one might ask, would we not allow ourselves to develop our sensual and sexual beings through fantasy?

Fantasies actually are quite common among both men and women. Kinsey found that 72 percent of the men and 50 percent of the women in his sample reported having sexual fantasies most times they masturbated (Kinsey et al., 1953). Although the specific content of fantasies varies widely with the individual, a few general themes commonly occur. Participants in the Hunt study (1974) reported common fantasy themes that involved having intercourse with a stranger, engaging in group sex, being forced or forcing someone to have sex, doing sexual things one would never do in reality, and having sex with a person of the same gender. It should be noted that while heterosexuals usually have heterosexual fantasies and homosexuals usually have homosexual fantasies, some crossing over may occur. For example, it is not uncommon for heterosexuals to have occasional homosexual fantasies and for homosexuals to have occasional heterosexual fantasies (Masters & Johnson, 1979).

Cultural stereotypes of male and female sexuality seem to play a part in determining male and female sexual fantasies. In general, men most commonly fantasize about having impersonal sex and about situations where they assume the role of aggressor. Women are more likely than men to fantasize about situations that involve romance or being forced to have sex (Hunt, 1974).

Some who are plagued by guilt or inhibitions about sexual matters might claim that thinking about a particular sexual experience is the same as engaging in that experience. If that is true, then are we millionaires, famous actors or actresses, or astronauts because we think or fantasize about these things? Of course not. While there may be disturbed individuals who inappropriately act upon their destructive fantasies, this represents the exception rather than the rule. Some people rob banks and some people act out distorted fantasies, but this does not make banks or fantasies bad in and of themselves.

The wish for variety in sexual life is normal. If this ideal is reached within marriage or other long-term relationships, there is considerably less likelihood that either partner will seek it elsewhere. Imagination and a willingness to experiment, together with an air of confidence and consideration, will serve most couples very well.

The Erogenous Zones

Erogenous zones are areas of the body, genital and nongenital, that are rich in the nerve endings whose stimulation causes sexual arousal. The most sensitive erogenous zones for both sexes are the genitals and the area surrounding them. Although stimulation of these areas is sexually arousing under favorable conditions, response can be obstructed by fear, pain, guilt, or distaste.

In addition to those zones that are common to most people, other areas of the body can take on erogenous sensitivity through conditioning. For example, if a man were to tickle the sole of his partner's foot each time they had enjoyable intercourse, foot-tickling would come to be associated with pleasurable intercourse, and the sole of the foot would become a conditioned erogenous zone for that particular woman.

A knowledge of the erogenous zones of one's own body is essential for the development of one's full capacity for sexual responsiveness. Sexual responsiveness is learned through experience and experimentation, beginning with one's own body. The person who is most sexually responsive has developed a sensuous enjoyment and appreciation for the sight, smell, taste, feel, and use of the body in all its infinite capacities.

Developing One's Sexuality

Probably the most successful way of learning to respond to one's full sexual capacity is through **masturbation**, the self-stimulation of the genitals through manipulation. A healthy and beneficial means of reducing sexual frustration and tension, masturbation (the incidence of which will be discussed in Chapter 11) is practiced by the majority of both men and women, married and single (Kinsey et al., 1948, 1953). Men usually masturbate by gripping the penis and moving the hand back and forth, so that the glans is stimulated in much the same manner as it is in the in-and-out movements of coitus. The degree of pressure and the speed of movement vary from man to man. Women usually masturbate by stroking the clitoris, again varying the intensity of pressure and the speed of movement to suit their individual preferences. Most women prefer stroking the side of the clitoris rather than its glans. Some women prefer vaginal stimulation and insert phallus-shaped objects or a finger into the vagina during masturbation. A few women prefer stimulation of the urethral opening,

Sexual-ity's "Dark Ages"

From before the birth of Hippocrates, down through the ages to the early 1900s, the medical world remained largely ignorant of cause and effect in sexual behavior. Objectivity and a scientific approach were notoriously lacking in the few investigations that were made. Occasionally some brave scientific soul would reach out for enlightenment, but such people were rare. Struggles through these dark ages toward an understanding of human sexuality were dealt a near death-blow in the middle eighteenth century when S.A.D. Tissot wrote his *Onana, a Treatise on the Diseases Produced by Onanism*. Projecting his personal problems, to say nothing of his unique ignorance, into his writings, Tissot wrote of the viciousness of "self-abuse," attributing most of the known medical disorders—including consumption, epileptic seizures, gonorrhea, and insanity—to the loss of semen through masturbation. It was Tissot who introduced the totally unscientific idea that the loss of one drop of seminal fluid causes more bodily damage and weakness than the loss of forty drops of blood.

Hysteria over masturbation reached such a pitch in the late nineteenth century that "depraved" women who resorted to it were frequently forced by their families to submit to a clitoridectomy (the surgical removal of the clitoris) as a method of control. French medical men, furthermore, expressed their dismay at an occupational hazard peculiar to seamstresses: the masturbatory up-and-down movements of their legs as they treadled their sewing machines were apt to cause orgasms. In at least one establishment, a matron was appointed to circulate among the seamstresses to detect runaway machines as the women became caught up in this "horrible" by-product of their profession.

and a small percentage are able to attain orgasm by rhythmically pressing their thighs together.

Other masturbatory techniques useful in heightening women's genital sensitivity include directing a stream of water onto the vulval area while bathing or showering and applying an electric vibrator directly to the clitoral area. Women report that the continuous pressure of running water produces an orgasm just slightly less intense than that produced by an electric vibrator. Of the vibrators, most women prefer the type that has rubber-knotted attachments that can be applied to the side or glans of the clitoris. Stimulation of this intensity seldom fails to bring a woman to multiple orgasms, and the orgasms she experiences are usually of a much greater intensity than those she experiences by any other means. Some women who enjoy vaginal stimulation insert a battery-driven penis-shaped vibrator directly into the vagina (although usually only slightly penetrating the opening), either as the sole masturbatory technique or in conjunction with manual- or electric-vibrator stimulation of the clitoral area.

A woman first using a vibrator should realize that she will remain "in control." Given time to get used to the vibrator, a woman can begin to appreciate the erotic sensations it can provide. While the vibrator can provide intense erotic pleasure for many women, they need not worry that it will overwhelm them or take over their sex lives (Steinhart, 1980).

By employing masturbatory techniques, men and women can discover what is most stimulating to them; and they can, in turn, give this information to their sexual partners. There are wide differences in individual reactions to various arousal techniques. Sexual partners cannot be clairvoyant; it is impossible for anyone to know what is most enjoyable for another person without being told.

Although there are many myths about the dangers of masturbation to body or mind, none has any foundation in fact. Masturbation does not "weaken" a man, nor does it lead to insanity, moral depravity, or hair on the palms of his hands! The only thing that masturbation leads to is pleasurable sensations, including orgasm (and in a man, ejaculation), with an accompanying release of sexual tension. In addition, there is no such thing as "excessive masturbation." The body regulates itself by refusing to respond when a state of sexual satiation is reached. Therefore the amount of sexual activity engaged in by any one person is normal for that person.

A young couple who have fondness and sexual attraction for each other may feel that sexual intercourse should be postponed until marriage—either to each other or to others. For these couples, mutual masturbation allows them relief from the uncomfortable congestion of the genitals that can occur when sexual tensions are not released by orgasm. Mutual masturbation also gives them the emotional fulfillment of providing sexual pleasure to each other. Young people are sometimes warned that petting to orgasm will prevent their being able to achieve orgasm through intercourse when they marry. On the contrary, those people who enjoy petting and who are capable of freely responding to it are the ones most capable of freely responding to coitus and of deriving the most pleasure from it (Ellis, 1958, 1960, 1963; Ficher, 1979; Kinsey et al., 1953).

Forms of Heterosexual Arousal

Among the most effective of all sexual stimulants are the hands, a fact that some tend to forget. **Petting, foreplay,** love play—whatever one chooses to call it—is the most satisfying when hands and fingers are freely employed. And while petting is the royal road to intercourse, it can also be highly pleasurable in its own right.

In the first stages of sexual arousal, both men and women become stimulated by gentle, slow, generalized stroking, but the caressing should become more specific as sex play progresses. Lightly and gently at first, and then more boldly, the hands should dart and slide over the partner's body—stroking, holding, caressing, squeezing, and massaging—alternating strokes with the palms of the hands with light, silky stroking of the fingertips. The stroking should gradually move toward the genital area in an advance-retreat-advance approach.

The man should be aware of the sensitivity of the woman's skin, and of the thinness and delicacy of the tissue of the vulva and vagina. These areas should not be manually stimulated unless the man's fingernails are clipped and smooth and unless the vulval region is well moistened either with bodily secretions or with a commercial lubricating product such as K-Y Sterile Lubricant. The clitoris is especially sensitive and cannot long tolerate direct and uninterrupted manipulation. The cervix and the walls of the vagina, with the exception of the anterior wall and the upper front area, contain few nerve endings and are somewhat insensitive to stimulation (Hoch, 1980).

Stimulation of the sensitive nerve endings in the pubococcygeal muscle encircling the vaginal opening may produce highly pleasurable sensations in many women. Further, by contracting their pubococcygeal muscles during coitus,* women may heighten their sexual pleasure (Kaplan, 1975; Dailey, 1980b).

Both men and women are sexually aroused by breast stimulation (Kinsey et al., 1953; J. L. McCary, 1966). The man can gently massage his partner's breasts, interspersing the manipulation with a light brushing of the nipple and an occasional gentle pinch of its sensitive tip. Caressing of the breast with the hands may be alternated with soft moist kisses and an exploring tongue. The tempo of the tongue's movements should be changed occasionally, allowing it to dart back and forth across the nipple in a firm, rapid manner, before resuming once more the soft moist stimulation. This kind of oral contact is equally pleasing to both men and women. Men are also sensitive to stimulation of their nipples. The woman may gently roll his nipples between her thumb and finger or lightly rake her fingernails across their tips.

Kissing, the usual forerunner of all sexual activity, should be continued during sex play. Like caressing, kissing should be varied in a teasing manner: open mouth, closed mouth; light lip pressure, heavy lip pressure, moist lips, dry lips; soft lips, nibbling teeth and lips; a darting tongue, a soft sensuous tongue. The lover's face and body should be covered with kisses, and the tongue should participate in this exploration. Ordinarily, kissing of the mouth should precede kissing of other parts of the body, except perhaps the hands. The woman may be particularly pleased if the man tenderly kisses her hands or nibbles her fingertips.

Sexual stimulation should continue until both lovers are ready to proceed with intercourse. Because both men and women have traditionally used the man's sexual response and capability as the gauge of "the way it is done," many women—and men, too—fail to realize that women are capable by natural endowment of multiple orgasms and, in fact, frequently require such multiple responses during a single sexual episode in order to be sexually satisfied. Many women, for example, are able to have six or more orgasms during a single period of sexual activity; about 15 percent of women regularly have multiple orgasms. By contrast, only about 6 to 8 percent of men are able to have more than one orgasm during each sexual experience; when the capacity for multiple orgasm exists, it is usually found only in very young men.

Since women are multi-orgasmic and since each successive orgasm is more intense than the preceding one, many women find they achieve greater satisfac-

* The Kegel or pubic floor exercise, whereby vaginal and urethral sphincter muscles are contracted and released, is done by alternately "holding in" and "letting go" of the same muscles that control urine flow. It strengthens the muscles for childbirth as well as for sexual pleasure.

tion if they are brought to orgasm one or more times before coitus. In this way, they are not left unsatisfied after the man has ejaculated and is no longer able to continue intercourse. Some men, of course, are capable of delaying their own orgasm in prolonged sexual intercourse; their sexual partners can therefore experience multiple orgasms during a lengthy coital act.

Keeping the man sexually excited and pleasurably engaged in bringing her to orgasm as often as she requires for complete satisfaction will necessitate timing and finesse on the woman's part. With her caresses and kisses, she should keep him just below the point of greatest sexual excitement, with an occasional teasing stimulus that will momentarily heighten his arousal level. She should be aware, for example, that stimulating the glans and frenum of his penis for any length of time may cause ejaculation to be imminent, and she should therefore avoid such intense stimulation unless she is ready for penetration. By enthusiastic response and pleasurable manipulation of the partner's body, she can, with practice, keep him at a prolonged state of erection, adding to the enjoyment of both.

Oral Sex

One form of sexual activity that is intensely pleasurable for both sexes is oral-genital stimulation. This stimulation is also a very effective means of bringing both a man and a woman to orgasm. **Cunnilingus,** the tongue-stroking of the woman's vulval area by the man, usually centers about the clitoris, although other parts of the vulva, particularly the labia minora, are also sensitive to oral stimulation. The sensitive glans of the clitoris can be stimulated in much the same manner as the nipples of the breasts are stimulated by the tongue. Beginning with light, teasing strokes of the tongue, interspersed with bold darting motions, the man should vary the technique to keep pace with the woman's heightening sexual excitement. As the woman's climax nears, the man should maintain a steady, constant stimulation of the clitoral area. (At the height of sexual tension the clitoris withdraws under its prepuce, and direct contact can no longer be maintained.) If the woman desires another orgasm, the same licking movements frequently will quickly bring another one about.

Fellatio, the stimulation by mouth and tongue of a man's penis, is highly pleasing to a man both for its physiological stimulation and also because it indicates that his partner enjoys a part of his body that is very important to him. Starting by covering the penis with soft kisses, the woman should gradually take the erect penis into her mouth. With tongue movements similar to those used in cunnilingus, the woman stimulates the penis, particularly at the glans and frenum. She can vary her technique according to the man's preferences, now lightly and softly kissing the penis, now sucking it closely, all the while stroking and fondling the testicles and scrotum. This kind of stimulation seldom fails to arouse a man to intense excitement, and a woman should be aware that the more intense and rapid her movements are, the more likely they are to bring a man to a height of arousal that can easily terminate in orgasm. She should therefore time her stimulation of the penis to coincide with her own state of sexual arousal.

Although some people have a negative attitude toward oral-genital sex, it is practiced by the majority of men and women who are college educated (Kinsey et al., 1948, 1953). It has been recommended by many authorities in the field of sex and marriage as a desirable and vastly pleasurable form of sexual behavior. If either partner, after attempting at least some experimentation with both giving and receiving oral-genital stimulation, finds that the technique is objectionable, then that individual should abstain from this form of sexual activity for the time being.

Anal Sex

Anal intercourse as well as oral and manual stimulation of the anus may be distasteful to many couples, but such forms of stimulation may be sources of erotic arousal to others. Anal intercourse in particular may cause physical discomfort for some people, especially initially. The discomfort can be minimized, however, if the couple proceed at a gentle, relaxed pace and care is used to apply a sterile lubricant around the anal opening and on the penis. Following anal contact, the man should exercise care in washing his penis thoroughly before penetrating his partner's vagina. Such a precaution is necessary to avoid certain vaginal infections that may result if bacteria ordinarily found in the rectum are introduced into the woman's vagina.

Anal eroticism, once thought to be practiced almost exclusively by homosexuals, has apparently increased in recent years in popularity among heterosexual couples. Hite (1976) reported that about half the women in her sample enjoyed being touched anally. About 40 percent of those who did so preferred simply being touched anally, 30 percent preferred anal penetration by finger, and 30 percent, penile-anal penetration. Recent evidence indicates that the incidence of anal sex may be as high as 90 percent for homosexual males (Lewis & Lewis, 1980a).

Male homosexuals and, to a lesser extent, heterosexuals make use of the space between the thighs to bring about ejaculation. This practice is called *interfemoral sexual intercourse*. Scientific opinion is that there is nothing physically or psychologically wrong with nonvaginal methods of coitus.

The freedom of both partners to explore all arousal techniques and to refrain from those techniques that are objectionable to either partner is essential for the fullest pleasure of both the man and the woman. Because of individual and combined personalities and preferences, each couple needs to discover—through open discussion and experimentation—just what brings them the greatest erotic pleasure.

Positions in Sexual Intercourse

The number of possible positions that two people can adopt for sexual intercourse is almost limitless, and each couple must arrive at its own preferences through experimentation and practice. Indeed, continued experimentation and adaptation of preferred positions add spice to the sexual act and prevent it from becoming monotonous. There is no one "normal" position, and any and all positions that both partners find satisfactory and pleasurable should be freely enjoyed by them (Greenhill, 1971).

The four most common positions in sexual intercourse are face-to-face, man above; face-to-face, woman above; side position, face-to-face; and the rear-entry position. There are endless variations on these positions, of course, and with an uninhibited approach, each couple can work out their own adaptations.

The *face-to-face, man-above position* is so common in European and American cultures that it is often and erroneously referred to as the "normal" position. Its popularity in Western cultures is attributable in part to the early Christian teachings of St. Augustine. St. Augustine and other early Christian leaders taught that the man-atop-woman position was the only acceptable position for sexual intercourse (Bullough, 1980). However, some other cultures consider the position uncommon and refer to it with amusement as the "missionary position."

Intromission is easily achieved in the face-to-face, man-above position when the woman lies on her back with legs apart and knees bent (Figure 8.1). The man, supporting himself on his elbows and knees, is largely in control of the couple's bodily movements. He should try to keep contact with the clitoris by putting pressure on the upper part of his partner's vulva. Pressure on her pubic bone is helpful to sandwich the clitoris between it and his pubic bone, thus providing clitoral friction. In this position, the woman may vary the position of her legs, sometimes closing them, sometimes pulling her knees to her shoulders or locking her legs around her partner's body (Figure 8.2).

The *face-to-face, woman-above position* offers numerous advantages that vary with the individual (Witkin, 1980). Clitoral contact is frequently easier and the friction more intense, for example, and the woman can control the tempo of movement and depth of penetration (Figure 8.3). This position is less sexually stimulating to the man because his body is less active; his muscles are more relaxed, so that he is frequently able to delay ejaculation for a longer period. Since the woman has primary control of coital movement, the man can relax and abandon himself to the pleasures of erotic fantasy and his partner's caresses. This position can be varied by the man's resting on his elbows and raising his bent knees for the woman to lean back against as she sits astride him. She can also lie full length against him, thus maintaining full body contact.

In the *face-to-face side position*, both partners lie on their sides facing each other (Figure 8.4). In this position, they can share control of the movements of intercourse. This position is sometimes assumed after the partners have achieved intromission in another position and have rolled onto their sides, giving them complete freedom to maneuver their legs, arms, and hands. Often the couple can go to sleep without losing contact after the completion of intercourse. One of the chief advantages of this position is that neither partner is supporting the weight of the other. It is therefore especially helpful to as-

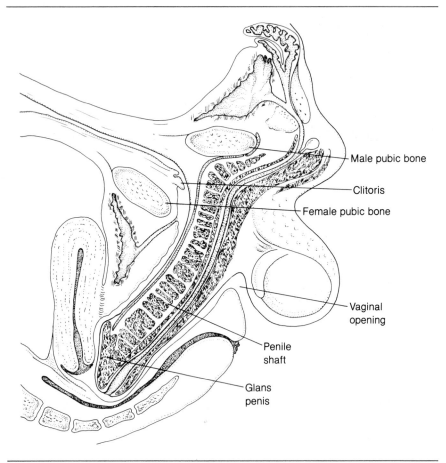

Male pubic bone

Clitoris

Female pubic bone

Vaginal opening

Penile shaft

Glans penis

Figure 8.1   Representation of the erect penis inserted into the vagina.

sume this position when either partner is fatigued or in ill health, or if one partner is considerably taller than the other. Since both partners can easily regulate their pelvic thrusts, sexual activity before orgasm can often be prolonged. Penile withdrawal and reinsertion are possible without much change of position or adjustment, and a steady coital rhythm can easily be sustained (Ellis, 1960; L. R. Rosen, 1980).

The *rear-entry position* may be assumed in a variety of ways (Figure 8.5). Both partners can lie on their sides, or the woman can kneel, lie on her stomach, or sit on the man's lap with her back to him (Heiman et al., 1976). There are numerous other variations. In the side-by-side rear-entry position, the placement of the woman's buttocks prevents deep penile penetration, but whatever degree of penetration is possible can be easily regulated by the man. A man often finds the pressure of his partner's buttocks against his body exciting. In this position, his hands are free to encircle the woman's body and to

Figure 8.2   Face-to-face coital position, man above.

Figure 8.3   Face-to-face coital position, woman above.

Figure 8.4   Side coital position, face-to-face.

Figure 8.5   Rear-entry coital position.

caress her breasts, clitoris, legs, or other erogenous areas (Ellis, 1960). Contact is usually lost in this position after the man's orgasm.

A more active position is the knee-chest rear-entry position, in which both partners assume a kneeling position, the woman with her head and arms on the bed. The position in which the woman lies on her stomach and her partner attempts rear-entry penetration while lying on top of her is generally too awkward and insufficiently pleasurable to be used by many couples. Sitting positions offer variety and novel enjoyment to some couples, although they allow such deep penetration that they are sometimes uncomfortable for the woman (Figure 8.6).

One of the chief factors affecting a couple's choice of coital position is their feeling about the psychological implications of the various positions. Some men feel uncomfortable in coitus involving any of the woman-above positions, because having the woman in a "superior" position makes them feel passive and controlled. Conversely, some women are uncomfortable in woman-above positions because they prefer to be "dominated" by the man, and the woman-above positions seem too aggressive to them. These feelings are, of course, related to the sex roles perpetuated by our society.

It is a burden for either partner *always* to have the responsibility for initiating and leading in a sexual relationship. Although it is important to recognize one's own feelings in this regard, the ideal relationship permits both the man and the woman to be active and passive in turn, as needs vary.

Figure 8.6   Variations of the basic coital positions.

A knowledge of the variety of possible sexual positions is helpful to facilitate experimentation and avoid monotony; however, a couple should take care to avoid exaggerated·concern with the "how" of sexual intercourse while engaging in it. Coitus may otherwise become artificial or mechanical, which can detract from the freedom and spontaneity of the relationship. Coitus is not a gymnastic feat, an endurance contest, or one in a series of laboratorylike experiments. Rather, it is an act intended to bring mutual pleasure through a variety of techniques and postures. Any technique of sexual arousal or position of sexual intercourse that affords a couple pleasure should be freely enjoyed by them.

Sexuality and Disability

As we mentioned in Chapters 3 and 4, uninhibited giving and receiving of sexual pleasure is not limited to physically able individuals (Pepmiller, 1980). To be sure, physically disabled people experience some degree of impairment of their orgasmic functioning. However, many handicapped men and women who have adjusted to their physical disabilities learn to express their sexuality freely and give of themselves to their sexual partners.

In addition to the physically handicapped, individuals who are mentally retarded or who suffer emotional disturbances also experience needs for love, intimacy, and sexual expression. In the past, society has not recognized these needs and has not fully accepted the right of mentally or emotionally handicapped individuals to freely express their sexuality.

Sometimes, in fact, it seems that society has viewed sexual expression among such individuals as an outgrowth of their intellectual deficiencies or their emotional disturbances. Probably, some element of fear underlies the reluctance of family members, health care personnel, and society-at-large to accept sexual expression among these individuals. Nevertheless, it is important to recognize that the emotionally and mentally handicapped have as great a need to express themselves sexually as the rest of us.

As we overcome our fears and ignorance about the concerns of the handicapped, we will grow in our knowledge, understanding, and sensitivity to the human condition. The handicapped will benefit from our increased awareness as we help and encourage them in finding appropriate means and outlets for their sexual expression. Society will benefit because our irrational concerns and fears will be alleviated and our sexual and emotional growth will be enhanced.

Aphrodisiacs and Anaphrodisiacs

Throughout history, people have sought to control sexual appetite through a variety of foods, drugs, mechanical devices, and physical activities. Most often the search has been for means of increasing sexual desire, but in some instances, means of decreasing desire have also been sought. An **aphrodisiac** is anything that increases sexual desire; an **anaphrodisiac** has the opposite effect.

Certain foods have long been thought to have sexually stimulating properties. The rarity or newness of some food (such as the potato when it was first brought to England) may arouse the hope that a sexual stimulant has been discovered. In other cases, certain foods have shapes or properties that resemble a particular sex organ, and the superstitious belief arises that sexual strength can be gained by eating such food. This belief, called the "doctrine of signatures," leads to the consumption of certain foods for their assumed erotic properties (MacDougald, 1961).

One well-known example is the idea that the oyster (which resembles the testicle) has sexually arousing properties. Chemical analysis, however, shows that the oyster consists of water, protein, and carbohydrates, plus small amounts of fat, sugar, and minerals—none of which can in any way affect sex drive or performance (Neiger, 1968).

Other cultures have their own applications of this theory. Many Chinese and Asiatic Indians, for example, place unshakable belief in the potency of powdered rhinoceros horn. It is not difficult to see how the succinct word *horny* has come to mean "having strong sexual desire " in the vernacular.

Such myths undoubtedly persist because the psychological impact of *believing* certain foods are aphrodisiacs are sometimes strong enough to produce, temporarily at least, an elevation in sexual desire and performance. The result is that the person believes a sexual triumph is directly related to eating raw bull's testicles ("prairie oysters") or clams or celery or tomatoes or any one of the other foods reputed to be aphrodisiacs. Thus, the individual's belief tends to perpetuate itself, and to be passed to other people.

Another reason for the widespread belief in the aphrodisiac qualities of certain foods is the strong association in the minds of most people between sex and hunger for food. It is certainly true that highly nutritious food is essential to physical well-being and that the well-nourished person is likely to have a more satisfying sex life. It is also true that certain sensuous people derive a distinct aphrodisiac effect from a gourmet meal elegantly served in an atmosphere of candlelight and lovely music. The effect is psychological, however; food in itself cannot be an aphrodisiac.

Alcohol is probably the most famous of the alleged sexual stimulants, but the truth is that alcohol is a depressant. In sufficient quantities, it narcotizes the brain, thus retarding reflexes, and dilates the blood vessels, thus interfering with the capacity for erection. However, in small quantities, alcohol acts to remove an individual's sexual inhibitions, and many men and women report that their sex drive and sexual enjoyment are increased by alcohol consumption. Results of one study indicate that women experience orgasm more readily when they do not drink alcohol. However, women may subjectively experience stronger sexual arousal and a more pleasurable orgasmic experience after moderate drinking (Malatesta et al., 1982).

If sexual drive and ability habitually increase after the use of alcohol, or if the person is unable to function sexually without the use of alcohol, one of two forces (perhaps both) is at work: either the stresses of daily living have acted as temporary inhibitors to sexual impulses, or some real emotional block exists in the area of sex. Thus, any increase in sex drive following consumption of alcohol is based on temporary removal of psychological barriers rather than an increase in physical prowess. Getting past the strains of the crisis of the moment or ridding oneself of emotional conflicts concerning sexuality would probably do more to increase sexual capability and enjoyment than would consumption of alcohol.

Another drug widely considered to be aphrodisiac is cantharides, or "Spanish Fly." Derived from a beetle native to southern Europe, the drug is produced when the insects are dried and heated until they disintegrate into a fine powder. When this powder is taken internally, an acute irritation of the genitourinary tract, accompanied by an increase in the dilation of the associated blood vessels, results (MacDougald, 1961). The increased blood supply to the irritated tissue can produce penile erection, but without an increase in sex drive. Taken in excessive doses, Spanish Fly can cause violent illness or even death.

Africans have long used another drug for sexual arousal. Taken from a tree that is native to that region, yohimbine is primarily used in most nations as a diuretic (a substance that increases urination) and in the treatment of disorders such as neuritis and meningitis. Its aphrodisiac qualities are reportedly due to its stimulation of the nerve centers that control erection. While there is some doubt about its effectiveness, yohimbine is generally conceded to be the most widely used drug for increasing sexual drive.

Claims are also made for the aphrodisiac effects of various addicting or illicit drugs, such as opium, morphine, cocaine, LSD, hashish, and marijuana. Like alcohol, these drugs release inhibitions; but, also like alcohol, they tend to have an anaphrodisiac effect if taken in large enough quantities.

Marijuana has gained many devotees as a sexual stimulant. Its effect appears to be to enhance the enjoyment of sexual activity rather than to increase the sex drive. Because the drug heightens sense perception and distorts time perception, orgasm is subjectively prolonged and seems more pleasurable. No evidence exists, however, that marijuana is sexually stimulating in and of itself (Churchill, 1968).

Amphetamines and cocaine act as brain-center stimulants. Reports (unconfirmed) of their aphrodisiac properties have been made. But if, in fact, any increase in sensual pleasures follows their use, it most likely results from misplaced confidence in them or the loosening of excessive sexual controls rather than from their actual aphrodisiac properties. In any case, with continued use, the drugs become addictive and in time would inevitably diminish sexual capacity rather than enhance it (Kaplan, 1974, 1979).

A drug alleged to be an intensifier of orgasmic pleasure is amyl nitrate. Inhaling this drug at the instant of orgasm is reported by some individuals to enhance the pleasure of the experience. (One wonders, however, how they can avoid being distracted by the mechanical operations necessary for amyl-nitrate sniffing at such a moment!) The drug apparently acts to relax the smooth muscles and consequently produces dilation of the veins in the genitourinary tract. Some of the side effects of amyl nitrate are dizziness, headache, fainting, and, in rare cases, death (Kaplan, 1974, 1979). Obviously, its use should be under the direction and prescription of a physician, as should that of any other drug mentioned.

Certainly it seems logical to assume that the centers of the brain controlling sexual response are capable of being influenced by various pharmacologic substances and other stimuli. To date, however, about the only effects that drugs appear to have on human sexual behavior are inhibitory rather than enhancing (Kaplan, 1974, 1979). Because any drug is only one variable in the complex system of sexuality, its effect on any two given people may differ vastly. Indeed, even the same person may experience quite different results from one episode to another in using the same drug in conjunction with sex (Table 8.1).

Androgen is the only substance now known that can increase sexual interest, drive, and performance in both men and women. And when its administration proves effective, it does not appear to cause other behavioral changes. Androgen is a male hormone, but it is produced by both sexes, and its natural secretion appears to be the chief libidinous control in both. When androgen deficiency exists, especially in males, sexual interest (and potency) is impaired. Androgen replacement therapy in such cases will increase libido and performance. But if the sexual problem is not clearly related to androgen deficiency, the usefulness of this therapy to increase sexual desire is debatable (Kaplan, 1979).

Another hormone, luteinizing hormone-releasing factor (LH-RF), apparently helps increase sexual desire and may enhance libido when androgen therapy is ineffective. Thyroxine, a hormone used to correct hypothyroid states and to lift depression, also reportedly enhances desire (Kaplan, 1979).

Erotic pictures, songs, and literature, as well as recordings of squeaking bedsprings accompanied by heavy breathing, moans, and gasps, have been used to titillate sexual interest and drive. Erotic films or books are sometimes suggested by marriage counselors for couples whose sex life has become lackluster and apathetic. While new sexual excitement can occur when one is exposed to erotic stimuli, immunity to such stimulation rapidly develops if the exposure is overdone.

All in all, the most effective aphrodisiacs remain good health, plenty of rest and sleep, adequate diet and exercise, and freedom from emotional tension. Anxiety may be alleviated, physiological functioning may be improved, the aging process may be slowed, and sexual desire and performance may be enhanced through programs of physical exercise (Frauman, 1982). Medical checkups, coordinated with appropriate attention to physical and emotional health, will likely ensure an active and continuing interest in sex.

Techniques used to decrease sexual interest and drive have varied through the ages: from taking cold baths, as suggested by Plato and Aristotle (MacDougald, 1961); to wearing chastity belts and penis cages, as suggested by the Romans and the British at one time; to using tranquilizers and other chemicals today.

The substance best known as a reputed anaphrodisiac is saltpeter, or po-

Table 8.1   Effects of Some Common Drugs on Human Sexual Response

| Drug | Medical usage | Phase of sexual response affected[a] | | |
		Desire	Excitement	Orgasm
Sedative-hypnotics Alcohol Barbiturates Chloral hydrate Methaqualone (Quaalude)	For insomnia and to lower anxiety.	In low doses, may increase because of lessened inhibitions, although expectations may influence behavior. In high doses, decreased.	Prolonged with low doses due to decreased sensitivity or due to intimacy or shared feelings; impotence with high chronic alcohol and barbiturate use.	With high doses, inhibited.
Mild tranquilizers Librium Meprobamate Tranxene Valium	To reduce anxiety and muscle tension; also for convulsive states.	May be enhanced slightly due to lessened anxiety; diminished in high doses.	None reported.	With usual doses, no effect; with very high doses, orgasm delayed.
Narcotics Codeine Methadone Morphine	For relief from pain and control of diarrhea and coughing; for withdrawal from narcotics (methadone).	In high doses, absent.	With high doses, impotence.	With high dosage, inhibited.
Major tranquilizers Haldol Mellaril Stelazine Thorazine	Sedative effect for control of psychiatric disorders.	May be decreased in high doses. (Delay of ovulation and menstruation in females reported with Thorazine.)	Impotence is reported rarely; some erectile difficulties.	Inhibition of ejaculation and retrograde ejaculation reported with Mellaril.
Antidepressants Tricyclics (Elavil, Tofranil) MAO inhibiters (Marplan, Nardil, Norpramine)	For depression.	Probably none.	None.	Very rare ejaculatory problems as side effects; some females report delay of orgasm.
Lithium carbonate	For manic states and possibly prevention of manic/depressive cycles.	Urgency and desire may be reduced.	Very rare potency problems as side effects.	

Source: Adapted from Kaplan (1979) and Sandler et al. (1980).
[a]Discussion of the excitement and orgasmic phases is found in Chapter 9.

tassium nitrate. Actually, this is an almost completely neutral chemical and is an absolute failure as an anaphrodisiac. Its only physical effect is that it is a fairly effective diuretic, and this may account for its far-flung but undeserved reputation as a sex deterrent. Experimentation with the drug Ismelin (guan-ethidine sulphate), used in the treatment of high blood pressure, showed that erectile potency, ability to ejaculate, and intensity of climax were all reduced significantly by intake of the drug. Side effects of stomach cramps, diarrhea, and general loss of physical energy were reported by one-half the subjects (Money & Yankowitz, 1967). Limited success has been reported from pre-scribing certain tranquilizers and other drugs in an attempt to decrease sexual desire. Some physicians are reluctant to use these drugs, however, fearing that removal or reduction of emotional blocks may result, producing aphrodisiac effects or unusual sexual behavior.

Men who are treated for various illnesses with the female hormone es-trogen almost always experience a decrease or cessation in sexual drive and interest. In contrast, male hormones have the opposite effect in women. Cypro-terone acetate, an experimental drug used to treat compulsive sexual disorders, reportedly leads to a loss of desire in both men and women (Kaplan, 1979).

Most information regarding aphrodisiacs and anaphrodisiacs is based more on folklore than on scientific evidence. In those cases where there seems to be a change in sexual desire or ability, the cause is usually psychological rather than physiological. Although the desire for a bottled cure for faltering sex interest is understandable, positive changes in sexual adjustment are al-most always the result of the individual's increased understanding of his or her own feelings about sex.

Summary

Fewer differences between the sexes and the responses to sexual stimuli and erotica exist than most of us believe. Women have as powerful a sex drive as men and as great a need psychologically and physically to express their sexuality.

In order to enhance their sexual relationships, men and women are en-couraged to become aware of the importance of personal grooming and hy-giene in sexual attractiveness. People who follow a slow and gentle pace in their sexual interactions and who vary their approach in sexual settings avoid boredom. Adding novelty and a little imagination helps keep sexual relation-ships alive. Men and women who use fantasies to augment their sexual arousal and are willing to experiment with one another are likely to have more exciting relationships.

In their sexual interactions, couples enhance arousal through stimulation of the erogenous zones—those areas of the body possessing a large concentra-tion of nerve endings. Sexual responsiveness in men and women is largely a learned phenomenon. One of the most important ways to learn full sexual re-sponse is through masturbation. People who learn about their own sensuality through masturbation, by exercising their tactile senses, and by learning erotic tongue movements and developing appropriate muscle control enhance their sexual relations. Couples can engage in such highly pleasurable sexual activities as petting or extended foreplay, breast manipulation, kissing, vibrator stimulation, cunnilingus, fellatio, and anal stimulation.

The four basic positions in which a couple may engage in the act of sexual intercourse are as follows: (1) the face-to-face, man-above position; (2) the face-to-face, woman-above position; (3) the face-to-face, side position; and (4) the rear-entry position. Through experimentation and practice a couple can arrive at those coital positions most pleasurable and satisfactory to them. Variations of the four basic oital positions are possible.

Uninhibited giving and receiving of sexual pleasure is not limited to physically able individuals. Men and women who suffer from varying degrees of impairment in their physical, mental, and emotional functioning also experience needs for intimacy and sexual expression.

Aphrodisiacs are foods, drugs, and devices used in an attempt to stimulate sexual desire. The aphrodisiac qualities of drugs—including alcohol, *cantharides* or Spanish fly, yohimbine, cocaine, marijuana, amphetamines, and amyl nitrate—have been extolled by users. However, the effects of such drugs in increasing sex drive are probably psychological. The hormone androgen is known to increase sex drive in both men and women. Anaphrodisiacs are drugs and techniques used to decrease sexual interest. Potassium nitrate, Ismelin, and cyproterone acetate have been employed as anaphrodisiacs. The results of such use have been neutral or of limited success.

TRUE OR FALSE: THE FACTS

Oral-genital sex is perverted and animalistic.
False. Although some people have a negative attitude toward oral-genital sex, it is practiced by the majority of men and women who are college educated and has been recommended by many authorities in the field of sex and marriage as a desirable and vastly pleasurable form of sexual behavior. *(144)*

Masturbation is practiced by most men and women.
True. Masturbation is practiced by the majority of both men and women, married and single. *(139)*

Alcohol is a sexual stimulant.
False. Alcohol is a depressant; however, in small quantities it can remove an individual's sexual inhibitions so that sex drive and sexual enjoyment are increased. *(151–152)*

Vaginal-penile intercourse is only one normal method of having sex relations.
True. Scientific opinion is that there is nothing physically or psychologically wrong with nonvaginal methods of intercourse. *(144)*

SUGGESTED READING

Bing, Elisabeth, and Colman, Libby. *Making love during pregnancy.* New York: Bantam Books, 1977.
This well-illustrated practical guide for expectant and new parents emphasizes sexual behavior during pregnancy. The guide also stresses education in prenatal development and changes in the woman's body during pregnancy.

McCary, James Leslie, and McCary, Stephen P. *McCary's human sexuality* (4th ed.). Belmont, Calif.: Wadsworth, 1982.
Chapters 9 (Techniques in Sexual Arousal), 10 (Aphrodisiacs and Anaphrodisiacs), and 11 (Positions in Sexual Intercourse) form the foundation for the material in this chapter.

Rabin, Barry. *The sensuous wheeler: Sexual adjustment for the spinal cord injured.* San Francisco: Multi Media Resource Center, 1980.
Stressing the importance of sexual expression, this creatively written book is a valuable practical guide for the spinal-cord injured to sexual satisfaction.

Raley, Patricia E. *Making love: How to be your own sex therapist.* New York: Avon, 1980.
This well-illustrated sexual self-help guide is intended for the adult reader of any sexual orientation who is interested in maximizing satisfaction in relationships. Systematic guidelines are provided for exploring significant aspects of erotic life.

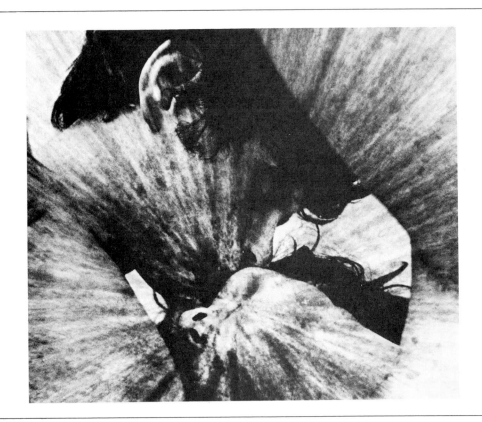

TRUE OR FALSE?

Sexologists are in agreement that women experience only one type of orgasm, produced by direct or indirect stimulation of the clitoris.

❧

Simultaneous orgasms are not necessarily more satisfying than those experienced separately and are, moreover, not necessary for sexual compatibility.

❧

Both men and women experience a refractory period (period of resistance to sexual stimulation) following orgasm.

Orgasm

CHAPTER 9

The Excitement Phase
The Plateau Phase
The Orgasmic Phase
The Resolution Phase
The Question of Simultaneous Orgasms
Summary
Suggested Reading

No matter what methods or techniques are employed or how intense the enjoyment is, the frequent (although certainly not the sole) goal in sexual activity is orgasm. An **orgasm** is the highly pleasurable, tension-relieving experience that is the summit of physical and emotional gratification in sexual activity. In both sexes, the approach of orgasm is marked by a rise in blood pressure and pulse rate, faster and deeper breathing, engorgement of erectile tissues with blood, and finally, an explosive release of muscular and sexual tension. This release is followed by a rather quick return of the body to its nonstimulated state.

Orgasm is a short-lived experience (usually lasting about three to ten seconds, ordinarily longer for women than men), but it is among the most intense of human experiences. This intensity may be difficult to understand. However, if another body need—for example, hunger—were to be satisfied in an equally short period of time, perhaps a similar intensity of reaction would be experienced.

The subjective sensation of orgasm is centered in the pelvic region for both men and women: the penis, prostate, and seminal vesicles in men; and the clitoris, vagina, and uterus in women (Masters & Johnson, 1966). Most specialists in human sexuality recognize that orgasm is a total body response, although men tend to be more "genitally focused" than women (Brotman, 1980; deMoya & deMoya, 1973). Some men even experience prostate orgasms (that is, orgasms resulting from finger massage of the prostate) that they describe as being "more generalized" or "deeper" than orgasms resulting from stimulation of the penis (Hite, 1981).

Many physiological changes occur in men and women as their sexual tension mounts to orgasmic release. Orgasm in the man is ordinarily accompanied by ejaculation. Recent research has shown that women may also experience an ejaculatory phenomenon that accompanies their orgasm (Ladas et al., 1982) (see page 54). The sexual responses of men and women are thus very similar and often parallel one another.

Some individuals, the majority of whom are women, have difficulty in reaching orgasm; in fact, this failure is the most common complaint of women seeking help from sex therapists. The reason is almost always psychological and should be handled accordingly. It is unfortunate, however, that orgasm is usually singled out as the most important criterion of sexual satisfaction and that both partners tend to feel unhappy or inadequate if the man or woman fails to achieve it. Many women report that emotional intimacy, tenderness, closeness, and sharing of deep feelings with a loved one are as rewarding as orgasms per se (Hite, 1976). Understand, however, that many women in our culture have been socialized to believe that orgasm is important for men but not for themselves. While some women undoubtedly have satisfying sexual lives that do not always include orgasm, many women enjoy and prefer the sexual release that orgasm provides on at least some occasions.

Because of the many nerve endings in the region of the clitoris and vulva and the almost negligible number in the vagina, many women find that mastur-

What Does an Orgasm Feel Like?

Two hundred fifty university students enrolled in an undergraduate marriage, family, and sex education course were asked to describe what experiencing an orgasm feels like. Some of the responses given by the women were these:

- "It's like having to urinate for a really long time and then the final relief that comes with urination."
- "Never have experienced."
- "A tingle, a warm feeling all over, a natural high, an accomplishment, a jerky movement inside. . . ."
- "Shooting stars!"
- "It's like a warmth that begins in the stomach and that suddenly explodes into a beautiful rush of tingling heat that extends from the top of my head to the tips of my toes."
- "Like a chocolate sundae . . . rich and fattening and fun, fun, fun!"

Some of the responses given by the men were these:

- "Everything goes so fast . . . all you can see is stars! It all comes to a boil in just a few seconds, then the whistle blows and it's all over and we come to a stop."
- "I used to get orgasms, but I didn't know what they were. I just knew they felt good."
- "Mount St. Helens."
- "Electrifying! . . . To be struck by lightning at just the right place."
- "Out of control."
- "A powerful feeling . . . like Superman. You feel all pumped up."

bation and other forms of direct stimulation, rather than coitus, bring them more orgasms, in faster succession, and with a more intense physical response. This point has been supported by research and by laboratory observation of women engaging in various sexual acts (Masters & Johnson, 1966; Wilcox & Hager, 1980). However, many women report experiencing a deeper, more satisfying orgasm when they experience a vaginal orgasm (Ladas et al., 1982). Some women may find that several clitoral orgasms are needed to achieve the same degree of satisfaction attained from a single vaginal orgasm. Coital orgasms are considered to be more emotionally satisfying, tension-reducing, and vaginally soothing (Hite, 1976).

Most men, on the other hand, find it easier and more satisfying to achieve orgasm through coitus than through other methods. As stated earlier, there has long been debate over women's capacity for multiple orgasms, despite the abundance of clinical evidence attesting to this capability. It has now been established that women are indeed capable by natural endowment of multiple orgasm. Furthermore, the women in Masters and Johnson's sampling reported that, subjectively, they found the second and third orgasmic responses to be more intense and more pleasurable than the first.

Through carefully controlled laboratory studies spanning an eleven-year period, bodily changes during the various phases of the sexual response cycle have been observed and recorded by Masters and Johnson (1966). They divide their description of the sexual response cycle into four phases: the excitement phase, the plateau phase, the orgasmic phase, and the resolution phase. They

The Difference between Vaginal and Clitoral Orgasms

Since and perhaps even before the profound influence of Sigmund Freud, controversy has existed concerning the difference between clitoral and vaginal orgasms—that is, orgasm resulting from some type of stimulation of the clitoris as opposed to orgasm resulting from penile-vaginal intercourse or manual-vaginal stimulation. Indeed, the early psychoanalysts and others have believed that mature women experience vaginal orgasms, while women who experience clitoral orgasms only are narcissistic and sexually inadequate. Freud thought that an emotionally immature girl would experience orgasm through clitoral stimulation, but that as she developed into a mature woman, the predominant focus in sexual response would change from the clitoris to the vagina. Masters and Johnson (1966) and other modern sex researchers, on the other hand, have emphasized the importance of direct or indirect clitoral stimulation in leading to women's orgasmic responses and in effect have downplayed the role of and importance of vaginal orgasms.

Recent evidence indicates that many women are capable of experiencing vaginal, clitoral, and/or "blended" orgasms and that they are able to have gratifying and satisfying sexual responses regardless of the type of orgasm (Ladas et al., 1982). Still other women do not experience orgasm at all, and some of them undoubtedly have enjoyable and fulfilling sexual lives. Perhaps the kind of orgasm is less important than the quality of the overall sexual experience.

In short, there may be no "better" or no "worse" way for women to experience orgasm. Whatever is gratifying and fulfilling for the woman—either alone or with her sexual partner or partners—is probably more important than the kind of orgasm she experiences. Thus, regardless of the form of sexual stimulation, it appears more important that women enjoy their sexuality rather than be overly concerned with the particular means by which they experience orgasm.

---

have found that a variety of physical and psychological stimuli will encourage the development of these phases and that adverse stimuli can interrupt their development.

No one is consciously aware of all the many physiological events that take place during the sexual act. But anyone wishing to understand orgasm, to heighten his or her awareness of the experience, and to know something of what his or her partner is experiencing will want to look at the orgasmic responses of men and women in some detail, as we shall do in this chapter.

The Excitement Phase

The **excitement phase** is the initial stage of the sexual response cycle. Any form of sexual stimulation that is appealing to an individual will initiate the excitement phase; and, if the stimulation is continued, it leads to the other phases of response and usually produces an orgasm. The excitement phase can be extended by interruption and subsequent resumption. It can also be stopped completely by totally withdrawing the stimulation; if the stimulation becomes objectionable or if extraneous factors interfere with the stimulation, the excite-

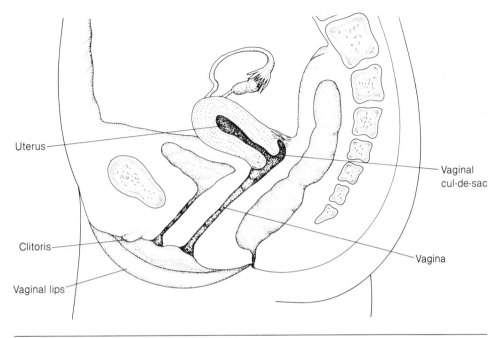

Figure 9.1   Female genitalia in preexcitement state.

ment phase may be stopped. Under any of these circumstances, the bodily changes that have occurred disappear in a relatively short time.

Sexual stimulation produces basically the same bodily reactions in both the man and the woman. Among these reactions are increased muscular tension (called **myotonia**) and an engorgement of the blood vessels (called **vasocongestion**), which causes the surrounding tissue to swell. Vasocongestion is especially pronounced in the genital organs.

A woman's physiological response to sexual stimulation in the excitement phase includes lubrication or "sweating" in the vagina, and marked vasocongestion in both the external and internal genital areas (Figure 9.1). It causes the labia majora to become congested with blood. If the women has not borne children (in which case she is referred to by scientists as a **nullipara**), the lips thin out and become somewhat flattened. As they flatten, the lips also elevate slightly, upward and outward, flaring away from the vaginal opening to allow the man freer access. This flattening process is not usually complete until late in the excitement phase or until the beginning of the plateau phase.

In a woman who has borne children (she is called a **multipara**), the major lips become greatly engorged, often increasing in size by two or three times. Although the lips hang in a rather loose and pendulous manner, there is a marked gaping away from the vaginal opening so that the man will not be impeded in penetration.

The labia minora also begin enlarging in the excitement phase. By the end

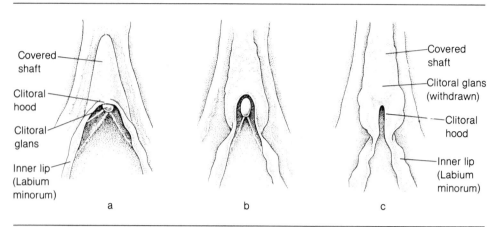

Figure 9.2   Representation of clitoris during sexual activity, showing (a) normal unstimulated state; (b) response during excitement and plateau phases; and (c) response at end of plateau phase and during orgasmic phase.

of this phase, or perhaps early in the plateau phase, they are two to three times thicker than their normal size. This thickening of the inner lips adds a centimeter or more to the length of the vaginal barrel and is further preparation for reception of the erect penis.

The clitoral shaft also swells during this phase, and the loose, wrinkled external skin that surrounds the clitoris fills out as the glans tissue beneath it expands (Figure 9.2). There is an increase in both the diameter and the length of the clitoral shaft, but the increase in size of the clitoris is usually not visible to the naked eye. If the increase in clitoral size becomes observable, it will be only after sexual tension has progressed into the late part of the excitement phase. Direct manipulation of the clitoral region will produce more rapid and greater enlargement of the clitoral glans than will other stimulation, such as fantasy, breast manipulation, or sexual intercourse.

Within ten to thirty seconds after sexual stimulation—whether psychological or physiological—has begun, the vagina begins to lubricate itself through a "sweating" phenomenon. Small droplets of clear fluid appear on the walls of the vagina; as sexual tension increases, the droplets coalesce to form a moist coating of the entire vaginal wall, completely lubricating the vaginal barrel.

The vasocongestion that causes the "sweating" in the vagina also causes a color change in the vaginal tissue. From its usual purple-red color, it changes slowly to a darker, rather patchy deep purple. The entire vaginal barrel becomes consistently darker in the subsequent phases.

Under nonexcited conditions the walls of the vagina—especially in women who have never borne a child—are touching. During the excitement phase, the wrinkled surface of the vagina stretches and flattens, and the vaginal mucosa thins with the expansion. Toward the end of the excitement phase, the entire uterus is drawn upward, pulling on the vagina and making its inner two-

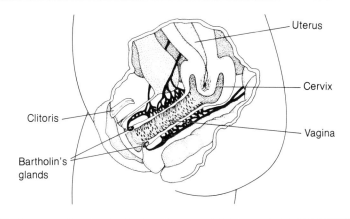

Figure 9.3   Female pelvic region, showing enlargement of vaginal blood vessels and "sweating" of vaginal walls during sexual arousal and climax.

thirds much wider and longer in a ballooning or tenting effect that helps to prepare the vagina for penetration. The entire vagina becomes dilated, but the marked expansion is limited to its inner two-thirds (Figure 9.3).

During the early part of the excitement phase, rapid and irregular contractions begin in the uterus. The uterus also response with vasocongestion during this phase. If the excitement or plateau phase is sustained for an excessively prolonged period, the uterus may become two or three times larger than its normal size.

Male genitalia show the same marked engorgement of the tissues with blood. A man's first physiological response to sexual stimulation is erection of the penis as its three spongy cylindrical bodies of erectile tissue fill with blood. This is a parallel response to vaginal lubrication in women. When the excitement phase is prolonged with varied stimuli, an erection may be lost and regained many times. Distractions such as loud noises, noticeable changes in lighting or temperature, or feelings of anxiety or fear can cause a partial or a complete loss of erection, regardless of the amount or type of stimulation. With penile erection, the urethra, of course, also lengthens. As the excitement phase progresses, the penile urethral passage becomes twice as large in diameter as it is in an unstimulated state, and the urethral opening widens.

Sexual excitement causes the skin of the scrotum to become thick and congested, limiting the space within the scrotal sac. The testes rise higher in the scrotum, with a slight rotation of the axis of the testes. If the excitement phase is prolonged more than five to ten minutes, the scrotal sac may relax again and the testes descend, but when sexual tension progresses to the plateau phase, they will quickly elevate again, and the scrotal wall will rethicken.

Erection of the nipples occurs during the excitement phase in almost all women and in about 60 percent of men. In women, increased sexual tension causes the **areolae**, the pigmented areas of the breasts surrounding the nipples, to become engorged and swollen. Women's breasts enlarge significantly, but the size of men's breasts is not similarly affected by sexual stimulation.

A measleslike rash, called the **sex flush,** appears in about three-fourths of sexually stimulated women and in about one-fourth of sexually stimulated men, although it may not appear in men until the plateau stage. It begins in the stomach region and at the throat and neck, and it spreads quickly to the breasts. As a rule, the intensity of the flush is in direct proportion to the intensity of the stimulation received.

Myotonia of voluntary muscles—and to a limited extent, of some involuntary muscles—is observable during the excitement phase, especially the latter part. There is muscle tension in the abdominal region and in the long muscles of both legs and arms. As excitement increases, the movements of both men and women become more restless, forceful, and swift. As sexual tension builds, there is a corresponding increase in heart rate and an elevation of blood pressure.

The Plateau Phase

During the **plateau phase,** sexual tension continues to mount, and physiological changes are intensified. If sexual stimulation is withdrawn during this period, an orgasm will not occur, and the built-up sexual tensions will decrease very gradually over a prolonged period of time.

Several marked changes occur during this phase in the genitalia; most of the changes are elaborations of the changes that began during the excitement phase. In women, there is a vivid color change, called the sex-skin reaction, in the engorged labia minora. There is a definite correlation between the intensity of the color change and the degree of sexual excitation. The marked color change is evidence of an impending orgasm.

The clitoris exhibits its most singular response to sexual stimulation during the late plateau phase. The body and glans of the clitoris withdraw and pull back deeply underneath the foreskin or hood, so that there is a 50 percent reduction in total length of the clitoris just before orgasm. If sexual stimulation is removed during the plateau phase, the clitoris will resume its normal position; if stimulation is reapplied, the clitoris will withdraw again.

The outer third of the vagina, which had become slightly dilated during the excitement phase, becomes congested with blood. The distended muscles involuntarily contract, causing the vagina to tighten around the penis as the woman nears orgasm. The congested outer third of the vagina and the engorged labia minora have been given the name **orgasmic platform** by Masters and Johnson (1966). The rapid and irregular contractions of the uterus intensify as the response cycle progresses from early excitement to late plateau phase, and further vasocongestion of the uterus produces additional enlargement.

Genital reactions in the male during the plateau phase are mostly an intensification of the reactions begun in the excitement phase. Late in the plateau phase the corona of the glans of the penis becomes more swollen, and there may be a deepening of the mottled reddish-purple color of the glans and the

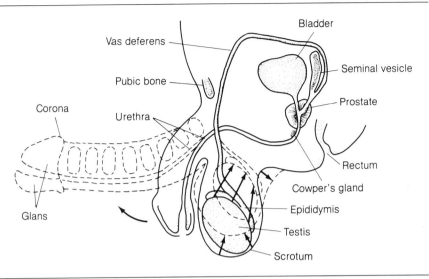

Figure 9.4   Male genitalia in preexcitement state. Dotted lines represent organ positions in excitement and plateau phases. Note that testis and scrotum move up, toward body cavity.

area just below the corona, but this color change is not as marked as the sex-skin color change in women. A few drops of secretion from the Cowper's glands are usually discharged from the penis during this phase, especially if the excitement phase has been prolonged and orgasm has been delayed. This fluid is in advance of the true ejaculate.

By the end of the plateau phase, the testes are fully elevated in the scrotum, indicating that orgasm is imminent. Vasocongestion in the testes causes them to increase in size, sometimes as much as doubling. The more protracted the plateau phase is, the more vasocongestion there is and the more marked the increase in testicular size.

Women's breasts reach their peak of expansion during the plateau phase. The areolae become so enlarged that they partially cover the erect nipples, giving the illusion that there is a loss of nipple erection. This is especially true of breasts that have never suckled a baby.

If a sex flush appeared on the woman during the excitement phase, much of her body will now be flushed. Late in this period, the intensity of the color and the expanse of the flush reach their peak. The man may now show the first signs of a sex flush, beginning under the rib cage and spreading over the chest, neck, and face. Fewer men than women have this response, and in those men who do, it may not occur during every response cycle.

Increased muscular tension is the most marked bodily response in both sexes during this period, but it is perhaps more pronounced in the man (Figure 9.4). Both voluntary and involuntary muscles are involved. Involuntary muscle contractions lengthen the vaginal barrel. Both sexes often purposefully make the muscles in the buttocks more tense in their striving for orgasm. Pelvic

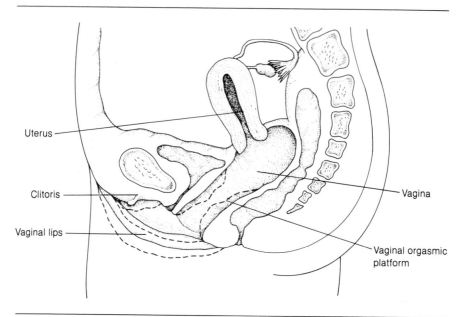

Figure 9.5   Female pelvic region, showing changes in size and position of organs and tissue during increasing sexual excitement and orgasmic response. Note ballooning and tenting effect of inner portion of the vagina. Dotted lines show organ positions during orgasm.

thrusts are at first voluntarily controlled by both men and women during this phase, but as excitement mounts, their motions become rapid, forceful thrusting, which is essentially an involuntary reaction, especially in men.

As the plateau phase continues, the heart rate elevates, sometimes increasing to more than twice the usual rate of about seventy beats per minute. During the latter part of this phase, there is also a marked elevation of blood pressure. Hyperventilation (increase in respiratory rate) begins during the plateau phase.

The Orgasmic Phase

The **orgasmic phase** consists of those few seconds when the sexual tension evidenced by muscular spasm and engorgement of blood vessels reaches its maximum intensity and is discharged in orgasm—a highly pleasurable, totally involuntary response.

The vagina shows a unique response during the orgasmic phase (Figure 9.5). The orgasmic platform, first noticeable during the plateau phase, contracts strongly in intervals of about 0.8 second. There are at least three or four of these contractions, and there may be as many as fifteen. They decrease in frequency and intensity after the first few, and their strength varies from woman to woman, with variations in individual experiences.

At about the same time that the sexual response cyle advances from the plateau to the orgasmic phase in the man, contractions of the accessory organs

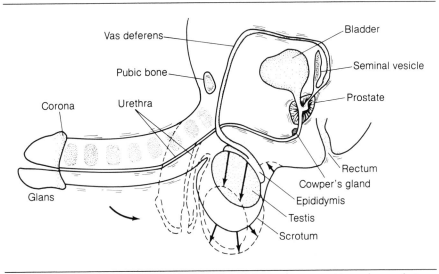

Figure 9.6   Male genitalia in orgasmic phase. Dotted lines represent positions after resolution phase. Note that testis and scrotum move down, away from body cavity, during resolution phase.

of reproduction—the vas deferens, the seminal vesicles, the ejaculatory duct, and the prostate—work to collect sperm and seminal fluid, which are compressed into the entrance to the prostatic urethra. The urethral bulb becomes greatly distended, and this signals the inevitability of orgasm in the man. He is unable to hold back from the climax after this moment. Ejaculation of the seminal fluid is caused by regularly recurring contractions of the urethra and of muscles at the base of the penis and around the anus. The intervals between contractions are roughly the same as those between orgasmic vaginal contractions (Figure 9.6).

If there has been a sex flush, the intensity of the flush during the orgasmic phase is proportionate to the intensity of the orgasm. Women sometimes have an involuntary distention of the external opening of the urethra during orgasm. The distention disappears and the opening returns to its normal state before the orgasmic phase is over. Women also occasionally feel an urge to urinate during or immediately after orgasm, and there may be a loss of urine as sexual tension mounts.

The Resolution Phase

The **resolution phase** is a period of return to the nonstimulated state. During this phase, women generally remain capable of continued orgasms if there is continued stimulation, but for men this phase includes a time (**refractory period**) during which restimulation is impossible.

As vasocongestion disappears in women, the labia majora return to normal size. As the excess blood drains from the labia minora, they usually return to a light pink color within ten to fifteen seconds, and the sex-skin color is usually totally normal within five minutes after orgasm.

The clitoris, which was retracted and invisible during the late plateau and orgasmic phases, now returns to its normal position within five to ten seconds after orgasm. Congestion of the clitoral glans and shaft may remain, however, for five to ten minutes after orgasm and occasionally may persist for as long as thirty minutes.

The outer third of the vagina quickly returns to normal as the vasocongestion that produced the orgasmic platform disappears, and the opening of the vagina returns to its normal size. The vaginal walls regain their rough, wrinkled surface, and the deep color of the vagina fades. The entire vagina returns to a normal state within ten to fifteen minutes after orgasm.

In men, return of the penis to its normal flaccid state occurs in two stages. In the first stage, about 50 percent of the erection is quickly lost soon after ejaculation. During the second stage, the remaining erection is lost at a slower rate, which varies according to the amount of continued sexual stimulation. If the penis is kept in the vagina or if the partner is held close for a time after ejaculation, the penis may retain a partial erection for a longer time. If the man stands up, urinates, smokes, or does some other sexually unrelated act, **detumescence** will occur rapidly in both the primary and secondary stages.

In most men, the scrotal skin rapidly returns to its relaxed, loosely wrinkled, prearousal state as congestion disappears. The testes return to their normal lowered position, lose their vasocongestion, and return to normal size. The longer the plateau phase, the slower the testes are in returning to normal size during the resolution phase.

The sex flush disappears, muscles return to a relaxed state, and nipple erection is lost. Heart rate, blood pressure, and respiratory rate quickly return to normal after orgasm. About a third of all men and women develop a perspiratory reaction immediately after orgasm. This perspiration may cover the entire body in both sexes, but it is usually confined in men to the soles of the feet and the palms of the hands. In women, it frequently covers the back, thighs, chest, underarms, upper lip, and forehead. This film of perspiration is not related to the physical exertion of coitus, since the response occurs regardless of the degree of physical activity in the first three phases. The amount of perspiration parallels the strength of the orgasm.

The Question of Simultaneous Orgasms

The desirability of simultaneous orgasms has long been a subject of speculation (Ellis, 1960). Naturally, if both partners prefer orgasms at the same time—and many couples do—then they should strive for this goal. However, there are some aspects of sexual response that should be considered before a couple embark upon the uneven struggle toward simultaneous orgasms or before they accept the premise that it offers the ultimate in sexual achievement.

The effort to give one's partner the fullest measure of concern and satisfaction is essential to rewarding sexual activity. If either person is primarily concerned with gratifying himself or is caught up in his own impending orgasm, he cannot give full attention to his partner. Similarly, if one is concentrating only on the partner's sexual gratification, appropriate concentration on one's own responses and pleasure is impossible.

Furthermore, men and women react quite differently in bodily movements at the time of orgasm. The man's tendency is to plunge into the vagina as deeply as possible at the moment of orgasm and to hold this position, followed perhaps by one or two deep, deliberate thrusts. The woman's tendency, on the other hand, is to want the same stroking, plunging movements of the excitement and plateau phases continued during the orgasmic reaction, with perhaps an acceleration of the thrusts and an increase of pressure in the vulval area. These two highly pleasurable patterns of movement are obviously incompatible. Since both cannot be executed at the same time, whichever pattern is carried out during simultaneous orgasm must detract from the full pleasure of one of the partners.

The arguments would appear to be stronger against than for simultaneous orgasm. It is easier for a man to achieve orgasm, but he is usually capable of only one. The sensible approach to orgasm would therefore seem to be that the man delay his own climax until his partner is fully satisfied. The couple can thereby devote full attention to giving the woman as many orgasmic responses as she wishes, and both can then concentrate wholly on providing the man with as satisfying an orgasm as possible.

Couples would do well to remember that it is the quality of the sexual relationships that deserves attention rather than the number, type, or timing of their orgasms. Couples who make orgasm the primary goal of their sexual interactions may find that they are paying too much attention to performance issues and thereby setting the stage for sexual dysfunctions or feelings of sexual inadequacy. In sum, couples may shortchange themselves if they become more concerned with reaching orgasm than with fully enjoying the entire love-making experience.

The quality of an orgasm—that is, its intensity, length, and overall pleasure—varies from person to person and within the same person from one act of coitus to another. Recency and frequency of occurrence can influence the quality of the next sexual experience, as can such factors as anxiety, guilt, depression, anger, indifference toward one's partner, and distaste for one's surroundings. These factors not only can affect the quality of the orgasm but also, if strong enough, can block the response altogether. As would be expected, women, because of their being subjected to the double standard, report a greater variability in the subjective quality of their orgasms than men do (Marmor et al., 1971).

Although the material in this chapter has focused on the physiological aspects of the sexual act, the importance of the emotional aspects must not be overlooked. For many, a close relationship and deep emotional involvement—love, if you wish—are of paramount importance to a complete and fulfilling sexual experience. Physiological sexual needs can be relieved without love, closeness, or even understanding. But many feel that they cannot really attain complete emotional; physical, and sexual satisfaction without the intermingling of those elements.

Summary

Orgasm is an intensely pleasurable, tension-relieving experience that leads to physical and emotional gratification for both sexes. Orgasmic sensations and responses appear to be essentially the same for both men and women. Some women experience an ejaculatory response, as men do.

The methods that most readily lead to orgasm for women are masturbation and other forms of direct stimulation of the clitoris. In contrast, most men report they find it easier and more satisfying to achieve orgasm through coitus.

Human sexual response may be conceptualized as being divided into four phases: excitement, plateau, orgasmic, and resolution. Many physiological changes, such as increased muscle tension (myotonia), engorged blood vessels (vasocongestion), increased heart rate, and heightened breathing, occur in men and women as their sexual tension mounts to orgasmic release. The four phases of sexual response are similar in both sexes except that after orgasm, men enter a refractory period (a state of temporary resistance to sexual stimulation). Women do not usually enter such a period and generally remain capable of returning to earlier phases of the cycle.

The experience of orgasm leads to a release of sexual tension for both men and women, although overconcern with simultaneous orgasms and emotional factors can lessen pleasure and lead to problems in sexual relationships. It is important to emphasize that the emotional aspects of human relationships are intermingled with the physical aspects and affect the degree of gratification that can be attained in sexual interactions.

TRUE OR FALSE: THE FACTS

Sexologists are in agreement that women experience only one type of orgasm, produced by direct or indirect stimulation of the clitoris.
False. Recent evidence indicates that women experience vaginal, clitoral, and/or "blended" orgasms and that they have satisfying sexual responses regardless of the type of orgasm. *(162)*

Simultaneous orgasms are not necessarily more satisfying than those experienced separately and are, moreover, not necessary for sexual compatibility.
True. Because men and women react differently in bodily movements at time of orgasm, because concentration on one's own or one's partner's gratification precludes concentration on the other's, and because a man can usually achieve only one orgasm, there is no evidence that simultaneous orgasms provide the ultimate in sexual satisfaction. *(170–171)*

Both men and women experience a refractory period (period of resistance to sexual stimulation) following orgasm.
False. Women remain capable of continued stimulation after orgasm, but men do experience a refractory period during which restimulation is impossible. *(169)*

SUGGESTED READING

Barbach, Lonnie Garfield. *For yourself: The fulfillment of female sexuality.* New York: Anchor/Doubleday, 1976.
This book is an excellent practical guide for women who have orgasmic difficulties or other sexual concerns.

Ladas, Alice K., Whipple, Beverly, and Perry, John D. *The G spot and other recent discoveries about human sexuality.* New York: Holt, Rinehart & Winston, 1982.
Written in nontechnical language for the general reader, this book offers a thorough description and discussion of the Grafenberg spot, an anatomical structure located on the anterior wall of the vagina that, when stimulated, enhances sexual pleasure for many women. The authors also discuss the phenomenon of female ejaculation, kinds of female orgasm, and similarities in sexual functioning between men and women.

McCary, James Leslie, and McCary, Stephen P. *McCary's human sexuality* (4th ed.). Belmont, Calif.: Wadsworth, 1982.
Chapter 12 summarizes the scientific work on human sexual response developed and reported by Masters and Johnson and other researchers.

Masters, William H., and Johnson, Virginia E. *Human sexual response.* Boston: Little, Brown, 1966.
This book is a landmark in sex research. Based on the authors' laboratory and clinical findings, the book documents the physiological reactions of men and women during the phases of the sexual response cycle.

Nowinski, Joseph. *Becoming satisfied: A man's guide to sexual fulfillment.* Englewood Cliffs, N.J.: Prentice-Hall, 1980.
This book is a practical guide for men who have sexual concerns. The book is designed to enhance understanding of sexuality and to aid in dealing with erectile problems, overcoming sexual tension and fear of women, and many other problems.

Raley, Patricia E. *Making love: How to be your own sex therapist.* New York: Avon, 1980.
This well-illustrated sexual self-help guide is intended for the adult reader of any sexual orientation who is interested in maximizing satisfaction in relationships. Systematic guidelines are provided for exploring significant aspects of erotic life.

TRUE OR FALSE?

Sexual behavior exists in very young children.

❦

Children experience a period of sexual latency between the ages of six and twelve during which sexual thoughts, feelings, and interests become dormant.

❦

Sexuality ends during the middle or later years of life.

Sexuality throughout the Life Cycle

CHAPTER 10

Infancy and Early Childhood (Birth to Five Years)
Forms of Sexual and Sensual Expression
Awareness of Roles Based on Gender

Latency: Myth or Fact? (Six to Twelve Years)
Sexual Behavior
Growing Heterosocial Interests

Adolescence (Thirteen to Nineteen Years)
The Adolescent: Child or Adult?
Sexual Behavior

Adult Development
Young Adulthood
Marital and Sexual Adjustment
Transitions in Middle Age
Late Adulthood

Summary

Suggested Reading

Throughout history, humans have assumed that a person's sexuality appeared magically at puberty and came to an abrupt halt during the middle and later years of life. During the seventeenth century, for example, children were viewed as being "sexually innocent" and childhood sexuality was seen as nonexistent. Then, around the turn of the century, Sigmund Freud introduced the notion that children experience sexual urges and engage in sexual behavior and that the most important aspects of development take place during the first few years of life (Murray, 1982). In recent years, however, social scientists have departed from Freudian tradition and have begun to view sexuality as a process that, like other aspects of human growth and development, continues throughout the life cycle.

This chapter will examine sexuality as it unfolds across the life span. Specifically, this chapter will focus on the development of sexual expression across the life span. This approach to understanding the human sexual experience has contributed greatly to a fuller appreciation of the process of sexual "unfolding" that occurs from infancy through childhood, adolescence, adulthood, and later age.

Infancy and Early Childhood (Birth to Five Years)

As we discussed in Chapters 2–4, genetic and hormonal factors have an impact on sexual development from the point of conception to puberty. Environmental and sociocultural variables also have an impact on individual sexual development. The predominant view among social and behavioral scientists is that biological and environmental variables combine to determine our uniqueness as human beings (Meyer-Bahlburg, 1980). There is, however, wide variety with respect to rate of maturation and emotional development, and in many cases it is difficult to isolate the differential impact that biological and environmental variables have on an individual's growth.

Whatever the effect of biological and environmental factors, it appears clear that our "basic sexual identity as male or female; our primary erotic orientation to the same or to the opposite sex; what arouses us sexually or turns us off; our sense of security and comfort as sexual beings; our sexual fears and preoccupations; all these and more are fixed or first established in childhood" (Constantine & Martinson, 1981). Western cultures typically have held the attitude that children are not born as sexual beings and that their exposure to sexual ideas or values should be minimized at all costs. The prohibitive and repressive influence on sexual expression in childhood that results from this attitude has existed for many generations in Western society.

In general, American society has embraced the notion that, during the first two decades of life, sex and love are entirely distinguishable concepts and that sex is evil and forbidden but love is good and encouraged. During the third decade of life, sex then becomes endorsed within the context of marriage and is assumed to result from love. Thus, sexual expression is discouraged among children because it is viewed as unacceptable and is disturbing for parents. Frequently children may be punished for showing any interest at all in sexual matters. In recent times repression of sexuality among young children has become less stringent as parents and society have accepted the idea that sexual expression among children is a healthy, natural sequence of events. In recent years, Western society has developed a somewhat more tolerant attitude toward sexuality in general, and this attitude has led to recognition of the natural forms of sexual expression that begin even during infancy (Currier, 1981; J. L. McCary, 1980).

Forms of Sexual and Sensual Expression

As evidence that sexual development begins early, one can even look to the period of prenatal development. Observers have noted that fetuses sometimes suck their fingers, thumbs, or toes in utero and can be responsive to external pressure or touching. Male babies are frequently born with penile erections, and some evidence shows that female infants experience vaginal lubrication (Murray, 1982). Infants will curiously explore their bodies and occasionally will fondle their genitals. Masturbation is a natural form of sexual expression among infants, and genital stimulation is a source of pleasure and relaxation for many infants. Pelvic thrust movements may be observed in some infants as young as eight to ten months. Many infants and young children have been observed to derive much comfort or satisfaction from sensual experiences such as thumb-sucking and suckling their mother's breast. Early experience involving self-stimulation, as well as the bonding that occurs between child and mother, lays the groundwork for further sexual and sensual development.

The importance of the attachment (pair-bonding) that occurs between infants and their mothers or primary caretakers cannot be overemphasized. If parents hold and cuddle their children and respond to them with affection, sensitivity, and understanding, then their children are likely to develop positive self-images, and their sexual and emotional growth is likely to be secure and healthy. If, on the other hand, parents are insensitive to their children and minimize or discourage physical contact, then children's sexual and emotional growth may be impeded, and their self-image may be negatively affected. Parents can thus provide important influences in the home environment that can shape and mold their children's development and define their realm of experience (Higham, 1980; J. L. McCary, 1980).

As children grow and mature, they will probably make more self-directed efforts at masturbation. Further, by age five, many children are capable of having autoerotic experiences that culminate in orgasm (Kinsey et al., 1948, 1953). Many young children develop the capacity to engage in sensual or sexual fantasies; and, by age five, many children have developed the capacity to relate to others in sensual, intimate, or erotic ways. Clearly, children can have sexual feelings and experience gratification before puberty (Langfeldt, 1981a, 1981b; Martinson, 1980, 1981a; Murray, 1982).

Awareness of Roles Based on Gender

Children's emerging sexuality is not just physical. By age two and three children become aware of their gender and begin to identify with the same-sex parent. Children begin to recognize differences that exist between them and

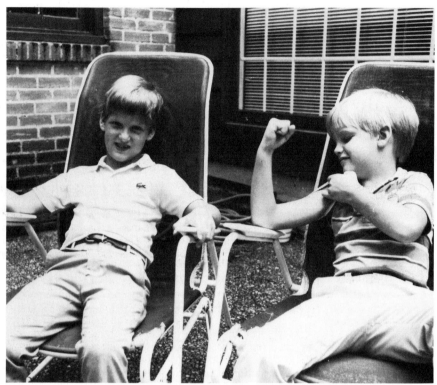

Sexual growth and awareness of gender role continues through childhood. *Larry Hanselka.*

their parent of the opposite sex as well as opposite-sex peers. Even small children may observe the physical differences that exist between themselves and their peers, and they may have an interest in fondling or displaying their genitals to others as well as having others display their genitals. Children often are intrigued by "doctor and nurse" games and become involved in family role-playing games (Gundersen et al., 1981). Thus, children become aware of their "maleness" or "femaleness," and they typically begin to develop the **gender roles** endorsed by the culture.

By late childhood many children play games where they fantasize about being involved in marriage and family relationships. Children may even declare that they are going to marry their opposite-sex parents (psychoanalytic theorists call this the Oedipus complex in boys and Electra complex in girls). Children may experience sexual desire for their opposite-sex parents and develop concerns about how their same-sex parents would react if they were aware of these desires. These early fantasies may be important foundations for children in forming their sexual identities and in establishing that they are accepted and cared for by the opposite sex. Feelings of guilt and anxiety or concerns about leaving out their same-sex parents may prompt children to resolve this initial relationship dilemma (Higham, 1980; Meissner, 1980; Murray, 1982). As chil-

The Seeds of Androgyny

A young boy boldly strolls, legs bowed, across his living room in childish imitation of a figure in a television cowboy show. With a serious gleam in his eye and his hand clenched on his toy pistol, he readies himself for a showdown with his villainous adversary. Then, suddenly he draws his pistol and fires, and in make-believe fashion pretends he has conquered his foe—in this case, his younger sister.

Meanwhile, his sister is oblivious to his commotion. Instead, she is absorbed in playing with her doll and setting up her dollhouse. She won't be bothered by his "silly boy games."

Both children are playing out their gender roles—roles that are approved of and reinforced by parents, peers, and society. Yet, ultimately the effects of these learned roles may not be discerned until the children reach adulthood. For instance, our rough-and-tumble young cowboy may grow up to believe that he is expected to dominate or control romantic and sexual interactions, while our passive and demure young lady may come to expect that she will wait for men to take the dating and sexual initiatives.

Some parents have attempted to modify such rigidly defined gender roles by engaging in "androgynous child-rearing." Such parents strive to select toys for their children that allow boys to become exposed to dolls or cooking utensils and girls some opportunity to play with mechanical games. Boys are taught that it is all right to express emotions, and girls are encouraged to be competitive. Boys and girls see their fathers assuming responsibility for domestic chores and family obligations and their mothers engaging in work and pursuing educational or career objectives outside the home. A blending of gender roles is more likely to occur in androgynous households where rigid or stereotypical male and female roles are abandoned so that the realization of equality between the sexes can be achieved.

Perhaps the present generation of growing young cowboys and young mothers will feel freer to sometimes exchange roles when they become adults and thus expand their conceptions of gender-appropriate role behaviors. Perhaps young cowgirls can grow into more assertive women and young chefs can develop into sensitive and caring men (Murray, 1982).

dren's realms of experience increase and as they gain experience in interacting with peers, the transition to thoughts about other types of relationships occurs.

Children learn sex roles by observing how they are treated differentially by their parents and others. Young girls are touched more frequently by their parents than are boys, and they may learn that it is appropriate for them to express themselves in an affectionate, demure manner. Murray (1982, p. 7) observes, "Girls are cuddled while boys are tossed about and generally receive rougher handling. Pain and crying are discouraged in boy babies while girls are comforted. Mothers of daughters touch and talk to their children more than do mothers of sons."

In recent years, however, gender roles seem to have become more flexible. The social status of the sexes has become more equal, and societal proscriptions regarding appropriate roles for boys and girls have been less rigid. This increased flexibility might allow boys and girls to develop without adopting narrowly defined, stereotypical roles based on gender. Nevertheless, it is true that American society still is not as tolerant of boys deviating from traditional masculine roles—perhaps because society fears that boys might develop homosexual or variant lifestyles.

Latency: Myth or Fact? (Six to Twelve Years)

Freud and his psychoanalytic disciples, as well as psychologists and social scientists of other theoretical orientations, have long recognized that rapid sexual development takes place from birth to age five. However, Freud postulated that sexuality becomes dormant as an area of interest in children between the ages of six and twelve. Freud referred to this period of development as the *latency stage*, and he believed that sexuality does not become a prominent concern again until children experience the hormonal and emotional changes of puberty. Psychological, sociological, and anthropological investigations have revealed evidence strongly suggesting that there is no latency period in sexual development. In fact, evidence indicates that sexual development progressively "unfolds" throughout childhood.

Sexual Behavior

Many children between the ages of five and twelve gain experience with masturbation. Kinsey (1948, 1953) reported that 45 percent of men and 15 percent of women had begun to masturbate by age thirteen. Data reported almost a generation later indicate that 63 percent of men and 33 percent of women begin to masturbate before they reach their teens (Hunt, 1974).

Many children also tend to engage in sexual exploratory activities with same-sex peers, and these homosexual activities are considered to be a normal part of growing up (Murray, 1982). Results of one study of children aged four to fourteen revealed that 52 percent of the boys and 35 percent of the girls had engaged in some homosexual activity (Elias & Gebhard, 1969). That homosexual play among children is likely to occur is not surprising when one considers that the social organization of preadolescent children involves a separation of the sexes—that is, boys tend to socialize mainly with boys and girls tend to socialize mainly with girls.

Children may participate in homosexual activities that include mutual masturbation and displaying and fondling each other's genitals. Boys, for example, may participate in group sex activities such as a "circle jerk," where the members of the group masturbate together. Girls do not appear to be as likely as boys to engage in such group homosexual activities.

Boys and girls often hear about and express interest in sexual intercourse during preadolescence. Many youngsters share sexual information and jokes with their peers (Langfeldt, 1981b), and some may even attempt coitus. Because children often become aware of societal or parental restrictions on their expression of sexuality, they may become more secretive or modest about their sexuality when they are in the company of adults (Gundersen et al., 1981;

Murray, 1982). Children also may become more interested in developing friendships with same-sex peers, and they may temporarily exclude the opposite sex from their play relationships. This camaraderie with one's peers allows the child to further establish a sense of sexual identity and to share with friends thoughts, feelings, and fantasies about social and sexual relationships. Thus, the fact that many preadolescents become responsive to erotic stimuli, engage in more masturbatory and homosexual activity, and begin to anticipate heterosexual interactions argues against the existence of a latency period.

Growing Heterosocial Interests

As children mature there is a growing interest in heterosocial parties and dating. Many preadolescents develop "crushes" on older adults such as teachers, and they frequently develop sexual interest in their opposite-sex peers. They become interested in kissing games at parties, they want to learn how to dance, and their sexual and social interests generally become oriented more toward persons of the opposite sex. They begin to anticipate heterosocial dating activities of adolescence, and they may admire or emulate older siblings and peers who are involved in dating activities.

Perhaps the sexual development that takes place between the ages of six and twelve is not so rapid or intense as during the first few years of life or during adolescence. Nevertheless, the emerging awareness and expression of oneself as a sexual being and the growing attraction to persons of the opposite sex as sources of affection are important processes in the sexual, social, and emotional growth of individuals (Janus & Bess, 1981; Martinson, 1981b).

Adolescence (Thirteen to Nineteen Years)

Accompanying the physical and hormonal changes of puberty is an intensification of emotional, psychological, and social interests in sex. Masturbation provides release for many boys and girls, and homosexual contacts may be a prelude to later heterosexual interactions. Attempts at flirting and attracting the opposite sex become more prominent. Dating and the formation of satisfying peer relationships become more evident. First experiences with coitus occurs for many teens by middle or late adolescence—long after the onset of puberty in most teens.

The Adolescent: Child or Adult?

The first awkward attempts at reconciling the physical changes of puberty with the emotional changes that occur during adolescence provide a transition to more mature, adult relationships (Meyer-Bahlburg, 1980). Reconciling these physical and emotional changes is not any easy task since adolescents are no longer considered to be children and yet are not accepted as mature adults. Adolescents are in a state of limbo because there is now a persistent interest in engaging in sexual activity as well as in forming romantic attachments. Yet, young persons may lack the maturity to make responsible decisions about forming meaningful, satisfying relationships (Meyer-Bahlburg, 1980; Shah &

Adolescence is a time when young people learn more about the opposite sex through dating relationships. *Dianne Baasch.*

Zelnik, 1980). That today's adolescents experience such an awkward transition between childhood and adulthood is ironic because, as Constantine and Martinson (1981) point out, "The most common and media sex objects are in, or barely out of, their teens, nor is this any recent trend, for many of the great sexual romanticists in history and literature involved lovers who were barely teenagers."

Bombarded by such media and social pressure and influenced by hormonal and physical changes, it is no wonder that adolescence is often a period of stress and turmoil. Not only are there pressures to conform to parental and societal expectations and to achieve the acceptance and approval of peers, but conflict and confusion are experienced by many adolescents as they attempt to express the sexual and sensual feelings that have been growing in them since childhood. Further, issues such as premarital pregnancy, abortion, pornography, and sexually transmitted diseases become practical realities for adolescents to consider—realities that present challenges to their value systems. Thus, becoming integrated into society's social structure while finding appropriate means to express one's sexuality is no easy task, even for the most well-adjusted adolescents. Sometimes the problems encountered during adolescence spill over into adulthood, and some may never be resolved completely.

Most adolescents begin to grow socially and emotionally through peer relationships and dating. During the past several decades there has been a trend for adolescents to begin dating at younger ages, so that now for many youngsters dating begins in late preadolescence and early adolescence. Casual dating often begins between ages twelve and fourteen for many youngsters, and through these early dating relationships, adolescents begin to learn more about the opposite sex. As adolescents grow and experience many of the trials and tribulations of the teenage years, there may be a progression from casual dating to dating one person steadily, to "going steady," to being "engaged to be engaged," or even to engagement to be married by late adolescence or early adulthood (J. L. McCary, 1980).

Sexual Behavior

Because of the physical and hormonal changes of puberty, as well as increased societal emphasis on sexuality, adolescent boys and girls experience a heightened awareness of an interest in sexual expression. Teenage males may experience sexual release unconsciously while asleep via nocturnal orgasms or "wet dreams." The incidence of masturbation increases sharply for both boys and girls, particularly during the early years of adolescence. Most boys begin masturbating to orgasm by age fifteen, and they masturbate frequently, typically two or three times a week. Adolescent females, on the other hand, masturbate about once per month (Hass, 1979). Attitudes toward masturbation have changed toward the positive over the last several decades. Most adolescents today do not disapprove of masturbation (Hunt, 1974), and they are not as likely as youngsters of past generations to feel guilty about masturbating (Sorenson, 1973).

Adolescent males and females also find sexual release through homosexual activity with same-sex peers or adults. Current estimates indicate that about 11 percent of adolescent males and 6 percent of adolescent females have had homosexual experiences (Sorenson, 1973). However, teenage homosexual experiences typically are motivated by curiosity and are considered to be a normal part of sexual development. Such same-sex experiences do not seem to be indicative of adult sexual preferences.

As adolescents mature they become more interested in experiencing **heterosexual** petting and coitus, which by late adolescence becomes the primary source of sexual outlet. In addition to increased incidence of heterosexual

Remembering First Sexual Experiences

Two hundred and fifty university students enrolled in an undergraduate marriage, family, and sex education course were asked to describe anonymously how they remembered their first sexual experience. Some of the responses given by the women were these:

- "I felt grown up afterward."
- "I enjoyed it, but I felt a bit guilty."
- "Still waiting for it."
- "It made me feel closer to my partner."
- "Painful and upsetting . . . I didn't understand what was happening to me."
- "Boring, painful, uninteresting, dull, stupid, and embarrassing! Neither one of us knew what we were doing."
- "An innocent discovery."

Some of the responses given by the men were these:

- "It was a special, happy experience, but it happened so quickly that I was unaware of everything that was happening to me."
- "Scary. . . . We were afraid of getting caught, yet it was fun, enlightening, and exciting!"
- "It wasn't very good, and I was afraid of getting her pregnant."
- "Gang-bang! . . . it was purely physical."
- "Disgusting . . . but I was desperate and lonely."
- "I had sex with an older woman who taught me everything there was to know."
- "It was humorous. My girlfriend's mother almost caught us. The whole experience lasted just three minutes."

petting and coitus, adolescents also begin to experience oral-genital contact and use oral-genital techniques in their premarital sexual encounters. Seventy-two percent of the males in the Hunt (1974) study had experienced fellatio before marriage; 69 percent of the females had experienced cunnilingus before marriage.

Adult Development

If individuals have grown in healthy sexual environments from infancy through adolescence, then they probably will be able to experience mature, healthy sexuality in adulthood. However, many inhibiting influences from family, friends, and society may negatively influence sexual growth. Transitory emotional concerns such as guilt and anxiety; physical issues such as disease, injury, or differing levels of sexual desire between partners; life events such as births of children, divorce, or death of a spouse all can have dramatic effects upon adult sexuality. Thus, adulthood also can be viewed as a period of transition and continuing development. Because other chapters in this book are concerned primarily with the sexual attitudes, feelings, and behaviors of adults, this section will examine briefly from a developmental perspective some general issues that influence the experience and expression of adult sexuality.

Young Adulthood

In American society marriage remains the only relationship in which sexual behavior is fully sanctioned by those of all religions, ages, and educational levels. Thus the healthy development and expression of adult sexuality can best occur in marriage since the marriage relationship is fully approved of and endorsed by society. Marriage, however, is not always a smooth course, as evidenced by the recent soaring divorce rate—one divorce for every two marriages (J. L. McCary, 1980). Nevertheless, most people marry, though later in life than in years past (U.S. Bureau of the Census, 1978).

The decision to postpone marriage until later in life means that many young adults experience an extended period of being single. Having achieved independence from parents and no longer constrained by parental limits, young adults usually find that sexual opportunities become more plentiful than during adolescence. Many young adults today prefer to spend their single years searching for the "perfect" sexual and emotional relationship; others prefer to experiment with many sexual partners and enjoy a variety of sexual relationships before "settling down."

Some young adults have not yet resolved the pressing concerns of adolescence. Concerns about sexual self-image and doubts about lovemaking prowess may linger into adulthood. Some young adults may experience conflicts concerning sexual identity and may come to think of themselves as homosexuals or bisexuals.

Young adults may encounter special problems if their chosen values, lifestyles, or modes of sexual expression come into conflict with those sanctioned by society. Adults who choose **homosexual** or **bisexual** life-styles may face unusual difficulties because their sexual preferences continue to meet with societal disapproval. Adults who choose to remain single may face pressures from family and friends who prefer that they marry and have children to "carry on the family name." Adult partners who choose to live together also may face disapproval because they have not chosen to live within the bounds of traditional marriage. Adults who have physical handicaps also have sexual desires and emotional needs that have begun to be recognized and understood only recently by society. Individuals who must cope with such sexual and relationship issues have needs for sexual and emotional expression that in the past at least have met with resistance from others.

Marital and Sexual Adjustment

As we've said, the high divorce rate in the United States and other industrialized nations attests to the difficulty encountered by many couples in attempting to adjust to demands imposed upon individuals by the marriage relationship.

Changing sex roles may lie at the root of some of the friction that has existed between the sexes. Some strain may occur in relationships, for example, when women choose to forego traditional passive roles in order to pursue careers and to achieve social, sexual, and economic equality with men. Likewise, some men are opting to remain at home and become "house husbands," sometimes to the chagrin of family, friends, and society. Many couples actively try to allow for flexibility in their relationships so that they do not adhere rigidly to traditionally defined male and female roles.

Even when the individuals in a relationship make a satisfactory adjustment to their marriage, there are stresses and hurdles for the couple to overcome. The unique, idiosyncratic demands and desires of another person may require of an individual the capacity to change and be flexible. Further, married couples often must adjust to external demands such as those that occur in getting to know and gaining acceptance by new in-laws.

Many adults who marry and have children find that the demands of parenthood may reduce opportunities for privacy and lead to diminished activity or interest in sex. Further, often not until the family is already formed does a couple learn of the financial and emotional burdens that children can bring. Boredom permeates many relationships, and individuals may seek extramarital affairs or "swinging" to add spice to their relationships. Many couples may experience sexual dysfunctions or inadequacies that may have their root in inappropriate or deficient sociosexual interactions during the childhood or teenage years (Gundersen et al., 1981; Langfeldt, 1981b; Murray, 1982). Problems including guilt, shame, fear, and sexual ignorance may complicate the picture and create special strains and pressures for the marriage relationship.

In some marriages sex is almost or totally lacking, and yet affection exists between the individuals in their relationship. In such marriages sex may play an unimportant or even negative role, and sexual relations between the man and woman may occur only a few times a year or perhaps not at all. If the individuals in the relationship find this arrangement to be satisfactory, then they may be happy with a relationship that may be described as platonic. However, for many couples the lack of a regular and happy sex life leads to problems, and thus stress and pressures may occur in the relationship (J. L. McCary, 1980). Many couples experience emotional as well as sexual communication difficulties in their relationships, and they may seek outside expert advice in helping them to resolve their difficulties.

Many couples are able to weather the storms of early relationship difficulties and remain married. By their late thirties, individuals who have coped successfully with the demands of marriage and parenthood are likely to acquire a sense of maturity and satisfaction with themselves and with their lives.

Transitions in Middle Age

The early years of adulthood blend almost imperceptibly into middle age. Indeed many of the personal concerns remain the same. However, concerns often become accentuated during the middle years of life as adults observe subtle changes taking place. Relationships within the family are changing as parents deal with their teenage or young-adult children. Changes occur in self-image as sagging waistlines and graying hair sometimes lead men and women to question their physical and sexual attractiveness. Changes occur in career development and some might leave old friends and loved ones behind as they relocate to new geographical areas or as they climb the corporate ladder of success. Changes in self-image occur in many adults when they become aware that they have left behind their youthfulness and old age looms on the horizon.

These changes of middle age impose demands that require new adjustments. Adults who adapt to the changes that occur in the family constellation find that they continue to maintain satisfying relationships with their growing children. Adults who do not change may find their lives encumbered with additional stress and conflict because others around them continue to grow and change. Adults who accept the physical changes that naturally occur with the aging process and yet exercise and maintain balanced diets are more likely to retain their physical, emotional, and sexual vitality. Adults who deny or ignore these considerations may find they are developing defeatist attitudes toward life and that their overall self-image is deteriorating. Adults who adjust to changes in career demands are more likely to find new challenges and adventures lying ahead. Adults who resist change in career and other aspects of life may find themselves tenaciously clinging to outmoded concepts. Adults who embrace the challenges and joys that each new stage of life can bring will likely find their middle years easier to grow into without experiencing dramatic changes in self-image. Adults who cling to their youth and deny the aging process may find their self-images adversely affected.

Such changes and adjustments can affect how middle-aged adults perceive themselves as sexual beings. Those who make satisfactory adjustments to change can maintain an active interest and participation in sex, while those who regard themselves as "over the hill" are more likely to lose their sexual vitality and interest. Negativistic attitudes toward the self and the aging process are unfortunate. Those who inappropriately or ineffectively try to deny the aging process are engaging themselves in a conflict they cannot win. Those who "flow with" the aging process are likely to have a more enhanced physical, sexual, and emotional self-image.

Thus, adulthood is not a placid, serene state of life that follows the turbulent period of puberty. Adulthood is fraught with its own trials and tribulations requiring changes and adjustments, just as changes and adjustments are characteristic of the earlier stages of life. Those adults who are not afraid to change and grow are better able to cope successfully with the physical and emotional changes that occur in the middle and later years of life. Indeed, sociosexual development is not a static phenomenon; rather, it is a dynamic process that progresses into old age.

Late Adulthood

Crises arising from certain life events can have a profound effect on the self-image of older adults and upon their conception of the roles they are now expected to play in society. Children now have grown up and are no longer dependent; parents and peers may begin to experience problems of physical health or perhaps already have passed away; physiological and emotional changes accompanying menopause or the climacteric may have begun to occur; and the peak of career development may have been reached, with retirement looming as a reminder that one's productive years are over.

Older persons may interpret the inevitable physical changes that accompany aging as evidence that they are losing their ability to function sexually. Further, many older adults believe the culturally reinforced notion that physical, emotional, and sexual vitality are available only to the young and falsely conclude that sexual expression is not available to them. Those who have never particularly enjoyed their sex life may use this cultural expectation as a convenient excuse to stop nurturing their sexual and emotional relationships.

To be sure, problems such as hormonal changes and physical deterioration and disease are more likely to affect people as they age. However, there are also certain benefits that may be enjoyed as people mature. For example, older women reach the peak of their sex drive during their middle and later years and thus are likely to have a greater interest in sex. Older men, on the other hand, do not experience the same degree of urgency to attain sexual release as they did when they were younger (J. L. McCary, 1973). Thus, older men often have a greater physical and emotional capacity to become attuned to the sexual needs and desires of their partners (Laury, 1980). Whether individuals choose to continue to develop their sexual and emotional relationships perhaps depends more on their knowledge and attitudes about sexuality than on the biological correlates of the aging process. However, whether older adults continue to enjoy a satisfying sex life depends to some extent on the degree of sexual activity and interest they expressed during their younger years. In general, those who are sexually active as younger adults will tend to retain their sexual vitality as older adults (J. L. McCary, 1980; Silny, 1980).

The attitudes an individual holds about sex and about life in general often determine the quality of adjustment to later life. Many adults fear growing old and become preoccupied with their illnesses and problems associated with aging. Such individuals are more likely to abandon their sexual lives and to view sexuality as an aspect of living that now has passed. Other older adults have questions about sagging virility or desirability, or they experience boredom and lackluster relationships. Such individuals sometimes turn to extramarital affairs to bolster their egos or to recapture a sense of personal strength and influence. Some older individuals are able to experience healthy and fulfilling sexual and emotional lives as they adjust to the physical and emotional changes that occur across the life span.

For many older adults marital heterosexual coitus remains the chief mode of sexual expression. Additionally, extended foreplay and petting can provide rewarding experiences of intimacy and sexual stimulation for older persons, even if intercourse is not possible (Kirkendall, 1980; Laury, 1980). Some older adults may turn to homosexual relationships in order to gain the emotional warmth and comfort that may be missing from their lives (Calleja, 1967). Other older adults who have lost a partner to divorce or death may seek new emotional and sexual relationships. If such relationships are unavailable, then they may utilize masturbation as an outlet for their sexual tensions. Older adults attempt to cope with isolation and loneliness as do many younger adults, and the need for fulfilling and satisfying sexual and emotional relationships is equally as important in the later years.

Unfortunately, in the past older women have experienced greater difficulty than older men in finding satisfying and fulfilling sexual and emotional outlets. Society has been more tolerant and accepting of sexual expression among older men, and in fact older men often have been viewed as being more sexually desirable than younger men. Older women, on the other hand, often have been overlooked or rejected as being "over the hill" as the attention of society has been directed toward the young and voluptuous woman (Sontag, 1976). This attitude has been unfortunate not only for the older woman but perhaps for the older man as well, because the older woman has experience and sensitivity that the younger woman may well lack. This trend in society may be changing somewhat, however, as older women sometimes engage in social dating with younger men just as older men in the past have turned to dating younger women. During the past several years, society appears to have developed a more liberal attitude toward sexual expression among the young. Perhaps society is also beginning to recognize that older men and women have sexual needs and desires and to accept the right of older men and women to seek sexual expression and fulfillment.

Our sexuality unfolds and develops across the life span. Sexuality does not suddenly appear in childhood, then stagnate during the latency period, then blossom during puberty, then reach full expression in adulthood, and then abruptly end in old age. Rather, sexuality is an integral part of total personality functioning throughout the life cycle. As J. L. McCary (1980) concludes,

> ". . . human sexuality begins at birth and ends at death. It is not a facet of humanity that exists solely during the years from 16 to 60, as some would like us to believe, but is rather as much a part of being a person as breathing is, and lasts just as long as breathing does. The important factor in human sexuality is not *when* but *how*. If one's sexuality is expressed with respect for oneself and one's partner, with regard for the rights of others, and with full knowledge and acceptance of one's responsibilities, it can be one of the most rewarding aspects of a person's life."

Summary

Sexuality is a process that, like other aspects of human growth and development, continues throughout the life cycle.

Biological and environmental variables combine to determine our uniqueness as human beings. Our basic sexual identities are established in childhood and then are reshaped throughout the remaining stages of the life cycle.

It is clear that sexuality is an integral and important part of our lives from the earliest days of infancy. Infants will curiously explore their bodies, fondle their genitals, engage in masturbation, and relate to others in sensual, intimate, or erotic ways. The bonding that occurs between child and primary care-giver(s) lays the groundwork for further sensual and sexual development.

Children's emerging sexuality is not just physical. By age two or three children become aware of their gender and begin to identify with their same-sex parent. Children become aware of their "maleness" or "femaleness," and they typically begin to develop the gender-appropriate roles endorsed by the culture. By late childhood many children play games where they fantasize being involved in marriage and family relationships. They may even express a desire, for a brief period, to marry their opposite-sex parent.

Between the ages of six and twelve children are said to be in the latency period of development. However, sexual development and interests are hardly dormant during this period. Children gain experience with masturbation and engage in sexual exploratory activities with same-sex and opposite-sex peers. While sexual development during this age period may not be as rapid or intense as during early childhood or adolescence, sexual growth and change continues.

In adolescence, the physical and hormonal changes of puberty occur. Adolescents also become more interested in dating and in forming satisfying peer relationships. First experiences with adult forms of sexual expression, including coitus, may occur. Adolescents are in the position of being neither children nor adults, and finding appropriate means for expressing sexuality is no easy task. Conflicts also may arise in dating relationships because adolescent boys and girls differ in their interests and desires for sexual and affectional expression.

After the difficult times of adolescence, sociosexual development continues into adulthood. Some adults face special problems if they choose to live nonmonogamous or nontraditional life-styles. Even those who choose to live within the traditional context of marriage face concerns such as adjusting to the idiosyncratic demands of another person, gaining acceptance by in-laws, adjusting to the births of children, dealing with boredom that may permeate their relationships, and facing sexual dysfunctions or inadequacies.

During the middle and later years, one's children have grown up, physical problems are more likely to arise, and retirement looms as a reminder that one's most productive years are passing. The attitudes individuals hold about sex and about life in general often determine the quality of adjustment they will experience in later life. Older adults attempt to cope with isolation and loneliness as do many younger adults. The need for fulfilling and satisfying sexual and emotional relationships continues through the later years.

TRUE OR FALSE: THE FACTS

Sexual behavior exists in very young children.
True. Infants will explore their bodies and occasionally fondle their genitals; they masturbate; they derive comfort and satisfaction from thumb-sucking and suckling a mother's breast. (*177*)

Children experience a period of sexual latency between the ages of six and twelve during which sexual thoughts, feelings, and interests become dormant.
False. Children between six and twelve have sexual interests: they masturbate; engage in sexual exploratory activities with same-sex peers; and, as they approach adolescence, gain interest in heterosexual interactions. *(180–181)*

Sexuality ends during the middle or later years of life.
False. Adults whose self-image allows them to embrace the challenges of every new stage of life can continue to remain sexually active throughout their life. *(187–189)*

SUGGESTED READING

Brecher, Edward. *Love, sex and aging: A consumer union report.* New York: Random House, 1982.
This myth-shattering report on sexuality and aging reveals the sexual behavior and relationships of 4,000 American men and women past the age of fifty.

Constantine, Larry L., and Martinson, Floyd M. (Eds.). *Children and sex: New findings, new perspectives.* Boston: Little, Brown, 1981.
Consisting of articles by several leading contributors, this book presents the latest information concerning children and sex. Some topics include children's sexual behavior and development, sex in the family, and effects of childhood sexual experiences.

Gadpaille, Warren J. *The cycles of sex.* New York: Charles Scribner's, 1975.
The author approaches human sexuality from a developmental perspective, examining sexuality as it unfolds across the life span.

Morrison, Eleanor S., Starks, Kay, Hyndman, Cynda, and Ronzio, Nina. *Growing up sexual.* New York: D. Van Nostrand, 1980.
Based on anonymous autobiographical papers by students, this unique book tells in students' own words their feelings, thoughts, and experiences of sexual development. Topics include learning about sex, first sexual experiences, family styles, sex roles, self-image, contraceptive use, sexual exploitation, and personal sexual values.

Murray, Linda. *Childhood sexuality.* Washington, D.C.: American Association of Sex Educators, Counselors and Therapists, 1982.
This brief (thirty-six pages), easy-to-read booklet charts the unfolding of sexuality in children from before birth to the preadolescent years and discusses issues relevant to childhood sexuality.

Silny, Ann Johnson. Sexuality and aging. In B. Wolman and J. Money (Eds.), *Handbook of human sexuality.* Englewood Cliffs, N.J.: Prentice-Hall, 1980.
This essay reviews the research literature on sexuality and aging and discusses the changes in sex-related characteristics in men and women as they advance in age. The author outlines the main changes in sexual physiology, behavior, and attitudes among the elderly.

TRUE OR FALSE?

Religion has a direct negative impact on sexual attitudes and behavior.

❦

Parents today expect their children to adhere to a sexual ethic more conservative than they themselves hold.

❦

The difference in incidence between male and female premarital sexuality has not changed, indicating that the sexual double standard continues as strong as ever.

❦

Postmarital sexual activity still appears to be relatively uncommon.

CHAPTER 11

A Climate of Attitudinal Conflict and Change

Religious and Racial Influences on Sexual Attitudes

Attitudinal Formation in Young People

Forms of Sexual Expression

Masturbation

Nocturnal Orgasm

Heterosexual Petting

Heterosexual Intercourse
Premarital Heterosexual Intercourse
Marital Heterosexual Intercourse
Extramarital Sexual Behavior
Postmarital Sexual Activity

Summary

Suggested Reading

Some psychotherapists hold that the way we think about or "talk to ourselves" about life events determines how we will respond to those events. Indeed, our sexual attitudes and behaviors are greatly influenced by our beliefs, thoughts, and perceptions regarding sex. When sexual attitudes and behavior are seriously out of phase, some irrational thought process may be involved. In other cases, a discrepancy between attitudes and behavior may be the result of a lag between changes in attitudes and beliefs and changes in behavior (Ellis & Harper, 1976; Maultsby, 1975; Zastrow, 1979).

Of course the demands and expectations of a particular culture, as well as differences within the culture, also produce a wide variety of attitudes toward sex. It comes as a surprise to many Americans to learn, for instance, that their condemnatory views on premarital and postmarital sexual activity are not shared by the majority of the world's cultures. Indeed, many religious teachings of Eastern sects, Islam, Judaism, and segments of Christianity endorse the experiencing of sexual pleasure outside marriage as well as in marriage (Bullough, 1980). Anthropological investigations have consistently found that cultures that encourage women to be completely free in their sexual expression produce women who are as uninhibited as men. Cultures where there is approval of women having orgasms produce women who have orgasms. Cultures withholding such approval produce women who are incapable of orgasm (Kronhausen & Kronhausen, 1965).

People in every culture are inclined to cling to their traditional ways of thinking and behaving, whether in political, religious, or sexual matters. Reluctance to accept change or to be swayed by outside influences, however rational or beneficial, is found not only within cultures but within subcultures as well.

All cultures place restrictions on the sexual expression of their members to some extent. Restrictions vary widely from culture to culture, and psychoanalytical theorists believe that a sexual need not expressed in one manner *will* be expressed in another. Much of a person's behavior might be influenced by the inhibition and consequent displacement of sexual needs into other channels. For example, we are consciously disturbed by the thought of premarital or extramarital sexual relationships, yet we are excessively interested in them. Consider how many of us express horror over the less than conventional behavior of certain luminaries in the entertainment world, yet voraciously consume every account of it, however exaggerated.

We might satisfy our own desires, conscious or unconscious, by identifying with these people. At the same time, by pointing an accusing finger at them, we avoid self-guilt. Tensions accruing from the denial of our own desires are thus drained off through great interest, joking, and laughter (Ellis, 1958). Certainly no sensible person suggests that control and appropriate expression of our sexual needs according to time and place are unnecessary. But to establish unrealistic and unreasonable prohibitions, whether directly or through the mechanism of guilt, is to set the stage for trouble now or later.

During the last twenty years, there has been a growing liberalization of sexual attitudes and less adherence to the double standard. *Randy Matusow.*

A Climate of Attitudinal Conflict and Change

Recent research indicates that the incidence of sexual *activity* among young adults has increased, primarily in heavy petting and sexual intercourse within relationships of deep emotional involvement. The most significant change by far, however, has been a growing liberalization of sexual *attitudes* and less adherence to the double standard (Bauman & Wilson, 1976; Howat et al., 1979).

Changes in premarital sexual behavior and sexual attitudes are particu-

The Sexual Revolution

The pioneering research of Alfred Kinsey and his team of investigators in the 1940s and 1950s remains a landmark in the scientific study of sex. The data collected by these scientists first pointed clearly to the vast difference existing in American society between officially sanctioned sexual behavior and what is actually practiced. More recently, Morton Hunt has applied the greater sophistication and understanding of methodological issues gained during many years of sex research to produce what is widely considered to be the most thorough and accurate investigation since the work of Kinsey. In his study of sexual behavior in the 1970s, Hunt attempted to study the same behaviors classified by Kinsey, although in greater detail. The results of this recent investigation are particularly valuable when contrasted with the data obtained by Kinsey nearly twenty-five years ago. Such a contrast provides an interesting picture of how the sexual behavior of American men and women has changed (or remained the same) during the last twenty-five years. Following is a summary of the major findings of the two studies from the late 1940s and early 1970s, presented in tabular form. Readers can thus determine for themselves whether the so-called "sexual revolution" of the 1960s and 1970s has actually occurred.

Masturbation

	Kinsey	Hunt
Males		
By age 13	45%	63%
Ever	92%	94%
Females		
By age 13	15%	33%
Ever	62%	63%

Premarital Sex

	Kinsey	Hunt
Oral sex		
Female to male (fellatio)	15–20%	72%
Male to female (cunnilingus)	14%	69%
Intercourse		
Males, by age 25	71%	97%
Females, by age 25	33%	67%

Oral Sex (Marital)

	Kinsey	Hunt
Fellatio		
Noncollege males	61%	54%
College males	59%	61%
Noncollege females	46%	52%
College females	52%	72%
Cunnilingus		
Noncollege males	16%	56%
College males	51%	66%
Noncollege females	50%	58%
College females	58%	72%

Conclusions

Interpretation of these data reveal several important conclusions about sexual behavior since the time of Kinsey:

1. Men and women begin masturbating earlier in life.
2. Both men and women are more accepting of oral sex before marriage.
3. The incidence of premarital heterosexual intercourse has increased, especially among women.
4. Anal intercourse and oral sex in marriage have gained acceptance.
5. Extramarital sexual intercourse has *not* increased significantly, except among younger women.
6. The incidence of overt homosex-

Intercourse (Marital)

	Frequency per week (median)	
	Kinsey	Hunt
Age		
16–25	2.45	3.25
26–35	1.95	2.55
36–45	1.40	2.00
46–55	.85	1.00
56–60	.50	1.00

Anal Intercourse

Kinsey		Hunt	
		Have experienced anal intercourse	
	%	*Age*	%
Never tried	89	under 25	25
Tried successfully	3	25–35	25
Have experienced	8	35–44	14

Extramarital Sex

	Kinsey		Hunt	
Age	% *Male*	% *Female*	% *Male*	% *Female*
Under 25	39	8	32	24
25–34	38	19	41	21
35–44	34	20	47	18
45–54	31	18–20	38	12
54 and over	30	18–20	43	15

Homosexuality (incidence of any overt homosexual experience)

	% Male	
	Kinsey*	Hunt
Ever during lifetime	37	20–25
After age 15	25	12–13
Predominantly or exclusively after age 15	4	2–3

	% Female		
	Kinsey*	Hunt	
		Single	*Married*
Only while single	26		
Only while married	3		
Ever during lifetime		20	10–11
After age 15		10–12	3
Predominantly or exclusively after age 15	1–2	2	less than 1

* Several contemporary sex researchers have criticized Kinsey's data, suggesting that methodological errors resulted in highly inflated incidence figures. Downward adjustment of incidence figures to allow for these errors leads to figures that more closely approximate Hunt's findings.

ual behavior in both men and women has remained about the same.

Sources:
Kinsey, Alfred C., Pomeroy, W. B., and Martin, C. E. *Sexual behavior in the human male.* Philadelphia: Saunders, 1948.
Kinsey, Alfred C., Pomeroy, W. B., Martin, C. E., and Gebhard, P. H. *Sexual behavior in the human female.* Philadelphia: Saunders, 1953.
Hunt, Morton. *Sexual behavior in the 1970s.* Chicago: Playboy Press, 1974.

larly pronounced among young adult women. Many women have become clearly conscious of their sexual urges, and a majority of college women engage in heavy petting and approve of premarital coitus when love or a meaningful relationship exists between partners. A substantial number engage in premarital intercourse. In fact, a majority of both men and women find premarital coitus acceptable. A change in sexual attitudes within the general populace has also been apparent in the last few years. Sexual topics are discussed more freely in the various communication media, schools, churches, and governmental circles—as well as by the person on the street.

Many people who are unaccustomed to casual conversation on sexual topics fail to understand that talk and action are not necessarily the same. Attitudes—and ease in discussing them—are not to be confused with behavior. Rather, inconsistency between sexual attitudes and sexual behavior is still very much a part of the American culture. Young people, among whom the change in behavior is reputed to be the greatest, are themselves confused about the discrepancy between talk and behavior. The majority of college women in one study, for example, stated that their female classmates "slept around." In actual fact, only 20 percent of all college women at that time were experiencing premarital intercourse. Results of another study (Rubinson et al., 1981) showed that college students tend to overestimate the sexual activity of their peers. In fact, more conservative behaviors and less sexual activity reported by some college students today may indicate that the "sexual revolution" of the past fifteen years is waning.

Research data from the middle 1970s suggest that the double standard may disappear in the 1980s. The question asked by college students today is not so much whether coitus should occur before marriage, but in what kind of relationships it should occur. A stable, affectionate dating relationship—today described as "going together" or living together—rather than a formal engagement is the usually accepted norm for engaging in premarital coitus (King & Sobel, 1975; Howat et al., 1979). Hunt (1974) showed that, depending upon the degree of a couple's affection or emotional involvement, up to 84 percent of men thought premarital coitus was acceptable for males, and up to 81 percent considered it acceptable for women. Although less permissive, women (up to 73 percent of them) condoned male premarital coitus; up to 68 percent considered it acceptable for women.

Although several studies made in the 1970s revealed that only 65 percent to 75 percent of college males had actually experienced premarital coitus, up to 88 percent considered it acceptable behavior (Howat et al., 1979). Factors affecting this permissive attitude were race, age, semester in college, strength of religious beliefs, and region of the country. Although as many as 80 percent of college women approved of premarital coitus, less than 60 percent actually engaged in it (Davis, 1971; Howat et al., 1979).

One of the most significant social changes in recent years has been the movement to provide equal opportunities for women in American society. The freedom and equality that women are demanding—and, to some extent, receiving—have had a profound effect upon prevailing sexual attitudes. Most women today are unwilling to accept the notion that they are subject to different sexual standards than men are. They view the pleasures and responsibilities of sex as being equally applicable to both sexes (R. R. Bell, 1971a).

Furthermore, evidence indicates that men and women who are involved in equitable relationships are more satisfied with their relationships as well as their overall lives than are men and women who are involved in inequitable interactions. Men and women who feel equitably treated by one another also tend to be more satisfied in their sexual interactions and relationships overall than do men and women who feel inequitably treated by one another (Hatfield et al., 1982).

To be sure, certain differences between the sexual attitudes of the two sexes have continued to be forged by such factors as childhood rearing, societal expectations, and certain physiological forces. In addition, the struggle for equality has produced an interesting side effect: the sexual attitudes of American women in recent decades often have been considerably healthier than those of American men. Researchers and clinicians have found that women are far more open and honest in supplying personal sexual data than men are. Rubinson et al. (1981) suggest that women may be more truthful in discussing their sexual behavior with their peers. Men frequently become entrapped in questions of self-esteem and may attempt to compensate through boasting for what they feel is a threat to their self-image. As a consequence, the data they provide are often unreliable.

Religious and Racial Influences on Sexual Attitudes

In the past, almost all studies on the subject showed that intensity of religious belief greatly influenced sexual attitudes and actual behavior. The influence of religion on sexuality has at times been detrimental. Larsen et al. (1980) have observed that adherents of intense religious doctrines often preach the benefits of love, understanding, and tolerance, while in fact they frequently practice rejection, punishment, and intolerance. Other investigations into this subject have shown that it is *not* religion per se that influences sexual behavior, but sex-related guilt built up in certain individuals as a result of some religious training and experiences (Ogren, 1974; Primeau, 1977). Some researchers have suggested that sex anxiety, which may or may not be related to sexual guilt, might be the important factor that influences behavior (Janda & O'Grady, 1980). Whether the conceptualization is in terms of guilt or anxiety, however, it seems that those people who conduct their lives according to the philosophy of the Golden Rule rather than the dictates of strict "thou shalt nots" have the more mature, better-adjusted, more fulfilling sex lives.

Research studies have consistently shown that blacks have a more active sex life before marriage and begin it earlier than whites (Reiss, 1970; Shah & Zelnik, 1980). However, any person who is concerned about real or apparent differences between blacks and whites should never forget the endless variables between social groups that make it almost impossible to isolate "blackness" or "whiteness" as a contributing factor in measured differences. Studies have pointed out that *apparent* differences between whites and blacks are related not to skin color but to general attitudes of liberality or conservatism in other areas, such as politics, economics, religion, and marriage (Reiss, 1974).

While religious and racial factors per se do not seem to affect sexual attitudes and behavior, general cultural influences, such as those related to social class and educational group, are important in forming them. For example, lower-class youngsters have premarital coitus at an earlier age and with greater frequency than upper-middle-class youth; and college women have a more liberated sexual attitude than do lower-middle-class women. College women are more likely to plan premarital coitus and to use effective birth control methods.

Attitudinal Formation in Young People

Many changes in sexual attitudes are due to the protracted period of adolescence imposed on today's youth. Our society requires longer periods of scholastic and vocational training than ever before, although today's youth become physically mature at an earlier age. Thus, the period of social adolescence is now approximately twice as long as it was a hundred years ago (R. R. Bell, 1971a).

During this prolonged period of social adolescence, the two sexes begin to develop divergent attitudes toward premarital sexual activity. "Sex appeal" is presented by the media as a means to instant popularity, success, admiration, and security. Young men, whose heightened sex drives are paced only by their feelings of adolescent insecurity, are particularly susceptible to the idea that their masculinity is measured by their success in seduction. The further they go sexually, the more masculine they are in their own and their peer group's eyes.

Young women, on the other hand, become indoctrinated with the importance of being "sexy." They are lured to purchase an often ludicrous conglomeration of products guaranteed to increase their sexual attractiveness. To a maturing young woman, the push to be "sexy" and at the same time to be "good" often causes considerable confusion and conflict. Like her male counterpart, the adolescent female is unsure of herself and of her sex role.

Youngsters thus can come to feel that their worth is determined by their ability to perform well in certain narrowly defined sex roles. A woman's recognition becomes dependent upon her beauty, while a man's desirability is equated with his physical power or success. These attitudes become firmly entrenched; over 80 percent of men report that sexual attraction is a distinct factor in their selection of a partner, while only 50 percent of women look for sexual attractiveness in a prospective mate (Greene, 1970).

Young teenagers tend to accept the traditional sexual standards of their parents uncritically. But as they grow older and begin to evaluate those standards, they become influenced by outside values, particularly those of their peer group (R. R. Bell, 1971a; Reiss, 1961). They might reject the preachments of their parents and adopt a more permissive code of sexual behavior. Teenagers also learn from their peers how to keep from being "found out" and thus avoid parental or societal wrath. Sensible parents should anticipate these pos-

Is There Moral Decadence among Our Youth?

Since the beginning of recorded history, older generations have been in a state of shock over the supposed immorality of the younger generation. About 2,400 years ago Socrates wrote:

Children now love luxury. They have bad manners, contempt for authority. They show disrespect for elders and love chatter in place of exercise. Children are now tyrants, not the servants of their household.

And in the eighth century B.C., the Greek poet Hesiod wrote:

I see no hope for the future of our people if they are dependent on the frivolous youth of today, for certainly all youth are reckless beyond words. . . . When I was a boy, we were taught to be discreet and respectful of elders, but the present youth are exceedingly wise and impatient of restraint.

Parents have wondered about the morality of youth apparently since the beginnings of humankind. After all, with their energy and vitality—and their inexperience—youth frequently challenge many societally accepted attitudes, values, and behavioral standards. In a departure from the age-old pattern, however, today's more conservative sociopolitical climate might temper parents' concerns about the ideas and activities of their youth. Perhaps the parents themselves—who were raised in a different sociopolitical era—are more liberal. Perhaps today's youth are questioning whether there is moral decadence among their parents.

sibilities and acquaint their children with a realistic code of ethical behavior, a code that will retain its validity after the children have left the home and its direct influence. The edict "don't do it because you will be punished" simply will not hold over the years.

Suppression or control of teenage sexuality is a dubious goal when one considers that many men and women who experience difficulty reaching orgasm as adults also were not orgasmic earlier in their lives. Thus it may be important that parents encourage their teenage sons and daughters to seek responsible, healthy means of sexual expression rather than attempt to discourage them from acting on their sexual desires by threats of punishment. Children are less likely to become sexually active if their family relationship is close, accepting, and loving. Girls who get along well with their fathers and mothers are less likely to become sexually involved than those who do not. Daughters who come from unhappy homes have less stable and less gratifying relationships with their male partners than girls from happy homes and, further, have more sex partners (Kirkendall & Libby, 1969; Shah & Zelnik, 1980).

There is frequently a marked discrepancy between the past (or present) sexual behavior of parents and the code of sexual ethics that they profess to their children. One study found, for instance, that 46 percent of men and 31 percent of women find heavy petting acceptable for adolescents. Yet, 93 percent of the men and 76 percent of the women in the sample had themselves experienced heavy petting prior to marriage. In this same sample, 28 percent of men and 18 percent of women reported they find sexual intercourse acceptable for adolescents. However, 84 percent of the men and 61 percent of the women said they had experienced sexual intercourse prior to marriage. (In contrast, 52 percent of the women in the sample said masturbation is acceptable, whereas only 32 percent of the women stated they engaged in it.) These data generally indicate that parents apply more conservative standards in evaluating what is acceptable and normal for their children (Wyatt and Stewart-Newman, 1982).

The Wyatt and Stewart-Newman study is especially pertinent since psychotherapists have long observed more regret among women who remained virgins until marriage than among those who did not. Several investigations have shown that those women who have had premarital coition are not sorry, and they maintain that they would repeat their behavior if they had it to do over again (R. R. Bell, 1971a; Kinsey et al., 1953). They expect their daughters, however, to conform to a more conservative ethic.

Forms of Sexual Expression

In discussions of human sexuality, it becomes apparent that sexual behavior is determined by many physiological, psychological, and social influences. The degree of **sex drive** in an individual and his or her expression of that drive are intricately influenced by all these factors. The desire and ability for sexual expression therefore vary widely among men and women. Individual variations in sex drive are common in people of the same sex and age and in the same person at different times in life.

To some extent, sex drive is influenced by age. A young man in his teens ordinarily has a very strong sex drive and is capable of almost instant erection; four to eight orgasms a day are not unusual. He may be ready for another orgasm only seconds after his first one. He usually desires sexual release whether or not he has any emotional attachments and whether or not he is occupied with other matters, such as school or sports. If no sexual partner is available, he will achieve sexual release through masturbation and nocturnal emission.

As a man approaches his thirties, he remains highly interested in sex, but the urgency is less acute, and he is satisfied with fewer orgasms. Erections still occur quickly and recede slowly, but by his late thirties it may be thirty minutes or more before he is capable of another orgasm after his first one. Sexual slackening continues through the forties. By age fifty, the average man is satisfied with two orgasms a week, and they are usually no closer together than eight to twenty-four hours. At this age, the focus of sexual pleasure has usually shifted from an intense, genitally centered sensation to a more generalized, sensuously diffused experience (Kaplan & Sager, 1971).

There is far more individual variation among women than among men in the development of sexuality. Typically, women's sexual awakening is a slower process, not reaching its peak until the late thirties or early forties. In their thirties, and frequently after childbirth, women begin to respond more intensely to sexual stimulation and to initiate the sex act more frequently. The incidence of extramarital sex is greatest among women in their late thirties. Vaginal lubrication—the equivalent of male erection so far as sexual response is concerned—occurs almost instantly for women in this age group, and many experience multiple orgasms. Levels of sexual desire among women are probably higher than many would have thought (Hite, 1976). Results of a recent study (Wilcox & Hager, 1980) indicate that many women desire more frequent sexual relations than they are actually experiencing.

Human sexuality expresses itself most commonly in any of five ways: masturbation, nocturnal orgasm, heterosexual petting, homosexual relations, and heterosexual intercourse (Kinsey et al., 1948, 1953). (A sixth way, sexual contact with animals, is so rare that we shall not discuss it here.) Typically, the individual finds outlets for sexual feelings through several different forms of sexual behavior. The level of a person's formal education and the degree of religious commitment may influence both the amount and the forms of sexual expression chosen.

Masturbation

Any type of self-stimulation that produces erotic arousal may be considered masturbation (Kinsey et al., 1953). It is a practice common among both men and women in marital and nonmarital states. Boys and girls begin the practice at an early age. Many boys first begin masturbating between ten and twelve years of age. Boys usually begin masturbating at earlier ages than girls (Cowart & Pollack, 1979), although many girls report having their first experiences with masturbation between the ages of five and ten (Hite, 1981). Thirteen percent of both sexes in Kinsey's sample had masturbated by their tenth birthday (Kinsey et al., 1953). In addition to providing a means of self-discovery and sensory awareness, masturbation also provides a form of sexual relief for those who do not have sexual partners.

Kinsey (1948) found that 95 percent of men admitted to having masturbated to orgasm at some time in their lives. Almost all the men sampled in Hite's survey (1981), regardless of marital status, regularly engaged in masturbation. Other studies have shown that more men with college training have masturbated than men with high-school or grade-school education. A little more than two-thirds of all boys experience their first ejaculation through masturbation, and about three-fourths of them learn how to masturbate from verbal or printed sources (R. R. Bell, 1971a; Kinsey et al., 1948). On the average, adolescent boys masturbate about 2.5 times a week, although many may masturbate from 4 to 7 or more times a week. Some men continued to masturbate on a sporadic basis throughout adult life (Ford & Beach, 1966). Many men experience their most intense orgasms during masturbation.

Masturbation is second only to heterosexual petting among the erotic activities of unmarried young women, and it is second after coition among married women (Kinsey et al., 1953). Of all the types of sexual activity among women, masturbation is the most successful method of reaching orgasm—a climax is reached 95 percent of the time (Hite, 1976; Kinsey et al., 1953). Furthermore, women reach orgasm more quickly through masturbation than through any other sexual technique—three-fourths of all women reach orgasm in under four minutes. The majority of all women masturbate at one time or another in their lives, whether or not they are aware of it. Many women do not recognize that indirect, pleasurable stimulation of the genitals, in behavior such as squeezing the thighs together or riding horseback, can be considered a form of masturbation. The range of frequency of masturbation among women is from once or twice in a lifetime to 100 orgasms an hour. Of those women who masturbate to the point of orgasm, however, the frequency is usually once every two to four weeks, regardless of age or marital status.

In contrast to men, the incidence of masturbation to orgasm increases among women up to middle age and then remains fairly constant (Kinsey et al., 1953). Most women prefer to masturbate by genital manipulation, while a few others employ thigh pressure, muscular tension, or simply fantasy without physical stimulation. More than half the women who masturbate invariably use erotic fantasy to accompany their physical stimulation, and a few others use fantasy only occasionally.

Women who have previously masturbated to orgasm have been found to be far more likely to reach orgasm during coitus in the first year of marriage than women who have never masturbated to orgasm before marriage. Women who are devoutly religious are less likely to masturbate than are others (Hunt, 1974; Kinsey et al., 1953).

Nocturnal Orgasm

It has long been recognized that men experience **nocturnal orgasm** or "wet dreams." Women also have erotic dreams that frequently culminate in orgasm; although, since they do not ejaculate, they do not have nocturnal emissions.

Almost all men have experienced erotic dreams, and almost 85 percent have had dreams that end in orgasm. Erotic dreams occur most frequently among young men in their teens and twenties, but approximately half of all married men continue to have them. The incidence of nocturnal emission, unlike other forms of sexual behavior, bears little relationship to religious affiliation or strength of religious conviction.

Nocturnal orgasm among women is much more common than is usually supposed. As many as 70 percent of the women in Kinsey's sample (1953) had dreams of sexual content, although only about half report having had dreams culminating in orgasm. The incidence of sexual dreams to orgasm reaches a peak among women in their forties. There is no correlation between frequency of nocturnal dreams to orgasm and a woman's religious or educational background.

Heterosexual Petting

Heterosexual petting refers to sexual contact between men and women that does not culminate in intercourse (Kinsey et al., 1953). There is a distinct correlation between the frequency of petting and educational level. Men with the least formal education pet the least; men of the middle group are next; and college men pet most of all.

Almost all married women have had some sort of petting experience prior to marriage, and 90 percent of the entire female population, whether or not they ever marry, engage in petting at one time or another. Women who have attained an advanced level of education engage in heavier forms of petting than do less-well-educated women.

Like most other forms of sexual behavior in women, petting is significantly related to religious background. The more pronounced the commitment to a religion, the more restricted the sexual behavior. Interestingly, however, religion ultimately has little influence, one way or the other, on frequency of petting to orgasm, even among the most religiously devout. Once religiously devout women reach orgasm through petting, they engage in this sexual activity as often as less devout women (R. R. Bell, 1971a; Kinsey et al., 1953). Highly religious men and women are more likely to experience oral-genital sex before they experience sexual intercourse (Mahoney, 1980).

Oral-genital contact, a form of petting that has been more slowly accepted than others, is now widely utilized as an erotic outlet by the majority in the higher socioeducational groups. Even in the 1940s, at the time of the early Kinsey studies, about two-thirds of the younger women at the upper educational levels who had experienced coitus more than twenty-five times prior to marriage had also experienced oral-genital stimulation; slightly fewer of these women had orally stimulated the genitals of their partners. These percentages have risen significantly since the Kinsey studies were conducted. For instance, one study shows that over 90 percent of the married people twenty-five years old and younger have participated in both fellatio and cunnilingus (Hunt, 1974).

Heterosexual Intercourse

The average man or woman is more interested in coitus with a member of the opposite sex than in any other type of sexual outlet, although other methods are significant in the lives of both sexes. Coitus is traditionally thought of in terms of a marital relationship, but three other forms are important to a discussion of the subject—premarital, extramarital, and postmarital intercourse.

Premarital Heterosexual Intercourse

Premarital intercourse commonly refers to coition between two single persons, although the term is also used to describe the experience of the single partner in coition between a single person and a person who is married to someone else (Ehrmann, 1961). As discussed earlier, American culture still generally accords more latitude in sexual expression to men than to women.

American males are more sexually permissive and active than ever before; but the rate at which both their attitudes and behavior have relaxed is considerably below that of American women. The difference in incidence has gradually—and, at times, dramatically—narrowed. The fact that differences remain between the sexes with respect to premarital coitus is undoubtedly based on the fact that female sexuality is still suppressed, despite the social changes of the past several decades.

Kinsey's studies (1948) found that 98 percent of men with a grade-school education, 84 percent of men with a high-school education, and 67 percent of men with a college education had had sexual intercourse before marriage.

Recent estimates (Francouer & Hendrixson, 1980) indicate that over 50 percent of American adolescents between the ages of fifteen and nineteen are sexually active. The Hunt study (1974) revealed that premarital sexual experience has increased among college men. By age seventeen, for example, half those males who eventually went to college had experienced premarital sex, more than double the Kinsey figures. Even among the noncollege men of this age group, there was an increase, although much smaller, in premarital coitus. Of course, since Kinsey's college sample experienced less premarital coitus than the noncollege men did, the greater increase would be expected in the first group. College men today tend to have intercourse with a woman whom they love or care for deeply rather than with a prostitute or casual pickup, as their fathers would have done. College men are now faced at a somewhat earlier age with the necessity for integrating their sexual attitudes and behavior, their emotional feelings, and their standards of appropriate conduct (Davis, 1971).

The incidence of premarital sexual intercourse among men may range from the extremes of a single contact to thirty-five or more coitions a week (the latter pattern sometimes persisting for as long as five years or more). Many men, particularly those at the upper end of the socioeducational scale, limit their premarital coition to one woman—often the woman they eventually marry. Other men, particularly at the lower end of the socioeducational scale, may have sexual intercourse with as many as several hundred women (Kinsey et al., 1948).

In the Kinsey study in the 1940s, young women with little education were found to begin coital activity at an earlier age than women with more education. Between the ages of sixteen and twenty, 38 percent of the grade-school educated, 32 percent of the high-school educated, and about 18 percent of the college educated had had premarital intercourse. Of all women who have premarital intercourse, about half have only one partner, and only 13 percent have six or more partners. About one-third have from two to five partners. Since the attractive woman has more opportunity to engage in coitus, she is more likely to have premarital intercourse and to have a larger number of sex partners (Kinsey et al., 1953).

While a small percentage of women attending college and living away from home have coition in the college town, by far the greater number have it in their hometowns during visits and vacations. The first coital experience for both men and women is typically with someone near their own age whom they have known for some time. It quite likely takes place in the young woman's home, her partner's home, or the home of a relative or friend and is usually remembered without regret (Shah & Zelnick, 1980).

Today, the marked increase among women in both incidence and frequency of premarital coitus causes far less surprise and shock among the general public than it did two decades ago. For example, little concern was expressed over a *Redbook* survey of 100,000 women showing that 90 percent of those under age twenty-five had experienced premarital intercourse (Levin, 1975). Shah and Zelnik (1980) report that the trend of increased premarital intercourse among women is continuing. Further, the age at which women first experience intercourse is dropping.

Marital Heterosexual Intercourse

According to the legal and moral codes of our Anglo-American culture, coitus between husband and wife is the one totally approved type of sexual activity. Although intercourse is the sexual outlet most frequently utilized by married couples, the sexual relationships in at least one-third of all marriages have been found to be inadequate to some degree (R. R. Bell, 1971a). Masters and Johnson (1970) have set the figure as high as 50 percent. An unsatisfactory sexual relationship in marriage usually generates other problems, partially because so much is expected of sex. On the other hand, problems in nonsexual areas of the marriage can generate problems in the sexual relationship.

Men's sex drive is usually somewhat greater than that of women during the early years of marriage among younger age groups. Such may not be the case among individuals who marry or remarry later in life. Nevertheless, as a group, husbands desire sexual intercourse (or at least report that they desire it) more frequently than their wives do. Results of the Hite survey (1981) confirm that men, regardless of marital status, want more intercourse than they actually experience. Further, men report that they want intercourse more for the emotional and physical closeness and enhancement of a "sense of male identity" it brings than for orgasm per se. Fifty-two percent reported they had coitus two to three times weekly, 41 percent reported having coitus four to eight times monthly, and the remaining 7 percent experienced the extremes of daily or little or no coitus (Hite, 1981).

Among less educated people, the belief exists that men are much more highly sexed than women and that a woman's sexual gratification is less important than a man's. According to this belief, the woman's gratification comes from knowing that her partner has been satisfied. College educated women and increasing numbers of others hold that women have as much right to sexual fulfillment as their partners. These women are consequently more satisfied with their sex lives than less educated women. In contrast to men with less education, highly educated men are sensitive to the sexual needs of their wives. Among men with some college education, 82 percent express concern for their partner's satisfaction, in contrast to a mere 14 percent of men with no college education (Masters & Johnson, 1966).

Practically all married women participate in sexual intercourse, although there is a gradual decline in frequency after the first two years of marriage. The frequency of intercourse declines more among women than among men with advancing years. Curiously, marital coition is the only form of sexual outlet among women that undergoes such a decline with advancing age (Kinsey et al., 1948, 1953). This decline in frequency is puzzling in light of research findings that women reach their peak of sexual desire between the ages of thirty-one and forty. It is probably the aging of men that causes the decrease in women's marital coital frequency, since men's sexual drive peaks between the late teens and the age of twenty-five and thereafter shows a steady decline (Kinsey et al., 1953).

The decline in frequency of marital intercourse after the first two years of marriage does not, of course, necessarily imply that interest in other forms of sexual activity declines. The incidence of masturbation and nocturnal dreams involving orgasm increases after marriage, remaining fairly steady at its maximum level until women become sixty years of age or even older.

A decline in marital satisfaction was noted in another *Redbook* study (Levin & Levin, 1975). Eighty-two percent of women who had been married less than one year rated sex with their husbands as "good" or "very good," while 68 percent of women married one to four years rated marital sex as "good" or "very good." The percentage of women expressing satisfaction with marital sex leveled off at 67 percent among women married five years or longer. Pietropinto (1980) reports research that supports these percentages.

Early investigations (Kinsey et al., 1953; Terman, 1938) concluded that more than 15 percent of all women regularly respond with multiple orgasms; it is a capacity naturally existing in all women (Masters & Johnson, 1967). The reason more women do not experience multiple orgasms can be traced to sexually ignorant or indifferent male partners, or to misconceptions held by the women concerning their sexual capacity and what is "normal" in sexual behavior.

There is little evidence that aging produces a decline in the sexual capacity of women. Apparently, women struggle with some success through the early marriage years to throw off inhibitory shackles forged by the taboos of their early sex education. Once they reach their maximum sexual peak, they maintain this level. By this time, however, the husband's interest in sexual intercourse typically begins to slacken. The unfortunate result is often all-round frustration, which frequently leads the wife to seek other means of sexual gratification.

While the amount of education a woman has appears to be highly significant in many areas of sexual activity, it does not appear to be a factor in the frequency of marital coitus. The incidence of orgasm in coition increases during the later years of marriage for all educational levels, but the incidence is consistently greater among women with higher education.

Extramarital Sexual Behavior

Extramarital sexual behavior customarily means **adultery** to most people. In this discussion it will refer to nonmarital sexual intercourse between a man and woman, at least one of whom is married at the time to someone else.

For men, the frequency of extramarital coitus decreases with age, but for women, both the frequency of extramarital coitus and the percentage of total outlet that it represents increase with age. Recent research indicates, however, that the incidence of extramarital coitus has increased for young women under age twenty-five (Williams, 1980). Because of society's attitude toward extramarital affairs, the participants will usually go to rather extreme lengths to hide or deny their adultery. As a result, it is difficult to arrive at the true incidence and frequency of extramarital coition. Even psychotherapists find their patients are reluctant to admit to adulterous conduct, despite the confidential nature of the therapeutic relationship. Notwithstanding the conscious or unconscious motivations in infidelity, both men and women generally rate marital sex as being more pleasurable than extramarital sex, although both rate extramarital coitus as pleasurable. Inexperience, guilt, or anxiety may be factors that lead individuals to perceive extramarital sex as being less satisfying than marital sex (Williams, 1980).

The shift in present-day ethical values suggests greater leniency of attitudes toward both premarital and extramarital sexual activity. Yet social, religious, and even legal condemnation remain strong enough that adultery is often destructive of a marriage (Williams, 1980). A large sample of college students at a midwestern university during the 1970s continues to express negative and conservative attitudes toward extramarital coitus, indicating that a sexual revolution with respect to this behavior is not likely to occur in the near future (Howat et al., 1979).

A recent study of politically liberal, well-educated young men and women of high socioeconomic status revealed that men who seek extramarital coitus usually begin their affairs sooner after marriage than women do. The first affair occurs within five years of marriage for almost three-fourths of the men and for more than half of the women. Hite (1981), in her survey of over 7,000 men, found that 16 percent experienced extramarital sex during their first year of marriage and 23 percent during their first two years. It is noteworthy that once women begin to have affairs, however, they have extramarital intercourse with about the same frequency as men.

Almost three-fourths of all married men admit to at least an occasional desire to have an extramarital affair, and a conservative estimate is that from 50 to 75 percent of them actually do have extramarital coitus at some point during their marriage (Ellis, 1972; Kinsey et al., 1948; Terman, 1938). Men of lower education have more extramarital coitus during the early years of marriage than men of other educational levels, although the less educated men become involved in extramarital intercourse less often as their marriages continue. Among college educated men, however, the incidence of extramarital intercourse increases with advancing years.

Seventy-two percent of the men in the Hite (1981) sample who had been married for two years or more had experienced extramarital sex. Further, the majority of the men had not told their wives of the affairs. Most men believed their affairs had had no real negative impact on their marriages. Most men said they loved their wives and did not intend to leave their wives for a new lover. Men typically cited a boring or unsatisfactory sex life at home as reason for seeking extramarital adventure.

Among white American married women, 7 percent have had extramarital intercourse by age twenty-six, and 26 percent by the age of forty (Kinsey et al., 1953). While it is generally accepted that the incidence of married women having had extramarital coitus has increased significantly since Kinsey's time—perhaps doubling his figure of 26 percent (Athanasiou et al., 1970)—the incidence found varies considerably from study to study. Again, whether or not one will admit to adulterous affairs depends largely on the confidence one has in the therapist or researcher.

Almost a third of all college-level women have had extramarital intercourse by the age of forty, whereas only about one-fourth of those in the same age group with only grade-school or high-school education have had similar experiences. About half of all women who have extramarital coitus believe that their husbands know of it or suspect it. When these figures are added to the percentage of wives whose husbands have no suspicion whatever of their wives' affairs, it indicates that for about three-fourths of the adulterous wives no marital difficulty develops because of their activity (Kinsey et al., 1953).

Of those women who experience extramarital coitus, more than two-thirds also experienced premarital intercourse. A large percentage of those women who have not had extramarital coitus state that they do not expect to do so, but more than half of those who have had extramarital intercourse intend to renew their activity (Kinsey et al., 1953).

One survey (Levin, 1975) showed that 33 percent of all married women have had extramarital coitus, with a positive correlation between length of marriage and the likelihood of its occurrence. Most of those having affairs are full-time wage earners, and about half reported being happy with their marriages and with marital sex. A recent survey (Gittelson, 1980) found that 33 percent of the female respondents acknowledged having been "unfaithful." Many of these women expressed the opinion that their affairs had had the effect of strengthening their marital relationships. In fact, the majority of those who have had an extramarital affair are not in retrospect distressed by the experience to the extent that they would not repeat the behavior in similar circumstances.

Postmarital Sexual Activity

Little research has been done on the subject of postmarital sex—that is, of men and women who are separated, divorced, or widowed (S-D-W). Most of the studies done were conducted among men and women who were quite old and therefore do not reflect the accurate incidence of postmarital behavior in the general population. In one early study of S-D-W women carried out by the Kinsey Institute (Gebhard et al., 1958), 76 percent of the separated, 73 percent of the divorced, and 72 percent of the widowed reported continuing coitus after their marriages terminated; such sexual patterns are therefore the rule rather than the exception. (Almost 20 percent of these women became pregnant in the postmarital period.)

Given the liberalization of sexual attitudes and behavior of recent years, it is expected that today the S-D-W women (and men)—especially the younger groups—will continue their sexual activity on a regular basis after a reasonable period of adjustment to their new roles. Further, since most divorces occur during the early years of marriage, it is likely that many people are opting for postmarital sexual experiences (Glick, 1980).

Summary

Our sexual attitudes and behaviors are greatly influenced by our beliefs, thoughts, and perceptions regarding sex. Cultural demands and expectations, as well as religious teachings and doctrines, also help shape our attitudes toward sex. One aim of growing up in a society is to learn how to express sexuality appropriately, without the burden of unreasonable prohibitions or excessive anxiety and guilt.

During the past two decades, there has been a growing liberalization of sexual attitudes and a decreasing adherence to the double standard. Changes in attitude toward premarital coitus, anal intercourse, erotically explicit material, and oral-genital sex have become evident. Particularly significant is the emergence of women in a more equal position in American society. Despite this revolution in attitudes and behavior, there appear to be few supporting reasons for the opinion of a growing moral decadence among today's young people.

Investigations of the impact of religious and social influences on sexual attitudes have shown that religion per se does not have a negative impact on sexual behavior, but that sex-related guilt acquired as a result of religious training and experience may affect behavior. Racial factors do not appear to have causative influence in the emergence of different sexual attitudes and behavior; however, social and educational factors appear to have such a causative effect.

The influence of the peer group and the sexual imagery found on TV programs also influence attitude formation in young people. Young women grow up believing that attractive appearance is the key to recognition, while young men learn that physical power and/or success are the indicators of male desirability.

Parents can play a vital role in shaping their children's sexual attitudes and perceptions by promoting close, accepting, loving family relationships. However, parents sometimes go to the other extreme by expecting the children to conform to a sexual ethic even more conservative than that of the parents.

The common forms of sexual expression include masturbation, nocturnal orgasm, heterosexual petting, homosexual relations, and heterosexual intercourse. The degree of sex drive differs from person to person and depends upon factors such as age, physical well-being, and psychological circumstances. Men experience the peak of their sex drive in the late teens or early twenties with a gradual decline in sex drive thereafter. Women typically do not reach the peak of their sex drive until the late thirties or early forties.

Masturbation is a common sexual practice among both males and females in premarital, marital, or postmarital states. An overwhelming majority of men masturbate at some time during their lives. Most women masturbate at one time or another in their lives, and, in contrast to men, the incidence of self-stimulation to orgasm increases up to middle age and remains fairly constant thereafter.

Erotic dreaming, often accompanied by nocturnal orgasm, is another form of sexual outlet for men and women. Together with orgasm, men experience nocturnal emissions or "wet dreams." Women also report having dreams that culminate in orgasm.

Heterosexual petting is a form of sexual expression enjoyed at one time or another by most men and women. Oral-genital contact is a form of petting now practiced by many people.

Heterosexual intercourse—whether it is premarital, extramarital, or post-marital—is the sexual outlet of greatest interest to both men and women. Premarital heterosexual intercourse—coition between two single persons—has increased in the United States. American males are more sexually permissive and active than ever before, but the difference in incidence between male and female premarital sexuality has narrowed, indicating that the sexual permissiveness and activity of females has increased at an even more rapid rate. Men today more frequently choose to have coition with a woman whom they love or care for deeply than with a prostitute or casual pickup. Socioeducational and other factors influence the degree of premarital sexual activity in both sexes.

Heterosexual intercourse within marriage is an approved type of sexual activity according to the legal and moral codes of our culture. Nevertheless, it is estimated that up to 50 percent of marital sexual relationships are unsatisfactory. Highly educated men tend to be more sensitive to the sexual needs of their mates than less educated men. Both sexes experience marital coitus less frequently in later life, with a steeper decline among women. Since they reach the peak of their sexual desire between the ages of thirty-one and forty while men reach their peak between the late teens and age twenty-five, it is probably the aging of men that leads to this decrease in women's marital coital frequency. The incidence of nocturnal dreams involving orgasm and masturbation increases after marriage for women, remaining fairly steady until they become sixty years of age or older.

Extramarital sexual intercourse, or adultery, refers to coitus between a man and a woman, at least one of whom is married at the time to someone else. Generally, the frequency of extramarital coitus decreases with age for men while it increases with age for women. Perhaps 50 percent of men and 25 percent to 33 percent of women become involved in extramarital sexual intercourse at some point in their marital lives.

Postmarital sexual activity, or the continuation of sexual activity by men and women who are separated, divorced, or widowed, is probably common —especially since the liberalization of sexual attitudes and behavior in recent years.

TRUE OR FALSE:
THE FACTS

Religion has a direct negative impact on sexual attitudes and behavior.
False. Religion itself does not influence sexual behavior but rather certain religious training and experience might build up sex-related guilt. Some adherents of intense religious doctrines practice intolerance while preaching love, understanding, and tolerance. (*199*)

Parents today expect their children to adhere to a sexual ethic more conservative than they themselves hold.
True. Parents expect their children to adhere to a certain code of sexual ethics, which they profess to their children, although it might be opposed to their own past sexual behavior. (*201–202*)

The difference in incidence between male and female premarital sexuality has not changed, indicating that the sexual double standard continues as strong as ever.
False. Changes in premarital sexual behavior and sexual attitudes are especially pronounced among women; there is less adherence to the double standard. (*196–197*)

Postmarital sexual activity still appears to be relatively uncommon.
False. Although little research has been done, in one early study, approximately three-fourths of the women who were separated, widowed, or divorced reported continuing coitus after their marriages ended. (*210*)

SUGGESTED READING

DeLamater, John, and MacCorquodale, Patricia. *Premarital sexuality: Attitudes, relationships, behavior.* Madison, Wisconsin: University of Wisconsin Press, 1979. This book presents a comprehensive analysis of contemporary premarital sexuality based on results of a large-scale survey.

Hass, Aaron. *Teenage sexuality: A survey of teenage sexual behavior.* New York: Macmillan, 1979. Reporting large-scale survey results, this book reveals teen attitudes, feelings, and experiences related to a wide range of topics in sexuality.

Hite, Shere. *The Hite report: A nationwide study on female sexuality.* New York: Macmillan, 1976. This best-selling book reports results of a national survey of female sexuality. Though not scientifically precise, the report reveals interesting descriptions by women of their sexual attitudes, feelings, experiences, and behavior.

Hite, Shere. *The Hite report on male sexuality.* New York: Alfred A. Knopf, 1981. This book is the companion volume to the original *Hite report.* Though lacking in scientific precision, the survey reveals interesting descriptions by men of their sexual feelings and experiences.

Hunt, Morton. *Sexual behavior in the 1970s.* Chicago: Playboy Press, 1974. Based on conclusions drawn from an extensive national survey, this book provides statistical information on the sex lives of American men and women as well as analyses and interpretations of the data.

Kinsey, Alfred C., Pomeroy, Wardell B., and Martin, Clyde E. *Sexual behavior in the human male*. Philadelphia: Saunders, 1948.
This book is the first of the famous Kinsey reports and a pioneering study of human sexual behavior. Its data point clearly to the vast difference existing in American society between officially sanctioned sexual behavior and what is actually practiced.

Kinsey, Alfred C., Pomeroy, Wardell B., Martin, Clyde E., and Gebhard, Paul H. *Sexual behavior in the human female*. Philadelphia: Saunders, 1953.
This book is the companion volume to the epic study of male sexual behavior published five years earlier by the Kinsey group. This survey contains findings on female sexual behavior as well as comparative data on female and male sexual behavior.

McCary, James Leslie, and McCary, Stephen P. *McCary's human sexuality* (4th ed.). Belmont, Calif.: Wadsworth, 1982.
Chapter 15 consists of a thorough review of American attitudes toward sex. Chapters 14, 16, and 19 are directly related to the study of sexual behavior.

TRUE OR FALSE?

Women who have strong sex drives, come to climax easily, and are capable of multiple orgasms are nymphomaniacs.

A transvestite and a transsexual are the same, and both are homosexuals.

Sex molesters of children are usually under sixty-five years of age.

Sexually arousing materials (erotica) have a corruptive effect on people's minds and behavior, especially children's.

Rape is a crime that results from uncontrollable sexual lust.

CHAPTER 12

Variance in Methods of Sexual Functioning and Quality of Sexual Striving
Sadism
Masochism
Exhibitionism
Scopophilia and Voyeurism
Troilism
Transvestism
Transsexualism
Gender Identity Disorders of Childhood
Variance in Choice of Sexual Partner or Object
Pedophilia
Bestiality
Pornography and Obscenity
Fetishism
Incest
Mate-Swapping
Variance in Strength of Sexual Drive
Nymphomania and Satyriasis
Promiscuity
Prostitution
Rape
Summary
Suggested Reading

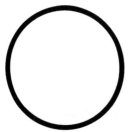

ne major problem in the field of sexology today—and, indeed, in the entire realm of mental health—centers on the question of what is "normal" sexual behavior and what is "abnormal" sexual behavior.

Many people are ready to stigmatize as perverted any sexual activity that deviates from their own sexual behavior. Yet in the course of human history, sexual practices and ethics have varied widely within and among different cultures (Tannahill, 1980). What is usual in one culture may be unusual and branded abnormal in another, although unusual sexual behavior is not perverted simply because it is out of the ordinary for a given culture.

Many terms have been used by the public and by professionals to describe sexual behavior that differs from the norm: sexual abnormality, deviation, aberration, perversion, and variance. The American Psychiatric Association, in its *Diagnostic and Statistical Manual of Mental Disorders*, employs the term *paraphilia* to describe disorders in which "unusual or bizarre imagery are necessary for sexual excitement" (DSM III, 1980). True sexual abnormality is difficult to define and pinpoint. Hence, the term *variance* may be the fairest word to use since it is the one that seems least emotionally charged or suggestive of disapproval. It should be noted, however, that many sexual thoughts, feelings, and behaviors may be merely atypical or unconventional. Thus even the term *variance* may be inappropriate in many instances.

It is possible for individuals to label themselves "perverted" simply because they lack basic knowledge about what conventional sexual behavior really is. They consequently believe that their fantasies and behavior, or the frequency of either, deviate markedly from the norm (Everett, 1971). When individuals do engage in truly abnormal sexual behavior on a continuing, compulsive basis, however, the behavior might be unrelated to sexual needs. Rather, the behavior could reflect deep-seated personal problems and could be an ongoing attempt to meet personal needs that actually are unrelated to sex. Pharmacologic treatments used in conjunction with psychotherapy can often be effective in helping disturbed individuals control or modify their behavior (Money, 1981; Money & Bennett, 1981).

Sociologists and other behavioral scientists have recently begun to view sexual variance as a social process rather than a social disease (Denfield & Gordon, 1970). Society seems to be progressing toward a more liberal definition of what constitutes normal sexual activity. Generally speaking, many authorities in the field believe that if the sexual behavior is not harmful to the participants, if it is carried out by consenting adults who are willing to assume all responsibility for their acts, if it is without any sort of coercion, and if it is out of sight and sound of unwilling observers, the behavior should be considered acceptable, whether or not others would care to participate in similar acts. These criteria serve as a valid basis on which to judge what is and is not variant sexual behavior.

Sexual variance may be said to fall into three categories: (1) variance in the method of sexual functioning and quality of sexual striving; (2) variance in the choice of the sexual partner, either person or object; and (3) variance in the degree of desire and strength of the sexual drive (Thorpe et al., 1961).

Variance in Methods of Sexual Functioning and Quality of Sexual Striving

Sadism

Sadism is a sexual variance in which the disturbed person gains sexual gratification, or at least an increase in sexual pleasure, by inflicting either physical or psychological pain upon his or her sexual partner. The aggressive act has no purpose except to secure sexual gratification (DSM III, 1980). Sadism appears to be a rare form of sexual expression in our society. Only 2.5 percent of the respondents of the Hunt study (1974) reported having any sadistic experience during the previous year.

The causes of sadism are as varied as the means of expressing it. A person may have been taught, consciously or unconsciously, to have disgust for anything sexual. Because normal sexuality is unacceptable, the acts of cruelty are a punishment of the partner for engaging in something so shameful. In a man, another source of sadism is fear of castration (feelings of inferiority); the sadistic acts reassure the sadist that he is more powerful than his partner and therefore need have no fear.

Whipping, biting, pinching, and slapping are typical acts of the sadist. Sometimes, of course, normal sexual expression includes lightly biting, pinching, and scratching during sex play; but if these acts are not motivated by cruelty or the desire to inflict pain, they do not reflect sadism. When such actions are of a violent, hostile nature and are the goal of the sexual act itself, they would be called sadistic. If sadism is expressed verbally, it is in the form of sarcastic remarks, belittling, threatening, teasing, or bullying.

Masochism

Masochism is the mirror image of sadism. The person receives sexual pleasure or gratification from being hurt, physically or mentally, by the sexual partner (DSM III, 1980).

Masochism, like sadism, develops from an attitude of shame and disgust toward normal heterosexual relationships, but it is much more common than sadism. Masochists use the pain and punishment inflicted on them to wash away the guilt associated with sexual desires. In other cases, they dominate the partner through the ability to endure punishment—which, in their way of thinking, proves their strength and superiority and also serves to make them the center of attention. Often, the sexual partner is identified with a parent figure who dominated them during childhood. For example, the masochist may remember experiencing sexual excitement in childhood while being beaten, a sensation centered in the erogenous zones of the skin and muscles about the buttocks. In most cases, it appears that the masochist is so fearful of rejection that he or she is willing to be subjected to almost any humiliation or punishment that will please the partner and win affection and acceptance (Coleman, 1972). This aberration may also take the form of mental masochism wherein the individual seeks out mental rather than physical suffering.

Pain per se is not what the masochist, or even generally the sadist, wants. To the sadomasochist (S/M), accidental pain is neither sexual nor pleasurable; it must be "planned pain." The S/M typically follows an elaborate script wherein the partner has allegedly done something for which he or she must be punished. The confrontation of "evil-doing" is followed by a period of threat and suspense, then by punishment (Gebhard, 1976).

Exhibitionism

Exhibitionism is a variance in which sexual gratification is derived from exhibiting the genitals to unwitting (and typically unwilling) observers. Occasionally an individual will masturbate while exhibiting himself (DSM III, 1980).

It is considered abnormal because sexual satisfaction is gained in a vicarious manner rather than through a straightforward sexual experience. A relatively common sexual problem, exhibitionism is involved in 35 percent of all arrests for sexual violations (DSM III, 1980). Far more men than women are exhibitionists, although just how many women do actually exhibit themselves is impossible to determine.

This behavior begins, classically, with the exhibitionists' feelings of insignificance or inadequacy; they hope to gain the notice they crave through exhibition. The usual male exhibitionist is a quiet, timid, submissive individual who lacks normal aggressiveness and who is beset with feelings of inadequacy and insecurity. He is usually described as being "nice" but immature. Characteristically, he was reared in a family atmosphere of overstrict and puritanical attitudes toward sex, and his formative years were dominated by a powerful, engulfing mother. The most common age for the onset of exhibitionism is during a man's early or middle twenties. Later onset of exhibitionism may reflect major emotional disturbances such as dementia, alcoholism, psychosis, or depression (Bastani, 1980; DSM III, 1980). Despite the fact that most of these men are married, their sexual relationship is likely to be a poor one.

Since the exhibitionist obviously hopes his actions will have a profound shock effect on the viewer, the woman who responds hysterically to his behavior merely feeds his disturbance. If one is confronted by an exhibitionist, the most sensible approach is to ignore his behavior calmly, possibly suggesting that he seek psychological help.

It should be remembered that the exhibitionist is more of a nuisance than a menace. He rarely becomes involved in more serious crimes, and when he does, his criminality is classically of a nonsexual nature. The exhibitionist seldom exposes himself while he is close to his victim. He chooses, rather, to remain at a safe distance—usually 6 to 60 feet away (Gebhard et al., 1965).

Pseudoexhibitionism is often confused with true exhibitionism. Pseudoexhibitionists are under stress, because heterosexual relations are not available, and they exhibit themselves only as a poor substitute for the preferred sexual intercourse.

Nudism is regarded by some as a variance because they erroneously link it with exhibitionism. Social nudism, however, is not a sexual deviation. As a matter of fact, the overall atmosphere in most nudist camps is, because of rigidly enforced rules of behavior, more suggestive of asexuality than of sexual permissiveness (M. S. Weinberg, 1971). The average nudist is also the average citizen, although he or she may be freed of certain taboos to which the rest of us still cling.

Scopophilia and Voyeurism

Scopophilia and **voyeurism** are disturbances in which the viewer of sexual acts and erotic material derives unusual pleasure and gratification simply from looking. Scopophilia refers to sexual pleasure gained from observing sexual acts and genitalia; voyeurism is the scrutinizing of nudes. The voyeur (commonly called a "Peeping Tom") usually does his or her viewing secretly. In efforts to observe the sexual activity or nude bodies of others, they peer through windows, or may go to such lengths as to bore peepholes through walls and doors of toilets, dressing rooms, and guest rooms. Only a small number of women are known to be voyeurs. According to FBI reports, nine men to one woman are arrested on charges of "peeping."

Like other sexually variant behaviors, these are believed to develop as defense mechanisms against what the individual feels is a threat to his or her self-esteem. By engaging in surreptitious examination of sexual details, rather than in more overt sexual behavior, they guard against any personal failure in sexual activity while at the same time enjoying a feeling of superiority over those whom they secretly observe.

The desire to view the naked body of one's sexual partner is certainly normal; so also is the pleasure a couple experience in viewing themselves by way of mirrors in the act of coitus itself. Viewing becomes abnormal only when it is consistently preferred to petting or sexual intercourse, or when it becomes a compulsive act (DSM III, 1980).

Troilism

Troilism (also *triolism*) is the sharing of a sexual partner with a third person who may participate in the sexual interaction or who may simply look on. It may involve two couples having sexual relations at the same time in sight of each other. Threesomes usually involve two members of one sex and one member of the other sex, but homosexual triangles also may occur. Even in predominantly heterosexual triangles, however, bisexuality may be involved. In any case, troilism is far more prevalent among men than among women: men usually instigate the behavior pattern and derive the greatest pleasure from it—at least initially. Perhaps the most significant problem that can arise in threesomes centers on the feelings of isolation and jealousy that might occur in the individual who might be temporarily excluded from the focus of the interaction (Frank, 1980).

Transvestism

Transvestism, or *cross-dressing*, refers to excitement or gratification, either emotional or sexual, derived from dressing in the clothes of the opposite sex (DSM III, 1980). The practice usually begins in childhood and is often brought about by parental rejection of the child's sex. The "petticoat punishment" of attempting to humiliate a young boy by forcing him to dress in girls' clothing may backfire and instead cause him to pursue cross-dressing (DSM III, 1980; Krueger, 1980).

Most transvestites engage only in normal and acceptable sexual activities, their strange dressing habits on "special occasions" being their only variance. Most of these people are able to make a satisfactory adjustment to sex and marriage, especially when they receive understanding and cooperation from their marriage partner.

Authorities agree that the majority of transvestites are not homosexual. The majority of transvestites are heterosexual males, typically married and often fathers (Krueger, 1980; Wise & Meyer, 1980). In one study of male transvestites, only 25 percent admitted having had a homosexual experience to the point of orgasm at least once in their lives (Benjamin, 1967). This figure is especially interesting since Kinsey found that 37 percent of all men have had at least one homosexual contact to the point of orgasm (Kinsey et al., 1948). Transvestism, furthermore, is typically a secret pursuit involving only one person; homosexuality obviously must involve two people. The homosexual must reveal himself as a homosexual in order to attract a partner, while the transvestite has no such need to reveal his transvestism.

There is considerable difficulty in estimating what the true number of transvestites is, since perhaps 90 percent keep their cross-dressing habits a secret. Estimates vary, but transvestism exists in 1 to 3 percent of the population (Krueger, 1980).

The pattern of cross-dressing varies among male transvestites. In one instance, women's apparel is worn only periodically. In another, the man has a fetishlike fondness for a particular article of women's clothing—such as panties or a brassiere—which he habitually wears under his own masculine clothing. In yet another, the yearning to wear women's finery may be so deeply ingrained that the transvestite discards men's clothing entirely to embark upon a lifelong masquerade as a woman.

Treatment of transvestism includes psychotherapy, especially the use of aversive conditioning techniques. However, the majority of transvestites do not seek treatment, and those who do often do not benefit much from the therapeutic experience (Wise & Meyer, 1980).

The transvestite is seldom a transsexual as well. In fact, the majority establish normal heterosexual relationships and would cringe at the suggestion of a sex-transformation operation.

Transsexualism

Transsexualism, also called *sex-role inversion*, is a phenomenon in which an individual's sexual anatomy and his or her sex role (gender identity) are incompatible (Green & Money, 1969). With few exceptions, the transsexual is genetically a male. He possesses normal male genitals, internally and externally; and he is capable of impregnating a woman. In no instance is the difference between the *sex* assigned by nature and the **gender identity** acquired through social conditioning more dramatically demonstrated than in the transsexual. The man knows that he is a male, yet he rejects his maleness totally. Not content with dressing as a female, as the transvestite is, he wishes to go all the way and live the life of a woman—emotionally, physically, sexually. The male sex organs become such hated objects that attempts at self-castration or suicide are not uncommon among transsexuals.

The causative factors of transsexualism appear to be much the same as those of transvestism and homosexuality. The transsexual's mother is typically an unhappy woman who engages her son in an intensely close relationship from which the father and the other children in the family are excluded. Thus, one of the most common predisposing factors to transsexualism is a troubled parent-child relationship (DSM III, 1980).

There are an estimated 10,000 transsexuals in the United States, and about 3,000 to 4,000 have undergone sex-reassignment surgery. Until recently, American transsexuals had to go to Europe or Casablanca for such an operation. American hospitals and clinics that perform the operation do so only after exhaustive consideration of each applicant. In order to receive sex-conversion surgery, the male transsexual must have lived as a member of the opposite sex for a considerable time and must have undergone female hormonal treatment. It is significant that persons approaching such operations—which involve, in a man, the removal of testicles and penis, leaving sufficient skin to form an artificial vagina—very rarely get "cold feet" and back out. Their determination to shed the appendages of their hated genetic sex is that strong.

Many doctors shrink from what is to them a mutilation of the human body. But all forms of psychotherapy have been singularly unsuccessful in helping these people who, in company with the transvestite and homosexual, are notably resistant to change. Since the transsexual's mind cannot be made to adjust to his body, the only sensible and humane course to follow is to make the body adjust to the mind.

Although sex-conversion surgery has been performed on a few females, the procedure is much more complicated and less esthetically and functionally successful than it is in the case of male transsexuals.

Transsexuals may have a previous sex history that is asexual, homosexual,

Dr. Richard Raskind before sex change operation. *Wide World Photos.*
Dr. Reneé Richards after sex change operation. *United Press International.*

or heterosexual in character. Those transsexuals with previous homosexual experiences or arousal patterns may claim, however, that their sexual behavior was really heterosexual since they were women in their mindset. Other transsexuals have never had any intense sexual feelings, and still others have had extensive heterosexual experiences (DSM III, 1980).

Typically, a man will undergo transsexual surgery because he wishes to be loved as a woman by a "straight" man. He does not wish to be loved by a homosexual, whose love object is another man. He is firmly convinced that some cruel caprice of nature has imposed upon him the body of a male and the emotionality and mentality of a woman.

Reports of individuals who have undergone sex reassignment surgery have become more known to the public in recent years. One story has recounted the life of an individual who served seventeen years in the Navy and later, after sex reassignment surgery, joined the Army as a woman. The individual reportedly was married twice as a man and fathered a child in his first marriage. Nevertheless, the individual elected to undergo a sex change operation at the age of thirty-seven (Shearer, 1981).

Gender Identity Disorders of Childhood

A child who expresses an extreme distaste for his or her sexual identity will often identify strongly with the other sex. Such a child may deny or repudiate his or her sexual organs and insist that he or she will grow up to be the other sex. Not unexpectedly, such a child will often experience social conflicts or ostracism by his or her peers. A boy who exhibits this disorder may be interested in playing *only* with dolls or dressing up in girls' clothing; a girl who exhibits this disorder may be interested in playing *only* sports or in identifying with traditional male roles.

Excessive emotional and physical closeness between a male infant and his mother, with the relative lack or absence of a father figure, may lead to gender identity problems for a boy. Lack of or absence of a mother figure in the early life of a female infant may cause her to excessively identify with her father and thus lead to gender identity problems for a girl. While gender identity disorders of childhood appear to be rare, such disorders, when they do occur, initially manifest themselves before a child's fourth birthday (DSM III, 1980).

While most children with gender identity disorders eventually acquiesce to social pressures and give up their identification with the opposite sex, a small number of boys and girls remain in conflict over their gender identity and grow up as transsexuals. Up to one-half of boys, and a lesser percentage of girls, who exhibit gender identity disorders as children may become aware of a homosexual orientation by the time they reach adulthood (DSM III, 1980).

Variance in Choice of Sexual Partner or Object

Pedophilia

Pedophilia is a form of sexual variance in which adults derive erotic pleasure from relationships of one form or another with children. Pedophilic practices include exposure of the genitals to the child and manipulation and possible penetration of the child. Of all sex offenders, about 30 percent are classified as pedophiles, most of them being men. This group is usually less aggressive and forceful than rapists, although public outrage against them is often stronger.

Many child molesters are mentally dull, psychotic, alcoholic, and asocial. Most are between the ages of thirty and forty years, the average being thirty-seven (Coleman, 1972; DSM III, 1980; McCaghy, 1971). Child molesters direct their sexual interests toward opposite-sex children twice as frequently as toward same-sex children (DSM III, 1980). Older offenders typically seek out very young children, while younger offenders usually concentrate their attention on adolescent girls.

The child molester is among the world's most feared and despised men. He is typically branded as a "sex fiend," "sex maniac," "dirty old man,"or "pervert." Yet excessive physical violence occurs in probably no more than 3 percent of all cases of sexual molestation; and only about 15 percent of all adult-child sexual contacts involve any kind of coercion, including threats (McCaghy, 1971). Nevertheless, Fritz et al. (1981) report that girls who respond to the "benevolent" inducements of the child molester might experience sexual maladjustment in their adult lives. Some women apparently experience guilt or self-blame for having succumbed to the positive advances of the molester.

Typically, the child molester is not a stranger lurking in the shadows as many parents think. Studies consistently show that from 50 to 80 percent of all child molestation is committed by family friends, relatives, or acquaintances.

Fritz et al. (1981) report that 4.8 percent of the males and 7.7 percent of the females in their college sample were molested as children. Heterosexual molestation of females as well as males most frequently occurs, although results of the Fritz study indicate that 10 percent and 40 percent of the molested females and males, respectively, experience homosexual molestation. Males appear to have experienced fewer negative aftereffects of their sexual molestations, perhaps because they "are likely to view prepubescent contacts as sexual *initiation* while females view such encounters as sexual *violation*."

Pedophilia usually develops as an attempt on the part of the pedophile to cope with a fear of failure in normal interpersonal and heterosexual relationships, especially with a sexually experienced woman, or as an attempt to satisfy a narcissistic love of himself as a child. Efforts to rehabilitate pedophiles through psychotherapy have shown promising results, although some become recidivists (relapsed offenders). The rate of recidivism among homosexually oriented child molesters is between 13 percent and 28 percent. The rate of recidivism among heterosexually oriented child molesters is about one-half the rate of the homosexually oriented child molesters (DSM III, 1980). While a prison sentence does little to alter the subsequent behavior of sexual deviates, society is, of course, protected from them during their term of imprisonment (Coleman, 1972).

Not all men charged as sex offenders against children are psychologically disturbed. Some may simply respond to what they perceive to be "seductiveness" on the part of some precocious children. While such "seductiveness" among children probably is the exception rather than the rule, some children apparently are willing or voluntary participants in their sexual interactions with adults. Further, the effect of such sexual experiences on children may not be negative as is often presumed. Some children may experience their sexual interactions with adults as being positive, especially if affection and emotional warmth are lacking in their home environments. Early sexual experiences do not always have traumatic effects on children (that is, if force or brutality is not involved), and later psychological stability and sexual orientations of children do not appear to be altered significantly. Early sexual contacts do not appear to have harmful effects on many children unless the family, legal authorities, or society reacts negatively (Bernard, 1981; Constantine, 1981; Ingram, 1981).

The role of family reactions to childhood sexual experiences cannot be emphasized enough. Constantine (1981), reviewing the effects of childhood sexual experiences, states the following:

Negative reactions of parents (and other important adults) to a child's sexual encounters, aside from their function in inducing guilt, can be, at least in a minority of cases, the most psychonoxious aspect of the entire experience. When communication in a family is good and when the family functions well, however, and especially when at least one parent can be highly supportive, even the effects of brutal assault can be minimized. (p. 241)

Certainly no sensible, caring parent would wish adult-child sexual experiences for their children. Some children, depending on personality factors and the nature of the sexual interaction, may experience adverse effects of their early sexual encounters with adults. Nevertheless, in many instances, the parents and society, rather than the children, are most traumatized if early sexual experiences come to light.

Bestiality

Bestiality (sometimes called *zoophilia*) is sexual gratification obtained by engaging in sexual relations with animals. The Kinsey investigators (1948) reported that 17 percent of men reared on farms have reached orgasm through sexual relations with animals, and many others probably have had some sort of sexual contact with them.

If the pattern of behavior becomes fixed, bestiality might be considered a mechanism to avoid feared failure with the opposite sex. In other cases the individual shows his hostility or contempt toward women by identifying them with animals, or by choosing animals in preference to them.

Pornography and Obscenity

Pornography is written or pictorial material that is deliberately designed to cause sexual excitement (Gebhard et al., 1965). However, to avoid confusion in terms, it is helpful to distinguish between *pornography*, a popular term, and the legal concept of **obscenity**. Obscenity consists of utterances, gestures, sketches, and the like that are judged repugnant according to the mores of society. Sexually arousing material may be obscene, but the responsibility of so labeling it lies with the courts. People often are confused by definitions and sometimes label inoffensive material "obscene," when it is merely sexually arousing (Primeau, 1977).

The attitude of Americans toward pornography is varied indeed. Many consider it informative or entertaining. Others believe that it leads to rape or moral breakdown, that it improves a couple's sexual relationship and leads to innovation in their coital techniques, that it eventually becomes only boring, that it causes men to lose respect for women, or that it serves to satisfy normal curiosity. More people than not report that the effects of erotica on themselves have been beneficial. However, those who judge pornography dangerous tend to see its effects harming others, not themselves. Those with a passion for purity and a determination to control the moral behavior of others typically cite two reasons why someone (usually themselves) should sit in judgment on what others may or may not read: (1) children's minds are corrupted by such material, and (2) it provokes sexual criminality or other sexual acting out.

Just what constitutes pornography? No matter how many laws are passed, erotica, like beauty, remains in the eye of the beholder. A massive Rubens nude will evoke admiration for its artistic merit in one person, some degree of sexual

The legal dilemma: What is pornographic and what is obscene? *Charles Gatewood.*

arousal in another, and moral indignation in a third. The same nude might evoke in a fourth only thoughts of the local reducing salon. Is the Bible pornographic? Is Shakespeare? Chaucer? St. Augustine? John Donne? Benjamin Franklin? All have, amazingly, been subjected to censorship, which is an indispensable tool in the business of purification.

DOES PORNOGRAPHY HARM CHILDREN?   Young adults, it is generally agreed, are particularly vulnerable to the arousal of strong sexual desires as a result of reading erotic material. But the contention that pornography has a degenerative effect upon them—or even upon children—is highly debatable. Certainly there is no research or clinical data to support the argument. In the most recent refutation, the President's Commission on Obscenity and Pornography—a nineteen-man team of experts conducting a two-year study—stated among its preliminary conclusions in August 1970: "There is no evidence to suggest that exposure of youngsters to pornography has a detrimental impact upon moral character, sexual orientation, or attitudes."

SEX-RELATED CRIMINALITY AND PORNOGRAPHY.   The consensus of such professionals as psychiatrists, psychologists, sex educators, social workers, and marriage counselors is that sexual materials cause neither adults nor adolescents any harm. Yet the argument persists that pornography stimulates people to commit criminal sex acts.

     As with the allegation that pornography harms children, there is no scientific evidence supporting a link between pornography and sexual criminality.

The preliminary report of the President's Commission mentioned earlier concluded that erotic materials do not contribute to the development of character defects or operate as a significant factor in antisocial behavior or in crime. The Commission found no evidence that exposure to erotica operates as a cause of misconduct in either youths or adults (Commission on Obscenity, 1970). A careful examination of imprisoned sex offenders shows that they grew up in strict families in an atmosphere of sexual repression, suggesting that this repression, not stimulation by pornography, led them to sex crimes. As Athanasiou (1980) concludes, there is virtually no scientific evidence that indicates a causal connection between exposure to pornography and antisocial behavior.

IS VIOLENT PORNOGRAPHY HARMFUL?   Erotic materials that combine sexual arousal and violence can be harmful. Recent studies not reviewed by Athanasiou (1980) suggest that depictions of sexual acts that involve force or violence against women, often portrayed in hard-core pornographic materials and even in the popular media, can cause some men to exhibit increased aggression or hostility toward women (Donnerstein, 1980; Donnerstein & Hallam, 1978). Violent pornography that links sex with aggression toward women may increase the viewer's sexual arousal to the aggressive stimuli and perhaps inadvertently reinforce the perception that such aggressive sexual behavior is acceptable.

Obviously, one important implication of this research is that violent pornography may increase the likelihood of aggressive acting out on the part of potential rapists and others who may be predisposed to commit violent acts. Further, while no evidence exists that erotic materials designed merely to incite sexual arousal have any deleterious effects on children's sexual development, sexually explicit materials that combine sex with violence might provide violent role models and thus promote children's learning of aggressive sexual behavior patterns (Bart & Jozsa, 1980; Russell, 1980). Thus, in any discussion of pornography and its potential negative effects, it might be most important to distinguish whether erotic materials are merely sexually arousing or whether they arouse by emphasizing violent or aggressive components.

PORNOGRAPHY AND SEXUAL ACTING OUT.   The President's Commission (1970) concluded from its investigation, according to its preliminary report, that during the twenty-four hours following the viewing of highly erotic material there may be some sexual arousal and, in some cases, increased sexual activity. But, the Commission observed, basic attitudes and sexual patterns do not change because of it. Furthermore, following erotic exposure people show greater tolerance towards others' sexual behavior than they did before, although their own standards do not change.

Few would deny that the young are more vulnerable to what they read than are those who are older, more sophisticated, and more critical. However, by extrapolating from Mayor Jimmy Walker's observation that no girl was ever ruined by a book, one can safely say that pornography has a negative effect only on the mind that was disordered to begin with.

WHO ARE THE PATRONS OF PORNOGRAPHY?   Approximately 85 percent of adult men and 70 percent of adult women in America have been exposed at some time during their lives to material of explicitly sexual content in either visual or textual form.

Many factors appear related to the incidence of individual exposure to erotica. Men are more likely to be exposed to it than women, young adults more likely than older ones, and people with more education more likely than the less well educated. The more socially and politically active have greater exposure than those who are less active. Those who attend religious services often are less likely to have contact with erotic material than those whose attendance is less regular (Commission on Obscenity, 1972).

Several recent studies of high-school and college-age youths confirm that minors today have considerable exposure to erotica, much of it in preadolescent and adolescent years. More than half of the boys were so exposed by the age of fifteen, and the girls, a year or two later. By the time they reach the age of eighteen, roughly 80 percent of boys and 70 percent of girls have seen pictures of coitus or have read descriptions of it (Commission on Obscenity, 1972).

Persons younger than twenty-one rarely purchase pornography, and very little is obtained through the mail. By far the most common source of erotica is friends, the exposure usually occurring in a social situation where the material is freely passed around. There is some evidence that the less socially active young person is less likely to see erotica than more social youth. Exposure to erotica in adolescence, then, is widespread, and occurs primarily in a group of peers of the same sex (or several members of both sexes). These experiences seem to have more social overtones than sexual ones.

Patrons of so-called "adult" bookstores and cinemas are predominantly white, middle-class, middle-aged, married males. The men who go to see pornographic films typically are dressed in business suits or neat casual attire; they usually attend the film alone, perhaps on an impulse while out shopping. Women in the past have not been as interested in explicit erotic material as men have. Evidence is growing, however, that women are increasingly interested in the same erotica that once was assumed to appeal only to men, and that they respond to it similarly (Athanasiou, 1980). Almost no one under twenty-one is observed in these establishments, even when it is legal for them to be there.

INDIVIDUAL JUDGMENTS OF PORNOGRAPHY.   A study investigating the factors leading an individual to judge pictures or books as pornographic indicates that persons of lower socioeconomic status tend to rate nudity as obscene, even if no genitalia are shown. They are more likely than subjects of higher socioeconomic and educational strata to regard any nude photo as being sexually exciting (Higgins & Katzman, 1969). Black-and-white photos are judged more obscene than color photos; pictures of poor photographic quality more obscene than those of higher quality; unattractive models more obscene than attractive ones, regardless of the pose; and erotic scenes in an indoor setting more obscene than those in an outdoor setting.

No one denies that genuine pornography and obscenity exist. However, apart from the fact that they present sex often unrealistically, and sometimes as something ugly and inhuman, the chief objection must lie in their literary, theatrical, or pictorial worthlessness, rather than in their power to corrupt.

Any legal curbs on pornography and obscenity imply the imposition of censorship—an eventuality that any thinking person would wish to avoid. As early as 1644, John Milton—a Puritan among Puritans—addressed Parliament in opposition to censorship, which he regarded as the handmaiden of tyranny. He argued that reading everything one wishes is the means of attaining knowledge of the good and evil and the ugly and beautiful that flourish indiscriminately in the world. Corrupting forces, he said, are everywhere present, and they can only be met by building up an inner discipline and *the ability of rational choice*. Censorship serves no such purpose, especially since its course, as history reveals, has led inevitably to the imposition on the masses of the prejudices, tyrannies, and, usually, the stupidity of the few.

No one admires or wishes to encourage pornography (except, of course, the writers or purveyors thereof). But the alternative to it is censorship—which would mean that the biblical *Song of Solomon* could be in as much danger as an East coast publication called *Screw*.

EROTICA VERSUS PORNOGRAPHY. Helping to reduce further the ambiguity concerning what constitutes pornography, the recent feminist-led campaign against pornography has provided a clear and important distinction between sexually explicit **erotica** and **pornography** (Steinem, 1980). For instance, the feminist perspective does not suggest that all sexually arousing materials can be considered pornographic, even if they depict sexual abuse and degradation. Rather, according to the feminist view, the key factor in determining whether the material is pornographic is the underlying personal message of violence or male conquest and the use of sex as a way to create or maintain male dominance and control over women in society. If the material contains the positive theme of sexual sharing and physical pleasure between men and women who are portrayed as equals, then the material may be termed erotica. This important distinction between erotica and pornography is becoming better understood as this viewpoint becomes more widely accepted.

Fetishism

Fetishism is a psychosexual variance in which an individual's sexual impulses become fixated on a sexual symbol that substitutes for the basic love object. Fetishes are not limited to articles of female attire and do not include sexually stimulating objects such as vibrators (DSM III, 1980). Usually the articles that are the focus of the fetish are fondled, gazed upon, or made part of masturbatory activities. Among the most commonly used symbols are underclothing, shoes (especially high-heeled shoes), and gloves. Articles made of rubber have very strong appeal to the fetishist. Or the object of the fetishist's fixation may be a bodily part of the opposite sex, such as hair, hands, thighs, feet, ears, or eyes. The fetishist is almost always male, and in acquiring his sex symbols he often commits burglary or even assault.

Fetishism is actually an intensification of normal tendencies existing in all people. Men, for example, find certain objects more sexually exciting than others—sweaters, hair, breasts, buttocks, or legs. They often jokingly refer to themselves as being "breast men," or "leg men," or "fanny men." It is therefore understandable that the symbol of the basic love object can become the love object itself in certain personality structures. Childhood experiences and habits, reinforced by unsatisfactory interpersonal relationships, are the most frequent antecedents of the fetishist's seeking comfort and sexual pleasure in objects rather than in people.

Incest

Incest is sexual intercourse between two persons, married or not, who are too closely related by blood or affinity to be legally married. All fifty states have laws against incest; however, laws relating to incest bear little uniformity from state to state and are often highly confusing. Further, mental health professionals often consider the psychological consequences of intrafamilial sexual contacts of any kind and tend to define incest more broadly (Courtois & Hinckley, 1981).

Incest actually is much more common than has previously been acknowledged by participating adults or children or than has come to professional or public attention. Estimates indicate that one in ten families and from 1.5 to 5 percent of individuals are involved in incest. However, the hidden incidence may range from five to ten times higher than these estimates indicate (Murray, 1982).

Recent investigations have indicated that incest often occurs in middle- and upper-class and educated families (Murray, 1982). Thus incest is not a phenomenon associated strictly with disadvantaged and lower socioeconomic groups. Incestuous behavior still remains shrouded in an atmosphere of secrecy and often is not discussed or communicated by the participants to anyone else. Guilt feelings and fears of condemnation and punishment by others may inhibit participants in incestuous encounters from revealing their behaviors.

Although incest traditionally has been viewed as a psychologically damaging experience, individuals sometimes remember incest experiences as being positive or neutral in emotional impact. This may not be surprising when one realizes that intrafamilial sexual experiences often occur among persons who have close, warm interpersonal ties. Further, when incest occurs among older adolescents or adults, there is greater likelihood that the experience can be understood and perhaps accepted as a constructive growth experience.

Incest is apparently more likely to be perceived as a negative and harmful experience when an individual uses explicit or implicit force, exploitation, or manipulation against another and when an age difference of several years exists between partners. Young children and the younger partners in incestuous relationships are more likely not to fully understand the experience or to feel overpowered by the older partner (Finkelhor, 1981; Nelson, 1981; Symonds et al., 1981).

The person who commits incest against children often comes from an unhappy home background, experiences feelings of loneliness or low self-esteem, shows a preoccupation with sex, and drinks heavily (Courtois & Hinckley, 1981; Murray, 1982). The person is often unemployed and therefore is at home with the children. The incest offender against adults is typically conservative, moralistic, restrained, religiously devout, traditional, and uneducated.

The most common form of incest is probably brother-sister, especially in families where children of both sexes must share a bedroom. The next most common form of incest, and the type most frequently reported to legal sources, is father-daughter incest (Coleman, 1972; G. A. Bernstein, 1979). Sometimes the daughter does not report the relationship to authorities because she craves parental affection and she interprets her father's advances as being an indication of love or caring. The typical victim is an only or oldest daughter, and the father-daughter incestuous experiences often begin when the girl is approaching puberty. The daughter in some instances may be an infant or young child when the incestuous experiences begin. The father in such relationships often is experiencing sexual maladjustment with his wife. Thus the daughter is turned to, to satisfy sexual and emotional needs that the parents cannot fulfill for each other. The father is usually in his thirties or early forties, and he frequently has unconscious homosexual strivings, psychopathic tendencies, and noticeable paranoid traits (G. A. Bernstein, 1979).

Mother-son incest appears to be rare; its incidence may be somewhat higher than is suspected, however, because neither party is likely to report it. Cases of grandfather-granddaughter incest can occur, and in fact research estimates indicate that 10 percent of intrafamilial contacts may involve this form of incest (Courtois & Hinckley, 1981). Other cases of incest may involve aunts, uncles, stepparents, stepchildren, and other relatives.

Mate-Swapping

Mate-swapping (also called *swinging*) is the sexual exchange of partners among two or more married couples (R. R. Bell, 1971b). The phenomenon has not been as rare as people might think; approximately 1 million Americans have reportedly engaged in mate-swapping (Bartell, 1971). However, recent research (Fang, 1976) shows that swinging is on the decline, perhaps on its way to becoming an outmoded form of sexual diversion. Nevertheless, estimates have indicated that 1 to 5 percent of Americans have engaged in mate-swapping and that as many as 1 to 2 percent have done so on a regular basis (Karlen, 1980).

Subjective assessment of marital happiness revealed no difference between swingers and nonswingers. There was no difference in the reported personal habits of the two groups, nor in their emotional health, although childhood relationships with parents had been less gratifying for swingers than for nonswingers (Gilmartin & Kusisto, 1973). Mate-swappers, to the surprise of many, frown on an extramarital affair unless all the marriage partners involved are fully aware of it. They believe that the real danger to marriage in extramarital sex lies in the risk of romantic involvement with another person and the dishonesty inherent in a secret affair. Swappers maintain that they engage in swinging to improve and support their marriage as well as to add fun and variety to their sex lives. Issues of sexual jealousy and risks of emotional attachments developing with other sexual partners arise among mate-swappers, but many swingers are able to resolve these concerns (Karlen, 1980; H. S. Rosen, 1971).

Most mate-swappers appear to be conventional, conservative, hardworking individuals who lead ordinary lives in other respects. Research into the psychodynamics of mate-swappers suggests that swingers are not sexual perverts, nor are they mentally or emotionally disturbed (Karlen, 1980; H. S. Rosen, 1971).

Variance in Strength of Sexual Drive

Nymphomania and Satyriasis

Nymphomania refers to the behavior of a woman whose abnormally voracious sexual hunger overshadows all her other activities. It is sometimes, although rarely, the outgrowth of certain physiological disorders; more often, however, the disorder is psychological (Auerback, 1968; Goodman, 1982).

When true nymphomania exists, it involves an uncontrollable sexual desire that must be fulfilled when aroused, no matter what the consequences. The sexual craving is unquenchable regardless of the number of orgasms and the pleasure received from them. Nymphomania is compulsive sexual behavior in the true sense of the term, driving the victim to irrational and self-defeating activities, with all the stresses and problems that any compulsion causes (Ellis & Sagarin, 1964). It must be stressed, however, that few words in our language are as misapplied as *nymphomania*. It is bandied about by the man on the street; it is a popular theme in X-rated films and a frequent topic of discussion in fraternity houses; and everyone from the minister to the mailman claims to know at least a half-dozen such women. Yet, as a true sexual disorder, nymphomania is quite rare.

Most men are sexually fulfilled after one orgasm and care very little about continuing sexual activity afterward. Sexually mature women, however, may not be satisfied with one climax. Men who do not understand this normal sexual need are likely to believe they are involved with a sensual freak who refuses to recognize the end of a good thing when she arrives there. Thus, such men often label a perfectly normal woman a nymphomaniac simply because she happens to have a healthy sexual appetite.

Satyriasis is an exaggerated desire for sexual gratification on the part of a man. One investigator reported a case of satyriasis in which a twenty-four-year-old male stated he had sexual intercourse three times a day and in addition he masturbated three or four times each day. The young man also experienced nocturnal emissions several times a week and had sexual fantasies that sometimes caused him to ejaculate. Reportedly, he also engaged in variant sexual activities, including frottage (rubbing or pressing against the desired person) and voyeurism (Moore, 1980). The public does not show as much concern over men who are "oversexed" as it does over similarly "afflicted" women. As might be expected, this disparity in attitudes has its roots in the traditional sexual role of females. Women's deviation from the sexually passive role as-

Nymphomania: A Case Study

Mrs. M was a white, nineteen-year-old female who came from a lower-middle-class background. She was an attractive though somewhat overweight young woman, and she was the mother of an eight-month-old infant. She was seen by a neurosurgeon, having been referred by her family physician because she was experiencing severe, persistent headaches and lower back pain. No physical basis for her symptoms could be determined, and she was referred for psychological evaluation and psychotherapeutic treatment. Her evaluation indicated that she was preoccupied with sexual concerns, loneliness, suicide, and hostility.

Mrs. M readily discussed her early sexual experiences and insatiable sexual desires. She stated that she and her twenty-year-old husband had sexual relations each night for several hours—or for as long as he could keep up with the pace. Her husband was a kind and caring man who thought it was his obligation to satisfy his wife's sexual needs. Nevertheless, he was perplexed by his wife's overwhelming sexual demands, and he could not comprehend why she remained just as sexually unsatisfied after hours of sexual intercourse and numerous orgasms as she had been at the initiation of sexual activity. Mrs. M reported that on rare occasions she was sexually satisfied to some extent, and afterwards her headache would disappear temporarily for a day or so.

The dynamics of her case were fairly easy to understand. She had begun having coitus at the age of nine with her stepfather. She had enjoyed sexual activity from the beginning. Since her father left home when she was a young child, she had missed male attention. She enjoyed coitus with her stepfather, primarily because of the attention she gained from engaging in sex with him. She continued having intercourse with her stepfather several times a week for seven years. She also found that she could attract the attention of other older males, and she subsequently became sexually involved with her uncles and a few other older men in her neighborhood. Sometimes the men initiated the sexual activity and sometimes she initiated the activity.

At about age fourteen Mrs. M began feeling guilty about her sexual involvement with her stepfather, and she confessed her sexual behavior to her mother. Mrs. M's mother refused to believe her and accused her of being a seductress and a worthless person. Mrs. M's sexual involvement with her stepfather continued for two more years. Finally, her guilt feelings became so intense that she broke off the sexual relationship. Not surprisingly, her stepfather left her mother at this time, and he was not heard from again. At this point Mrs. M first developed her headaches; and her subsequent sexual experiences were unsatisfying, except in rare instances with her husband.

Mrs. M's relationship with her mother and with other relatives continued to deteriorate until she met her husband. At this time she became involved in a warm, affectionate relationship with him and she developed a close relationship with her in-laws as well. She continued to have her headaches, however, and her sexual problems persisted.

Once Mrs. M entered psychotherapy, efforts were directed toward helping her develop a more positive self-image and toward persuading her to believe that her husband's love was sincere and valuable. Her husband received counseling also, and gradually Mrs. M came to understand the dynamics of her behavior. She learned that she did not have to engage in seductive or sexual behavior to prove her worth as a person. She found that she did not have to use sex exclusively in order to gain love and affection. She eventually came to lead a happy, productive life (J. L. McCary, 1972).

signed by society is likely to be more noticeable. The incidence of true satyriasis and nymphomania is about the same—both are very rare disorders—and each can usually be successfully treated with psychotherapy.

Promiscuity

Promiscuity is generally defined as the participation in sexual intercourse with many people on a more or less casual basis. A person whose own sexual activity is limited in frequency and restricted in expression tends to condemn the more liberal sexual behavior of others as promiscuity. Thus, the term is often used more as a derogatory evaluation than as a widely recognized scientific or sociological label.

Studies involving personality and family backgrounds of promiscuous women indicate that they have generally made an uneven and perhaps incomplete progression to physical, emotional, intellectual, and social maturity. They have difficulty accepting responsibility for their own behavior and characteristically they blame parents, husbands, and friends for their own failures and shortcomings. Their promiscuity is not caused by a strong sex drive; rather, it results from their attempt to use sex to cope with other emotional problems. To a large extent, men follow the same behavioral patterns in their promiscuity (which has been called "Don Juanism," after the legendary Spanish libertine) as women do. In the case histories of almost all the men studied, promiscuous behavior proved to be the result of feelings of inadequacy, emotional conflicts, and other personality problems. There is no evidence that the sex drive of these men is stronger than that of average men (Kirkendall, 1961).

Changes in standards of sexuality and great variety of individual differences have contributed to the difficulty in determining how much sexual activity constitutes excessive or promiscuous behavior. Arbitrary standards of "normal" sexual frequency may not be appropriate criteria in determining hyperactive sexual behavior. Perhaps a more accurate criterion of promiscuity would be the degree to which frequent sexual activity harms other aspects of social functioning (Sandler et al., 1980).

Prostitution

Prostitution is participation in sexual activities for monetary rewards. Two elements are essential: first, sexual favors are offered for an *immediate* return of money or valuables; second, the selection of partners is relatively *indiscriminate* (Gebhard, 1973).

Kinsey and his associates (1948) found that 69 percent of white males had had some experience with prostitutes. However, over the past several decades there apparently has been a steady decrease in the number of professional prostitutes in America and in the frequency with which men visit them. For example, the 1948 Kinsey study revealed that about 20 percent of its college-educated sample had had their first coital experience with a prostitute. But in the 1967 comparative study, this figure had fallen to an estimated 2 to 7 percent (Rubin, 1969a). College-age men are more likely to have sexual relations with young women in the context of an emotional relationship, while married, middle-aged men are becoming the most frequent customers of prostitutes (Boles, 1980).

Men visit prostitutes for many reasons: they want variety in their sex life; they are too shy, too embarrassed, or too physically handicapped to find heterosexual outlets elsewhere; they may need to gratify their variant sex urges, such as sadomasochistic or fetishistic tendencies, and can pay to have them satisfied; they wish to have sexual activity without the obligations associated with less anonymous sexual intercourse; or perhaps their wives are pregnant, or a child has been born and they feel in competition with it for the wife's affection. In associating with prostitutes, however, men often forget that, since prostitution is illegal, they run the risk of blackmail, arrest, and scandal, to say nothing of the dangers of contracting sexually transmitted diseases, or of being robbed.

Very few women become prostitutes because they are highly sexed and actually enjoy the sexual experience prostitution affords them. Most are not sexually responsive to their clients, although they may very well thoroughly enjoy sex with their men friends or husbands (Gebhard, 1969).

One study has revealed that the attitude of the prostitute toward her clients is similar to that of anyone else providing a service to customers: she likes some, dislikes others, and feels indifferent toward still others. Over 66 percent of those surveyed expressed no regrets over having entered the profession (Gebhard, 1969). Prostitutes are, however, subject to certain occupational hazards. For example, about 66 percent of one sampling of prostitutes had contracted sexually transmitted disease (Gebhard, 1969). Yet contact with prostitutes accounts for only about 5 percent of STD cases in this country. In fact, uneducated, sexually active teenagers are more likely to be transmitters of disease than are prostitutes (Townley, 1980).

The male prostitute generally serves a male clientele, although from time to time brothels have been established for the pleasure of women. The award-winning film *Midnight Cowboy* gives an excellent characterization of a young man attempting to earn money specifically from his sexual services to women. (A man's failure in this profession is no doubt attributable to his physiological inability to function beyond the point of sexual satiation, whereas a woman can function endlessly despite the absence of any erotic desire.) The "gigolo" is often thought of as a male prostitute, but he is usually employed more as a companion or escort than for sexual services (Hoffman, 1972).

Some male prostitutes ("hustlers") are homosexual; some are not. Most, however, are young men who think of themselves as being quite masculine in appearance and orientation. They allow themselves to be "picked up" by men, usually older ones, in order to make some easy money. The hustler allows his male client to perform fellatio on him, for which privilege he receives money; there is rarely more to the relationship. A homosexual seeking a male prostitute wants a "straight" partner. A hustler therefore attempts to magnify his masculine image by wearing such attire as a leather jacket, boots, and skin-tight bluejeans (Hoffman, 1972).

It has been estimated (Lloyd, 1976), and police do not dispute the figure, that some 100,000 boys aged thirteen to sixteen are actively engaged in homo-sexual prostitution, a sizable part of their customers being older married men. These boys are, for the most part, runaways from working-class or welfare homes.

Rape

In the general consensus, **forcible rape** is defined as sexual intercourse forced on an unconsenting person, male or female. Rape typically has little to do with uncontrollable lust. The rapist is motivated primarily by the wish to dominate and by hostility and aggression toward his victims (Groth & Gary, 1981; Hite, 1981). The assault victim is often chosen as a matter of chance, and bears the brunt of the rapist's need at that moment to vent his feelings of violence. Male homosexual rape in prison is likewise typically not associated with great sexual need. It is an attempt to reaffirm the prisoner power structure. Further, the prisoner seeks to reaffirm the sagging image of his masculinity by proving his ability to control others by force (Money & Bohmer, 1980; Sagarin, 1976).

The legal definition of forcible rape includes cases where the victim con-sents only because of fear, force, or fraud, or is incapable of rational consent because of mental retardation. Rape can also be charged if the woman is asleep, is unconscious from drugs or alcohol, or is tricked into coitus by a man pretending to be her husband (Czinner, 1970).

Statutory rape is another form of criminal intercourse. It implies coitus with a female below the age of consent, which is usually eighteen. A man can be convicted and imprisoned on statutory rape charges even though the girl appeared quite old enough or lied about her age. Most rape convictions are based on statutory grounds (Slovenko, 1971). Women can be convicted of rape if they are an accessory in forcing coitus on another woman or in persuading an underaged girl to have intercourse. Women have also been convicted, al-though extremely rarely, of statutory rape involving an underaged boy and of forcible rape (even more rarely) involving an adult man. In every state rape is a felony.

Rape victims are usually between the ages of eighteen and twenty-five, although some are young children and older women. The rapist is tyically between twenty and twenty-four years old, from a low-income, culturally deprived background, and of dull-normal intelligence. The convicted rapist scores significantly lower on IQ tests than do nonrapists convicted of violent crimes (Ruff et al., 1976). He is likely to have had emotionally unstable parents who imposed little supervision on him in his youth, and a weak, often alco-holic father. The majority of rapists, however, come from broken homes. The rapist is usually emotionally immature and frequently physically unattractive (Gebhard et al., 1965; Rubin, 1966). Interestingly, rapists are strong believers in the double standard and place great value on a woman's virginity (Griffin, 1976). A high percentage are either married at the time they commit rape or have been married at some time during their adulthood (Rada, 1975). Others have several women friends and what appear to be satisfactory, nonviolent re-lationships with them. Nevertheless, most rapists report experiencing diffi-

Rape Prevention

In order to prevent a sexual assault, women and men are advised to consider potential resistance methods they might use. Women, and men as well, can take courses in self-defense and assertiveness training to develop physical skills and self-confidence and thereby help reduce their vulnerability to attack. Those who are more self-assured and who take measures to prevent rape may thwart a potential rapist by not appearing to be weak, available, or easy prey. Some of the following precautions have also been recommended (Kollias & Tucker, 1974; Pepitone-Rockwell, 1980):

- Carrying a whistle to attract attention if one is bothered
- Owning an attentive pet or watchdog
- Exercising discretion in telephone listings of name and address
- Not going out alone on dark city streets
- Walking in the middle of a sidewalk rather than close to a building or curb where someone might be lurking
- Avoiding deserted areas, such as abandoned buildings and alleys
- Riding a bus rather than a subway, and hiring or hailing taxis only from a recognized company
- Driving with windows up and doors locked
- Locking the car when it is parked
- Not entering an elevator alone with a man or letting a stranger into one's apartment or home for any reason
- Using security locks on windows and doors in apartment or home

culties in being able to relate to women and in being able to form meaningful interpersonal relationships in general. Rapists often express feelings of inadequacy and low self-esteem in general (Pepitone-Rockwell, 1980).

Alcohol plays a central role in sexual assault. With unusual consistency, various studies of rape show that approximately 50 percent of rapists were drinking at the time of their attack. Alcohol may serve any of several purposes—to give the rapist courage, to remove intellectual control over behavior, or to provide an after-the-fact excuse. These generalizations do not rule out the possibility that a highly intelligent, seemingly respectable, handsome young man might become a rapist, becaue such is sometimes the case. Rapists do, however, have a greater tendency to express violence and rage than other men do.

Rape is one of the fastest rising crimes of violence in America. In 1979, 75,989 sexual assaults were reported, and it is generally thought that, for every reported case, between eight and ten go unreported (FBI, 1979). Group or gang rape (two or more rapists) has been estimated to account for up to 70 percent of all rape cases (Steen & Price, 1977).

Strong vestiges of the attitude that the woman is somehow responsible for rape cling and are reflected in the law and judicial procedures following rape. Sexual assault is the only crime of violence wherein the victim must defend her part in it; only recently have strenuous efforts been made to change this position. Nevertheless, the outrage of the woman's family (perhaps also self-directed), the often inhumane attitude of hospital attendants where she seeks treatment, and the humiliating questions posed by police investigators cause many rape victims to remain silent after the attack. The greatest injustice occurs, however, in the witness box, where the victim is frequently twisted into the posture of a defendant by the defending counsel—"she asked for it"; "she is of loose moral character anyway"; "she didn't fight hard enough." Not infrequently the victim is completely shattered emotionally by the treatment accorded her on the witness stand (Brownmiller, 1975).

In legal theory, a man cannot be accused of forcing sexual union on his wife, as permanent consent to coitus is considered part of the marriage contract (Brownmiller, 1975). Recently, however, the problem of marital rape has come to societal attention as some women have pressed legal charges against their husbands for rape. While marital rape is usually not reported, authorities estimate there may be as many as 2 million offenses per year (Groth & Gary, 1981).

Men are by no means exempt from rape. Prison rape, as mentioned previously, is seen by penal authorities as epidemic (Money & Bohmer, 1980). Once raped, that reputation follows the person for the rest of his sentence, wherever he may be transferred. Many of these youths return to the outside world full of shame and hatred.

Every major American city now has a rape crisis center to which victims may turn. These centers provide personal counseling, information on medical and legal procedures, and advice on rape prevention. The centers attempt as well to help make the victim's contact with hospital and police a more positive experience (Kollias & Tucker, 1974). Personal counseling can help in a woman's reactions—both acute and long term. Acute reactions include physical injury, often serious; muscular tension; and gastrointestinal and urinary disturbances. Among the psychological reactions are severe anxiety, fear, and depression. The overall social adjustment, as well as the work, economic, leisure time, and family adjustments, of rape victims may be impaired, especially in the first few months following the rape incident (Resick et al., 1981).

Summary

Sexual practices, ethics, and behavior vary widely within and among different cultures. What is usual or normal in one culture may be variant or abnormal in another culture. Generally, sexual behavior can be considered acceptable if three conditions are met: that it is not harmful to the participants, that it is carried out by consenting adults, and that it is out of sight and sound of unwilling observers. Sexual behavior may be variant or abnormal depending upon (1) the method of functioning and quality of sexual striving, (2) the choice of the sexual partner or object, and (3) the degree and strength of the sexual drive. Men typically reveal a greater tendency toward variant sexual behavior than do women.

One form of sexual variance is *sadism*, wherein sexual gratification is derived by inflicting either physical or psychological pain on the sexual partner. *Masochism* is the mirror image of sadism because the masochist receives sexual pleasure or gratification from being hurt, physically or mentally, by the sexual partner.

Exhibitionism involves sexual gratification that the individual, typically male, derives from exhibiting the genitals and occasionally masturbating before unwitting and unwilling observers. *Pseudoexhibitionism* may occur when heterosexual relations are not available and persons exhibit themselves only as a poor substitute for preferred sexual intercourse. *Scoptophilia* and *voyeurism* refer to sexual pleasure gained from observing sexual acts, genitalia, and nudes. *Social nudism* is not a sexual deviation, but it is regarded as a variance by some because it is erroneously linked to exhibitionism. *Troilism* involves the sharing of a sexual partner with another person or persons.

Transvestism, or *cross-dressing*, usually engaged in by heterosexual males, refers to emotional or sexual gratification that is derived from dressing in the clothes of the opposite sex. *Transsexualism*, or *sex-role inversion*, refers to an obsession or compulsion to become a member of the opposite sex through surgical changes. *Gender identity disorders of childhood* involve a child who expresses an extreme distaste for his or her sexual identity and insists that he or she will grow up to be the other sex.

Pedophilia is a form of sexual variation in which the adult engages in or desires sexual activity with a child. *Bestiality* refers to sexual gratification obtained by engaging in sexual relations with animals.

Erotica is written or pictorial material that is deliberately designed to arouse sexual excitement. *Pornography* is sexually explicit material. *Obscenity* refers to utterances, gestures, sketches, and so on that are judged abhorrent according to the mores of our society. No significant evidence exists showing that children's minds are corrupted by pornography or that pornography provokes sexual criminality or other sexual acting out. Most men and women in the United States have been exposed at some time to material of explicitly sexual content. There is no evidence that these individuals or society are harmed by exposures to erotica, although recent evidence suggests that exposure to violent pornography may be harmful. Whether sexually explicit material is judged obscene depends more upon the evaluating individual's psychological characteristics, occupation, and socioeconomic, political, and educational background. Curbs on pornography and obscenity through censorship often result in adverse consequences for society rather than the presumed benefits.

Fetishism is another sexual variance in which an individual's sexual impulses become fixated on a sexual symbol or object, such as an article of clothing or a bodily part such as hair, hands, thighs, feet, or eyes.

Incest involves sexual relations between close relatives, such as a brother and sister or father and daughter. *Mate-swapping*, or *swinging*, refers to the exchange of sexual partners between married couples.

Nymphomania, a rare disorder, refers to the uncontrollable or excessive sexual desire in a woman that must be fulfilled when she is aroused with no regard for the circumstances. *Satyriasis*, also rare, refers to the excessive or exaggerated desire for sexual gratification on the part of a man. *Promiscuity* refers to the participation in sexual relations with many people on a casual basis.

Prostitution involves the engagement of sexual activity for money or valuables. For the past several decades there has been a steady decrease in the number of professional prostitutes in America and in the frequency with which men consort with them. Now, college-age men appear to be seeking sexual relations with young women in the context of an emotional relationship; and, as a result, married middle-aged men are the most frequent customers of prostitutes.

Forcible rape involves sexual intercourse with a person who does not give consent or who offers resistance. *Statutory rape* refers to coitus with an individual below the age of consent. While women can be convicted of rape, most rapists are men beset with feelings of inadequacy and low self-esteem. Rape is an act of aggression and has little to do with uncontrollable lust. Male homosexual rape in prisons is also known to occur.

Rape victims have at times been reluctant to press charges against rapists because of fears that their families, hospital staffs, or legal authority figures may be unsympathetic toward them. However, changes in societal attitudes and development of sources to which victims may turn, such as rape crisis centers, have led to a more understanding and sympathetic approach to the victim. Furthermore, women may learn how to lessen their chances of being raped by taking courses in self-defense and assertiveness training in order to develop their physical skills and self-confidence.

TRUE OR FALSE: THE FACTS

Women who have strong sex drives, come to climax easily, and are capable of multiple orgasms are nymphomaniacs.
False. A strong sex drive is not a sign of a nymphomaniac; a nymphomaniac's abnormally voracious and uncontrollable sexual hunger overshadows all other activities. (*234*)

❦

A transvestite and a transsexual are the same, and both are homosexuals.
False. A transvestite (cross-dresser) is rarely a transsexual (person who experiences sex-role inversion); the transvestite usually establishes normal heterosexual relationships, and a transsexual might have a history of asexuality, heterosexuality, or homosexuality. (*222–224*)

❦

Sex molesters of children are usually under sixty-five years of age.
True. Most child molesters are between thirty and forty years old. (*225*)

❦

Sexually arousing materials (erotica) have a corruptive effect on people's minds and behavior, especially children's.
False. The President's Committee on Obscenity and Pornography has stated that "There is no evidence to suggest that exposure of youngsters to pornography has a detrimental impact upon moral character, sexual orientation, or attitudes." (*228*)

❦

Rape is a crime that results from uncontrollable sexual lust.
False. Rape typically has little to do with uncontrollable lust, but rather with a wish to dominate and with hostility and aggression toward the victim.
(*238*)

SUGGESTED READING

Athanasiou, Robert. Pornography: A review of research. In B. Wolman and J. Money (Eds.), *Handbook of human sexuality.* Englewood Cliffs, N.J.: Prentice-Hall, 1980.
This article surveys studies concerning physiological response to pornography, the effects of pornography on social behavior and personality, and social and sex differences in response to erotica. The variety of definitions of pornography with respect to local statutes is considered.

Brownmiller, Susan. *Against our will: Men, women and rape.* New York: Simon & Schuster, 1975.
This important book presents the feminist perspective of rape, the historical and contemporary status of the problem.

Bullough, Vern L. *Sexual variance in society and history.* Chicago: University of Chicago Press, 1976.
This scholarly volume examines historical and cross-cultural attitudes toward sexual behavior stigmatized as "deviant." Western society is emphasized in the discussion, which includes homosexuality as variant behavior.

Groth, Nicholas. *Men who rape.* New York: Plenum, 1980.
The author examines the personality and psychological characteristics of rapists.

Lederer, Laura (Ed.). *Take back the night: Women and pornography.* New York: William Morrow, 1980.
This book is a collection of articles by women on the history, ethics, politics, economics, and effects of pornography. This book is a product of the feminist effort to stop pornography, providing interesting perspective for the general reader.

McCary, James Leslie, and McCary, Stephen P. *McCary's human sexuality* (4th ed.). Belmont, Calif.: Wadsworth, 1982.
Chapter 17 presents detailed information on the major forms of sexual variance. Chapter 19 discusses legal aspects of sexual variance.

Meiselman, Karin C. *Incest: A psychological study of causes and effects with treatment recommendations.* San Francisco: Jossey-Bass, 1978.
Integrating previous literature with the author's own findings, this book describes incest cases and discusses causes and effects of incest. Anthropological and sociological views of incest are presented, and research methodological issues are considered.

TRUE OR FALSE?

People are either totally heterosexual or totally homosexual.

☙

Homosexuals are usually identifiable by their appearance.

☙

Childhood involvement with an adult homophile does not always result in an individual's later becoming a homosexual.

☙

Bisexuals are comparable to homosexual groups but not comparable to heterosexual groups.

Homosexuality

CHAPTER 13

Incidence

Suggested Causes
Hereditary Theory
Environmental Theory
Hormonal Imbalance

Homosexual Patterns and Practices

Attitudes toward Homosexuality

Homosexuality and Children

Bisexuality

Summary

Suggested Reading

Homosexuality refers to sexual activity between same-sex partners. Sexual contact leading to orgasm is often but not always involved. In our society, homosexuality usually has been deplored as a mode of sexual activity, although legal and social sanctions are changing. Some sexologists regard the homosexual experience as being so diverse, and the psychological, social, and sexual aspects so varied, that to use the words *homosexual* or *homosexuality* to describe anything more than the individual's sexual choice at a particular time is misleading and inexact (A. P. Bell, 1976).

Many data exist on the subject of homosexuality, but one must remember that information coming from clinicians has often been gathered from homosexuals in treatment, and these data may represent a biased picture of homosexuality. To counteract what they consider distortions of their image, homosexuals have formed organizations (the Mattachine Society and the Daughters of Bilitis are the two oldest) to create more accurate and favorable public opinion. In recent years, homosexuals also have formed political action groups to encourage changes in public policy that they think have worked unfairly against homosexuals.

Incidence

Kinsey and his co-workers (1948) established that homosexuality and heterosexuality are by no means absolute and devised a seven-point continuum as a way to illustrate the degrees of homosexuality (Figure 13.1). At one extreme is exclusive heterosexuality. This is followed by predominant heterosexuality with only incidental homosexuality. Then follows predominant heterosexuality, but with more than incidental homosexuality. At the midpoint, there is sexual function at equal levels. Still further along the continuum is predominant homosexuality, but with more than incidental heterosexuality; then predominant homosexuality with only incidental heterosexuality; and, finally, exclusive homosexuality with no heterosexual leanings at all. Kinsey and his associates found that half of American males were classified somewhere between a score of 0 ("exclusively heterosexual") and a score of 6 ("exclusively homosexual"). Women also varied in their classification on this scale, although fewer women were found to be exclusively homosexual (Bell & Weinberg, 1978). Note that a person's classification on this scale refers to the degree of sexual responsiveness to others of the same and opposite sex.

To sum up the Kinsey findings, which are still pertinent today, 60 percent of males and 33 percent of females have engaged in at least one act of overtly homosexual sex play by age fifteen. The researchers also found that 37 percent of the male and 13 percent of the female population engaged at least once in their lives in some form of homosexual activity to the point of orgasm. A study of 20,000 well-educated, liberal men and women of high socioeconomic status confirmed Kinsey's early conclusions that more than one-third of all men and nearly one-fifth of all women have had at least one homosexual experience in-

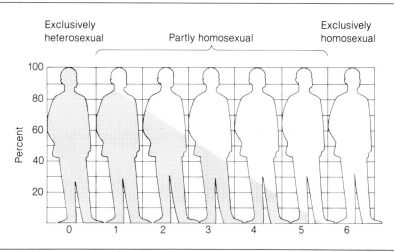

Figure 13.1   Schematic representation of the Kinsey continuum of male heterosexuality-homosexuality.

volving orgasm. A substantial number of other women (22 percent) have considered engaging in homosexuality. Hunt (1974) found that 10 to 12 percent of single women had had at least one homosexual experience past the age of fifteen. Both homosexual men and women have their first *heterosexual* intercourse at an earlier age than heterosexuals. About 17 percent of the homosexual women and 18 percent of the homosexual men sampled had their first coitus before the age of fifteen, as compared with only 6 percent and 9 percent, respectively, of heterosexual women and men (Athanasiou et al., 1970; Kinsey et al., 1948, 1953). Thus, homosexual individuals are not especially lacking in heterosexual experience, but they appear to find such experiences less satisfying or pleasurable than do heterosexual individuals (A. P. Bell et al., 1981). The average male homosexual has his first homosexual experience sometime before age fourteen, and the average female homosexual at about nineteen or twenty (Kaye, 1971). Other findings indicate that homosexuals who report having preadult homosexual feelings tend to experience them at about ages thirteen and sixteen, respectively, among males and females. "Advanced" homosexual experiences tend to follow two to four years after homosexual individuals first have homosexual feelings (A. P. Bell et al., 1981).

Sociologist William Simon, a long-time research associate at the Kinsey Institute, has estimated that only 2 to 3 percent of the male population have a long-term serious homosexual pattern; and an additional 7 to 8 percent have casual or occasional homophile experiences. Therefore, the total would be about 10 percent of the male population who have had more than experimental or fleeting homosexual contacts in their lives (Karlen, 1971). These figures were substantiated by Hunt (1974), who found that only 10 percent of his married subjects and 11 percent of the single ones had any homosexual experience at all after the age of fifteen.

Only about 1 to 3 percent of the female population between the ages of twenty and thirty-five in Kinsey's sample were exclusively homosexual, although an additional 2 to 6 percent in this age bracket were "more or less exclusively homosexual" (meaning that there might have been a rare heterosexual contact). Of all women who have engaged in any form of homosexual activity, Kinsey's study has indicated that about 33 percent have fewer than ten experiences, and many have only one or two experiences.

Of the women participating in the Hite study (1976), 8 percent said they preferred sex with women, another 4 percent identified themselves as "bisexual," and an additional 5 percent claimed they had experienced sex with both men and women, but gave no preference. These figures are considerably higher than those reported in other surveys, and perhaps reflect a bias of the Hite sample from whom information was gathered. Of the men participating in the Hite survey (1981), 11 percent reported they preferred sex with men and 4 percent reported they liked sex with both men and women. It would appear from these data that homosexuality continues to be a form of sexual expression experienced by a sizable proportion of men and women today.

Consensus among authorities is that male homosexuals outnumber lesbians (female homosexuals) about two or three to one, although the cause of this imbalance is frequently debated. It is extremely difficult, of course, to do more than estimate the true number of homosexuals in the United States, because most are still "in the closet"—that is, they keep their sexual preference hidden. It is generally accepted by sexologists that about 4 percent of white males in the United States are exclusively homosexual throughout their sexual lives, 8 percent are exclusively homosexual for at least three years between the ages of sixteen and fifty-five, and 37 percent have experienced at least some form of overt homosexuality to the point of orgasm in their lifetimes. Furthermore, 10 percent of all men have some homosexual experience after marriage (Kinsey et al., 1948).

As indicated earlier, homosexuality is somewhat less common among women than among men. The occurrence of both exclusive and partial homosexuality among women is only two-thirds of that among men (Cory, 1961). It is generally found, too, that most female homosexuals are bisexual. Either they have had heterosexual experiences, or they will have them in the future, or they will shift back and forth between homosexuality and heterosexuality. Only 33 percent of declared lesbians are exclusively homosexual (Bieber, 1969; Peplau, 1981). In one study of lesbians (Kaye, 1971), 67 percent of those who declared themselves to be exclusively homosexual at the time of questioning reported earlier heterosexual relationships. Over 80 percent of A. P. Bell and Weinberg's (1978) lesbian sample reported previous heterosexual coitus, but 33 percent denied orgasm as a result of such activity. Kinsey's study (1953) showed that female homosexuality is largely confined to single women and, to a lesser extent, to the previously married. Just over 30 percent of Masters and Johnson's (1979) lesbian sample had been previously married, from less than six months to thirteen years. Although 19 percent of Kinsey's total female sampling had had active homosexual contact by the age of forty, when the marital status of this group was considered the pattern of active homosexual incidence for the same age group shifted: 24 percent of the women had never been married, 9 percent had been previously married, and only 3 percent were married women. Hunt (1974) found that 9 percent of married women and 15 percent of the single ones in his sample had had at least one homosexual experience.

Of those women surveyed by Kinsey who had the most extensive homosexual experience, only 20 percent expressed definite regret. Almost 90 percent of all the women with homosexual experience themselves declared that they would keep as a friend any woman with a history of lesbianism. They were less accepting (74 percent) of male friends with a history of homosexuality.

Homosexual behavior also might occur when people are deprived of heterosexual outlets. This is called *deprivation* or *situational homosexuality*. In situational homosexuality, "heterosexual" men or women may engage in homosexual activity while they are in prison, in the military, or in similar circumstances where heterosexual outlets are unavailable. These individuals usually return to heterosexuality when their circumstances change and they once again can find satisfactory partners of the opposite sex. Such persons are not homosexual, as they do not identify as homosexuals or prefer a homosexual lifestyle. Rather, their homosexual behavior may be a means of establishing human contact or ending loneliness while their deprived circumstances exist.

Suggested Causes

Theories concerning the causes of homosexuality usually fall into three categories: hereditary tendencies, environmental tendencies, or hormonal imbalance.

Hereditary Theory

"Nativistic" theorists argue that homosexuality is inborn. They point out that most gays grow up in a culture that encourages heterosexuality and that they are usually ignorant of their homosexual tendencies until they reach pubescence and first encounter opportunities for homosexual attachments and expression. Therefore, these theorists reason, the homosexual tendencies must have been inborn and not learned. Even Freud believed that homosexuality had a genetic causality, and that the individual's early experiences either reinforce or extinguish the tendency.

A. P. Bell et al. (1981) cite evidence that suggests there may be a biological foundation underlying homosexuality. These researchers note that learning experiences may play a part in the development of homosexuality among bisexual individuals, while inborn, biological factors appear to operate more strongly among exclusively homosexual individuals. These researchers further suggest that "bisexuals are probably more susceptible to having their sexual responses altered by behavior 'therapy.' Exclusive homosexuality, we suspect, is probably much more resistant to change because it seems more deeply ingrained" (p. 217).

In support of hereditary theory in general are the studies that have indicated that the intelligence, interests, personality characteristics, and so on, of identical twins are often quite similar, regardless of whether the twins are reared together or apart (Bower, 1979; Coleman, 1972). However, other conflicting evidence has seriously questioned the idea that there are direct genetic components underlying human behavior as complicated as homosexuality (Diamond & Karlen, 1980).

Environmental Theory

There is more convincing evidence that homosexuality is the outgrowth of environmental pressures and other conditioning factors (Coleman, 1972; Kinsey et al., 1948, 1953; Pomeroy, 1966b; Thorpe et al., 1961). The individual might seek homosexual outlets, for instance, as the result of an accidental but pleasurable homosexual incident in childhood or because of segregation with others of the same sex for long periods of time (such as in a boarding school or correctional institution).

The most likely explanation centers around factors in the home environment. One report (Saghir & Robins, 1973) studying the childhood of adult male homosexuals revealed that 72 percent, compared with 12 percent of a control group of heterosexuals, had lost one or both parents before the age of fifteen. Furthermore, 50 percent of the gays but only 17 percent of the straights recounted that severe marital problems existed between their parents. Another study (Whitam, 1977) found several "childhood indicators" of later adult male homosexuality. These indicators were: interest in dolls, cross-dressing, preference for company of girls rather than boys in games, preference for company of older women to older men, assessment by other boys as being a sissy, and sexual interest in other boys rather than girls in childhood sex play. Not only did adult homosexual males reveal a significantly higher number of childhood indicators than did the heterosexuals, but the stronger the homosexual orientation, the greater the number of childhood indicators exhibited. Interestingly, A. P. Bell et al. (1981) point to childhood indicators of gender nonconformity as reflecting that homosexuals are probably affected by a genetic predisposition toward their sexual preferences.

Unhealthy patterns in homosexuals' family lives have often been noted. In one survey (Saghir & Robins, 1973), 41 percent of the male homosexual respondents, in contrast to twenty-three percent of the heterosexuals, asserted that their mothers had overcontrolled them. Many other psychological pressures may act together or separately to veer a boy toward homosexuality, and similar forces influence a girl toward lesbianism. The father may have been weak, aloof, and an ineffectual force in his son's life, leaving the boy to develop an excessive mother attachment that he never outgrows. The more common father-son interaction that can culminate in the son's homosexuality, however, is the one in which the father is harsh, overly aggressive, and too much of a "tough guy" to allow his son to enter into a close relationship with him. The boy does not identify with his father and does not learn the masculine role in life. Frequently this sort of father attempts to teach his son to be a real "he-man," but he prevents the very thing he wants for his son by not establishing a healthy relationship rooted in tenderness, acceptance, understanding, and love.

The Status of Homosexuality in Ancient Times

At least as old as history, homosexuality was a well-known phenomenon in ancient Rome, where it was practiced openly and widely. Not only did the ancient Greeks regard homosexual behavior as natural (at least, for persons within higher intellectual ranks), but it was also a form of love more exalted than heterosexual affection. To the Greeks, the full experience of beauty and love were best embodied only in the male, and thus relationships between two males were not only condoned but also were valued. However, it is noteworthy that the Greeks did not exclude women from the expression of homosexual love. Sappho, a poetess who lived on the Greek island of Lesbos, wrote erotic poems intended for her female students, thus leading to the modern use of the term *lesbianism* to refer to female homosexuality.

Male-female alliances represented practicality—an ordered household, a tax refuge, and a means of producing children. Homosexual love was more typically woven into the fabric of the philosophical, intellectual, and spiritual pursuits so prized by the Greeks.

Thus, one comprehensive investigation revealed that 84 percent of the male homosexuals, as opposed to 18 percent of the male heterosexuals, felt that their fathers had been emotionally distant and indifferent (Saghir & Robins, 1973). Again, however, A. P. Bell et al. (1981) argue that familial difficulties may result from the fact that the prehomosexual child is "different" from the very beginning. In other words, it can be suggested that "an inborn predisposition toward gender nonconformity might lead to rather than proceed from the kinds of family relationships that have traditionally been held responsible for gender nonconformity" (p. 218).

Sociological forces acting upon particularly vulnerable adolescents can be powerful. For example, a boy's relationship with girls might have been so unsatisfactory and threatening that he seeks the companionship of his own sex in order to avoid a repetition of his failures. Similarly, a sensitive girl who has been callously rejected by a boy she loves might decide never again to run the risk of another rejection and turn to women for warmth and acceptance. Experiences such as these have led some behavioral scientists to conjecture that homosexuality is always associated with an unconscious fear of heterosexual relationships (Marmor, 1965).

Hormonal Imbalance

According to the third theory, homosexuality is caused by an imbalance of sex hormones. The urine of any man or woman reveals hormones of both sexes; in some, the same-sex hormone dominates. It is suggested that if the dominance is reversed, homosexuality will result. This theory has alternately gained and lost support over the years, and while it is not usually considered significant in a study of homosexuality, the sex research team of Masters and Johnson has in recent years revived interest in biological correlates. When testosterone and sperm-count levels of a group of homosexual and heterosexual males eighteen to thirty-five years old were compared, endocrine variants in bisexual homosexuals did not differ from those in heterosexuals. But those subjects who were predominantly or exclusively homosexual displayed "diminished plasma testosterone concentrations and impaired spermatogenesis" (Kolodny et al., 1971). A. P. Bell et al. (1981) cite other research that notes that hormonal levels, physical structures, patterns of sleep, and blood chemistry can be different in homosexual and heterosexual individuals.

In a review of recent endocrine studies into the causes of homosexuality, Masters and Johnson (1979) cite several lines of investigation that have produced conflicting results. They point out that many such studies have methodological difficulties, that homosexuality is a diverse phenomenon (as is heterosexuality), and that the origins of heterosexuality are as obscure as those of homosexuality. Thus, researchers have been unable so far to determine whether the anomaly is gonadal, pituitary, or hypothalamic in origin. They also warn that similar endocrine dysfunctioning has yet to be found in a majority of homosexuals. Even if such dysfunctioning were to exist, however, it might be primarily the result rather than the cause of homophile psychosexual orientation.

Homosexual Patterns and Practices

What homosexuals do when they have sexual relations is a mystery to many people. In fact, homosexual practices are the same as those of heterosexual couples; except for penile-vaginal coitus, there are no heterosexual practices that cannot be performed by a homosexual couple. Usually preceded by kissing and petting, these acts in males include oral-genital contact, mutual genital stimulation, anal intercourse, and interfemoral coitus. In the Masters and Johnson study (1979), it was found that committed homosexual couples differed consistently from their heterosexual counterparts in the amount of time spent in prolonged foreplay. The homosexuals took more time, appeared to be more relaxed, and were more completely and subjectively involved than were the heterosexual couples. Thus, homosexuals appear to be more empathic lovemakers than heterosexuals.

The sexual expressions of greatest importance to and most cherished by lesbians (in company with many heterosexual women) are embracing and close total body contact. Genital activity and orgasm frequently are of secondary importance (A. P. Bell & Weinberg, 1978; Kaye, 1971; Peplau, 1981). The sexual practices of American lesbians are limited only by the imagination of the particular couple. However, three seem more common than others: mutual manual-genital stimulation, cunnilingus, and *tribadism* (one woman atop the other, both making rhythmic pelvic thrusts to stimulate each other's clitoris and vulva). Positions may vary, of course, as they do among straight couples, and many sex acts common to lesbians are quite similar to practices of heterosexuals (A. P. Bell & Weinberg, 1978; Lyon & Rosen, 1974; Peplau, 1981).

It is a fallacy that homosexuals are usually identifiable by appearance. Only about 15 percent of men with extensive homosexual experience and 5 percent of lesbians can be identified by appearance or mannerisms (Pomeroy, 1966a). A high degree of effeminacy is evident in about 21 percent of male gays under age twenty-six, the percentage dropping to about 7 percent as these men grow older. Effeminate characteristics are learned, and they can be unlearned. There are, to be sure, such stereotypes as limp-wristed, lisping, highly effeminate "queens." However, such "queens" represent a very small proportion of homophiles and tend to be shunned by the rest of the homosexual community. At the other extreme are homosexuals bent on presenting themselves as supermasculine.

It is typically thought that male homosexuals play one of three roles in their sexual encounters: active, passive, or mixed. Homophiles themselves prefer to play no fixed role, changing it according to their partner's preferences and aggressiveness. That they tend to switch roles during a single sexual encounter further blurs the distinction between active and passive.

The life-styles of lesbians—to the public eye, at least—appear to be less flamboyant and less promiscuous than those of male gays. They do not often go to gay bars searching for pickups. If they do go, it is with a friend, seeking sociability rather than social contacts. According to one study done by A. P. Bell and Weinberg (1978) in the San Francisco area, less than a fifth of the lesbians had visited a gay bar in search of a sexual partner during the previous year. More than two-thirds of the male homosexuals, on the other hand, had visited a gay bar to seek out a sexual partner or partners. Some men engage in homosexual practices with numerous partners. This seems to be because homosexual men do not ordinarily concern themselves with finding a steady or permanent partner until they are about thirty. Prior to that, they seem intent upon seeking the satisfactions of the moment rather than establishing a lasting relationship (Peplau, 1981; Sonenschein, 1968).

Lesbians are much more likely than male gays to pair off and establish lasting relationships. This is easier for women than men because of the differences in society's role expectations. Lesbians melt into the community more easily and are subjected to far less harassment by the police. The duration of established lesbian relationships is comparable to that of heterosexual relationships. About 65 percent of the lesbians in one study (Rubin, 1969b) had remained one to nine years in a single partnership, and 17 percent had remained for ten or more years. A. P. Bell and Weinberg (1978) found similar stability in their study. In comparison, Rubin (1969b) found 48 percent of the heterosexual women in his study had stayed for one to nine years with one male partner, and 40 percent for ten or more years.

Although some clinical data suggest that the roles in a lesbian relationship are likely to be clearly defined, the A. P. Bell and Weinberg (1978) and Peplau (1981) data suggest it is rare to find a lesbian relationship in which one of the partners does all or even most of the "masculine" or "feminine" tasks. Public opinion to the contrary, most lesbians would not choose a man as a sexual partner in preference to a woman, no matter how great his charms and persuasiveness or his skill in making love. A. P. Bell and Weinberg (1978) found that nearly two-thirds of the lesbians in their sample expressed no regret over

Lesbian couples are much more likely than male gays to establish lasting relationships. *Michael Hanulak, Photo Researchers, Inc.*

their homosexuality, nor had they ever seriously considered discontinuing homosexual activity. Most of those who did attempt to give up homosexuality did so only once, and few attempted marriage.

Attitudes toward Homosexuality

Despite changes in public acceptance of homosexuality, the attitude of the average American toward gays and gay life-styles is still quite negative and differs from that of many other cultures. A study of seventy-six primitive societies (Ford & Beach, 1951) showed that 64 percent approved of homosexual relations. Another study of 193 societies throughout the world (Murdock, 1934) showed that 28 percent accepted male homosexuality, at least to an extent, but only 11 percent accepted female homosexuality. In the typical American community, however, the reverse of these acceptance patterns is generally true. Male homosexuality is severely denounced, often to the point of violence, while female homosexuality receives less restrictive disapproval.

Larsen et al. (1980) have developed a scale to measure current attitudes of heterosexual college students toward homosexuality. These investigators have found that "being male, a business student, frequent church attender, responsive to negative peer attitudes, fundamentalist in religiosity, and authoritarian" are factors associated with antihomosexual attitudes. Conversely, women who are liberal arts students and nonfrequent church attenders tend to have more tolerant attitudes toward homosexuality. Positive peer attitudes, low religiosity, and low authoritarianism are also related to more tolerant views toward homosexuality.

There are regional differences in the acceptance of homosexuality. For example, in the Bay area around San Francisco the gay population is more accepted and therefore highly visible. Homophiles hold public office and are recruited by the police department, and there has not been a raid on a gay bar for nearly twenty years. In contrast, the Pennsylvania House of Representatives censured the governor in 1979 for proclaiming a "Gay Pride" week. And even in the same area there can be conflicting notions of acceptance. In the early summer of 1980, police in Houston raided a gay bar during Gay Pride week on the eve of the annual police-versus-gays softball game.

Some evidence, then, points to a recent change in public attitude toward homosexuality, a swing from almost total condemnation to a position of greater tolerance—at least toward gay civil rights, if not toward widespread acceptance of homosexuality as a life-style. It was almost unheard of a generation ago for academicians, doctors, lawyers, and ministers to publicly identify themselves as members of a once despised and feared group. Yet over 70 percent of Americans still view homosexuals as sexually abnormal, perverted (50 percent), or mentally ill (40 percent) (Weinberg & Williams, 1976).

In a reversal of its century-old position, the American Psychiatric Association in 1973 struck homosexuality from its list of mental disorders. Only those who are in conflict about their sexual orientation—or, rather, those whose conflict is great enough that they wish to change sexual directions—are considered disturbed and hence in need of psychological help. Further, some mental health professionals have come to agree with A. P. Bell et al. (1981), who suggest that "exclusive homosexuality probably is so deeply ingrained that one should not attempt or expect to change it. Rather, it would probably make far more sense simply to recognize it as a basic component of a person's core identity and to help the client develop more positive feelings about and respect for his or her own sexual proclivites" (p. 211).

The Status of Homosexuality in Modern Times

The military's traditionally rigid ban against homosexuals has not softened, despite the courageous efforts of several service personnel. U.S. Air Force T/Sgt. Leonard Matlovich challenged the policy by openly declaring himself a homosexual and thus forcing a discharge hearing. He was considered to be a "perfect case" for such a confrontation because of his twelve-year unblemished military record—the lack of which has derailed other challenges. Although the military board that heard the case handed down a general discharge (less than honorable), which often becomes a barrier to civilian employment and VA benefits, a review board later upgraded the discharge to honorable. Thus the Air Force—and the country—lost a dedicated public servant, once again leaving one to wonder how many other valuable public servants are lost because of their fear of exposure. In December 1978, the U.S. Court of Appeals, ruling in the case involving Matlovich, declared that the military cannot discharge gay persons without specific, appropriate reasons in addition to homosexuality.

Of course, discrimination against homosexuals exists not only in the military. No doubt many homosexuals continue to be discriminated against in government and private-industry jobs although most are good citizens and productive members of society. Interestingly, homosexual contact is considered a crime in many states; and, in 1982, Texas became only the twenty-sixth state to end the criminalization of consensual homosexual practices by adults in private. Still, according to various surveys, homosexuality continues to be regarded by many Americans as a greater menace to society than abortion, prostitution, or adultery. In yet another poll, respondents felt that only communism and atheism outweighed homosexuality as the greatest threat to the nation. Although increasing numbers of people dispute the view that homosexual behavior among consenting adults should be considered a crime, there are still many who do not favor decriminalization or social acceptance of homosexuality.

In September 1976, the Council of Representatives of the American Psychological Association adopted a resolution that stated: "The sex, gender identity, or sexual orientation of natural parents, or of prospective adoptive or foster parents, should not be the sole or primary variable considered in custody or placement cases."

The 1980 edition of the American Psychiatric Association's *Diagnostic and Statistical Manual of Mental Disorders* further reflects the changing nature of homosexuality in that profession. In line with its 1973 position, homosexuality is not included as a separate diagnostic entity. The manual contains an entry for "Ego-dystonic Homosexuality" that refers to ". . . a desire to acquire or increase heterosexual arousal so that heterosexual relationships can be initiated or maintained, and a sustained pattern of homosexual arousal that the individual explicitly states has been unwanted and a persistent source of distress" (DSM III, 1980, p. 281). Civil rights groups and the homosexual community viewed these pronouncements as a great victory.

Sgt. Leonard Matlovich, avowed homosexual, after his honorable discharge from the United States Air Force. *United Press International.*

Homosexuality and Children

It is an unfortunate experience for a youngster between the ages of seven and sixteen to be seduced by a homosexual or heterosexual adult, but the effects on future sexual preference are seldom permanent. Boys seduced by an older homosexual male are no more liable to become homosexuals than are boys who have not been seduced, and the evidence is that they later marry and lead quite normal lives (Constantine, 1981; "From the Editor's Scrapbook," 1965). What of those cases where there is close, frequent contact between a child and a homophile? Although a few local decisions have upheld the right of homosexuals to teach in the schools, parents are often apprehensive. Yet there is no evidence that a homosexual teacher will lure a child into the gay world, or that such a teacher is more likely than a heterosexual teacher to molest a child sexually. Some teachers *are* homosexual, without a doubt; but they keep their sexual preference to themselves, as do heterosexual teachers.

Nor does evidence exist that a homosexual parent will be less loving and effective than a heterosexual parent. Recently, several court decisions have given custody of children to lesbian mothers. In one case in California, the state supreme court awarded two lesbian mothers custody of their children, finding that their sexual preferences did not create a harmful child-raising environment ("Forum Newsfront," 1979). In adoption cases, an openly gay male couple recently has been permitted to adopt a child (Vetri, 1980), and a homosexual minister has been granted the right to adopt a child in New York ("Forum Newsfront," 1979). Still, the right of the professed homophile to have custody of children remains unresolved. As an example: responding to the plaintiff's plea not to let a child become the victim of "someone else's social experiment," a Dallas jury awarded custody of a nine-year-old boy to his father. The mother, a nurse and an avowed lesbian who had been living with another woman since her divorce, was also ordered to pay part of the child's support.

It can be seen that many moral, ethical, attitudinal, and legal issues remain to be resolved within our society in regard to homosexuality. Certainly, homosexuality continues to be a sensitive subject for many people, and many of our values are brought into question when the straight world confronts and struggles to assimilate the gay community. Even the concrete provisions of the law are not so concrete when issues concerning homosexuality are heard in our courts. Our values and our laws concerning homosexuality continue to be in a state of flux, and our views of the gay community are constantly being reshaped and remolded.

Bisexuality

Past research has focused on the differences, and sometimes similarities, that exist in the values, attitudes, and behaviors of homosexual and heterosexual groups. One general conclusion of such research is that diverse and different personalities exist in the homosexual community just as diverse and different personalities exist in the heterosexual community. It has heretofore been accepted that heterosexual individuals may differ from one another in every aspect of their life circumstances other than sexual orientation, and it has even been recognized that heterosexual individuals may express themselves sexually in different ways. The contribution of past research has been to show that homosexuals may also differ in each of the aspects of their life circumstances other than sexual orientation and that they too might express themselves sexually in different ways.

One contaminating factor in past research has been that **bisexuals**—men and women who enjoy sex with members of both sexes—have often been lumped into the homosexual groups in studies of sexual attitudes, values, and behaviors. However, contemporary research is beginning to recognize that bisexual individuals should be studied as a discrete group as are homosexual and heterosexual groups. In fact, it may be especially important that bisexuals be studied as a separate group since they may constitute a greater segment of our population than people who are exclusively homosexual. Technically, if one extrapolates from the Kinsey scale of 0–6 (that is, exclusive homosexuality to exclusive heterosexuality), perhaps up to 45 percent of the men and 35 percent of the women in the United States can be considered as belonging to the bisexual group. By these percentages, as many as 40 million people in the United States can be considered to be bisexual.

Researchers are beginning to recognize that a diversity of personalities quite likely exists within the bisexual community as within the homosexual and heterosexual communities. Bisexuals not only differ in their general life circumstances, but they might also differ in the way they express themselves sexually. For instance, some bisexuals might have a predominantly homosexual orientation or a predominantly heterosexual orientation or perhaps an equally homosexual and heterosexual orientation. Bisexuals might engage in their differing sexual orientations on a transitory, temporary basis or on a long-term, enduring basis. Just like exclusive homosexuals or exclusive heterosexuals, they might be monogamous or they might be promiscuous. They might have an emotional interest in one gender and yet a sexual interest in another gender. Researchers have many questions to answer regarding the attitudes, values, and behaviors of this segment of our population.

With the help of media attention and the support of bisexual groups, such as the Bi Center in San Francisco and The Forum Center, Inc., in New York City, the special problems and issues faced by bisexuals are beginning to be confronted. Future research will give us a greater unerstanding of those individuals who are bisexual—especially since they have been overlooked and ignored for so long (Macdonald, 1982).

Summary

Homosexuality refers to sexual attraction to or sexual activity with members of one's own sex. Attitudes, values, and perceptions toward homosexuality are changing, and homosexuals are forming organizations and political action groups to protect and enhance their public image.

Homosexuality and heterosexuality are not necessarily totally separate and distinct human behaviors. Kinsey and his co-workers devised a seven-point continuum indicating that sexual behavior varies from exclusive heterosexuality at one extreme to a combination of heterosexual and homosexual behavior to exclusive homosexuality at the other extreme. That much overlap exists in the expression of human sexual behavior is demonstrated by evidence indicating that more than one-third of all men and nearly one-fifth of all women have had at least one homosexual experience involving orgasm. While probably 10 percent or less of men and women have had extensive homosexual experience, many men and women have had homosexual feelings or some sort of homosexual response at some point in their lives. Male homosexuals outnumber female homosexuals by two or three to one, and it is noteworthy that most female homosexuals are bisexual.

Contrasting theories exist to account for the supposed causes of homosexuality. One of these theories is that homosexuality has a hereditary basis and is based on one's genes. The environmental theory suggests that homosexuality develops as a result of the psychological pressures and conditioning factors coming from the home and family. A third theory postulates that homosexuality is caused by an imbalance of sex hormones.

Regardless of the causes of homosexuality, evidence indicates that homosexual practices are the same as those of heterosexual couples, except for penile-vaginal coitus. Kissing and petting, oral-genital contact, mutual genital stimulation, anal intercourse, interfemoral coitus, and rhythmic pelvic thrusts, such as those involved in tribadism, are among the practices of homosexuals. The majority of homosexuals cannot be identified by their appearance. Lesbians (female homosexuals) do tend to be less flamboyant and less promiscuous than male gays, however, and are more likely to pair off and establish lasting relationships.

Despite the changes in public acceptance of homosexuality, most Americans still maintain a negative attitude toward this form of human sexual expression. In our society male homosexuality is severely denounced while female homosexuality receives less restrictive disapproval. The American Psychiatric Association and the American Psychological Association have adopted positions that no longer view homosexuality as a mental disorder.

It is unfortunate when a young person is seduced by a homosexual, but even in such instances few if any of the potentially negative effects are permanent. Homosexuals are no more inclined to seduce children than are heterosexuals. Many homosexuals are loving and affectionate parents, and recently some courts have allowed homosexuals to gain custody or adopt children. Homosexuality is still a sensitive subject in our society with many moral, ethical, attitudinal, and legal issues to be resolved.

Rather than having exclusively homosexual relationships, some men and women opt for bisexual relationships in which sex can be enjoyed with members of both sexes. Researchers are beginning to recognize that a diversity of personalities quite likely exists within the bisexual community as within the homosexual and heterosexual communities.

TRUE OR FALSE: THE FACTS

People are either totally heterosexual or totally homosexual.
False. Kinsey and his associates found that half of American males were classified somewhere between "exclusively heterosexual" and "exclusively homosexual"; women also varied in their classifications. (246)

Homosexuals are usually identifiable by their appearance.
False. Only about 15 percent of men with extensive homosexual experience and 5 percent of lesbians can be identified by appearance. (252–253)

Childhood involvement with an adult homophile does not always result in an

individual's later becoming a homosexual.
True. Boys seduced by an older homosexual male are no more likely to become homosexuals than are boys who have not been seduced. (257)

Bisexuals are comparable to homosexual groups but not comparable to heterosexual groups.
False. Bisexuals might have a predominantly homosexual orientation, a predominantly heterosexual orientation, or an equally homosexual and heterosexual orientation. (259)

SUGGESTED READING

Bell, Alan P., and Weinberg, Martin S. *Homosexualities: A study of diversity among men and women.* New York: Simon & Schuster, 1978.
This book presents a comprehensive exploration of homosexual behavior and life-styles, exploding many myths. The authors review a wide range of topics pertinent to homosexuality, such as the gay sexual experience, problems of social adjustment, and various psychological issues.

Bell, Alan P., Weinberg, Martin S., and Hammersmith, Sue Kiefer. *Sexual preference: Its development in men and women.* Bloomington, Ind.: Indiana University Press, 1981.
Based on data derived from the authors' personal interviews with approximately 1,500 individuals, this book discusses the development of both homosexuality and heterosexuality in men and women.

Klein, Fred. *The bisexual option.* New York: Arbor House, 1978.
This book presents a penetrating look into the world of bisexuality and shatters many myths.

Marmor, Judd (Ed.) *Homosexual behavior: A modern reappraisal.* New York: Basic Books, 1980.
This book is a collection of articles examining homosexual behavior from biological, social, and clinical viewpoints. Advances in understanding homosexuality are appraised, and many issues are examined, including development of sexual identity, the stigma of the homosexual label, homosexuality and aging, genetics in homosexual etiology, gay culture, and cross-cultural approaches.

Masters, William H., and Johnson, Virginia E. *Homosexuality in perspective.* Boston: Little, Brown, 1979.
Based on the authors' research and clinical experience, this book attempts to dispel the many myths surrounding homosexuality and to establish a better understanding of homosexual behavior. The authors discuss treatment of sexual dysfunctions among homosexuals and report results of treatment for conversion and reversion.

McCary, James Leslie, and McCary, Stephen P. *McCary's human sexuality* (4th ed.). Belmont, Calif.: Wadsworth, 1982.
Chapter 18 details the incidence and causes of homosexuality as well as homosexual patterns and practices and attitudes toward homosexuality.

Silverstein, Charles. *Man to man: Gay couples in America.* New York: Simon & Schuster, 1981.
This book presents a personal examination of the lives and experiences of a number of gay men based on the author's personal interviews. Many important issues faced by gay couples are addressed, including religion and gay love and "coming out." This book would appeal to a wide variety of readers, regardless of sexual orientation.

Sexual inadequacies or dysfunctions exist in only a small percentage
of marriages.

❦

Sexual dysfunctions are typically caused by emotional rather than
physical factors.

❦

Lack of sexual desire among men and women is rare.

Sexual Dysfunctions

CHAPTER 14

The Nature of Sexual Dysfunction

Male Sexual Dysfunction
Erectile Dysfunction (Impotence)
Ejaculatory Dysfunction

Female Sexual Dysfunction
Female Sexual Unresponsiveness
Orgasmic Dysfunction
Vaginismus
Dyspareunia

Inhibitions of Sexual Desire

Seeking Professional Counseling

Summary

Suggested Reading

I t is estimated that up to 50 percent of American marriages are flawed by some form of **sexual inadequacy** or dysfunction—a gloomy commentary on one of humankind's oldest institutions (Lehrmann, 1970; Masters & Johnson, 1970). A marriage is affected by sexual inadequacy because the distress experienced by one partner directly affects the other, and relationships with every other family member are usually affected as well. (It should be noted, however, that some couples whose sexual relationship is poor might nonetheless have a good, loving relationship in other areas of their marriage.) One survey (Mace, 1971a) has revealed that the average physician encounters about three cases a week in which problems of sexual maladjustment exist. The actual number of patients with sexual problems is undoubtedly considerably higher than this survey indicates. Many physicians do not routinely inquire into the sexual aspects of their patients' lives for the obvious reason that their medical specialty precludes it. A more compelling reason is that they are beset with sexual problems themselves and are uncomfortable discussing sex with their patients.

Studies have consistently shown that the physician who asks patients specifically about their sexual adjustment will uncover far more sexual problems than the physician who waits for them to volunteer such information (Pauly & Goldstein, 1970). Psychiatrists, psychologists, social workers, and other specialists in human behavior report that as many as 75 percent of their patients have sexual problems that require help (Wiener, 1969).

The overwhelming majority of complaints to physicians comes from wives. They are distressed that they cannot achieve orgasm easily or are lacking in sexual desire. They are distressed because they feel no affection for their husbands. Or they complain that they find sex too overwhelming an experience, or that it is physically uncomfortable, if not painful. The questions that husbands most frequently ask their doctors concern impotence or premature ejaculation, the infidelity of their wives, and the frequency with which coitus should normally occur (Mace, 1971a). In many instances, the basis of the problem lies in simple ignorance about sexual techniques or in general misinformation about sexuality, which can easily be corrected with sex counseling. In other instances, the causes are more complicated. Persons can become impaired in their sexual functions by fear of failure, a need to remain under conscious control during sexual activity, or a distressing fear of rejection if they do not perform adequately. These patients can usually be helped by brief sex therapy, the primary thrust being to open up the couple's ability to communicate.

Another group of patients also suffers from performance anxiety and fear of rejection, but are more difficult to treat. Still other patients are unconsciously "fearful of romantic or sexual success" (Kaplan, 1979). Their sexual problems are associated with negative thoughts and attitudes toward themselves and internal feelings of conflict and profound insecurity. In these cases, sex therapy must be directed toward alleviating a basically disturbed relationship between the sexes and problems of fragile self-esteem and guilt following the pleasures of sex.

What Happens in Sex Therapy?

Different and varied approaches have emerged over the years in the practice of sex therapy. Approaches have varied from the traditional "talking" therapies at one extreme to more unorthodox methods such as group masturbation programs for women who experience orgasmic difficulties at the other extreme. Sex therapy programs that include medical-anatomical examinations along with "talking" therapy may be seen as falling somewhere in the middle of the continuum.

Most sex therapy programs today involve "talking" therapy, where treatment paradigms developed by Masters and Johnson and Helen Singer Kaplan are applied in treating clients who have problems related to their sexual functioning. Often, a detailed sex history is taken by the sex therapist so that in-depth knowledge related to the individual's or couple's sexual concerns can be gained. Among the questions sex therapists frequently ask clients are these:

Did your sexuality develop normally? Do you recall any specific event that affected your sex life? When do you first remember having sexual thoughts? Sexual feelings? When did you first masturbate? How did you feel about it? What things were you told about masturbation? How was each of the many aspects of sex discussed in the family? What was your first sexual experience? What were your feelings about it? What homosexual experiences did you have as a child? How did you feel about them? What has excited you sexually in the past? What excites you sexually now? What stirs up sexual guilt or shame in you now? Under what circumstances can you function satisfactorily now? What circumstances cause you *not* to function satisfactorily now? How do you achieve orgasm? How do you feel about clitoral stimulation? Oral sex? How do you account for these feelings? How do you feel about ejaculation during oral sex? How do you feel about your partner's genital odor? Vaginal secretion? What do you think excites him (her) the most? How do you feel about doing it? Why? How do you feel about your body? Do you think you or your partner takes too long or too short a time to climax? Must his (your) penis be stimulated physically to become erect? How much pressure? How do you feel when he is (you are) slow to get an erection or cannot do so at all? How do you feel if she (he) fails to reach orgasm? How do you feel if you do not? How do you feel, knowing that she (he) can masturbate to orgasm but cannot respond to orgasm with you? How do you feel about the size of his (your) penis, her (your) vagina, her (your) breasts? How do you feel about multiple orgasms?

Taking a sex history, employing clinically established sex therapy techniques, and using educational aids are common in most sex therapy settings. Medical follow-up or consultation may be indicated if physical problems are suspected. For many people, the most difficult sex therapy session is the first one. However, once a couple has met with a sensitive and qualified sex therapist, fears and concerns often are alleviated, and thus subsequent sessions can proceed much more smoothly.

Consultation with a qualified sex therapist can help many couples overcome their sexual diffi-culties. *Larry Hanselka.*

Some individuals overestimate the sexual activity of others, and they come to base their sexual expectations of themselves on their perception of the sexual involvements or behaviors of others. This tendency to try to live up to heightened sexual expectations may cause individuals to experience frustration, anxiety, or guilt because they "are thinking and behaving as others would have them do, rather than for sexual fulfillment." Sex therapy in these cases can be directed toward helping the affected individuals to modify the performance demands or expectations that they have imposed upon themselves (Rubinson et al., 1981). A final group of patients are not at all appropriate candidates for brief sex therapy. Their problems involve profound personal psychopathology, such as deep depression, pervasive paranoia, and marked marital hostility. Or they have built such rigid defenses against personal inter-relationships that they need extensive psychotherapy before they can begin to benefit from sex therapy (Kaplan, 1974, 1979). Fortunately, persons in this category rarely present themselves for treatment of sexual dysfunction alone.

In isolated cases, sexual dysfunction is the result of some physical disor-der—birth defect, trauma, diabetes. However, the vast majority of sexual inadequacies are the emotional by-products of early conditioning—in or out-side the home—or the result of simple ignorance in sexual matters and about human relationships. These problems often surface in people who have no psy-chological difficulties in other spheres of their lives (Kaplan, 1974). In prac-tically all instances, psychogenic sexual dysfunction could have been circumvented had the individual received an adequate, well-timed sex education (Masters & Johnson, 1970). It is generally the case that very young children have pleasurable, positive sensations and attitudes relating to sex. But before they reach their teens, these normal reactions typically have been distorted by society's prevailing attitude that sex is dirty and evil. Added to this negativism are the fears, ignorance, and misinformation concerning sex that young people so easily absorb from their environment.

A basic part of most therapeutic programs, therefore, is an attempt to reestablish the positive, pleasurable sensations and attitudes natural to early childhood. Masters and Johnson use what they call *sensate focus* (Helen Kaplan prefers the term *pleasuring*), the keystone of which is the sense of touch. By touching, feeling, caressing, and exploring all the skin surfaces and mounds of his or her sexual partner's body with his or her fingers and palms, the patient is brought back into contact with sensory reactions. Instructions for those beginning pleasuring exercises vary from couple to couple, according to their particular problem, anxiety level, and cultural background. In all cases, however, the therapists should be well-trained professionals, relaxed and free of sexual conflicts themselves, especially in the matter of touching.

The Nature of Sexual Dysfunction

In both males and females, sexual response consists of two distinct and somewhat independent components. First is genital **vasocongestion,** which produces penile erection and vaginal lubrication and swelling of vaginal and labial tissue. Second is the reflex or involuntary clonic (alternating tensing and relaxing) muscle contractions involved in both male and female orgasm (Kaplan, 1974, 1975). Thus in the male, potency and ejaculatory disorders are controlled by different parts of the autonomic nervous system and are different clinical entities. Similar differences are found in women because sexual dysfunctions involve general sexual inhibitions and/or specific orgasmic problems.

There are six forms of sexual dysfunction, three affecting each sex. In the male, **erectile dysfunction** (also known as male **inhibited sexual excitement** and **impotence**) implies that erectile ability is impaired, with the inhibition limited to the vasocongestive aspects of sexual response. The second and third forms of sexual dysfunction in the male are composed of two types of ejaculatory dysfunctions. The first is **premature ejaculation,** in which a man is unable to exercise proper voluntary control over his orgasmic reflex. The result is that he climaxes before he wants to. The second type is **retarded ejaculation** (also known as *ejaculatory incompetence* and *ejaculatory inhibition*), in which he is troubled with involuntary overcontrol, causing his ejaculatory reflex to be excessively delayed, if it occurs at all, despite the fact that he receives what ordinarily would be considered adequate stimulation.

The first form of female dysfunction is **sexual unresponsiveness** (with alternate names of *female inhibited sexual excitement* and *general sexual dysfunction*), in which the woman derives little sexual pleasure from sexual contact. This condition roughly parallels male erectile dysfunction, in that vaginal vasocongestion and lubrication fail to occur. The second form, **orgasmic dysfunction** or *inhibited female orgasm*, occurs when a woman, although sexually responsive otherwise, experiences difficulty in achieving orgasm. This condition is not unlike male retarded ejaculation. The third form, **vaginismus**, has no counterpart in the male. Muscles ringing the vaginal opening go into spasm-like contractions when penetration is attempted, making coitus impossible (DSM III, 1980; Kaplan, 1974, 1975).

Kaplan (1974) also discusses *sexual anesthesia* in women as a fourth type of sexual disturbance, although she considers the problem technically to be a disorder rather than a dysfunction. In sexual anesthesia, a woman suffers from a hysterical conversion neurosis, and as a result she "feels nothing" when sexual stimulation is attempted, even though she may enjoy the warmth and pleasure of the physical closeness that it affords. Clitoral stimulation produces nothing more than a sensation of touch, and she may be unable to discern when the penis enters the vagina.

Male Sexual Dysfunction

Erectile Dysfunction (Impotence)

In the context of sexual dysfunction, erectile dysfunction or impotence can be defined as a man's inability to attain or maintain an erection of sufficient strength to enable him to perform the act of intercourse (Figure 14.1). Three types are recognized: *organic, functional,* and *psychogenic.*

The first of these, organic impotence, is relatively rare and is caused by some anatomical defect in the reproductive or central nervous system. Functional impotence involves physiological difficulties also, in that erection and other functions of the sexual system are dependent upon adequate hormonal activity, a satisfactory vascular supply, and an intact, properly functioning nervous system. Problems in any one of these areas can result in defective potency (Kaplan, 1975). Functional impotence may be caused by a nervous disorder, excessive use of alcohol or certain drugs, circulatory problems, diabetes, the aging process, physical exhaustion, or other conditions. In cases of functional impotence, the specific cause or causes may be discovered by a thorough medical examination and may be treated by appropriate medical regimens.

Psychogenic impotence is the type most frequently encountered, accounting for a majority of known cases (Kaplan, 1975). This malfunctioning is usually caused by emotional inhibitions that block or interfere with certain impulses from the brain that act upon the neural centers of the spinal cord controlling erection. Psychogenic impotence has been classified as either primary or secondary.

Primary impotence means that the man has *never* been able to achieve or maintain an erection of sufficient firmness to engage in coitus. Secondary impotence is a sexual dysfunction in which the man has had at least one successful coital experience but is now incapable of coital performance. A single failure to achieve erection does not mean that a man is impotent. Virtually all men at one time or another, particularly when they are upset or very tired, are

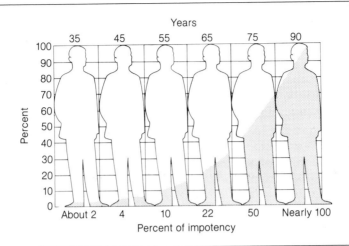

Figure 14.1   Schematic representation of the incidence of impotence in men. The shaded areas indicate the average percentage of men who usually suffer from impotence at various ages.

unable to attain an erection or maintain it long enough for penetration (Ellis, 1963; Laury, 1980). When a man fails to achieve penile erection in 25 percent of his sexual attempts, however, the condition may be correctly diagnosed as secondary impotence (Masters & Johnson, 1970).

The man who suffers from secondary impotence is typically successful in his first attempt at sexual intercourse and continues to be effective in dozens or perhaps thousands of coital encounters thereafter. But the day arrives when, for one of many reasons, he fails to achieve an erection. A first-time failure or several failures occurring within a short period of time can generate such fear and apprehension that the man can no longer function sexually. As he puts more and more pressure on himself to perform and becomes more and more anxious about possible failure, he becomes increasingly tense and less likely to be able to achieve an erection. Thus, fear of failure becomes a self-fulfilling prophecy, and a pattern of failure is established.

Some older men are led to believe that they have grown too old to function sexually. They may become so convinced that their age prevents them from having erections that they do indeed become impotent, despite the fact that they continue to have morning erections and erections during sleep. Any man who can achieve a morning erection *is* capable of having an erection; his failure at other times is psychological rather than physical. Almost all men have erections every sixty to eighty minutes during sleep (and sleeping women develop vaginal lubrications at about the same time intervals), whether or not they are capable of erections during the waking state (Masters & Johnson, 1971).

SOME CAUSES OF ERECTILE DYSFUNCTION.   Masters and Johnson have listed these causes of secondary impotence, in descending order of frequency: a history of premature ejaculation, intemperate alcoholic consumption, excessive maternal or paternal-domination in childhood, inhibitory religious orthodoxy, homosexual conflict, inadequate sexual counseling, and certain physiological inhibitors (Lehrman, 1970).

In those cases in which premature ejaculation is the herald of impotence, the evolution of the problem usually follows a predictable course. The man regularly ejaculates prematurely. At first his partner is tolerant. But as time passes she complains more and more. The man, who perhaps has been insensitive to the severity of his partner's sexual frustration, finally internalizes her accusations. He comes to view himself as a grossly inadequate lover and decides that at all costs he must learn to delay ejaculation.

He tries all manner of techniques to take his mind off the pleasurable sensations of coitus, but he succeeds only in blocking his full emotional involvement. In his anxiety, and not wishing to risk additional failure, he begins to avoid coition altogether, using any excuse possible. Sooner or later, however, his partner approaches him sexually and he discovers to his horror that he does not respond with an erection. He is now struck with the thought that he has a problem of considerably greater magnitude than premature ejaculation—he is totally incapable of coitus. Thus failure generates fear, and fear generates further failure (Masters & Johnson, 1970).

Alcohol figures prominently in the life of a man whose impotence is related to immoderate use of it—martinis at business luncheons, highballs for relaxation before dinner, and a parade of evening business or social gatherings at which spirits flow freely. Despite the man's greater-than-average consumption of alcohol over the years, his sexual functioning has remained satisfactory. Then some incident occurs that alters everything. Perhaps he somehow angers his wife in the course of an evening during which he has had many drinks. He decides to make amends by making love to her. To his dismay he cannot achieve an erection, partly because of the alcohol and partly because of his reaction—fear, anger, shame—to his wife's anger. His wife, because she is still irritated with him, does nothing to stimulate him sexually, either physically or psychologically.

A day or so later the man finds himself pondering this sexual failure. He firmly determines to accomplish that night what he had failed to do two nights before. Evening comes; there are several drinks "to relax" and a heavy meal with wine. But, unfortunately, determination is the only firm thing in the picture as erection once again fails to occur. This failure is almost inevitable because the burden of anxiety and fear bred by the first failure has been physiologically complicated by a heavy intake of alcohol and food. In attempting to "will an erection," the man has effectively ensured a second failure. Fear and failure reinforce one another, and a vicious circle is thus welded.

Secondary impotence in some men stems from unhealthy mother-son relationships, which may have bred unconscious incestuous desires or association of all women with the mother image. Some men become sexually incapable because of conscious or unconscious disgust, anger, or hostility toward their wives. The ills resulting from inadequate sex education have already been firmly established in this text. Guilt and shame, usually relating to some child-hood experience or stemming from faulty sex education, are common contrib-utors to sexual inadequacies.

Ejaculatory Dysfunction

PREMATURE EJACULATION.   Premature ejaculation occurs in men at all socio-economic levels, and there seems to be no correlation between it and any spe-cific sexual conflicts or particular form of psychopathology (Kaplan, 1974). Many people assume that premature ejaculation is primarily the result of a physical condition, such as a penis made abnormally sensitive by circumcision. But neurological and clinical testing of tactile discrimination (sensitivity to touch) has failed to reveal any difference in the sensitivity of a circumcised and an uncircumcised penis. Even in those cases in which the prepuce does not fully retract, the response to stimulation of the penis, circumcised or uncircumcised, is the same.

From the outset of this discussion, however, it is well to settle the question of what premature ejaculation is—and is not. Some authorities declare ar-bitrarily that ejaculation is premature if it occurs before penetration or within ten seconds thereafter. They say, further, that ejaculation occurring anytime after ten seconds of intromission, but not within the man's conscious control, must be considered "early ejaculation." Other authorities state that the man who cannot control his ejaculation for at least one full minute after penetration should be described as a premature ejaculator (Kinsey et al., 1948). Others be-lieve that the number of pelvic thrusts a man is capable of making after pene-tration and before ejaculation is the determinant. Still others define premature ejaculation in terms of the sexual requirements of the individual partners and are not concerned about specific periods of time. Prominent in this group are Masters and Johnson, who designate ejaculation as premature if the man can-not delay it long enough after penetration to satisfy his sexual partner in at least half of their acts of sexual intercourse together (1970). For many reasons, none of these definitions is completely satisfactory. For example, is a man a premature ejaculator if he can delay his climax only twenty-five minutes while his partner requires thirty minutes of coital stimulation? And what of the man who cannot last longer than sixty seconds after intromission, yet whose part-ner climaxes after only thirty seconds? The crucial measure of prematurity is "the absence of voluntary control over the ejaculatory reflex, regardless of whether this occurs after two thrusts or five, whether it occurs before the fe-male reaches orgasm or not" (Kaplan, 1974).

In any discussion of premature ejaculation, a word of caution must be injected. It is important to understand that at one time or another almost every man has ejaculated more quickly than he or his partner would have liked. The essential thing is that the man not become anxious over possible future failures. Otherwise, what is a normal, situational occurrence may become a chronic problem.

As with erection, the penis does not control ejaculation, premature or oth-erwise: the brain does. And the psychological forces involved are many. An element of revenge is often present in premature ejaculation—toward the particular woman or toward women in general. Or the man may be tense, tired, or lacking in self-confidence in his sexual abilities. Intercourse may have been preceded by an overlong period of sexual abstinence; or the man may have been through a prolonged period of sexual excitement, because of foreplay, before intromission was attempted.

Young men of today typically have their first sexual encounter with young women of their peer group. Often, these experiences take place in a parked car, in the imminent danger of being spotlighted by the police; or on a couch in the living room of the young woman's parents, where at any moment her father is liable to bound into the room, shotgun in hand and blood in his eye. The anxiety thus generated serves to condition many younger men to the pattern of quick ejaculation. Certainly anxiety is a major factor in blocking a man's perception of the sensations that signal impending ejaculation. Kaplan hypothesizes that the premature ejaculator has not learned to control his ejaculation because he fails to identify the sensations immediately preceding orgasm. The anxiety that he has experienced in the past during this brief period has interfered with his learning process. Unlike erection, which cannot be brought under voluntary control, ejaculation and orgasm can be. With proper training, men can learn to detect the sensations that herald orgasm and then learn to control ejaculation.

Another common form of teenage sexual behavior can also condition premature ejaculation. After extensive petting, the youth, possibly fully clothed, lies atop the girl, rubbing his penis over her vulval region by moving his body back and forth, as is done in intercourse, until he ejaculates. Thus the youth is conditioned to ejaculate through rubbing and body pressure rather than from prolonged penetration. There is also the man who has had wide sexual experience as a teenager, in the process of which he has developed a near-total lack of regard for women. The female exists, in his thinking, solely for his gratification, an instrument for his sexual release. Her needs and welfare are of no concern. Intercourse, in his selfishness, is truly a mounting process, in which delay of orgasm is neither necessary nor desirable. In fact, this utter disregard for their partners' sexual satisfaction was Masters and Johnson's most consistent and significant finding in their study of the early sexual histories of premature ejaculators.

Lastly, the practice of coitus interruptus (withdrawal) as a birth-control technique sometimes conditions premature ejaculation. The man finds himself unable to control ejaculation because he has never had to do so.

Only rarely does premature ejaculation have a physical basis, as has been pointed out. The glans may be abnormally sensitive because of, say, a chemical irritation. Or the prostate or the verumontanum (a part of the urethra) may be infected. But beyond these rare incidents, premature ejaculation is usually caused by emotional or psychological factors.

RETARDED EJACULATION.   Retarded ejaculation or ejaculatory over-control is a relatively rare form of sexual inadequacy in which a man has difficulty ejaculating while his penis is in a woman's vagina. He may, however, be able to ejaculate by masturbating or during a homosexual encounter, or, in the case of some married men, with a woman to whom he is not married (Masters & Johnson, 1970). Or he may not be able to ejaculate at all (Ovesey & Meyers, 1970). McCarthy (1981) reports clinical data indicating that perhaps up to 15 percent of men experience some form of ejaculatory inhibition occasionally or in certain situations.

Sometimes a man with a quite satisfactory normal ejaculatory ability loses it because of a psychologically traumatic experience. In other cases, the dysfunction is rooted in his distaste for his partner. The failure to ejaculate is merely a means of rejecting her. In other instances, fear of impregnating, the partner's known adultery, and the danger of children's walking in on the couple during coitus can cause a man, consciously or unconsciously, to withhold his ejaculate. Examination of a man's sexual attitudes, feelings of anxiety, sexual performance skills, and heterosocial interaction skills can lead to a better understanding of and more effective treatment of retarded ejaculation (McCarthy, 1981).

Female Sexual Dysfunction

The nation's leading sex therapists, Masters and Johnson (1970) and Helen Kaplan (1974, 1975), use somewhat different classifications to describe sexual dysfunctions in women. For example, Masters and Johnson have discarded the term **frigidity** in favor of *female orgasmic dysfunction*. They argue that frigidity has so many meanings for different people that more precise terminology is needed. A man desiring coitus seven times a week may consider his partner frigid because she wants it, or is orgasmic, only three times; the man who desires coitus three times weekly would consider her sex drive perfectly normal. (The third man who desires sex only once a week might well call her a nymphomaniac!) Kaplan tends to use the terms *frigidity*, *general sexual dysfunction*, and *female sexual unresponsiveness* interchangeably, and includes the problem (whichever term is used) as one of her four classifications of female sexual dysfunction.

Despite these differences in classification, there is a general agreement among sex therapists regarding the nature, cause, and treatment of the various forms of female dysfunction (Ard, 1974; Hartman & Fithian, 1972; Kaplan, 1974, 1975; Masters & Johnson, 1970; McCarthy et al., 1975). For our purposes, Kaplan's (1974) terminology will be used: (1) female sexual unresponsiveness (also called general sexual dysfunction), (2) orgasmic dysfunction, and (3) vaginismus. As mentioned earlier, sexual anesthesia (the fourth classification) is not a true sexual dysfunction and will not be included here.

Causative factors in a woman's sexual difficulties may be *organic, relational*, or *psychological* (Ellis, 1961). Organic causes include injuries to or constitutional deficiencies in the sexual apparatus, hormonal imbalance, disorders of the nervous system, imflammation or lesions of the internal or external genitalia and surrounding areas, excessive use of drugs or alcohol, and the aging process.

Relational factors suggest that the man may be a "sexual moron" whose

Sex Therapy for the Handicapped: A Case Study

Sexual expression among disabled men and women is a problem that has largely been ignored in settings where rehabilitation services are provided. Handicapped individuals have been regarded as nonsexual beings, and their rights of sexual expression generally have been denied. Recently, however, health professionals and society-at-large have begun to view the sexual needs of the disabled individual with greater empathy and understanding. The following case study provides an example of how the sexual needs of a woman with cerebral palsy were met through a sex therapy program (DeWolfe & Livingston, 1982).

The client in this case is a twenty-five-year-old woman who has had cerebral palsy since birth and who has experienced extreme physical limitation as a result of her condition. Her body is constantly in a state of nonpurposeful, spastic movement, and she frequently experiences muscle spasms. She spends many of her waking hours in a wheelchair with her arms restrained. Her hands are of only marginal use to her. She has some control over the movements of her head, and her speech, although slurred and unclear, can be understood. Personal aids or nursing staff help her with the majority of her daily activities.

During the course of her illness, neither health professionals nor her parents ever discussed the possibility that she might have sexual needs and desires and the wish to express them. She did not become aware of her sexuality until she became involved in a short-lived sexual relationship with a young man. Their sexual relationship had been satisfying to her, and she experienced oral-genital contact, coitus, and orgasm. After a few months, the young man ended the relationship for no known reason and with no discussion. She was unable to contact him and she felt abandoned, hurt, and angry. Although she felt powerless to do anything about the relationship, she resolved that she would deal with her sexual feelings and find an appropriate means of sexual release. She discussed

selfishness, overeagerness, or stupidity stifles romance and fills his partner with revulsion toward sex. Resentment, for whatever reason, can inhibit or destroy sexual functioning. So can any of a number of other forces, realistic or unrealistic. A common cause is a woman's inability to accept her mate. She may find him sexually unattractive or undesirable; he may be a poor provider; or he may not be the man she wanted to marry. For whatever reason, he does not fit her concept of "the right man" (Masters & Johnson, 1970). Because a woman is usually aware that sexual capability is highly important to a man, she can, by withholding her sexual response, express her conscious or unconscious hostility toward him (McGuire & Steinhilber, 1970).

The most common and by far the most important causes of female sexual dysfunctioning are psychological, typically such emotional problems as shame, guilt, and fear. In women under conflict about sex, erotic feelings arouse anxiety. These women's defense against sexual anxiety is not only to avoid sexual stimulation, but also to build defenses that will prevent their becoming aroused. Usually these women have been indoctrinated in a negative sexual value system based on the implication that sex is bad, whether in or out of marriage (Mas-her problems with a social worker and arrangements were made for her to enter a sex therapy program that accounted for her feelings as well as her sexual needs.

The sex therapy program designed for this client involved five phases: (1) sex education and information giving, (2) assessment of her physical capabilities, (3) recognition of and exploration of her sensual and sexual feelings, (4) enhancement of her sexual feelings by developing sexual fantasies, and (5) development of a special mechanical apparatus by which she could receive direct vibrator stimulation of her clitoris. The therapy also involved "homework" assignments during each of the five phases.

When the client was ready to begin using the vibrator apparatus, she still required much assistance. She not only required help in moving from her wheelchair to her bed, but she also needed help in removing her underwear and in being appropriately positioned on the vibrator apparatus. Once in position on the vibrator apparatus, the therapist and staff left her by herself in her room. She masturbated for fifteen to twenty minutes, and she became orgasmic after her second session. She requested that a favorite nude male photograph be placed so that she could view it while masturbating. After masturbating, the staff would help her back into her clothes and into her wheelchair.

After therapy was terminated, the client continued to use the vibrator for an additional six months. She met another man with whom she developed a satisfying sexual and emotional relationship. She later contacted her therapist to discuss her progress and to indicate that she no longer needed the vibrator. She eventually married this man and left the residential rehabilitation setting to live with him.

Through the course of her therapy program, this woman experienced changes in her self-awareness and in her capacity to express her sensual and sexual feelings. Her sense of self-esteem improved and positive changes in her behavior were noted by her friends, her social worker, and the rehabilitation staff. She became better able to verbalize her feelings of anger regarding her brief affair, and she generally became more positively assertive.

ters & Johnson, 1970). Even if they cannot avoid sexual activity on the physical plane, they can minimize their participation by refusing to become involved in the interaction of sexual response. Other factors responsible for a woman's unresponsiveness are many and varied. She may expect physical pain in coitus and therefore dread it. She may fear rejection or condemnation by her lover if she lets herself go sexually; she may be frightened of becoming pregnant. She may have homosexual tendencies, be too emotionally tied to her father, or bear a repressed hostility toward men in general (Ellis, 1960, 1961).

Female Sexual Unresponsiveness

Sexually unresponsive women vary considerably in their capacity for erotic sensation or sexual pleasure. Some are completely devoid of desire and consider sexual contact an unbearable ordeal; some find coitus disgusting or frightening, and endure it only to preserve the relationship; some find no erotic pleasure in the act, but derive distinct emotional fulfillment from the physical closeness of coitus.

In classifying female sexual unresponsiveness and orgasmic dysfunction as separate entities, Kaplan (1974) points out that some women have no erotic feelings in sex play, show no physiological signs of arousal, and are "dry and tight"; yet they may respond to orgasm rather easily once coitus is initiated. The most inhibited woman is the most difficult to treat, quite naturally. The prognosis is considerably brighter if the patient presently has some responsiveness, or if she has been responsive in the past but now is not because of some situational circumstance.

A five-year study (Fischer, 1973) of the sexual responsiveness of middle-class married women in Syracuse, New York, failed to confirm many previously held beliefs about female sexuality. For example, no relationship was found between a woman's orgasmic responsiveness and the man's sexual technique, her source of sex education, her parents' attitudes toward sex, or her religiosity, femininity, general mental health, traumatic sexual experiences (or lack of them), sensitivity to stimulation, or premarital and marital experience. These findings confirm other research showing that women who experience orgasm through vaginal penetration are no more emotionally mature than those who achieve it through direct clitoral stimulation. In fact, about 66 percent of the women stated that, of the two, they prefer clitoral stimulation.

Orgasmic Dysfunction

The sexual dysfunction most commonly complained about by women is orgasmic difficulty: (1) the inability to achieve orgasm, (2) the ability to achieve orgasm by means other than coitus, but not through coitus, or (3) coital orgasms that are more slowly achieved than either they or their partners would like. Female orgasmic dysfunction is classified as either primary or situational. The woman in the primary category has never achieved an orgasm in her life through any method of sexual stimulation. The woman in the situational category has managed to achieve at least one orgasm in her experience, whether by coitus, masturbation, or some other form of stimulation, but no longer does so (Masters & Johnson, 1970).

The causes of orgasmic dysfunction are much the same as those causing female sexual unresponsiveness (or frigidity). Further, orgasm may have acquired some symbolic meaning, signifying to the woman submission to the male or loss of self-control; or the intensity of the orgasmic experience frightens her. Whatever the cause, the physiological result is an involuntary inhibition of the orgasmic reflex. The woman is afraid to "let herself go," and she unconsciously reinforces the control because it also holds her sexual anxieties at bay. The syndrome becomes so automatic that the woman is unable to climax even when she loves her partner, is unanxious, is sexually aroused, and wants to experience orgasm.

Both research results and clinical findings differ in their assessment of women's orgasmic capabilities. Estimates vary, but 90 percent or more of all American women are able to achieve orgasm by one means or another, although perhaps less than 50 percent of women reach orgasm regularly during coitus without additional clitoral stimulation (Kaplan, 1974; Wilcox & Hager, 1980). Recent research indicates that many women may be orgasmic with proper stimulation of the anterior vaginal wall (Hoch, 1980).

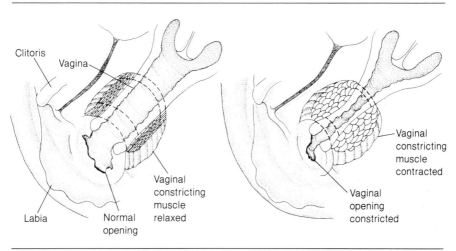

Clitoris
Vagina
Labia
Normal opening
Vaginal constricting muscle relaxed
Vaginal constricting muscle contracted
Vaginal opening constricted

Figure 14.2   Schematic representation of the vagina, showing vaginal muscles relaxed (left) and contracted (right) in spasms of vaginismus.

Certain women do not wish to have orgasms coitally or are unable to. They should be assured that they are in no way neurotic, maladjusted, or sexually inadequate, nor is their partner an inadequate or a poor lover. Some women who reach coital orgasm easily nonetheless prefer manual, vibrator, water-spray, or oral stimulation. Some people prefer vanilla ice cream, others prefer chocolate; the rationale is the same.

Vaginismus

Vaginismus is an extremely powerful and often severely painful contraction of the muscles surrounding the vaginal tract, which may persist for long periods of time (Figure 14.2). In severe cases, even the attempt to introduce the penis into the vagina will produce agonizing pain, making penile penetration impossible. In less severe cases, vaginal spasms merely delay intromission or make it more difficult. Vaginismus is considered a sexual dysfunction only when its severity is such that penetration is not possible (Wabrek & Wabrek, 1976).

Masters and Johnson assert that the chief cause of vaginismus is an impotent male whose repeated attempts at sexual intercourse followed by an equal number of failures have so frustrated his partner that she protects herself subconsciously by closing the vaginal doors. Other important causes are anticipated pain of first penile penetration; fear or guilt concerning coitus; inhibitions formed by emotionally traumatic experiences, such as rape; conflict growing out of homosexual tendencies; and physical abnormalities that make intercourse extremely painful (Masters & Johnson, 1970). The noted marriage counselor David Mace has suggested an additional dimension in the problem of vaginismus. He theorizes that in some instances the woman is saying to her partner, in effect, "I am afraid to let you come fully into my life by opening myself freely and trustfully to you" (Mace, 1971b).

Men as well as women must understand the dynamics behind vaginismus in order to avoid any behavior that will produce discomfort for either partner. A selfish, inconsiderate, and brutal man can do irreparable damage by forging ahead like a battering ram in his attempts at sexual intercourse when his partner is suffering these muscular spasms.

Vaginismus, strangely, seldom occurs in women of the lower socioeconomic-educational strata. It is an affliction almost exclusively of women in the upper levels of these groups.

Dyspareunia

A sexual problem often associated with vaginismus is **dyspareunia**, or painful coitus. Both men and women may experience it, although women are affected far more frequently. Genital injuries, such as tears, lacerations, bruises, or ruptures, can occur in women who experience intercourse that is too rough or vigorous (Beazlie, 1981). Men sometimes experience acute pain at the time of erection, but that is not actually dyspareunia. Men suffer from dyspareunia only when orgasm causes severe, jabbing pain. The pain is commonly the result of congestion of the prostate, seminal vesicles, or ejaculatory ducts, or an inflamed verumontanum. In other cases, the pain may be caused by an irritation of the glans penis in the uncircumcised male arising from poor hygienic habits. Peyronie's disease can also make coitus painful for a man. Otherwise, dyspareunia in men is extremely rare.

Dyspareunia in women frequently has its inception in tension, fear, or anxiety over initial sexual intercourse, and the pain can involve vagina, cervix, uterus, or bladder. The vaginal muscles become taut and coitus can be painful, especially if the man is clumsy or insensitive. Furthermore, depending upon the type and thickness of the hymen, pain may be experienced when the tissue is ruptured by penile penetration (Capraro et al., 1981; Ellis, 1960; Kaplan, 1979).

Coitus may be painful because of lesions or scar tissue formed in the vaginal opening as a result of an episiotomy, a crude nonprofessional abortion, or rape, especially gang rape (the last two quite predictably capable of causing as much emotional as physical trauma). Some women suffer considerable pain when the cervix is touched and moved by the penis during sexual intercourse; coitus, in fact, becomes impossible at times.

Dyspareunia in postmenopausal women frequently occurs because the mucous membrane of the vagina has become fragile and thin, sometimes shrinking to a fraction of its former thickness. It therefore does not secrete sufficient lubrication for easy penile intromission. Vaginal creams are frequently prescribed in such cases to act as a lubricant and to stimulate the mucous membrane.

A displaced or prolapsed uterus is another persistent cause of painful coitus in women. So also are polyps, cysts, and tumors of the reproductive system. Some women suffer pain during sexual intercourse because the vaginal barrel is irritated by the chemicals contained in contraceptive creams, foams, jellies, or suppositories. Other women react painfully to the rubber or plastic that condoms and diaphragms are made of, and to excessive douching. Still other women produce insufficient vaginal lubrication during coition, so that coital movements produce a painful or burning sensation. (In this last case, coital discomfort can be avoided by using a commercial lubricant.)

Medical opinion is that if dyspareunia persists over a period of time, small undetected lesions in the vagina (which cause 85 percent of the cases) are to be suspected. Furthermore, any infections of the vagina, uterus, bladder, or surrounding areas can obviously make intercourse painful for a woman.

Medical and surgical remedies are clearly of great value in many cases of dyspareunia. Nevertheless, the benefits of psychotherapy should not be overlooked when the foundations of the disorder appear to lie in emotional blocks and fears.

Inhibitions of Sexual Desire

Sexual dysfunctions can be understood within the framework of a biphasic model of sexual response. This model allows for sexual dysfunctions to be viewed as resulting from problems in the excitement or orgasmic phases. For example, impotence in males and general sexual dysfunction in females can be described as excitement phase disorders, and premature ejaculation in males and orgasmic dysfunction in females can be described as orgasmic phase disorders.

Helen Kaplan (1979) has emphasized that a triphasic model is necessary to more fully take into account the complete range of human sexual response. In addition to the excitement and orgasmic phases, the model recognizes the importance that a third phase, the *desire* phase, plays in human sexual response. The triphasic model thus leads to a more comprehensive understanding of human sexuality in general and of sexual dysfunctions in particular.

The importance of the third category in this triphasic model is seen in estimates that up to 40 percent of all sexual problems in men and women might result from inhibitions in the desire phase. The sexual conflicts that arise from desire phase disorders are often deep-seated and require intensive psychotherapeutic and psychosexual treatment. Anger, fear of failure, performance anxiety, sexual phobias, maladaptive communication patterns, fear of sexual success, and fear of intimacy may be at the root of desire phase disorders.

Kaplan's term for this third class of disorders is *inhibitions of sexual desire (ISD)*. She has found that the success rate of treatment is substantially less than the rate using the brief, supportive psychotherapeutic techniques and behavioral treatments for excitement and orgasmic phase disorders. Increasingly sophisticated treatment strategies, including desensitization techniques, sensate-focus exercises, insight-oriented psychotherapy, and sometimes medication, may improve the success rate of treatment of desire phase disorders.

Sometimes the emotional factors underlying desire phase disorders are so great that dramatic psychological reactions occur. One unusual case involved a man who became nauseated or developed headaches when sexual relations were initiated with his wife. His sexual aversion apparently developed when his mother moved into his home following the death of his father. The man's sexual guilt was so great that he could not respond sexually with his mother in the house. Unfortunately, the man was not amenable to any form of altered living circumstances or therapy, and thus his sexual aversion continued. Since the problem already had been evident for eight years, the man's wife was concerned that their sexual relationship would suffer until his mother died (Diana, 1981).

While specific cases such as the one just described may be relatively unusual, it is evident that desire phase disorders are more common than once realized. Indeed, some otherwise normal individuals may display a lifelong lack of interest in sexual activity that may not come to light until conflict or distress is expressed by their mates. Interestingly, desire phase disorders are now being observed more frequently in men, and it is becoming understood that these disorders are not limited to the wife's proverbial headache. Understandably, feelings of frustration, anger, depression, inadequacy, or fear may be manifested by persons involved in such relationships of sexual conflict (Jacobs, 1981).

Seeking Professional Counseling

Since the 1970 publication of Masters and Johnson's pioneering work, *Human Sexual Inadequacy*, concerning the treatment of sexual dysfunction, clinics and counselors specializing in sex therapy have multiplied throughout the country. Some are, of course, professionally qualified; many others are not. And, whether inspired by good intentions or by greed and their own personal problems, the latter have found it easy to prey on those seeking solutions to sexual problems. Needless to say, an untrained person passing himself or herself off as a sex therapist or counselor may only aggravate the patient's problems rather than relieve them. Since most people have no real means of knowing whether a particular clinic or therapist is legitimately qualified, what can they do?

Recognizing the need for special training and certification of sex therapists, in 1973 the American Association of Sex Educators, Counselors and Therapists (AASECT) took steps to protect the public. It appointed a group of the nation's most highly qualified professionals to establish guidelines for the training of sex counselors and therapists. AASECT next appointed a committee to review the qualifications of persons wishing to specialize in sex therapy. As a result, AASECT has become the best-known, although unofficial, organization of certification for sex therapists. Anyone seeking the names of qualified professionals in his or her part of the country should address inquiries to: AASECT; 2000 N Street, N.W. #110; Washington, D.C. 20036.

Summary

Specialists who study human sexual behavior have asserted that at least 50 percent of American marriages are flawed by some form of sexual maladjustment. Some sexual problems stem from ignorance about sexual techniques, whereas other problems are rooted in fears of failure, fears of rejection, or performance anxiety. Other sexual problems are more complicated, and the individuals

The Use of Surrogate Partners in Sex Therapy

One trend that has emerged in the treatment of sexual dysfunctions involves the use of surrogates in some sex therapy programs. In therapy programs where the services of a surrogate are applied, the surrogate works with the sexually dysfunctional client in accordance with supervisory instructions from the sex therapist who understands the therapeutic needs of the client. The surrogate may be a female who works with a sexually dysfunctional male, or the surrogate may be a male who works with a sexually dysfunctional female. In some instances, the surrogate may be employed to work with a homosexual client and thus may be a male working with a male or a female working with a female.

A sex therapist and client may elect to engage the services of a surrogate, particularly when there is no regular sex partner available to the client. In addition to the full range of male and female sexual dysfunctions, the services of a surrogate may be sought to help deal with concerns such as poor sexual self-concept or body image, questions about sexual orientation, special medical problems or physical disabilities (such as painful coitus or spinal-cord injuries), or sexual inexperience or naiveté.

The surrogate-client relationship usually involves emotional interaction as well as shared physical intimacy. Because of the special nature of this type of association, the surrogate-client relationship cannot be a typical businesslike interaction. On the other hand, the therapeutic goals of the relationship are primary in importance, and thus the therapist assumes an important role in developing the perspective of the sex therapy program. Most therapy programs are short term, lasting fifteen to twenty sessions on average, but the client often continues working with the therapist after the surrogate's participation in the sex therapy program has been discontinued. Occasionally an emotional attachment occurs between client and surrogate; and, if this occurs, it is important that the couple's feelings for each other be resolved, perhaps with the help of the therapist.

Sometimes a sex therapist will employ surrogates that the therapist supervises or trains individually to work with specific sexual problems. Other therapists turn to organizations such as the International Professional Surrogates Association to find trained, qualified surrogates for their clients. Many sex therapists elect to forego the use of surrogates and instead may rely on more traditional methods of treatment. Some therapists and lay people view the professional use of surrogates in sex therapy as an attempt to legitimize prostitution. On the other hand, those therapists who utilize surrogates in their sex therapy programs view the surrogate as being involved in an ongoing learning process that is aimed at helping the client develop more effective verbal and nonverbal communication skills. Obviously, the use of surrogate partners in sex therapy is a sensitive and controversial issue and is a form of interaction that is unacceptable to many (IPSA, 1982).

affected may require both sex therapy and psychotherapy. Those individuals affected by profound personal psychopathology require intensive psychotherapy rather than sex therapy.

The foundation of sex therapy programs to help sexually inadequate or disturbed individuals is the use of "sensate focus" or "pleasuring techniques," which key on developing the sense of touch.

Sex therapy programs have been used to treat sexual dysfunctions in both sexes. Those forms of sexual dysfunctions that affect men are: (1) *erectile dysfunction* (impotence), (2) *premature ejaculation*, and (3) *retarded ejaculation*. Those forms of sexual dysfunction that affect women are: (1) *sexual unresponsiveness*, (2) *orgasmic dysfunction*, and (3) *vaginismus*. *Sexual anesthesia* is also a type of sexual disturbance or disorder that affects some women.

Erectile dysfunction or impotence refers to a man's inability to attain or maintain an erection of sufficient strength to enable him to perform the act of intercourse. Three forms of impotence exist: (1) *organic impotence*, caused by some anatomical defect in the reproductive system or central nervous system; (2) *functional impotence*, caused by a nervous disorder, the excessive use of alcohol or drugs, circulatory problems, the aging process, or exhaustion; and (3) *psychogenic impotence*, caused by emotional inhibitions that block or interfere with sexual response. Psychogenic impotence is further classified as either *primary* (implying that the man has never been able to achieve or maintain an erection to engage in coitus) or *secondary* (indicating that the man has had at least one successful coital experience but is now incapable of it). Anxiety, guilt, or the anticipation of failure often underlies the problem of impotence.

Premature ejaculation refers to ejaculation prior to, just at, or soon after intromission. Different definitions establish different guidelines for what is considered premature ejaculation based on time of intromission, the number of pelvic thrusts, or the sexual requirements of the individual's partner. Only rarely does premature ejaculation have a physical basis. More often, it is the psychological forces (including anxiety) that act to block a man's perception of the sensations that lead up to orgasm.

Retarded ejaculation is a form of sexual inadequacy in which a man has difficulty ejaculating while his penis is in a woman's vagina. Fear, performance anxiety, or minimal commitment to the woman is often an underlying factor in this sexual dysfunction.

Organic, relational, and, more commonly, psychological causes are contributing factors in female sexual dysfunctions. Additionally, factors such as expectation of pain in coitus, fear of rejection, fear of becoming pregnant, or harboring hostility toward men in general can also be responsible for the unresponsiveness of a woman.

Women who experience female sexual unresponsiveness may be devoid of desire entirely. On the other hand, they may find coitus disgusting or frightening, or they may find no erotic pleasure during coitus although they derive emotional fulfillment.

The sexual dysfunction women most commonly complain of is orgasmic difficulty. Female orgasmic dysfunction is classified as "primary" if the woman has never achieved orgasm through any method of stimulation and as "situational" if the woman has managed to achieve at least one orgasm through coital or noncoital means but no longer does so.

Vaginismus refers to the presence of strong muscular contractions within the vagina that make penile penetration impossible. The causes of vaginismus include a fear of pain associated with penile penetration, fear, guilt, frustration concerning coitus, inhibitions formed by emotionally traumatic experiences, conflicts growing out of homosexual tendencies, and physical problems that make intercourse painful. Vaginismus occurs most commonly in women who are in the upper socioeconomic and educational strata.

Dyspareunia, a sexual problem often associated with vaginismus, is painful or difficult coitus. Men may suffer from dyspareunia, although women are more frequently affected. Emotional factors, physical traumas, disorders, diseases, infections of the reproductive system, and insufficient vaginal lubrication are among the factors that can cause dyspareunia in women. Medical and surgical techniques as well as psychotherapy are treatments for this sexual problem.

Recent evidence indicates that a triphasic model of human sexual response may exist and that a more comprehensive understanding of human sexuality may be gained by recognizing the roles played by the desire, excitement, and orgasmic phases of this model. This triphasic model has the particular strength of allowing for a clearer understanding of inhibitions of sexual desire. As a result, increasingly sophisticated and effective treatment strategies are being developed that soon may improve the success rate in treating the heretofore misunderstood or ignored desire phase disorders.

TRUE OR FALSE: THE FACTS

Sexual inadequacies or dysfunctions exist in only a small percentage of marriages.
False. Estimates say that up to 50 percent of American marriages are flawed by some sort of sexual inadequacy or dysfunction. (264)

❦

Sexual dysfunctions are typically caused by emotional rather than physical factors.
True. In both men and women, emotional or psychological factors are the most common and most important causes of sexual dysfunction. (268, 274)

❦

Lack of sexual desire among men and women is rare.
False. Some estimates say that up to 40 percent of all sexual problems in men and women might result from inhibitions in the desire phase. (279)

SUGGESTED READING

Barbach, Lonnie Garfield. *For yourself: The fulfillment of female sexuality.* New York: Doubleday, 1976.
This book is an excellent practical guide for women who have orgasmic difficulties or other sexual concerns.

Kaplan, Helen Singer. *Disorders of sexual desire.* New York: Brunner/Mazel, 1979.
The author uses detailed case studies drawn from her own experience as a clinician to demonstrate treatment of various sexual dysfunctions, especially problems of desire. Included in the Appendix are valuable tables covering the effects of drugs and physical illness on sexuality and the physical causes of dyspareunia.

LoPiccolo, Joseph, and LoPiccolo, Leslie. (Eds.). *Handbook of sex therapy.* New York: Plenum, 1978.
This outstanding source volume for clinicians provides comprehensive coverage of the etiology and treatment of male and female sexual dysfunctions and professional and ethical issues in sex therapy.

Masters, William H., and Johnson, Virginia E. *Human sexual inadequacy.* Boston: Little, Brown, 1970.
Based on the authors' intensive clinical research, this important source volume for professionals and students describes the causes and methods of treatment of sexual dysfunctions in men and women.

McCary, James Leslie, and McCary, Stephen P. *McCary's human sexuality* (4th ed.). Belmont, Calif.: Wadsworth, 1982.
Chapter 20 summarizes the research and treatment of sexual dysfunctions and forms the basis of this discussion.

Nowinski, Joseph. *Becoming satisfied: A man's guide to sexual fulfillment.* Englewood Cliffs, N.J.: Prentice-Hall, 1980.
This book is a practical guide for men who have sexual concerns. This book is designed to enhance understanding of sexuality and to aid in dealing with erectile problems, overcoming sexual tension and fear of women, and many other problems.

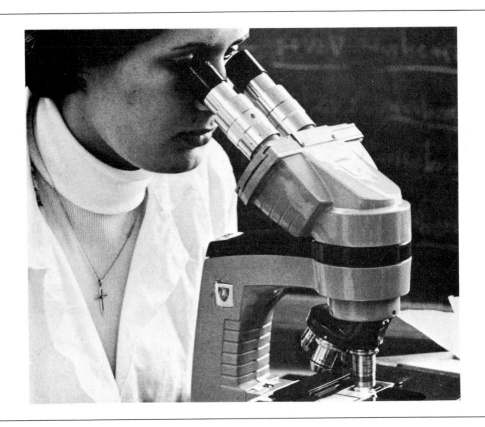

TRUE OR FALSE?

Sexual diseases are commonly picked up from toilet seats, public swimming pools, and so forth.

The symptoms of gonorrhea are readily detectable.

If a chancre associated with syphilis disappears or goes away, then one cannot assume he or she is no longer infected.

A woman does not need a Pap smear test until she has had a child or has reached middle age.

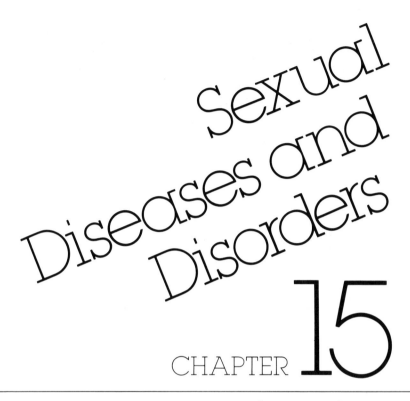

Sexual Diseases and Disorders

CHAPTER 15

Sexually Transmitted Diseases
Gonorrhea
Syphilis
Genital Herpes
Acquired Immune Deficiency Syndrome

Nonvenereal Diseases
Nonvenereal Syphilis
Leukorrhea
Trichomoniasis
Candidiasis or Moniliasis
Carcinoma
Dermatoses
Inflammation of Internal and External Genitalia

Sexual Disorders
Chromosomal Anomalies
Hermaphroditism

Summary

Suggested Reading

Sexually Transmitted Diseases

variety of diseases, infections, and inflammations can afflict the male and female genital organs. **Sexually transmitted diseases** or STD (formerly called venereal disease or VD) implies contagious diseases communicated mainly through sexual contact. Sexually transmitted diseases attack men, women, and children, and are considered to be among the most serious afflictions of humankind.

The discovery of penicillin and other antibiotic drugs has made it possible to control STD, but eradication remains only a hope. Control depends on adequate treatment of the infected individual and of every person with whom he or she has had sexual contact. Cases of STD should be reported to public health officials, who are responsible for contacting those who might have been infected by the person whose case is reported and arranging for their treatment. Many cases are not reported, however, making it difficult to locate and treat those who carry STD.

Infected individuals are often reluctant to seek treatment because of ignorance or guilt. Teenagers, in whom the increase in STD has been the greatest, frequently do not feel free to turn to their parents with a problem of this nature, and few of them have ready access to a physician in whom they can confide. Some individuals who contract STD are simply unwilling to disclose the identity of their sexual partners. In addition, physicians often fail to report cases that involve their private patients. As a result, the person who infected the patient—and those whom the patient has subsequently infected—are not contacted and treated.

The nature of the diseases themselves complicates the reporting and contacting process. **Syphilis** has an incubation period (the period between the infection of an individual and the manifestation of the disease) of about three weeks; this time lapse often permits health officials to seek out and treat those who have been infected before they become contagious. **Gonorrhea**, however, has an incubation period of only two to eight days. Persons who become infected with gonorrhea, therefore, may have already transmitted the disease to others before they can be contacted (Quinn, 1971). This, and the fact that there are no clinical symptoms of gonorrheal infection in about 80 percent of the women who contract the disease, have led to the current epidemic. The rate of increase in gonorrhea is 15 percent per year and shows no sign of abating (Quinn, 1971; Smartt & Lighter, 1971). Even if all cases were reported, adequate public funds are not available to assist medical authorities in searching out and treating infectious contacts. In the United States, public apathy continues to limit the efforts of agencies working to combat STD.

One segment of the population showing the greatest increase in venereal disorders in recent years has been the male homosexual group (Ginsberg, 1980; "Syphilis Trends," 1981). Studies reveal that as many as 60 percent of male homosexuals contract STD. This figure increases to 78 percent if other

Table 15.1. Sexually Transmitted Disease Rates per 100,000 Population, 1980

Age	Male	Female	Total
	Primary and Secondary Syphilis		
10–14	0.5	1.3	0.9
15–19	18.7	15.0	16.9
20–24	52.6	19.0	35.8
25–29	52.9	12.4	32.6
30–34	39.2	7.6	23.2
35+	6.8	1.3	4.1
Age	*Gonorrhea*		Total
10–14	23.6	74.8	48.7
15–19	930.0	1,414.5	1,168.3
20–24	2,102.2	1,458.6	1,780.5
25–29	1,449.8	636.3	1,040.7
30–34	727.8	245.9	484.0
35+	94.0	24.9	59.7

Source: U.S. Department of Health and Human Services, Public Health Service, *Sexually transmitted disease statistical letter, 1980.* Atlanta: Center for Disease Control, 1982b.

types of sexually transmitted disorders (such as head or crab lice) are considered. The risk of contracting a disease or disorder is greatest for those individuals who engage in sexual relations with many partners and for those who have casual, anonymous sexual encounters—for example, in public restrooms or gay baths ("Study Finds Sixty Percent," 1981). The same sexually transmitted infections are seen in the homosexual population and among heterosexuals, although the sites of infection may be different (Unger, 1975). In the general population, the incidence of syphilis and gonorrhea is highest among the group between twenty and twenty-four years old. Of those affected, 60 percent of the females and 80 percent of the males are single (Table 15.1).

Studies have revealed no "typical" teenager more likely than another to contract STD. The infected young people studied were of all personality types and represented the whole spectrum of American society. Of the cases treated at STD clinics, the majority, as might be expected, came from low-income minority-group families. The other infected youngsters were no doubt treated by their private physicians. Otherwise, the statistics showed that, although most of those infected had begun high school, only about 15 percent had graduated.

Factors other than heightened or more indiscriminate sexual activity in the general populace have also contributed significantly to the rise in STD observed in recent years. First, use of the condom, which offers protection against pregnancy and venereal infection alike, has not kept up with the increase in incidence of sexual intercourse. Second, several strains of gonococcus have demonstrated a measure of resistance to the usual dosage of penicillin, the treatment of choice, while at least one strain is altogether unaffected by it. Third, asymptomatic gonorrheal infection in both men and women is on the rise, meaning unwitting infection of others. A fourth factor has been the general ineffectiveness of public health agencies in tracking down sexual contacts of infected persons, and a fifth has been the addition to the STD roster of certain diseases (such as herpes) that were previously considered nonvenereal (Piemme, 1974).

When there is even the slightest suspicion that one's partner or oneself may have STD, prophylactics should be used during sexual intercourse. The simplest and best prophylactic for men, if they suspect their sexual partner is infected, is the condom, followed by a thorough soap-and-water cleansing of the genitalia after coitus. If a woman is going to have sexual intercourse with a partner of unknown hygiene, she should insist that he use a condom; and if there is any suspicion that sexually transmitted disease is present, she should use an antiseptic douche, followed by a soap-and-water cleansing of the genitalia.

Following is a discussion of a variety of sexually transmitted diseases. It is presented in the belief that sex instruction is incomplete without such information. It also rests on the conviction, supported by research, that knowledge can help contain the spread of STD.

Gonorrhea

Gonorrhea is both the most ancient and the most prevalent of all sexually transmitted diseases. Today the incidence of gonorrhea is second only to the common cold among communicable diseases in the United States. Gonorrhea is referred to in the Bible and in Chinese writings dating back as early as 2637 B.C. Before the advent of "miracle drugs" in 1943, it was not easily cured, and complications often resulted. The disease is usually considered relatively minor today and can easily be treated, although some strains of gonorrhea are apparently building resistance to the drugs used in treatment.

Primarily a disease of the young, gonorrhea's highest incidence is among men twenty to twenty-four years old. Its second highest incidence is among those fifteen to nineteen years old. After the age of twenty-five, the incidence declines steadily. Although gonorrhea is almost always contracted during sexual intercourse with an infected person, a recent study revealed that, even without the use of a condom, the risk of men acquiring gonorrhea by sexual contact with an infected woman is only about 20 to 30 percent after one or two acts of coitus (Holmes, 1975; Holmes et al., 1970). The gonococcus usually restricts itself to the genitourinary area, although the rectum may be infected during anal intercourse or, in the case of women, by spreading from the genitals (Oill & Guze, 1980). Homosexual males and heterosexual females who engage in fellatio and have gonorrhea in another body location have a pharyngeal infection in approximately 20 percent of cases (Ginsberg, 1980).

In a man, gonorrhea usually manifests itself by acute *urethritis*, an inflammation of the urethra. A thin watery discharge from the penis begins from two to seven days after infectious sexual contact, usually becoming thicker and greenish yellow in color within another day or two. There is usually a frequent and urgent need to urinate, and urination causes a burning sensation at the tip of the penis, which has become swollen and inflamed.

Painful and sometimes serious complications commonly result from untreated gonorrhea. One of the most agonizing is **epididymitis**, characterized by a swelling of the structures leading from the testes. The testes themselves may swell from the infection, sometimes becoming as large as an orange and extremely painful (Roen, 1981). Other possible complications include inflammation of the joints or of the eye, skin infections, and, more rarely, inflammation of the membranes of the heart or brain.

As many as 80 percent of women who contract gonorrhea manifest no visible symptoms (Ginsberg, 1980). When the disease does cause symptoms, the first is a vaginal discharge beginning two to seven days after infectious contact. The vulva becomes red, raw, and irritated. There is an urgent and frequent need to urinate, and urination is often accompanied by pain and a scalding sensation. Because women are so often unaware of the infection and hence do not seek medical attention, and because diagnosis and treatment are more difficult in women than in men, gonorrheal complications in women are considerably more common and severe than they are in men (Fletcher & Landes, 1970). Asymptomatic gonorrhea, if left untreated, may lead to **salpingitis**, or inflammation of the fallopian tubes, in about 50 percent of the cases. This condition, also known as pelvic inflammatory disease (PID), is painful and can cause sterility if scar tissue forms, thus blocking the fallopian tubes.

The majority of men and women with rectal gonorrhea are asymptomatic, but symptoms such as anal itching and discomfort and anal discharges may develop (Oill & Guze, 1980).

Although the source of gonorrheal infection is almost always sexual intercourse, children are sometimes infected through mutual masturbation, sexual exploration and experimentation, or sexual assault. At one time, nearly 33 percent of all blindness in children was the result of infection of the eyes acquired in the birth process from mothers with gonorrhea. This problem has now been almost completely eradicated by treating the eyes of newborn babies with a solution of silver nitrate (Blau, 1961).

The treatment of gonorrhea is usually quick and simple. For men, a single injection of 2.4 million units of penicillin is recommended. For women (and men with anal gonorrhea), the recommended dosage is double that, or 4.8 million units. The dosage is divided into two injections given during a single visit to a clinic. When the patient is allergic to penicillin, or is penicillin-resistant, one of the tetracycline drugs may be successfully substituted. Tetracycline drugs may be contraindicated, however, in women who are pregnant.

Nongonococcal urethritis (NGU) may affect both men and women. The symptoms of NGU are similar to those of gonorrhea, although it is ordinarily not considered a sexually transmitted disease. The difference between them is that in NGU the bacterium known to cause gonorrhea is not found in a smear of the urethral discharge. The urethritis may be caused by trichomonads, fungi, or other infectious agents (McCormack, 1976; Oriel, 1980).

Syphilis

In 1530 the physician Fracastoro published a poem, which achieved wide popularity, about a shepherd named Syphilis who had been stricken with a disease that, until then, had been known as "the great pox." The disease has been known ever since as syphilis.

It is still debated whether Christopher Columbus and his crew brought syphilis to America from Europe, or whether they contracted the disease from West Indian women and then carried it to Europe. It seems unlikely that Columbus and syphilis arrived simultaneously in America, however, since study of the bones of American Indians indicates that syphilis existed in America at least 500 years before Columbus's voyage. Whatever the reason, syphilis spread in epidemic proportions across the known world within a few years after Columbus and his men returned to Europe from their historic journeys. Columbus himself probably died, in 1506, from general **paresis**, one of the neurological disorders resulting from syphilitic infection (Coleman, 1972). About 400 years later, in 1905, the causative organism of syphilis, the **spirochete** *Treponema pallidum*, was discovered, and the relationship between syphilis and paresis was subsequently recognized.

Once the villain spirochete had been identified, extensive studies were made of the disease, and effective methods of diagnosis, such as the Wassermann test of blood serum, were developed. In the past, syphilis was treated by a combination of bismuth and arsenic administered alternately and slowly for as long as two years or more. This treatment was coupled with fever induced either by typhoid germs or by extensive applications of heat. Since 1943, when penicillin was discovered, syphilis has been treated quickly and easily, sometimes by one powerful injection. The recommended dosage for men is 2.4 million units given in a single injection. A penicillin-sensitive patient can be treated with tetracycline or erythromycin (Brown et al., 1971).

It is important to recognize syphilis during its early phase, the two years following infection. At that time, irreversible tissue damage has not yet occurred and the disease can be most easily cured. This is also the period when the patient is most infectious and is the greatest menace to public health. The early phase is subdivided into primary and secondary stages of infection. The *primary stage* of syphilis is easily identified by a lesion or a **chancre** (sore) that appears in the anal-genital area from ten to forty days after infectious sexual contact. In some cases, the sore may appear in the mouth or on the tonsils or lips, and the infection may be extragenital in origin (S.A.M. Johnson, 1981).

The chancre begins as a small red papule (a solid, cone-shaped lump on the skin) and then becomes eroded and moist. The only other sign at this stage is a painlessly swollen lymph gland near the site of infection. For example, if the chancre is on the penis or labia minora, the glandular swelling will be in the groin. If the disease is treated at this stage, all danger of further complications or of transmission to another person is removed. Without treatment, the primary chancre heals in four to ten weeks, removing the warning signal but not the danger of internal damage.

The *secondary stage* usually begins as a nonitching rash on the trunk of the body. The rash begins after six weeks and usually within three months of infection and sometimes is so indistinct as to escape notice. Other symptoms appear at this time, but they are usually not recognizable as syphilis-related

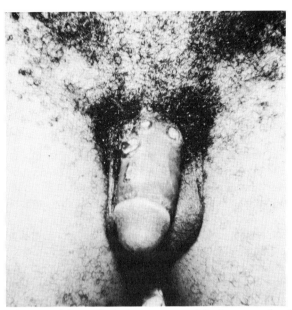

Multiple primary chancres of the penile shaft, a symptom of the first stage of syphilis. *Photograph courtesy of the Center for Disease Control, Atlanta, Georgia.*

except by a physician. They include glandular enlargement, throat infection, headaches, malaise, and a low-grade fever. Sometimes there is also a loss of eyelashes, eyebrows, and scalp hair, causing a "moth-eaten" appearance. Secondary lesions heal, without treatment, within a few weeks or months or possibly a year. No scar tissue remains as an indication of the presence of syphilis, and the only method of diagnosis after this stage is a blood serum test.

The *third stage*, or *latent period*, of syphilis begins from six months to two years after the initial infection. The disease is termed *early latent* when the patient has been infected less than four years or is under twenty-five years of age. Syphilis is considered *late latent* when infection has persisted longer than four years, or when the patient is over twenty-five. During the latent period there are no symptoms associated with syphilis, and the latency may last for months or years. Syphilitics do not infect contacts during the latency period, but the results of a blood serum test are always positive. Without treatment, the disease can now progress to the destructive stage of late syphilis.

The *fourth stage*, or *late syphilis*, may manifest itself in any organ, in the central nervous system and the cardiovascular system and, particularly, on the skin. These symptoms can appear as late as thirty years after the initial infection. Late lesions may appear in the mouth and throat and on the tongue. The lesions are usually accompanied by thickening of the tissue or by destructive ulcers and are responsible for the crippling and disfiguring effects of syphilis. A chronic inflammatory process may develop in this late stage, involving bones, joints, eyes and other organs, and, especially, the cardiovascular system.

In the United States, although the disease still rages, modern methods of diagnosis and treatment have eliminated syphilis as "the great scourge." In 1980, for example, some 27,000 new cases were reported—although undoubtedly many more cases were not reported. Primary and secondary cases of syphilis occur most often in urban communities of 200,000 population or greater. Syphilis rates per 100,000 people have shown a sizable increase from 9.5 in 1977 to 12.0 in 1980 ("Syphilis Trends," 1981).

Untreated syphilis remains deadly in about 25 percent of those infected. About 50 percent of untreated cases experience no disability or inconvenience; another 25 percent have some residual evidence of the disease, but suffer no disability or shortening of life (Blau, 1961). Some authorities believe that the absence of severe ill effects in such a high proportion of untreated syphilitics is due to resistance to the disease built up by administration of penicillin and other antibiotics in the treatment of other earlier illnesses.

Untreated syphilis may produce certain severely disabling neurological and psychiatric disorders, the two most common being **neurosyphilis** and general paresis. In the past, about 5 percent of all untreated syphilis progressed to general paresis, but the figure has recently dropped to about 3 percent (Coleman, 1972). Neurosyphilis occurs in about 10 to 25 percent of untreated cases of syphilis (Greenwood, 1980).

The incidence of syphilis at birth, called **congenital syphilis**, has greatly lessened in recent years due to improved prenatal care of syphilitic mothers. In 1941 there were 13,600 cases of congenital syphilis diagnosed in children under one year of age in the United States. More recent data indicate that the number of cases of congenital syphilis has decreased from 451 in 1971 to 107 in 1981 ("Syphilis Trends," 1981). It is during the early stage of a woman's infection, the first two years, that syphilis may be transmitted by the mother to an unborn infant. If the mother is properly treated before her fourth month of pregnancy, the child is usually born free of syphilis.

Although there are usually pathological symptoms of congenital syphilis, the appearance of symptoms may be delayed until the child is ten or fifteen years old. In some cases they are delayed until he or she is as old as thirty. The course of congenital syphilis is similar to that of the second and third stages in the contracted form of the disease. Various degrees of mental defect may exist in cases of congenital syphilis, and there are sometimes developmental defects such as an increase in the cerebrospinal fluid in the skull or a decrease in the size of the brain. Hardening of the affected tissues and convulsions are also occasional developments from congenital syphilis. In other cases, pupillary signs (unusual changes and reaction of the pupils) might be the only indication of the disease.

Genital Herpes

Herpes is an acute skin disease affecting the external genitalia. There are two forms of herpes, Type I and Type II. About 90 percent of Type I appears above the waist, typically as cold sores or fever blisters affecting the lips, nose, or mouth. About 90 percent of the Type II infection appears below the waistline and is usually sexually transmitted. Until about 1965, Type II herpes was

If You Get Herpes . . .

In recent years public health officials have voiced alarm at and public attention has become focused on the increasing incidence of genital herpes. Indeed, genital herpes presently ranks second only to gonorrhea in incidence among sexually transmitted diseases in the United States. Authorities estimate that up to 35 percent of the general population have been exposed at some point to the herpes virus, while up to 8 percent of patients seen in clinics manifest symptoms of genital herpes infection. Genital herpes has thus become one of the most significant health problems in America today.

Those who have contracted genital herpes are understandably quite concerned about the emotional and physical effects the disease might have on their lives. They may fear, for example, that their present and future sex life will be disrupted. Many acquire a negative sexual self-image or fear they will carry forever the social stigma of being "diseased." Herpes sufferers also are concerned that they will continue to experience distressing physical symptoms, and they lament that a foolproof, effective medical cure has not been found for the disease.

All is not lost, however, if one contracts genital herpes. Of course, those who are afflicted with genital herpes can experience recurrent outbreaks of the disease, but steps can be taken to modify the physical symptoms of the disease as well as related emotional factors. For instance, emotional stress has been implicated as a factor that may lead to or aggravate recurrent outbreaks of genital herpes, and a herpes sufferer can take steps on his or her own or through various forms of therapy to manage stress more effectively or modify the sources of stress. Support groups for herpes victims have been established, and such groups may be effective in helping herpes sufferers deal more effectively with their concerns. Further, since transmission of the herpes virus is most likely to occur during active outbreaks of the disease, avoiding intercourse during outbreaks of herpes sores will decrease the likelihood of spread of the disease.

Although genital herpes has become a pesky sexually transmitted disease, particularly in recent years, if contracted it does not spell the end of one's sex life. Consultation with one's physician or allied health personnel can provide productive alternatives in managing genital herpes (U.S. Dept. of HHS, 1982a).

almost never seen by physicians in the United States. But since that time its incidence has increased dramatically, until it now ranks second only to gonorrhea in incidence and accounts for about 13 percent of all sexually related or transmitted disease in the United States. Further, there is increasing though inconclusive evidence that herpes Type II can cause cancer of the cervix (Amstey, 1974; Blough & Giuntoli, 1979; National Institute of Allergy and Infectious Diseases, 1976; Reyner, 1975).

Because of the growing practice of fellatio and cunnilingus in recent years, a mixture of the two herpes types is being found with increasing frequency in both facial and genital regions (Fiumara, 1980; Johnson, 1981). Symptoms are wide-ranging: from the formation of small blisters that burst to form small ulcers or that dry and harden into the crust typically associated with Type I, to the large, painful vesicles and enlarged and tender inguinal nodes usually associated with Type II. In the latter example, patients are extremely uncomfortable and may require analgesics.

The disease can be spread on one's own body by self-infection and can involve the entire external genitalia. Because the herpes virus remains in the body after the initial herpes infection goes away, symptoms of genital herpes can occur again. Fever, sunlight, menstruation, and emotional stress may trigger recurrent episodes in some herpes patients (U.S. Dept. of HHS, 1982a).

Pain during urination is a particularly distressing symptom reported by women. Doctors often prescribe application of lidocaine (Xylocaine) to the affected area to relieve pain during urination. If this is unsuccessful, victims may be instructed to sit in a pan of water and urinate into it. If the latter is unfeasible, spraying the affected area with cold water from a plastic bottle with a spray top while urinating may mitigate the burning (Chang, 1974; Fiumara, 1980).

Relieving the symptoms and preventing the recurrence of herpes infections have proven exceedingly difficult. In fact, no safe, totally effective treatment has been determined. One controversial treatment used by some physicians involves painting the lesions with a light-absorbing dye and then shining a fluorescent light on them. The virus becomes hypersensitive to light and can be inactivated by exposure to it (Kaufman et al., 1973). Some physicians do not advocate use of dye treatment because of the theoretical possibility of causing a malignancy.

Recently, physicians and medical researchers have begun to report success in treating herpes infections with chemotherapeutic agents such as 2-Deoxy-D-glucose, vidarabine, and acyclovir. Acyclovir, recently approved for use by the Food and Drug Administration, appears to be an effective treatment for the initial outbreak of genital herpes but is of dubious value in treating recurrent episodes (Blough & Giuntoli, 1979; Check, 1977; Gunby, 1980; "Study Cites Herpes Drug," 1982).

Acquired Immune Deficiency Syndrome

Acquired Immune Deficiency Syndrome (AIDS) is a sometimes fatal condition, characterized by a breakdown in the body's natural system of immunity or resistance to infection. Up to 40 percent of the people afflicted with AIDS have died of various infections, many of them from Kaposi's sarcoma, a form of cancer. Although the cause of AIDS is still a mystery, researchers suspect that a virus transmitted by direct contact with body fluids, especially blood and semen, may play a role.

Cases of AIDS reported thus far have occurred predominantly among sexually promiscuous homosexual and bisexual men, Haitian immigrants to the U.S., intravenous drug abusers, and persons suffering from hemophilia, a hereditary bleeding disorder. AIDS thus appears to be transmitted among homosexual men by contact with an infected sexual partner. Recent evidence suggests that the partner receiving the ejaculate may be at the highest risk of developing AIDS. Hemophiliacs may contract AIDS by receiving blood transfusions from an infected donor. Drug addicts may acquire AIDS by sharing contaminated needles.

The latency period for AIDS seems to range from a few months to two years after exposure. Thus, there may be a significant time period from the time AIDS is contracted to the time when recognizable clinical illness occurs. AIDS symptoms may include night sweating, unexplained fever, unexplained weight loss, enlarged lymph nodes, and skin lesions. Skin markings may take the form of purple or pink blotches harder than the surrounding skin.

Cases of AIDS have thus far been concentrated in urban areas that have large homosexual populations, such as New York and San Francisco. However, AIDS has been reported in a number of states and countries. Preventive measures such as the use of condoms, more careful selection of sex partners, and blood donor screening may help in controlling the spread of AIDS (U.S. Dept. of HHS, 1983; Shearer & Shearer, 1983).

Nonvenereal Diseases

Many diseases, infections, and inflammations affecting the male and female sexual systems may have no relationship to sexual activity. But in each instance some part of the internal or external genitalia is affected and may possibly be aggravated by sexual contact.

Nonvenereal Syphilis

Nonvenereal syphilis, an endemic infection acquired in infancy, is caused by an invasion of a parasitic organism closely related to the treponemal organism causing venereal syphilis (hence its inclusion here). The disease is frequently referred to as *yaws* or *pinta*. It affects many people in widely separated parts of the world and typically thrives in warm, moist climates and in conditions of filth. Penicillin has been used successfully in many countries in mass eradication campaigns conducted by the World Health Organization.

Leukorrhea

Leukorrhea is excessive vaginal mucous discharge caused by a chemical, physical, or infectious agent. Its pathogenesis is varied, and it is not a disease entity in itself. Women taking the Pill, for instance, especially a type with high estrogen content, frequently suffer from it, as do those infected with such organisms as trichomoniasis and monilia. Some vaginal discharge, of course, is to be expected under certain normal circumstances. Sexual excitement causes vaginal secretions to increase, and the mucous discharge of most women is greater than average just before the menses and throughout pregnancy. The discharge can be considered abnormal when it stains clothing, causes local symptoms, or has an offensive odor (Fiumara, 1976).

When the Pill is responsible for leukorrhea, the discharge is clear and odorless. But if it is annoying, the condition can be corrected by lactic acid or vinegar douching (1 teaspoon per quart of water) to balance the vaginal pH, or by taking a pill of different hormonal content. Foreign bodies—forgotten tampons, diaphragms, IUDs, or pessaries—often cause leukorrhea. In these cases the discharge may be purulent, blood-tinged or brown, and malodorous (Swartz, 1981). The foreign bodies must be removed, of course, and the removal followed by douching with lactic acid or vinegar (Fiumara, 1976).

Trichomoniasis

Trichomoniasis, a parasitic infection afflicting 25 percent of all women, is the most common minor gynecological disease. (**Gynecology** is the branch of medicine that deals with the female reproductive system.) The first indication of infection is usually a white or yellowish vaginal discharge accompanied by itching and burning. The discharge frequently causes protracted inflammation and soreness of the external area of the vulva. A separation of the inflamed labia often reveals a thick, smelly, bubbly discharge in the vestibule (Swartz, 1981).

Trichomoniasis sometimes causes severe itching rather than soreness. In either case, the condition seems to worsen immediately before and after menstruation. The symptoms vary in women, from very mild to very severe. No matter how minor the symptoms seem, a doctor should be consulted immediately if there is the slightest indication of infection.

Men also may suffer from this annoying infection, although they seldom experience the bothersome symptoms of copious discharge, itching, and burning that are typical in women (Cibley, 1980; Felman, 1980). If one sexual partner is found to be infected with trichomoniasis, the other should be examined also, since it is possible for a couple to pass the infection back and forth for many years if only one partner is treated. If a man is aware that he is infected and he wears a condom while engaging in sexual activity over a three- to four-month period, then the parasites will most likely die and lead to an end of the reinfection occurrences (Cibley, 1980).

Authorities disagree about where the parasites originate or precisely how one contracts the disease (other than from an infected sexual partner). While some classify it as a venereal infection, others have found that it can be contracted in a swimming pool or bathtub. However contracted, the incubation period is thought to be between four and twenty-eight days.

The drug Flagyl is reported to be about 85 percent effective in the treatment of trichomoniasis. Obtainable by prescription only, it is administered orally and cures the condition within ten to fourteen days in both men and women.

Trichomoniasis is usually complicated by simultaneous infections of monilia and perhaps one or several other bacteria. Treatment of trichomoniasis and any other accompanying infection should be rigorously pursued. While the disease is not considered serious, it can be tormenting and is sexually inhibiting.

Candidiasis or Moniliasis

Candidiasis, or moniliasis (commonly called **monilia**), is a fungus infection of the genital region that can cause acute discomfort, primarily in women. More frequently than not, monilia accompanies other infectious organisms, such as trichomonads.

The genital area afflicted with monilia has white cheesy spots on the vulva, in the vagina, and on the cervix. There may also be minute ulcerations of the labia minora and in some cases a thick or watery vaginal discharge that may be malodorous (Swartz, 1981). All these symptoms can eventually lead to a raw, bleeding surface if treatment by a gynecologist is not prompt and careful. Women who have been overtreated with antibiotic vaginal suppositories are susceptible to infection, as well as women who are pregnant and those who are on the pill. It is also found sometimes in children. A cure can be obtained, however, with persistent and adequate treatment under the direction of a gynecologist (Felman, 1980; Fiumara, 1976).

Carcinoma

Cancer can strike any part of the sexual system. Its symptoms are diverse, and one should immediately consult a physician upon recognizing any suspicious signal, such as the seven outlined by the American Cancer Society:

- Unusual bleeding or discharge
- A lump or thickening in the breast or elsewhere
- A sore that does not heal
- Change in bowel or bladder habits
- Persistent hoarseness or cough
- Persistent indigestion or difficulty in swallowing
- Change in the size or color of a wart or mole

Some researchers maintain that smegma and other impurities collect more easily under the foreskin of uncircumcised men and that these impurities can predispose them to penile cancer or their sexual partners to cervical cancer. Other researchers dispute this theory and offer evidence that points to no higher incidence of either penile or cervical cancer in uncircumcised men and their partners.

Women who begin to engage in coitus early in life and continue to engage in it on a regular basis thereafter are more liable to develop cancer of the cervix than are women who marry later in life ("Reassessing the Pill's Risks," 1980; Sebastian, 1980). Research data from studies of nuns indicate that chastity might be related to a low incidence of cervical cancer. The incidence of cancer of the uterus, ovaries, or breasts appears to be unrelated to chastity or to infrequent intercourse.

Whether or not the foreskin of a man has been removed by circumcision and regardless of how sexually active a woman is, sensible precautions against cancer should be taken by both sexes. Regular gynecological examinations, including a **Pap smear** test, could save the lives of thousands of women annually. The Pap test is a simple and painless procedure that involves taking a sample of cervical fluid by means of a cotton swab and examining the fluid for the presence of cancer cells. It is important that all women, regardless of their age or whether they have borne children, receive an annual Pap smear examination. Frequently, the vaginal discharge that can accompany cervical cancer is pungent and malodorous (Swartz, 1981). While there is no test analogous to the Pap smear that will detect cancer in the male genital system, it is advisable for every man to have a thorough physical examination every year, since many of the possible sites of cancer are routinely inspected in such an examination. For example, inspection of the prostate gland may reveal early signs of prostatic cancer.

Breast cancer, representing over one-fourth of all the cancers, is responsible for 20 percent of cancer-related deaths in women. Carcinoma of the breast is the most frequent cause of death for women in the forty- to fifty-year-old age group, so self-examination and gynecological examinations become especially relevant once women reach their middle years. Unless advised otherwise by their gynecologist, women should begin to develop good health habits early and learn breast self-examination techniques in their late teens. The questions associated with breast cancer are how most effectively to detect it and how, once a positive diagnosis is made, to treat the malignancy. In the first instance there is manual examination and, more recently, thermography, a technique of heat-sensitivity scanning of the breast. There is also the X-ray technique called mammography, said to pinpoint minute lesions undetectable in other examination techniques (Marchant, 1980).

In the second instance, the matter of treatment, radical mastectomy has been the traditional approach—the removal not only of the breast, but also of the lymph glands in the armpit and the muscles of the chest wall. The resulting disfigurement is an added psychological trauma to many women, who are already distressed from the realization of having a dreaded disease. Today some doctors are opting for less radical measures, arguing that, by the time many breast cancers are detected, the cancer has already spread and will recur no matter what form of surgery is done. Destruction of the primary cancer is therefore the best that doctors can do, they maintain, and this can be accomplished by radiation as effectively as by surgery.

Prostatic cancer represents 10 percent of the malignancy occurring in men and showed a 20 percent increase in the twenty-two-year period (ending in 1969) surveyed by the American Cancer Society in 1975. One investigator recently has cited American Cancer Society data indicating that prostatic cancer claims 22,000 lives each year (Mazur, 1980). Surgery in the case of a cancerous prostate is a far more radical procedure than in noncancerous cases, since tissues around the prostate must also be removed as a safety measure. Furthermore, advanced prostatic cancer, even when metastasized throughout the body (it typically spreads to the bones of the pelvis and spine before the patient is aware that anything is wrong), may be controlled dramatically when castration is performed or the patient is treated with female hormones. Both treatments, of course, are unfavorable to the patient's retaining his potency.

Testicular cancer affects primarily young men in their early twenties. Tes-

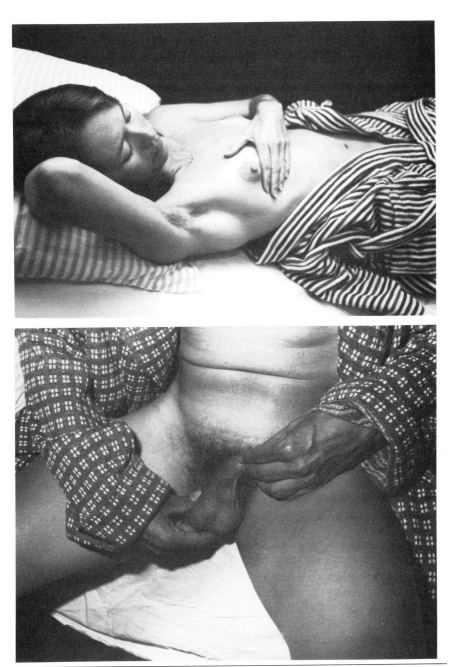

Female breast (top) and male testicular (bottom) self-examination techniques for early detection of lumps or irregularities. Self-examination techniques such as these are important aspects of preventive health care. *Larry Hanselka.*

ticular lumps may not cause pain in the affected testicle, but the disease may be indicated by other symptoms such as pain in the breasts and fluid accumulation or painful swelling of the scrotum. Early detection of this form of cancer is possible if men learn to make testicular self-examinations to check for unusual or possibly malignant lumps (Mazur, 1980).

Dermatoses

Dermatoses (skin diseases) of the genital region are fairly common. They have a wide variety of causes. Sometimes, for example, chemicals contained in soap that is not rinsed off after a bath or shower can collect in the sensitive areas of the genitalia and produce irritation or burns. Frequently the difficulty is compounded by the application of a medication that is too strong for the distressed area.

Tinea cruris, or *jock itch*, is a fungus infection that afflicts the genital region. Reddish, scaly patches develop into large, highly inflamed zones causing itching and pain—an infection strikingly similar to athlete's foot. Sweating, tight clothing, and inadequate drying of the genitalia after bathing provide a favorable environment for its development.

Scabies and pediculosis (*crabs*) are two of the dermatoses caused by parasites that can invade the genital area, as well as other areas—such as hands, wrists, and feet. **Scabies** is a highly contagious skin disorder in which a female mite burrows between the layers of skin and deposits her eggs. Little blisterlike vesicles housing the mite and her eggs appear on the skin surface and soon develop into papules, pustules, and a rash that itches formidably, especially at night. Medication prescribed by a physician can usually rid the victim of scabies in a short time.

In **pediculosis pubis**, the pubic hair is infested with crab lice, the bites of which cause an itchy skin irritation. Scratching produces further irritation, and a brownish discoloration of the skin may develop. The crab louse usually buries its head in the follicles of the pubic hair and attaches its body to the hair itself. These parasites, commonly passed from person to person through sexual contact, may also be picked up from a toilet seat or a bed. Medical treatment is available that kills the pediculi in the affected pubic area. Shaving the pubic hair is of no value in getting rid of the lice (Schneidman, 1980).

Inflammation of Internal and External Genitalia

The suffix *-itis* added to the name of an organ indicates inflammation of that organ. Many disorders of the internal and external genitalia of both men and women fall into this category.

Vaginitis, a fairly common irritation, may be caused by bacteria, foreign objects, or the use of strong chemicals. Douching with too high a concentration of chemicals, overmedication, tampons that are inserted and then forgotten, and incorrectly placed vaginal suppositories can all cause chemical burns and inflammation of the vaginal tract.

Excessive douching or the use of overly strong douches is frequently the basic evil, especially among the young and the newly married. Such douching destroys the protective organisms that naturally inhabit the vagina, reducing the acid condition and providing a suitable place for the development of hostile bacteria. In some cases, medicated douches may be useful as a treatment for vaginal disorders and as a preventive measure to eliminate infections associated with pelvic surgery (Connell, 1982). Most gynecologists agree, however, that a healthy vagina needs no douching, although studies have indicated that douching with water or with a mild vinegar or alkaline solution produces no harmful effects. Probably the best safeguard against vaginitis is good general physical health coupled with positive attitudes toward sex and personal hygiene.

Cystitis, inflammation of the bladder, may occur in a variety of ways. Symptoms include a severe burning sensation during urination, frequent urination, and sharp pain in the lower abdomen.

Irritation of a woman's bladder may occur as a result of frequent sexual intercourse due to the tendency of the bladder to become slightly displaced by the pressure of the penis and weight of the man's body. This condition frequently occurs during honeymoons when sexual intercourse is very frequent, and it is sometimes called "honeymoon cystitis." It is advisable for a woman to empty her bladder before sexual intercourse and to use a lubricating jelly when there is an insufficient amount of vaginal secretion. Both measures will decrease pressure on the abdominal organs through the vagina during coitus.

Sometimes cystitis is caused or aggravated by emotional factors, usually related to conflict over sexual matters. Whatever its cause, a physician should be consulted at the first sign of cystitis because early treatment helps to avoid complications. Daily cleansing of the external genitalia and of the urethral opening with surgical soap is an aid in treatment.

Epididymitis, a fairly common disorder among men, involves inflammation of the epididymis, the structure closely attached to each testicle. Gonorrhea is a major predisposing condition in epididymitis. In mild cases there might be only slight swelling and tenderness, while in severe cases the entire testicular structure may be greatly swollen and painful (Roen, 1981). Mild cases respond readily to medical treatment, but some cases of chronic epididymitis persist for years, and the condition can result in sterility.

Prostatitis, more common among older than younger men, is usually a chronic condition, although it can occur suddenly and become critical. There seems to be a clear relationship between infrequent sexual activity and the temporary enlargement of the prostate that accompanies chronic prostatitis. Prostatitis can also follow prolonged infection of other parts of the body. It is estimated that from 30 to 40 percent of American men between the ages of twenty and forty suffer from chronic prostatitis (Brosman, 1976).

Symptoms include a thin mucous discharge from the urethra and pain in the lower back, testicles, perineum, posterior scrotum, and sometimes the tip of the penis, especially at the time of ejaculation (Cawood, 1971). Prostatitis can also lead to painful or inadequate erection, premature and sometimes bloody ejaculations, impotence, and sterility. Treatment by a urologist includes prostatic massage, antibiotics, and prolonged warm baths to clear up the infection and to bring about drainage of the congested gland.

Sexual Disorders

Sexual disorders are customarily considered to be physical anomalies of the genitalia caused by hereditary, constitutional, or postnatal factors. These conditions are much more rare than most venereal and nonvenereal diseases.

Undescended testes are found in about one boy in fifty at the age of puberty; the incidence dwindles to approximately one in five hundred by adulthood. Pain does not necessarily accompany this condition (Roen, 1981); however, testes that remain undescended after puberty will progressively degenerate if their placement is not corrected. Hormonal treatment often causes a successful descent of the testicles unless there is some physical blockage. In this case, surgery is indicated.

Monorchism is a condition in which there is only one testicle in the scrotum. The existing testicle produces sufficient quantities of both hormones and sperm for normal physiological and sexual functioning. Sometimes one testicle is much smaller than the other, causing one to suspect monorchism. This inequality is not monorchism, however, since two testicles are present, and the small testis in such cases is usually functional, at least to some degree.

Congenital anomalies of the vagina, uterus, and fallopian tubes are more common than many realize. The vagina, for example, may be closed or missing entirely. If it is missing, an artificial vagina that is functional for sexual intercourse can be surgically constructed. Double vaginas also occur, or the vagina may be divided into two parts by a septum, as the nose is. Similar anomalies are also found occasionally in the uterus and in the fallopian tubes, or either of these might be missing altogether. Such congenital anomalies are usually the result of the failure of the Müllerian ducts (the embryonic forerunners of the female genitals) to fuse completely during prenatal development (Masters & Johnson, 1966; Netter, 1961).

An imperforate hymen is a condition in which the vagina is sealed off by a solid mass of hymenal tissue. It may go unnoticed until the onset of menstruation. Unless the hymen is punctured at the menarche, the menstrual fluid will be retained in the vagina, and the uterus must enlarge in order to contain the flow. Incision of the hymen corrects the condition easily and quickly. The hymenal tissue in this instance is inordinately thick and tough and must be surgically cut before penile penetration is possible (Capraro et al., 1981).

Abnormal uterine bleeding is the most frequent gynecological complaint encountered by physicians. Functional uterine bleeding refers to hemorrhages not precipitated by detectable abnormalities. If ovulation does not occur, too little or no progesterone is secreted, yet the secretion of estrogen continues. The result in some instances—although not all—is that the proliferation or growth phase of the menstrual cycle persists, and with it comes a thickening of the uterine lining.

In these circumstances there is no growth stimulation of the ovarian follicles because ovarian estrogen inhibits the release of the follicle-stimulating hormone from the pituitary gland. The uterine lining shows unnatural growth, and the follicles gradually convert into cystic structures. The irregular hormonal interplay frequently produces uterine bleeding that is abnormal both in frequency and amount.

Cervical erosion may result when any break in the cervical tissue, such as unhealed lacerations caused by childbirth, or any unusual exposure of the cervical mucous glands to the bacteria inhabiting the vaginal tract, makes the cervix susceptible to infection. Infection of this area, which is usually chronic and low-grade, might lead to erosion and ulceration of the cervical tissue, and correction might require a partial removal of the cervix.

Displacement of the uterus is said to exist when the womb becomes fixed in an abnormal position. The usual uterine position in a woman standing erect is approximately at right angles to the axis of the vagina, putting the uterus in an almost horizontal plane above the bladder. For various reasons, the ligaments supporting the uterus can become too taut or too loose, and the organ shifts to an unusual position, exhibiting a slight to great degree of deviation. The shift frequently causes painful menstruation, backaches, and pelvic congestion and makes sexual intercourse uncomfortable.

Endometriosis involves abnormal growth of the endometrium (lining of the uterus). Symptoms of the disorder may include sterility, painful and irregular menstruation, backaches, and painful sexual intercourse. The condition can occur as long as the ovaries produce hormones; it is most often found in women in their thirties. The tissue can begin to grow in any of various parts of the afflicted woman's body—the cervix, abdominal walls, intestines, Bartholin's glands, vulva; even the navel may be affected. Treatment depends upon the severity of the symptoms. If required, surgery usually involves removal of the organs or areas invaded, together with the surrounding tissue.

Menstrual cramps, when of a physiological origin, are usually caused by a tilted or infantile uterus, inadequate dilation or blockage of the cervical os, hormonal imbalance, endometrial disorders, or similar anomalies. Sometimes there is not a precise, specific, known physical cause, and psychological factors may be at the root of the problem (Dingfelder, 1980).

Congested ovaries and testicles occur following prolonged sexual stimulation without orgasmic relief. Since this is a common occurrence in women during an engagement period, the term "engagement ovaries" is frequently used. In men, the condition is referred to as "stone ache" or "blue balls."

Congenital and acquired anomalies of the breast are found in both men and women. The most frequent of these disorders among men is *gynecomastia*, in which there is an abnormal increase in breast size due to hormonal imbalance. Excess tissue can be shrunk by endocrine medication or removed by simple surgery.

Women may also possess abnormally enlarged breasts, or they can possess more than two breasts or nipples. Extra breasts and nipples usually are located somewhere in the milk line, which starts under the arm and extends through the breasts and down both sides of the abdomen in a line to the lips of the vulva, terminating in the inner thighs. Plastic surgery can correct all these abnormalities (Goin & Goin, 1980).

Chromosomal Anomalies

Several congenital sexual disorders are caused by chromosomal anomalies. The relationship between an abnormal karyotype (an arrangement of chromosomes) and certain disorders was first observed in 1938 and has since been studied in detail.

Best known of the chromosomal abnormalities are Turner's syndrome and Klinefelter's syndrome. These conditions are believed to arise from the faulty splitting of the 23 pairs of chromosomes during the formation of sperm or ova. The result is a germ cell (ovum or sperm) that contains an extra sex-determining (X or Y) chromosome or that is lacking one.

In **Turner's syndrome**, the total number of chromosomes contained in the fertilized ovum is only forty-five, rather than the normal forty-six: the sex karyotype is XO rather than XX (female) or XY (male). The abnormality will produce a woman having the primary external sex structure of a female, although poorly developed and infantile in size, but having no ovaries. Besides deficiencies in the primary and secondary sex characteristics, other typical indications of this disorder are a short stature, winglike folds of skin extending from the base of the skull to an area over the clavicle, and a broad, stocky chest. Deafness, urinary infections, cardiac defects, and mental deficiency are also fairly common. About one in 3,000 females is born with Turner's syndrome (Scott, 1980).

In **Klinefelter's syndrome** there is an extra female (X) sex chromosome in the fertilized egg, producing a man of incomplete virilization and distinctly feminine appearance. The testicles are small and incapable of producing mature sperm, and breast development is prominent. These men, furthermore, show a tendency toward mental impairment, and a large number can be characterized as having inadequate personalities. Predictably, their sex drive is low (Money, 1968).

A third form of chromosomal abnormality discovered in certain men, which has attracted considerable attention of late, involves extra Y (male) chromosomes. Some investigators have speculated that the disorder creates a "supermale," one who is more prone than average to undisciplined, aggressive, criminal, or sociopathic behavior (Gardner & Neu, 1972).

Hermaphroditism

Hermaphroditism is a rare congenital condition in which an individual cannot be clearly defined as exclusively male or female. Historically, the classifications of hermaphroditism that have been recognized are true hermaphroditism, male hermaphroditism, and female hermaphroditism. A fourth classification, dysgenetic hermaphroditism, has recently been discussed in the scientific literature (Money, 1980b; Money & Ehrhardt, 1972). Hermaphroditic classification is based on the form and structure of the gonads.

True hermaphroditism is a very rare condition in which an individual has the gonads of both sexes. That is, the true hermaphrodite possesses at least some ovarian and testicular tissue (Money 1968, 1980b; Money & Ehrhardt, 1972). At puberty the true hermaphrodite may develop a body that is ambigu-

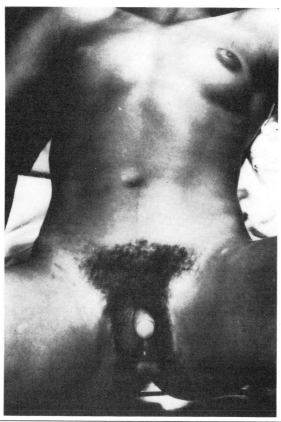

Photograph of a true hermaphrodite with a left ovary, a right testis, and forty-four-plus XX chromosome count. The subject always lived as a male and was married and a stepfather. *From Money*, Sex Errors of the Body. *Baltimore: The Johns Hopkins University Press, 1968.*

ous. Usually, however, the body of the true hermaphrodite becomes predominantly male or predominantly female in appearance (Money & Ehrhardt, 1972).

The *male hermaphrodite* has gonads that are testes, but the external genitalia are either ambiguous or feminine in appearance (Money 1968; Money & Ehrhardt, 1972). The gonads of the *female hermaphrodite* are ovaries, but the external genitalia are either ambiguous or masculine in appearance, even a penis and an empty scrotum. The male hermaphrodite sometimes develops a totally feminine body at puberty, irrespective of attempted treatment; the female hermaphrodite, untreated, may develop a totally male body at puberty.

Dysgenetic hermaphroditism occurs in the case of an individual who fails to develop completely the gonads of either sex and thus cannot be classified as either a true male or true female hermaphrodite.

One factor known to cause female hermaphroditism is the presence of androgen, the male sex hormone, during a critical stage in prenatal development. Because of a genetic defect the XX female fetus may be exposed erroneously to androgen instead of the correct hormone, cortisol. This is the **androgenital syndrome**, characterized by varying degrees of masculinization of the female sexual anatomy. The **androgen-insensitivity syndrome**, also genetically transmitted, occurs in XY male individuals. Cellular insensitivity to androgen in the prenatal environment can result in near or complete feminization of the sex organs (Mazur & Money, 1980; Money, 1968, 1980b; Money & Ehrhardt, 1972).

In the complete form of both syndromes, the affected babies are difficult to distinguish from normal boys and girls and are sometimes sex assigned and reared as members of the wrong sex. Childhood influences quite naturally predispose the individual to assume the interests, attitudes, and sexual behavior of one sex, however much his or her physical characteristics may be those of the opposite sex—another indication of the superiority of psychological over physiological factors in sexual matters.

Summary

The causative organisms of sexually transmitted diseases (STD) are ordinarily found only in human beings and are almost always acquired by direct sexual contact. The incidence of STD is particularly high among teenagers and young adults in their twenties. Young people infected with STD are of all personality types and represent the whole spectrum of American society. Gonorrhea is difficult to control because 80 percent of women have no clinical signs or symptoms of infection and thus do not know that they may be transmitters of the disease. Promiscuity, both heterosexual and homosexual, is definitely linked to STD, and there has been a great increase of STD in recent years among the male homosexual group. Men and women who suspect that they or their sexual partners may have STD can control the spread of infection by using prophylactics and paying close attention to personal hygiene after coitus.

Gonorrhea is the most ancient and prevalent of the venereal diseases. The causative organism (the *gonococcus*) usually attacks the genitourinary area, although rectal infections and pharyngeal infections can occur. In the male, gonorrhea is experienced through an urgent and frequent need to urinate accompanied by a burning sensation at the tip of the penis. Symptoms of gonorrhea in the female, when present, are usually shown through an urgent and frequent need to urinate accompanied by pain and a scalding sensation. For both sexes, penicillin is the treatment of choice for gonorrhea, although other drugs occasionally need to be substituted. Silver nitrate or penicillin solutions are put in the eyes of newborn babies to help protect them from the possibility of gonorrheal infection acquired in the birth process from an infected mother. *Nongonococcal urethritis* (NGU), a common infection with symptoms similar to those of gonorrhea, is differentiated from gonorrhea by the fact that in NGU the bacterium that causes gonorrhea is not found in the smear of the urethral discharge.

Syphilis is a disease caused by a corkscrew-shaped spirochete, or bacterium, known as *Treponema pallidum*. Penicillin or drugs such as tetracycline or erythromycin are used to treat syphilis. Early syphilis is divided into a primary stage, identified by a lesion or a chancre usually in the anal-genital area together with a swollen but painless lymph gland, and a secondary stage, characterized by a nonitching eruption or rash on the skin. Latent syphilis, which commences six months to two years after the initial infection, is dangerously deceptive. During this period all symptoms associated with syphilis disappear for months or years. Late syphilis may manifest itself in any organ, in the central nervous system and cardiovascular system, and on the skin. Symptoms can appear as late as thirty years after infection. Untreated syphilis may produce *neurosyphilis* or *general paresis*. Congenital syphilis, or syphilis existing at birth, can occur when a syphilitic mother transmits the disease to any child she conceives during the first two years of her infection.

Herpes is an acute skin disease caused by a virus that has two forms, Type I and Type II. Herpes Type I generally appears above the waist, while herpes Type II (usually sexually transmitted) is commonly found below the waistline. Occasionally a mixture of the two types is found. The sores from genital herpes can look like blisters or small bumps and can be painful. Effective cures for herpes infections have not yet been developed, although medical treatments are available to alleviate the symptoms.

Nonvenereal diseases also affect the male and female sexual systems but may have no direct relationship to sexual activity. *Nonvenereal syphilis* is a parasitic organism related to the organism causing venereal syphilis. It typically thrives in warm, moist climates and in conditions of filth. *Leukorrhea* is excessive vaginal mucous discharge caused by a chemical, physical, or infectious agent. *Trichomoniasis*, the most common of the minor gynecological diseases, often causes copious discharges, itching, burning, and a nagging odor for many women. Many men have only mild or no symptoms of trichomoniasis, although they can carry the parasites and pass them to (or back and forth with) their sexual partner. *Candidiasis* or *moniliasis* is a fungus infection causing itching and inflammation of the vagina. This disease often accompanies other infections such as trichomoniasis.

Carcinoma, or cancer, can affect the sexual systems of both women and men. Penile cancer can occur in men, and one theory suggests that the incidence of this form of cancer may depend on whether a man is circumcised or uncircumcised. In women, cervical cancer can be limited to early stages by taking regular Pap smear tests. Apparently, cervical cancer occurs most frequently in those women who begin coitus early in life and continue to engage in it on a regular basis. Breast cancer results in 20 percent of the cancer-related deaths of women. Manual examination of breasts, together with techniques such as thermography and mammography, can help in the detection of breast cancer. Prostatic cancer represents 10 percent of all malignancies occurring in men. Testicular cancer is a disease that primarily affects young men in their early twenties. Men can learn how to make testicular self-examinations so that early detection of the disease is possible.

Dermatoses, or skin diseases, of the genital region are fairly common and include problems such as *tinea cruris* (jock itch), scabies, and pediculosis (crabs). Inflammations of the internal and external genitalia may affect both men and women. *Vaginitis,* or vaginal irritation, is a fairly common disorder that may be caused by bacterial invasion, the introduction of foreign objects into the canal, and the use of strong chemicals. *Cystitis* refers to inflammation of the bladder; the symptoms usually include a severe burning sensation in the urethra during urination, a frequent need to urinate, and sharp pain in the lower abdomen. *Epididymitis* is a common disorder in men and involves inflammation of the epididymis. *Prostatitis,* the inflammation of the prostate gland, may be either acute or chronic.

Sexual disorders are physical anomalies of the genitalia. Those sexual disorders that affect males include undescended testes and *monorchism,* a condition where there is only one testicle in the scrotum.

Sexual disorders that affect females include (1) rudimentary, missing, extra, or divided vaginas, uteri, or fallopian tubes; (2) *imperforate hymens,* tissues that block or partly cover the external opening of the vagina; (3) *abnormal uterine bleeding* and functional uterine bleeding; (4) *cervical erosion,* because of infection, congenital defects, or childbirth injuries; (5) *displacement of the uterus* or abnormal positioning; (6) *endometriosis,* the aberrant growth of uterine tissue in other parts of the female pelvic cavity; and (7) *menstrual cramps* that might have a physical or psychological basis. Other problems that affect males and females are congested ovaries or testicles and congenital and acquired anomalies of the breast.

Chromosomal anomalies might occur such that an individual does not have the normal forty-six chromosomes (represented by forty-four autosomes and a pair of sex chromosomes). *Turner's syndrome* is a disorder affecting females, and *Klinefelter's syndrome* is a disorder affecting males. Males with extra Y chromosomes (such as XYY, XYYY, or XYYYY) might be prone to behavior that gets them in trouble with the law. *Hermaphroditism* (which includes true hermaphroditism, male hermaphroditism, female hermaphroditism, and dysgenetic hermaphroditism), occurs when the development of the gonads or external genitalia are ambiguous or incomplete, often leading to problems in identifying whether the individual is male or female.

TRUE OR FALSE: THE FACTS

Sexual diseases are commonly picked up from toilet seats, public swimming pools, and so forth.
False. Although some sexual diseases such as trichomoniasis might be contracted through swimming pools and so on, the majority of sexual diseases are communicated through sexual contact. (*288, 298*)

❦

The symptoms of gonorrhea are readily detectable.
False. Although gonorrhea in a man usually manifests itself by acute urethritis, as many as 80 percent of women who contract gonorrhea manifest no visible symptoms. (*291*)

❦

If a chancre associated with syphilis disappears or goes away, then one cannot assume he or she is no longer infected.
True. Without treatment, the primary chancre heals in four to ten weeks, removing the warning signal but not the danger of internal damage. *(292)*

A woman does not need a Pap smear test until she has had a child or has reached middle age.
False. All women need annual Pap smear tests. *(300)*

SUGGESTED READING

Barlow, David. *Sexually transmitted diseases: The facts.* New York: Oxford University Press, 1979.
This book contains detailed information for health care personnel and the general public on the etiology, diagnosis, and treatment of various sexually transmitted diseases and infections.

Cherniak, Donna, and Feinbold, Allan. *The VD handbook.* Montreal: The Montreal Health Press, 1977.
This brief yet highly informative guide delivers an abundance of practical information on sexually transmitted diseases.

McCary, James Leslie, and McCary, Stephen P. *McCary's human sexuality* (4th ed.). Belmont, Calif.: Wadsworth, 1982.
Chapter 21 contains material on sexual diseases and disorders.

Money, John, and Ehrhardt, Anke A. *Man and woman, boy and girl: The differentiation and dimorphism of gender identity from conception to maturity.* Baltimore: Johns Hopkins University Press, 1972.
Drawing upon the findings of many disciplines, this book presents comprehensive treatment of sexual differentiation and development and contributes to understanding of homosexuality, transsexualism, transvestism, and sexual anomalies.

Rowan, Robert J., and Gillette, Paul J. *The gay health guide.* Boston: Little, Brown, 1978.
This medical guide for homosexual men and women focuses on identification, transmission, diagnosis, and treatment of sexually transmitted diseases and how to avoid them.

GLOSSARY

A

abortion (ə-bôr-shən) Premature expulsion from the uterus of the product of conception—a fertilized ovum, embryo, or nonviable fetus. Abortion can be *therapeutic*, indicating that a threat to the mother's life or possible life abnormality exists, or *elective*, indicating that it is performed at the request of the expectant parent(s). Either is termed *criminal* when performed contrary to existing laws. *See also* **miscarriage.**

abortion, spontaneous *See* **miscarriage.**

abstinence (ab'-stə-nəns) A refraining from the use of or indulgence in certain foods, stimulants, or sexual intercourse.

adolescence (ad'ə-les'əns) The period of life between puberty (appearance of secondary sex characteristics) and adulthood (cessation of major body growth).

adultery (ə-dul'tə-rē) Sexual intercourse between a married person and an individual other than his or her legal spouse.

amenorrhea (ā-men'ə-rē'ə) Absence of the menses (menstruation).

amniocentesis (am'nē-o-sen-tē'sis) Also known as *amniotic tap*. A procedure in which amniotic fluid is drawn from the amniotic sac surrounding the fetus and is subjected to microscopic analysis.

amnion (əm'nē-ən) A thin membrane forming the closed sac or "bag of waters" that surrounds the unborn young within the uterus and contains amniotic fluid in which the fetus is immersed.

amniotic fluid (am-ni-ot'ic floo'id) The clear fluid, contained within the amnion, that surrounds the unborn child.

anal intercourse (ā'n'l in'têr-kôrs') Sexual activity in which the penis is inserted into the sexual partner's anus. It is sometimes called sodomy, particularly in its legal definition. *See also* **sodomy.**

anaphrodisiac (an-af'rə-diz'ē-ak') A drug or medicine that allays sexual desire.

androgen (an'drə-jən) A steroid hormone producing masculine sex characteristics and having an influence on body and bone growth and on the sex drive.

androgen-insensitivity syndrome Feminization of the male sex organs because of cellular insensitivity to androgen in the prenatal environment.

androgenital syndrome (an'drə-jən'ə-t'l sin'drōm) Masculinization of the female anatomy because of the presence of the hormone androgen in the prenatal environment.

aphrodisiac (af'rə-diz'i-ak') Anything, such as a drug or a perfume, that stimulates sexual desire.

areola (ə-rē' əl-ə) The ring of darkened tissue surrounding the nipple of the breast.

artificial insemination (är'tə-fish'əl in-sem'ə-nā'shən) Introduction of semen into the vagina or womb of a woman by artificial means.

B

Bartholin's glands (bär-thol'əns) Two tiny glands in the female, located at either side of the entrance to the vagina.

bestiality (bes'chē-al'i-tē) A sexual variance in which a person engages in sexual relations with an animal.

birth control Deliberate limitation of the number of children born, through such means as contraceptives, abstinence, the rhythm method, *coitus interruptus*, and the like.

bisexual (bī-sek' shoo-əl) Literally, having sex organs of both sexes, as in hermaphrodites; having a sexual interest in both sexes.

blastocyst (blas' tə-sist) The fertilized egg in the early stage of cell division when the cells form a hollow sphere.

breech presentation (brēch prez'ən-tā' shən) A birth position in which the baby is presented and delivered buttocks first.

312

C

caesarean birth (si zâr′ ē-ən) [or **caesarean section**] Delivery of a child through a surgical incision in the abdominal and uterine walls.

castration (kas ′trā-shən) Removal of the gonads (sex glands)—the testicles in the male, the ovaries in the female.

celibacy (sel′ə-bə-sē) The state of being unmarried; abstention from sexual activity.

cervix (sûr′viks) Neck; in the female, the narrow portion of the uterus, or womb, that forms its lower end and opens into the vagina.

chancre (shang′kər) The sore or ulcer that is the first symptom of syphilis.

chromosome (krō′mə-sōm′) One of several small rod-shaped bodies found in the nucleus of all body cells, which contain the genes, or hereditary factors.

circumcision (sûr′kəm-sizh′ən) Surgical removal of the foreskin or prepuce of the male penis.

climacteric (klī-mak′ter′ik) The syndrome of physical and psychologic changes that occur at the termination of menstrual function (that is, reproductive capability) in the female and reduction in sex-steroid production in both sexes; menopause; change of life.

clitoris (klit′ər-is) [adj. **clitoral**] (klit′ər-əl) A small, highly sensitive nipple of flesh in the female, located just above the urethral opening in the upper triangle of the vulva.

coitus (kō′i-təs) Sexual intercourse between male and female, in which the male penis is inserted into the female vagina; copulation.

coitus interruptus (kō′i-təs in′tə-rup′tus) [or **premature withdrawal**] The practice of withdrawing the penis from the vagina just before ejaculation.

colostrum (kə-los′trəm) A thin, milky fluid secreted by the female breast just before and after childbirth.

conception (kən-sep′ shan) The beginning of a new life, when an ovum (egg) is penetrated by a sperm, resulting in the development of an embryo; impregnation.

conceptus (kən-sep′tus) The first stage of cell division following fertilization.

condom (kon′dəm) A contraceptive used by men, consisting of a rubber or gut sheath that is drawn over the erect penis before coitus.

congenital (kən-jen′i-t′l) Existing at birth, but not necessarily inherited.

contraception (kon′trə-sep′shən) The use of devices or drugs to prevent conception in sexual intercourse.

copulation (kop′yə-lā′shən) Sexual intercourse; coitus.

corona glandis (kə-rō′nə gland′is) The rim surrounding the base of the glans penis in the male.

corpus luteum (kôr′pəs lōō′tē-əm) A yellow mass in the ovary, formed from a ruptured graafian follicle, that secretes the hormone progesterone.

couvade (kōō-väd′) The practice in some cultures wherein the man suffers the same symptoms during pregnancy as those his partner, the pregnant mother, is experiencing.

Cowper′s glands (kou′pərz) Two glands in the male, one on each side of the urethra near the prostate, which secrete a mucoid material as part of the seminal fluid.

crabs (krabs) See **pediculosis pubis**.

cunnilingus (kun′ə-ling′gəs) The act of using the tongue or mouth in erotic play with the external female genitalia (vulva).

cystitis (si-stī′tis) Inflammation of the bladder usually characterized by a burning sensation during urination.

D

detumescence (dā-tōō-mes′əns) Subsidence of swelling; subsidence of erection in the genitals following orgasm.

diaphragm (dī′ə-fram′) A rubber contraceptive used by women, which is hemispherical in shape and fits like a cap over the neck of the uterus (cervix).

dilation (dī-lā-shən) Stretching or enlarging an organ or part of the body, especially an opening.

douche (dōōsh) A stream of water or other liquid solution directed into the female vagina for sanitary, medical, or contraceptive reasons.

dysmenorrhea (dis'men-ə-rē'ə) Painful menstruation.

dyspareunia (dis"pă-ru' nĭ-ă) Coitus that is difficult or painful, especially for a woman.

E

ejaculation (i-jak'yə-lā'shən) The expulsion of male semen, usually at the climax (orgasm) of the sexual act.

embryo (em'brē-ō') The unborn young in its early stage of development—in humans from one week following conception to the end of the second month.

emission (ī-mish'ən) Discharge of semen from the penis, especially when involuntary, as during sleep (nocturnal emission).

endocrine gland (en'də-krin gland) A gland that secretes its product (hormone) directly into the bloodstream.

endometriosis (en'dō-mē-trē-o'sis) The presence of endometrial tissue (uterine lining) in other parts of the female pelvic cavity, such as in the fallopian tubes or in the ovaries, bladder, or intestines.

epididymis (ep'i-did'ə-mis) The network of tiny tubes in the male that connects the testicles with the sperm duct.

epididymitis (ep" ĭ-did" ĭ-mi'tis) Inflammation of the epididymis, a common disorder affecting men.

erectile dysfunction (i-rek't³l dis'fəg'shən) A form of inhibited sexual excitement where a man is unable to attain or maintain an erection of sufficient strength to enable him to perform the act of intercourse.

erection (i-rek'shən) The stiffening and enlargement of the penis (or clitoris), usually as a result of sexual excitement.

erogenous zone (i-roj'ə-nəs zōn) A sexually sensitive area of the body, such as the mouth, lips, breasts, nipples, buttocks, genitals, or anus.

erotica (i-rot'i-kə) Material that pertains to sexual love or sensation; sexual stimulation. *See* pornography.

estrogen (es'trə-jən) A steroid hormone producing female sex characteristics and affecting the functioning of the menstrual cycle.

excitement phase The initial stage in the human sexual response cycle that follows effective sexual stimulation.

exhibitionism (ek'sə-bish'ə-niz' əm) A sexual variance in which the individual—usually male—suffers from a compulsion to expose his genitals publicly.

F

fallopian tube (fə-lō'pē-ən tōōb) The oviduct or egg-conducting tube that extends from each ovary to the uterus in the female.

fellatio (fə-lā'shē-ō') The act of taking the penis into the mouth for erotic purposes.

fertility (fər-til'i-tē) The state of being capable of producing young; the opposite of sterility.

fertilization (fûr't³-li-zā'-shən) The union of egg (ovum) and sperm (spermatazoon), which results in conception.

fetishism (fet' i-shiz'əm) A sexual variance in which sexual gratification is achieved by means of an object, such as an article of clothing, that bears sexual symbolism for the individual.

fetus (fē'təs) In humans, the unborn young from the third month after conception until birth.

follicle (fol'i-kəl) The small sac or vesicle near the surface of the ovary in the female that contains a developing egg cell (ovum).

foreplay (fôr'plā') The preliminary stages of sexual intercourse, in which the partners usually stimulate each other by kissing, touching, and caressing.

foreskin (fôr' skin') The skin covering the tip of the male penis or the female clitoris; prepuce.

fornication (fôr nə-kā' shən) Sexual intercourse between two unmarried persons (as distinguished from adultery, which involves a person who is married to someone other than his or her coital partner).

frenulum (frē' nə-ləm) A delicate, tissue-thin fold of skin that connects the foreskin with the under surface of the glans penis; frenum.

frigidity (frij-id' i-tē) A common term for a form of female sexual dysfunctioning, implying coldness, indifference, or insensitivity on the part of a woman to sexual intercourse or sexual stimulation; inability to experience sexual pleasure or gratification.

G

gamete (gam′ēt) The mature reproductive cell of either sex—sperm (male) or ovum (female).

gender identity (jen′dêr i-den′tə-ti) One's view of self as masculine or feminine; an environmentally or psychologically determined feature.

gender role The realm of activities, culturally defined, that is associated with one's particular gender identity.

gene (jēn) The basic carrier of hereditary traits, contained in the chromosomes.

genital organs (jen′i-t'l ôr′gəns) [or **genitals** (jen′i-t'lz) or **genitalia** (jen′i-tā′ lē-ə)] The sex or reproductive organs.

germ cell (jûrm sel) The sperm (spermatozoon) or egg (ovum).

gestation (je-stā′shən) Pregnancy; the period from conception to birth.

glans clitoridis (glanz klit′ər-id′-is) The head of the clitoris.

glans penis (glanz pē′nis) The head of the penis.

gonad (gō′nad) A sex gland; a testicle (male) or ovary (female).

gonadotropic (gō-nad′ə-trap′ik) A hormone-like substance that has a stimulating effect on the gonads.

gonadotropin (gō-nad′ə-trō′pən) A substance having a stimulating effect on the gonads (sex glands).

gonorrhea (gon′ə-rē′ə) A venereal disease, transmitted chiefly through coitus, that is a contagious catarrhal inflammation of the genital mucous membrane.

graafian follicle (grä′ fē-ən fol′i-kəl) A small sac or pocket in the female ovary in which the egg (ovum) matures and from which it is discharged at ovulation.

gynecology (gī′nə-kol′ə-jē) A medical specialty that treats the problems of female sexual and reproductive organs.

H

hermaphrodite (hûr-maf′rə-dīt′) An individual possessing both male and female sex glands (ovary and testicle) or sex-gland tissue of both sexes.

herpes (hûr′ pēz) Clustered blisters on the surface of the skin or mucous membranes, caused by viral infection, which tend to spread and can be sexually transmitted.

heterosexuality (het′ ə-rə-sek′shoo-al′ i-tē) Sexual attraction to, or sexual activity with, members of the opposite sex; opposite of **homosexuality**.

homologous (hə-mol′ə-gəs) Corresponding in position, structure, or origin to another anatomical entity.

homosexuality (hō′mō-sek′shoo-al′i-tē) Sexual attraction to, or sexual activity with, members of one's own sex; the opposite of **heterosexuality**.

hormone (hôr′mōns) A chemical substance produced by an endocrine gland that has a specific effect on the activities of other organs in the body. Hormones secreted by the gonads (testes or ovaries) have an impact upon sexual development or functioning.

hymen (hī′mən) The membranous fold that partly covers the external opening of the vagina in most virgin females; the maidenhead.

hypothalamus (hī′pə-thal′ə-məs) A small portion of the brain that controls such vital bodily processes as visceral activities, temperature, and sleep.

hysterectomy (his′tə-rek′ tə-mē) Surgical removal of the female uterus, either through the abdominal wall or through the vagina.

I

impotence (im′pə-t'ns) Disturbance of sexual function in the male that precludes satisfactory coitus; more specifically, inability to achieve or maintain an erection sufficient for purposes of sexual intercourse.

incest (in′sest) Sexual relations between close relatives, such as father and daughter, mother and son, or brother and sister.

induced abortion An intentional effort to terminate pregnancy.

inhibited sexual excitement A form of sexual dysfunction affecting both men and women. In men it is defined as the inability to attain or maintain an erection of sufficient strength to enable him to perform the act of intercourse. In women it is defined as the absence or diminished capacity for erotic sensation or sexual pleasure.

intercourse, sexual (in'tər-kôrs', sek'shōō-al') Sexual union of a male and a female, in which the penis is inserted into the vagina; coitus.

interstitial cells (in'tər-stish'əl sels) Specialized cells in the testicles that produce the male sex hormones.

intrauterine device (IUD) (in'trə-yōō'tər-in di-vīs') A small plastic or metal device that, when fitted into the uterus, prevents pregnancy.

intromission (in'trə-mish'ən) Insertion of the penis in the vagina.

K

Klinefelter's syndrome (XXY) (klīn'fel-tərz) An abnormality, afflicting males, in which the sex-determining chromosomes are XXY, instead of the normal XY, one gamete having somehow contributed an extra X at the time of fertilization. Symptoms of the condition include small testicles, sterility, and often a distinctly feminine physical appearance.

L

labia majora (lā'bē-ə mə-jor'ə) [sing. **labium majus** (lā'bē-əm ma'jəs)] The outer and larger pair of lips of the female external genitals (vulva).

labia minora (lā'be-ə mī-nōr'ə) [sing. **labium minus** (lā'bē-əm mī'nəs)] The inner and smaller pair of lips of the female external genitals (vulva).

lactation (lak-tā'shən) The manufacture and secretion of milk by the mammary glands in a mother's breasts.

laparoscopic (lap'ə-ros'kō-pic) [also "Band-Aid" sterilization] Sterilization by cutting or cauterizing the fallopian tubes through minute abdominal incision(s).

lesbianism (lez'bē-ən-iz'am) Female homosexuality.

M

maidenhead (mād' ³n-hed') The hymen.

masochism (mas'ə-kiz'əm) A sexual vari-

ance in which an individual derives sexual gratification from having pain inflicted on him or her.

masturbation (mas'tər-bā' shən) Self-stimulation of the genitals through manipulation; autoeroticism.

mate-swapping [or **swinging**] A form of sexual variance in which two or more married couples exchange sexual partners.

meiosis (mī-ō'sis) Cellular reduction division, as in spermatogenesis and oogenesis, in which daughter cells are produced containing half the number of chromosomes present in the original cell. *See* **mitosis**.

menarche (mə-när'ke) The onset of menstruation in the human female, occurring in late puberty and ushering in the period of adolescence.

menopause (men'ə-pôz') The period of cessation of menstruation in the human female, occurring usually between the ages of forty-five and fifty-five; climacteric; change of life.

menstruation (men'strōō-ā'shən) The discharge of blood from the uterus through the vagina that normally recurs at approximately four-week intervals in the female between puberty and menopause.

Minipills (min'i-pils) Birth control pills containing small doses of progestin alone, as opposed to combination pills, which contain both progestin and estrogen.

miscarriage (mis-kar'ij) Spontaneous expulsion of a fetus from the onset of the fourth to the end of the sixth month of pregnancy.

mitosis (mī-tō'sis) Ordinary cell division involving nuclear and cytoplasmic fission and resulting in two new cells, each containing the full complement of forty-six chromosomes. *See* **meiosis**.

monilia (mo-nə' lī) [or **moniliasis** (mō-nə-lī-a'sis)] A yeastlike infective organism (fungus) causing itching and inflammation of the female vagina.

monogamy (mə-nog'ə-mē) Marriage between one man and one woman.

monorchism (mä'nor-kiz'əm) The condition of having only one testicle in the scrotum.

mons veneris (monz və-nə'ris) [or **mons pubis** (monz-pyōō'biz)] A triangular mound of fat at the symphysis pubis of the female, just above the vulval area.

Müllerian ducts (myül-ir′ē-ən) The primitive genital ducts that, under hormonal influence, evolve into the female genitalia.

multipara (mul-tip′ə-rə) [adj. **multiparous** (mul-tip′ə-rəs)] A woman who has given birth to two or more children.

myotonia (mi′ə-tō′nē-ə) Increased muscular tension.

N

neurosyphilis (nu″ro-sif′ĭ-lus) Syphilitic infection of the nervous system.

nocturnal emission (nok-tûr′n°l i-mish′ən) [or **nocturnal orgasm**] An involuntary male orgasm and ejaculation of semen during sleep; a "wet dream."

nullipara (nə-lip′êr-əs) [adj. **nulliparous** (nə-lip′ êr-əs)] A woman who has never borne a viable child.

nymphomania (nim′fə-mā′ nē-ə) Excessive sexual desire in a woman.

O

obscenity (əb-sen′i-tē) Disgusting, repulsive, filthy, shocking material—that which is abhorrent according to accepted standards of morality.

oogenesis (o′ə-jen′i-sis) The process of ova development.

oophorectomy (o″of-o-rek′to-me) The surgical removal of an ovary or ovaries.

oral-genital sex (ôr′l jen′ə-t°l) A form of sexual intercourse in which the mouth is used to receive the penis (**fellatio**) or the mouth and lips are used to stimulate the vulva, especially the clitoris (**cunnilingus**).

orgasm (ôr′gaz-əm) The peak or climax of sexual excitement in sexual activity.

orgasmic dysfunction (ôr′gaz′mik dis-funk′ shun) A form of sexual dysfunction in which the female experiences difficulty achieving orgasm or is unable to reach orgasm by either coital or noncoital means.

orgasmic phase The third stage in the human sexual response cycle during which the orgasm occurs.

orgasmic platform The area comprising the outer third of the vagina and the labia minora, which displays marked vasocongestion in the plateau phase of the female sexual response cycle (term used by Masters and Johnson).

ovary (ō′və-rē) The female sex gland, in which the ova are formed.

ovulation (ov′yə-lā′shən) The release of a mature, unimpregnated ovum from one of the graafian follicles of an ovary.

ovum (o′vəm) [pl. **ova** (ō′və)] An egg; the female reproductive cell, corresponding to the male spermatozoon, that after fertilization develops into a new member of the same species.

P

Pap smear (pap smēr) Simple and painless procedure of taking sample of cervical fluid by means of a cotton swab and examining the fluid for presence of cancer cells.

paresis (pə-rē′sis) A chronic syphilitic inflammation of the brain and its enveloping membranes, characterized by progressive mental deterioration and a general paralysis that is sometimes fatal.

parthenogenesis (par′ thə-nō-jen′i-sis) Reproduction by the development of an egg without its being fertilized by a spermatozoon.

parturition (pär′tōō-rish′ən) Labor; the process of giving birth.

pediculosis pubis (pə-dik′yə-lo′sis pyōō′bis) An itchy skin irritation in the genital area caused by the minute bites of the crab louse.

pedophilia (pə-dō-fē′lē-ə) A sexual variance in which an adult engages in or desires sexual activity with a child.

penile shaft (pēn′°l shaft) The body of the penis, composed of three cylindrical bodies and a network of blood vessels, which are encircled by a band if fibrous tissue and covered by skin.

penis (pē′nis) The male organ of copulation and urination.

penis captivus (pē′nis kap′tiv-əs) A condition in humans in which it is alleged that the shaft of the fully introduced penis is tightly encircled by the vagina during coitus and cannot be withdrawn. Most authorities say this condition occurs only in animals, notably the dog.

perineum (per'ə-nē' əm) [adj. **perineal** (per'ə-nē'əl)] The area between the thighs, extending from the posterior wall of the vagina to the anus in the female and from the scrotum to the anus in the male.

petting (pet'ting) Sexual contact that excludes coitus.

pituitary (pi-tōo' i-ter'ē) Known as the "master gland" and located in the head, it is responsible for the proper functioning of all the other glands, especially the sex glands, the thyroid, and the adrenals.

placenta (plə-sen'tə) The cakelike organ that connects the fetus to the uterus by means of the umbilical cord, and through which the fetus is fed and waste products are eliminated; the afterbirth.

plateau phase (pla-tō') The fully stimulated stage in the human sexual response cycle that immediately precedes orgasm.

polyandry (pol'i-an'dri) The form of marriage in which one woman has more than one husband at one time.

polygamy (pə-lig'ə-mē) The form of marriage in which a spouse of either sex may possess a plurality of mates at the same time.

polygyny (pə-lij'ə-nē) The form of marriage in which one man has more than one wife at the same time.

pornography (pôr-nog'rə-fē) The presentation of sexually arousing material in literature, art, motion pictures, or other means of communication and expression.

postpartum (pōst' pär'təm) Occurring after childbirth or after delivery.

potency (pōt'ən-sē) Having the male capability to perform sexual intercourse; capable of erection.

precoital fluid (prē-kwē'təl flōo'id) Alkaline fluid secreted by the Cowper's glands that lubricates the urethra for easy passage of semen.

pregnancy (preg'nən-si) The condition of having a developing embryo or fetus in the body; the period from conception to birth or abortion.

premature ejaculation (pre'mə-chōor' i-jak'yə-lā' shən) Ejaculation prior to, just at, or immediately after intromission. Ejaculation occurs before the woman can climax in at least 50 percent of the acts of intercourse.

premenstrual syndrome (prē-men'stral) Discomfort or pain occurring before menstruation.

prenatal (prē-nāt'əl) Existing or occurring before birth.

prepuce (prē'pyōos) Foreskin.

progesterone (prō-jes'tə-rōn') The female hormone (known as the pregnancy hormone) that is produced in the yellow body of corpus luteum, and whose function is to prepare the uterus for the reception and development of a fertilized ovum.

prolactin (prō-lak'tin) A hormone secreted by the pituitary gland that stimulates the production of milk by the mammary glands in the breasts (lactation).

promiscuity (prə-mis'kyōo-i-tē) The tendency to engage in sexual intercourse with many persons; engaging in casual sexual relations.

prophylactic (prō'fə-lak'tik) A drug or device used for the prevention of disease, often specifically sexually transmitted disease.

prostate gland (pros'tāt gland) The gland in the male that surrounds the urethra and the neck of the bladder.

prostatic fluid (pros'tat' ic flōo'id) A highly alkaline, thin, milky fluid produced by the prostate gland that constitutes a major portion of the male's semen or ejaculatory fluid.

prostatitis (pros'ta-ti' tis) Inflammation of the prostate gland, typically a disease of older men.

prostitution (präs-tə-tü'shən) Engaging in sexual relationships for payment.

pseudocyesis (süd-ō-sī-ē'səs) False pregnancy.

puberty (pyōo'bər-tē) [or **pubescence** (pyōo-bəs' ənz)] The stage of life at which a child turns into a young man or young woman: the reproductive organs become functionally operative and secondary sex characteristics develop.

R

rape, forcible (rāp) Forcible sexual intercourse with a person who does not give consent or who offers resistance.

rape, statutory Coitus with a partner under the age of consent (usually eighteen).

refractory period (ri-frak′ tə-rē pēr′ē-əd) A man's temporary state of psychophysiologic resistance to sexual stimulation immediately following an orgasmic experience (term used by Masters and Johnson).

resolution phase The last stage in the human sexual response cycle during which the sexual system retrogresses to its normal non-excited state.

retarded ejaculation (ri-tärd-ed i-jak′yoo-lā′shən) A form of sexual dysfunction in which the male is troubled with involuntary overcontrol of the ejaculatory reflex, causing it to be excessively delayed, if it occurs at all, despite adequate stimulation.

rhythm method (rith′əm meth′əd) A method of birth control that relies on the so-called "safe period" or infertile days in the female menstrual cycle.

S

sadism (sā′diz-əm) A sexual variance in which there is the achievement of sexual gratification by inflicting physical or psychological pain upon the sexual partner.

salpingectomy (sal′pin-jek′tə-mē) Surgical removal of a fallopian tube from a woman.

salpingitis (sal′pən-jīt′əs) Inflammation of the fallopian tube(s).

satyriasis (sā′tə-rī′ə-sis) Excessive sexual desire in a man.

scabies (ska′bēz) A highly contagious skin disorder caused by a mite that burrows into the skin to lay eggs. A rash results in affected areas.

scopophilia (sko-po-fil′e-ah) [or **scoptophilia** (skop-to-fil′e-ah)] A sexual variance in which a person achieves sexual gratification by observing sexual acts or the genitals of others. *See also* **voyeurism**.

scrotum (skrō′təm) The pouch suspended from the groin that contains the male testicles and their accessory organs.

secondary sexual characteristics The physical characteristics—other than the external sex organs—that distinguish male from female.

semen (sē′mən) The secretion of the male reproductive organs that is ejaculated from the penis at orgasm and contains, in the fertile man, sperm cells.

seminal emission (sem′ə-n²l i-mish′ən) or **seminal fluid** (sem′ə-n²l floo′id) A fluid composed of sperm and secretions from the epididymis, seminal vesicles, prostate gland, and Cowper's glands that is ejaculated by the male through the penis upon his reaching orgasm.

seminal vesicles (sem′ə-n²l ves′i-k²ls) Two pouches in the male, one on each side of the prostate, behind the bladder, that are attached to and open into the sperm ducts.

seminiferous tubules (sem′ə-nif′ər-əs too′byools) The tiny tubes or canals in each male testicle that produce the sperm.

sex drive Desire for sexual expression.

sex flush The superficial vasocongestive skin response to increasing sexual tensions that begins in the plateau phase (term used by Masters and Johnson).

sexologist (sek-säl′ə-jəst) A professional who engages in the scientific study of human sexuality.

sexual dysfunction (sek′shoo-əl dis-funk′shən) *See* **sexual inadequacy**.

sexual inadequacy (sek′shoo-əl in-ad′ə-kwa-sē) Any degree of sexual response that is not sufficient for the isolated demand of the moment or for a protracted period of time; frequent or total inability to experience orgasm.

sexual intercourse (sek′shoo-əl in′tər-kôrs) *See* **intercourse, sexual**.

sexually transmitted disease (STD) (sek′shoo-əl-i tranz-mit′-id di-zēz′) A contagious disease communicated by sexual activity.

sexual unresponsiveness (sek′ shoo-əl ən-ri-spän′siv-ness) A form of sexual dysfunction in which the female experiences absent or diminished capacity for erotic sensation or sexual pleasure. *See also* **inhibited sexual excitement**.

smegma (smeg′ mə) A thick, cheesy, bad-smelling accumulation of secretions under the foreskin of the penis or around the clitoris.

sodomy (sod′ə-mē) A form of sexual variance variously defined by law to include sexual intercourse with animals and oral-genital or anal-genital contact between humans.

sperm (spûrm) [or **spermatozoon** (spûr'mə-tə-zō'ən)] The mature male reproductive cell (or cells), capable of fertilizing the female egg and causing impregnation.

spermatogenesis (spûr' mat'ə-jen'i-sis) The process of sperm formation.

spermicide (spûr'mi-sīd) An agent that destroys sperm.

spirochete (spī'rə-kēt') A corkscrew-shaped microorganism; one type of spirochete causes syphillis.

sterility (stə-ril'ə-ti) The inability to produce offspring.

sterilization (ster'ə-li-zā' shən) Any surgical procedure by which an individual is made incapable of reproduction.

syphilis (sif'ə-lis) Probably the most serious venereal disease, it is usually acquired by sexual intercourse with a person in the infectious stage of the disease and is caused by invasion of the spirochete *Treponema pallidum.*

T

testicle (tes'ti-kəl) The testis; the male sex gland.

testis (tes'tis) [pl. **testes** (tes'tēz)] The male sex gland, or gonad, which produces spermatozoa.

testosterone (te-stos' tə-rōn') The male testicular hormone that induces and maintains the male secondry sex characteristics.

tinea cruris (tin'ē-ə krŏŏr'is) A fungus infection causing irritation to the skin in the genital region.

toxic shock syndrome (TSS) (tok'sik-shok sin'drōm) A rare cluster of symptoms in women (and sometimes men): vomiting, fever, diarrhea, skin rash, and rapid decrease in blood pressure, together with possible shock. A bacterium is suspected as the cause, whose growth may be made favorable by tampon usage.

transsexualism (trans-sek' shŏŏ-əl-iz-əm) A compulsion or obsession to become a member of the opposite sex through surgical changes.

transvestism (trans-ves'tiz-əm) A sexual variance characterized by a compulsive desire to wear the garments of the opposite sex; cross-dressing.

trichomoniasis (trik'ə-mə-ni'ə-sis) An infection of the female vagina caused by infestation of the microorganism *Trichomonas* and characterized by inflammation, usually resulting in a vaginal discharge and itching and burning.

troilism (trŏi'liz-əm) A sexual variance in which, ordinarily, three people (two men and a woman or two women and a man) participate in a series of sexual practices.

tubal ligation (tŏŏ'b'l lī-gā'shən) A surgical procedure for sterilizing a female in which the fallopian tubes are cut and tied.

tumescence (tŏŏ-mes'ənts) The process of swelling or the condition of being swollen.

Turner's syndrome (tər'nərz) An abnormality afflicting females in which one of the sex-determining pair (XX) of chromosomes is missing, leaving a total of forty-five rather than the normal forty-six chromosomes. Symptoms of the condition include incomplete development of the ovaries, short stature, and often webbing of the neck.

U

umbilical cord (um-bil'i-kəl kord) The flexible structure connecting the fetus and the placenta; navel cord.

undescended testes (un-di-send'ed tes'tis) A developmental defect in males in which the testicles fail to descend into the scrotum; cryptorchidism.

urethra (yŏŏ-rē'thrə) The duct through which the urine passes from the bladder and is excreted outside the body.

uterus (yŏŏ'trəs) The hollow, pear-shaped organ in females within which the fetus develops; the womb.

V

vagina (və-jī'nə) The canal in the female, extending from the vulva to the cervix, that receives the penis during coitus and through which an infant passes at birth.

vaginal lubrication (vaj'ə-n'l lŏŏ'brə-kā' shən) A clear fluid (like sweat) that appears on the walls of the vaginal barrel within a few seconds after the onset of sexual stimulation.

vaginismus (vaj′ə-nis′ məs) Strong muscular contractions within the vagina, preventing intromission of the penis when intercourse is attempted.

vaginitis (vaj′ə-nī′tis) Inflammation of the female vagina, usually as a result of infection.

vas deferens (vas def′ə-renz′) [or **ductus deferens** (duk′təs def′ə-renz′)] The sperm duct(s) in the male, leading from the epididymis to the seminal vesicles and the urethra.

vasectomy (va-sek′tə-mē) A surgical procedure for sterilizing the male involving removal of the vas deferens, or a portion of it.

vasocongestion (vas′ō-kən-jest′ yən) Congestion of the blood vessels, especially the veins in the genital area.

vas sclerosing (vas sklĕ-ro′sing) Male sterilization wherein the vas deferens is blocked, preventing passage of sperm.

venereal disease (VD) (və-nēr′ ē-əl di-zēz′) A contagious disease communicated mainly by sexual intercourse, such as syphilis or gonorrhea.

vestibule (ves′tə-byool) The area surrounding and including the opening of the vagina in the female.

virgin birth *See* **parthenogenesis.**

virginity (vər-jin′i-tē) The state of never having engaged in sexual intercourse.

voyeurism (vwä′ yə-riz-əm) A sexual variance in which a person achieves sexual gratification by observing others in the nude.

vulva (vul′və) The external sex organs of the female, including the mons veneris, the labia majora, the labia minora, the clitoris, and the vestibule.

W

"wet dream" *See* **nocturnal emission.**

Wolffian ducts (wul′fē-ən) The primitive genital ducts that, under hormonal influence, evolve into the male genitalia.

X

X chromosome (X krō′mə-sōm′) A sex-determining chromosome present in all of a female's ova and in one-half of a male's sperm; the fertilization of an ovum by a sperm having an X chromosome will result in the conception of a female (XX).

Y

Y chromosome (Y krō′mə-sōm′) A sex-determining chromosome present in one-half of a male's sperm; the fertilization of an ovum by a sperm having a Y chromosome will result in the conception of a male (XY).

Z

zoophilia (zō-o-fil′i-ə) *See* **bestiality.**

zygote (zi′gōt) The single cell resulting from the union of two germ cells (sperm and egg) at conception; the fertilized egg (ovum).

REFERENCES

Abortion amendment wins panel's approval. *The Houston Post*, December 17, 1981.

American Association of Sex Educators, Counselors and Therapists. *The professional training and preparation of sex counselors.* Washington, D.C.: Author, 1973.

Amstey, M. S. Herpes V.D.: A serious problem in pregnancy. *Medical Aspects of Human Sexuality*, August 1974, pp. 128–140.

Ard, B. N., Jr. *Treating psychosexual dysfunction.* New York: Aronson, 1974.

Arey, L. B. *Developmental anatomy: A textbook and laboratory manual of embryology* (7th ed.). Philadelphia: Saunders, 1974.

Athanasiou, R. Pornography: A review of research. In B. B. Wolman and J. Money (Eds.), *Handbook of human sexuality.* Englewood Cliffs, N.J.: Prentice-Hall, 1980.

Athanasiou, R., Shaver, P., and Travis, C. Sex. *Psychology Today*, July 1970, pp. 39–52.

Auerback, A. Satyriasis and nymphomania. *Medical Aspects of Human Sexuality*, September 1968, pp. 39–45.

Bach, G. R., and Deutsch, R. M. Intimacy. In M. E. Lasswell and T. E. Lasswell (Eds.), *Love, marriage, family: A developmental approach.* Glenview, Ill.: Scott, 1973.

Barclay, A. M. Biopsychological perspectives on sexual behavior. In D. L. Grummon and A. M. Barclay (Eds.), *Sexuality: A search for perspective.* New York: Van Nostrand Reinhold, 1971.

Baron, R. A., and Byrne, D. *Social psychology: Understanding human interaction* (2d ed.). Boston: Allyn, 1977.

Bart, P., and Jozsa, M. Dirty books, dirty films, and dirty data. In L. Lederer (Ed.), *Take back the night.* New York: Morrow, 1980.

Bartell, G. D. *Group sex.* New York: Wyden, 1971.

Bastani, J. B. Counseling the exhibitionist and his family. *Medical Aspects of Human Sexuality*, October 1980, pp. 81–82.

Bauman, K. E., and Wilson, R. R. Premarital sexual attitudes of unmarried university students: 1968 vs. 1972. *Archives of Sexual Behavior*, 1976, 5, 29–37.

Beazlie, F. S. Coital injuries of genitalia. *Medical Aspects of Human Sexuality*, August 1981, pp. 112–121.

Bell, A. P. The homosexual as patient. In M. S. Weinberg (Ed.), *Sex research: Studies from the Kinsey Institute.* New York: Oxford University Press, 1976.

Bell, A. P. and Weinberg, M. S. *Homosexualities: A study of diversities among men and women.* New York: Simon & Schuster, 1978.

Bell, A. P., Weinberg, M. S., and Hammersmith, S. R. *Sexual preference: Its development in men and women.* Bloomington, Ind.: Indiana University Press, 1981.

Bell, R. R. *Marriage and family interaction* (3d ed.). Homewood, Ill.: Dorsey Press, 1971. (a)

Bell, R. R. "Swinging," the sexual exchange of marriage partners. *Sexual Behavior*, May 1971, pp. 70–79. (b)

Belliveau, F., and Richter, L. *Understanding human sexual inadequacy.* New York: Bantam Books, 1970.

Benjamin H. Transvestism and transsexualism in the male and female. *Journal of Sex Research*, 1967, 3, 107–127.

Bennett, S. M., and Dickinson, W. B. Student-parent rapport and parent involvement in sex, birth control, and venereal disease education. *Journal of Sex Research*, 1980, 16, 114–130.

Bernard, F. Pedophilia: Psychological consequences for the child. In L. L. Constantine and F. M. Martinson (Eds.), *Children and sex: New findings, new perspectives.* Boston: Little, Brown, 1981.

Bernstein, G. A. Physician management of incest situations. *Medical Aspects of Human Sexuality*, November 1979, pp. 66–87.

Bernstein, I. C. Sterilization: Social and psychiatric considerations. *Medical Aspects of Human Sexuality*, March 1980, pp. 61–62.

Bieber, T. The lesbian patient. *Medical Aspects of Human Sexuality*, January 1969, pp. 6–12.

Blau, S. Venereal diseases. In A. Ellis and A. Abarbanel (Eds.), *The encyclopedia of sexual behavior* (Vol. 2). New York: Hawthorn Books, 1961.

Blough, H. A., and Giuntoli, R. L. Successful treatment of human genital herpes infections with 2-Deoxy-D-glucose. *Journal of the American Medical Association*, 1979, *241*, 2798–2801.

Boles, J. Age of prostitutes' customers. *Medical Aspects of Human Sexuality*, July 1980, p. 67.

Boston Women's Health Book Collective. *Our bodies, ourselves*. New York: Simon & Schuster, 1973.

Bower, T.G.R. *Human development*. San Francisco: Freeman, 1979.

Bragonier, J. R. Influence of oral contraception on sexual response. *Medical Aspects of Human Sexuality*, October 1976, pp. 130–143.

Brody, J. E. Sterilization is gaining acceptance in U.S. *International Herald Tribune*, May 10, 1976.

Brody, J. E. New forms of IUDs promise improvements in safety. *Houston Chronicle*, February 10, 1980.

Brosman, S. A. How frequency of coitus affects prostate. *Medical Aspects of Human Sexuality*, March 1976, p. 143.

Brotman, H. The pleasures of orgasm: How men and women differ. *Sexology Today*, November 1980, pp. 14–17.

Brown, W. J., Lucas, J. B., Olansky, S., and Norins, L. C. Roundtable: Venereal disease. *Medical Aspects of Human Sexuality*, April 1971, pp. 74–97.

Brownmiller, S. *Against our will*. New York: Simon & Schuster, 1975.

Bullough, V. Sex, pleasure, and sin. *Sexology Today*, December 1980, pp. 30–34.

Calderone, M. S. Love, sex, intimacy, and aging as a life style. In *Sex, love, and intimacy—whose life styles?* New York: SIECUS, 1972.

Calleja, M. A. Homosexual behavior in older men. *Sexology*, August 1967, pp. 46–48.

Capraro, V. J., Rodgers, B. A., and Rodgers, D. E. Vaginal anomalies: Effects on sexual function. *Medical Aspects of Human Sexuality*, September 1981, pp. 122–125.

Cavanagh, J. R. Rhythm of sexual desire in women. *Medical Aspects of Human Sexuality*, February 1969, pp. 29–39.

Cawood, C. D. Petting and prostatic engorgement. *Medical Aspects of Human Sexuality*, February 1971, pp. 204–218.

Cefalo, R. C. Toxemia of pregnancy. *American Family Physician*, 1979, *19*, 90–96.

Chang, Te-Wen. Relief of pain in women with genital herpes. *Journal of the American Medical Association*, 1974, *229*, 641.

Check, W. Herpes encephalitis is successfully treated. *Journal of the American Medical Association*, 1977, *238*, 1121–1126.

Churchill, W. Do drugs increase sex drive? *Sexology*, October 1968, pp. 164–167.

Cibley, L. J. Trichomonas Vaginalis vaginitis. *Medical Aspects of Human Sexuality*, March 1980, pp. 53–54.

Clark, L. Your personal questions answered. *Sexology*, November 1969, p. 36.

Clarren, S. K., and Smith, D. W. The fetal alcohol syndrome. *New England Journal of Medicine*, 1978, *298*, 1063–1067.

Coleman, J. C. *Abnormal psychology and modern life* (4th ed.). Chicago: Scott, 1972.

Collaborative Group for the Study of Stroke in Young Women. Oral contraceptives and stroke in young women: Associated risk factors. *Journal of the American Medical Association*, 1975, *231*, 718–722.

Comfort, A. *The joy of sex*. New York: Crown, 1972.

Comfort, A. Anxiety over penile size. *Medical Aspects of Human Sexuality*, September 1980, pp. 121–130.

Commission on Obscenity and Pornography. *The report of the Commission on Obscenity and Pornography*. New York: Bantam Books, 1970.

Commission on Obscenity and Pornography. Pornography: Patterns of exposure and patrons. In R. R. Bell and M. Gordon (Eds.), *The social dimension of human sexuality*. Boston: Little, Brown, 1972.

Connell, E. B. The uterine therapeutic system: A new approach to female contraception. *Contemporary OB/GYN*, December 1975, pp. 49–55.

Connell, E. B. Vaginal douching. *Medical Aspects of Human Sexuality*, March 1982, pp. 341–34J.

Constantine, L. L. The effects of early sexual experiences: A review and synthesis of research. In L. L. Constantine and F. M. Martinson (Eds.), *Children and sex: New findings, new perspectives*. Boston: Little, Brown, 1981.

Constantine, L. L., and Martinson, F. M. Child sexuality: Here there be dragons. In L. L. Constantine and F. M. Martinson (Eds.), *Children and sex: New findings, new perspectives*. Boston: Little, Brown, 1981.

Corbett, L. The last sexual taboo: Sex in old age. *Medical Aspects of Human Sexuality*, April 1981, pp. 117–131.

Cory, D. W. Homosexuality. In A. Ellis and A. Abarbanel (Eds.), *The encyclopedia of sexual behavior* (Vol. 1). New York: Hawthorn Books, 1961.

Courtois, C. A., and Hinckley, J. A. Grandfather-granddaughter incest. *Journal of Sex Education and Therapy*, 1981, 7, 37–42.

Coutts, R. L. *Love and intimacy: A psychological approach*. San Ramon, Calif.: Consensus Publications, 1973.

Cowart, D. A., and Pollack, R. H. A Guttman scale of sexual experience. *Journal of Sex Education and Therapy*, 1979, 6, 3–6.

Currier, R. L. Juvenile sexuality in global perspective. In L. L. Constantine and F. M. Martinson (Eds.), *Children and sex: New findings, new perspectives*. Boston: Little, Brown, 1981.

Czinner, R. The many kinds of rape. *Sexology*, January 1970, pp. 12–15.

Dailey, J. Help for the small or nonfunctioning penis. *Sexology Today*, March 1980, pp. 46–49. (a)

Dailey, J. Women's most versatile muscle: The PC. *Sexology Today*, July 1980, pp. 40–43. (b)

Davis, K. E. Sex on campus: Is there a revolution? *Medical Aspects of Human Sexuality*, January 1971, pp. 128–142.

DeLora, J. S., and Warren, C.A.B. *Understanding sexual interaction*. Boston: Houghton Mifflin, 1977.

deMoya, A., and deMoya, D. Viewpoints: What is the basis for the distinction many patients make between vaginal and clitoral orgasms? *Medical Aspects of Human Sexuality*, November 1973, pp. 84–103.

Denfeld, D., and Gordon, M. The sociology of mate swapping: Or the family that swings together clings together. *Journal of Sex Research*, 1970, 6, 85–100.

DeWolfe, D. J., and Livingston, C. A. Sexual therapy for a woman with cerebral palsy: A case analysis. *Journal of Sex Research*, 1982, 18, 253–263.

Diagnostic and statistical manual of mental disorders (DSM III). Washington, D.C.: American Psychiatric Association, 1980.

Diamond, M., and Karlen, A. *Sexual decisions*. Boston: Little, Brown, 1980.

Diana, L. Unusual sexual case: Complete sexual aversion. *Medical Aspects of Human Sexuality*, January 1981, p. 1240.

Dingfelder, J. R. Diagnosis and treatment of menstrual cramps. *Medical Aspects of Human Sexuality*, January 1980, pp. 117–118.

Donnerstein, E. Pornography and violence against women: Experimental studies. *Annals of the New York Academy of Sciences*, 1980.

Donnerstein, E., and Hallam, J. The facilitating effects of erotica on aggression against women. *Journal of Personality and Social Psychology*, 1978, 36, 1270–1277.

Eastman, N. J., and Hellman, L. M. *Williams obstetrics* (12th ed.). New York: Appleton, 1961.

Eddy, C. A. Detecting time of ovulation. *Medical Aspects of Human Sexuality*, December 1979, pp. 51–52.

Ehrmann, W. Premarital sexual intercourse. In A. Ellis and A. Abarbanel (Eds.), *The encyclopedia of sexual behavior* (Vol. 2). New York: Hawthorn Books, 1961.

Elias, J., and Gebhard, P. Sexuality and sexual learning in children. *Phi Delta Kappan*, 1969, 50, 401–405.

Elias, S. Advising patients about genetic amniocentesis. *Medical Aspects of Human Sexuality*, August 1980, pp. 51–52.

Ellis A. *Sex without guilt.* New York: Lyle Stuart, 1958.

Ellis, A. *The art and science of love.* New York: Lyle Stuart, 1960.

Ellis, A. Frigidity. In A. Ellis and A. Abarbanel (Eds.), *The encyclopedia of sexual behavior* (Vol. 1). New York: Hawthorn Books, 1961.

Ellis, A. *Sex and the single man.* New York: Lyle Stuart, 1963.

Ellis, A. *The civilized couple's guide to extramarital adventure.* New York: Wyden, 1972.

Ellis, A., and Harper, R. *A new guide to rational living.* North Hollywood, Calif.: Wilshire, 1976.

Ellis, A., and Sagarin, E. *Nymphomania.* New York: Gilbert Press, 1964.

Epstein, A. Supreme Court rejects abortion limits. *Houston Post*, June 16, 1983.

Everett, H. C. Competition in bed. *Medical Aspects of Human Sexuality*, April 1971, pp. 10–22.

Fang, B. Swinging: In retrospect. *Journal of Sex Research*, 1976, 12, 220–237.

Federal Bureau of Investigation. *Uniform crime reports.* Washington, D.C.: U.S. Department of Justice, 1979.

Felman, Y. M. Complications of some "minor" sexually transmitted diseases. *Medical Aspects of Human Sexuality*, September 1980, pp. 65–83.

Ficher, I. V. Value of extended foreplay. *Medical Aspects of Human Sexuality*, December 1979, pp. 12–23.

Fielding, J. E. Smoking and pregnancy. *New England Journal of Medicine*, 1978, 298, 337–339.

Finkelhor, D. Sex between siblings: Sex play, incest, and aggression. In L. L. Constantine and F. M. Martinson (Eds.), *Children and sex: New findings, new perspectives.* Boston: Little, Brown, 1981.

Fischer, S. *The female orgasm: Psychology, physiology, fantasy.* New York: Basic Books, 1973.

Fiumara, N. J. Differential diagnosis and treatment of venereally transmitted urethritis and vaginitis. *Medical Aspects of Human Sexuality*, March 1976, pp. 41–42.

Fiumara, N. J. Sexual behavior and primary and recurrent herpes genitalis. *Medical Aspects of Human Sexuality*, May 1980, pp. 151–152.

Fletcher, A., and Landes, R. R. Treatment of gonorrhea today. *Medical Aspects of Human Sexuality*, August 1970, pp. 50–61.

Ford, C. S., and Beach, F. A. *Patterns of sexual behavior.* New York: Harper, 1951.

Ford, C. S., and Beach, F. A. Self-stimulation. In M. F. DeMartino (Ed.), *Sexual behavior and personality characteristics.* New York: Grove, 1966.

Forum newsfront. *Playboy Magazine*, March 1979, p. 46.

Francoeur, R., and Hendrixson, L. The battle over sex education in New Jersey. *Sexology Today*, September 1980, pp. 18–25.

Frank, M. How threesomes work. *Sexology Today*, October 1980, pp. 22–27.

Frauman, D. C. The relationship between physical exercise, sex activity, and desire for sex activity. *Journal of Sex Research*, 1982, 18, 41–46.

Fritz, G. S., Stoll, K., and Wagner, N. N. A comparison of males and females who were molested as children. *Journal of Sex and Marital Therapy*, 1981, 7, 54–59.

From the editor's scrapbook. *Sexology*, January 1964, pp. 408–410.

From the editor's scrapbook. *Sexology*, March 1965, pp. 536–538.

Fromm, E. *The art of loving.* New York: Harper, 1956.

Gabbe, S. G. New ideas on managing the pregnant diabetic patient. *Contemporary OB/GYN*, 1979, 13, 109–113.

Gardner, L. I., and Neu, R. L. Evidence linking an extra Y chromosome to sociopathic behavior. *Archives of General Psychiatry*, 1972, 26, 220–222.

Gebhard, P. H. Misconceptions about female prostitutes. *Medical Aspects of Human Sexuality*, March 1969, pp. 24–30.

Gebhard, P. H. Prostitution. *Encyclopaedia Britannica*, 1973.

Gebhard, P. H. Fetishism and sadomasochism. In M. S. Weinberg (Ed.), *Sex research: Studies from the Kinsey Institute*. New York: Oxford University Press, 1976.

Gebhard, P. H., Gagnon, J. H., Pomeroy, W. B., and Christenson, C. V. *Sex offenders*. New York: Harper, Hoeber, 1965.

Gebhard, P. H., Pomeroy, W. B., Martin, C. E., and Christenson, C. V. *Pregnancy, birth, and abortion*. New York: Harper, 1958.

Gilmartin, B. G., and Kusisto, D. V. Some personal and social characteristics of mate-sharing swingers. In R. W. Libby and R. N. Whitehurst (Eds.), *Renovating marriage*. Danville, Calif.: Consensus Publications, 1973.

Ginsberg, M. M. Gonorrhea among homosexuals. *Medical Aspects of Human Sexuality*, February 1980, pp. 45–46.

Gittelson, N. Marriage: What women expect and what they get. *McCall's*, January 1980, pp. 87–89, 150–151.

Glick, P. C. Years of marriage most prone to divorce. *Medical Aspects of Human Sexuality*, July 1980, p. 11.

Goin, J. M., and Goin, M. K. Advising patients about breast reduction. *Medical Aspects of Human Sexuality*, May 1980, pp. 91–92.

Goldstein, P. J. Diabetes and pregnancy. *Medical Aspects of Human Sexuality*, March 1980, pp. 59–60.

Goodman, J. D. Nymphomania. *Medical Aspects of Human Sexuality*, February 1982, pp. 60–70.

Green, R., and Money, J. (Eds.). *Transsexualism and sex reassignment*. Baltimore: Johns Hopkins University Press, 1969.

Greenblatt, R. B., and Stoddard, L. D. The estrogen-cancer controversy. *Journal of the American Gerontological Society*, 1978, 26, 1–8.

Greene, B. L. How valid is sex attraction in selecting a mate? *Medical Aspects of Human Sexuality*, January 1970, p. 23.

Greenhill, J. P. What is the psychological significance of various coital positions? *Medical Aspects of Human Sexuality*, February 1971, pp. 8–16.

Greenwood, R. J. Diverse presenting symptoms of neurosyphilis. *Medical Aspects of Human Sexuality*, April 1980, pp. 31–32.

Gregg, S., and Ismach, J. Beyond "VD." *Medical World News*, March 1980, pp. 49–63.

Griffin, S. Rape: The all-American crime. In S. Gordon and R. W. Libby (Eds.), *Sexuality today and tomorrow: Contemporary issues in human sexuality*. N. Scituate, Mass.: Duxbury Press, 1976.

Groth, A. N., and Gary, T. S. Marital rape. *Medical Aspects of Human Sexuality*, March 1981, pp. 122–131.

Gunby, P. New anti-herpes virus drug being tested. *Journal of the American Medical Association*, 1980, 243, 1315.

Gunderson, B. H., Melas, P. S., and Skar, J. E. Sexual behavior of preschool children: Teacher's observations. In L. L. Constantine and F. M. Martinson (Eds.), *Children and sex: New findings, new perspectives*. Boston: Little, Brown, 1981.

Hanson, J. W., Strissguth, A. P., and Smith, D. W. The effects of moderate alcohol consumption during pregnancy on fetal growth and morphogenesis. *Journal of Pediatrics*, 1978, 92, 457–460.

Hardin, G. *Birth control*. New York: Pegasus, 1970.

Harris, R., Yulis, S., and LaCoste, D. Relationships among sexual arousability, imagery ability, and introversion-extraversion. *Journal of Sex Research*, 1980, 16, 72–86.

Hartman, W. E., and Fithian, M. A. *Treatment of sexual dysfunction: A bio-psycho/social approach*. Long Beach, Calif.: Center for Marital and Sexual Studies, 1972.

Hass, A. *Teenage sexuality: A survey of teenage sexual behavior*. New York: Macmillan, 1979.

Hatcher, R. A., Stewart, G. K., Guest, F., Finkelstein, R., and Godwin, C. *Contraceptive technology 1976–1977* (8th ed.). New York: Irvington, 1976.

Hatcher, R. A., Stewart, G. K., Stewart, F., Guest, F., Schwartz, D. W., and Jones, S. A. *Contraceptive technology 1980–1981*. New York: Irvington, 1980.

Hatfield, E., Greenberger, D., Traupmann, J., and Lambert, P. Equity and sexual satisfaction in recently married couples. *Journal of Sex Research*, 1982, *18*, 18–32.

Heiman, J. R. The physiology of erotica: Women's sexual arousal. *Psychology Today*, April 1975, pp. 91–94.

Heiman, J., LoPiccolo, L., and LoPiccolo, J. *Becoming orgasmic: A sexual growth program for women.* Englewood Cliffs, N.J.: Prentice-Hall, 1976.

Higgins, J. W., and Katzman, M. B. Determinants in the judgment of obscenity. *American Journal of Psychiatry*, 1969, *125*, 1733–1738.

Higham, E., Sexuality in the infant and neonate: Birth to two years. In B. B. Wolman and J. Money (Eds.), *Handbook of human sexuality.* Englewood Cliffs, N.J.: Prentice-Hall, 1980.

Hite, S. *The Hite report: A nationwide study on female sexuality.* New York: Macmillan, 1976.

Hite, S. *The Hite report on male sexuality.* New York: Alfred A. Knopf, 1981.

Hoch, Z. The sensory arm of the female orgasmic reflex. *Journal of Sex Education and Therapy*, 1980, 6, 4–7.

Hoffman, M. The male prostitute. *Sexual Behavior*, August 1972, pp. 16–21.

Holmes, K. K. Average risk of gonorrheal infection after exposure. *Medical Aspects of Human Sexuality*, February 1975, p. 83.

Holmes, K. K., Johnson, D. W., and Trostle, H. J. An estimate of the risk of men acquiring gonorrhea by sexual contact with infected females. *American Journal of Epidemiology*, 1970, *91*, 170–174.

Howat, P. A., O'Rourke, T. W., and Rubinson, L. G. Trends in sexual attitudes and behavior among selected college students. *Journal of Sex Education and Therapy*, 1979, 6, 78–83.

Hunt, M. *Sexual behavior in the seventies.* Chicago: Playboy Press, 1974.

Ingram, M. Participating victims: A study of sexual offenses with boys. In L. L. Constantine and F. M. Martinson (Eds.), *Children and sex: New findings, new perspectives.* Boston: Little, Brown, 1981.

International Professional Surrogates Association. Brochure. Los Angeles, 1982.

Jacobs, L. I. Lifelong indifference to sexuality. *Medical Aspects of Human Sexuality*, January 1981, pp. 140–149.

James, B. E. Marriages in which the wife is the sexual initiator. *Medical Aspects of Human Sexuality*, July 1980, pp. 16–24.

Janda, L. H., and O'Grady, K. E. Development of a sex anxiety inventory. *Journal of Consulting and Clinical Psychology*, 1980, 48, 169–175.

Janus, S. S., and Bess, B. E. Latency: Fact or fiction. In L. L. Constantine and F. M. Martinson (Eds.), *Children and sex: New findings, new perspectives.* Boston: Little, Brown, 1981.

Johnson, S.A.M. Dermatologic conditions caused by sexual activity. *Medical Aspects of Human Sexuality*, December 1981, pp. 90–96.

Kaplan, H. S. *The new sex therapy: Active treatment of sexual dysfunction.* New York: Quadrangle, 1974.

Kaplan, H. S. *The illustrated manual of sex therapy.* New York: Quadrangle, 1975.

Kaplan, H. S. *The new sex therapy. Vol. II: Disorders of sexual desire.* New York: Brunner/Mazel, 1979.

Kaplan, H. S., and Sager, C. J. Sexual patterns at different ages. *Medical Aspects of Human Sexuality*, June 1971, pp. 10–23.

Karlen, A. *Sexuality and homosexuality.* New York: W.W. Norton, 1971.

Karlen, A. Swingers: The conservative hedonists. *Sexology Today*, May 1980, pp. 12–18.

Kaufman, R. H., Gardner, H. L., Brown, D., Wallis, C., Rawls, W. E., and Melnick, J. L. Herpes genitalis treated by photodynamic inactivation of virus. *American Journal of Obstetrics and Gynecology*, 1973, *117*, 1144–1146.

Kaye, H. E. Lesbian relationships. *Sexual Behavior*, April 1971, pp. 80–87.

Keller, D. E. Women's attitudes regarding penis size. *Medical Aspects of Human Sexuality*, January 1976, pp. 178–179.

Kenan, E. H., and Crist, T. Counseling the spinal cord injured female and female partner of a spinal cord injured male. *Journal of Sex Education and Therapy*, 1981, 7, 29–32.

King, M., and Sobel, D. Sex on the college campus: Current attitudes and behavior. *Journal of College Student Personnel*, 1975, 16, 205–209.

Kinsey, A. C., Pomeroy, W. B., and Martin, C. E. *Sexual behavior in the human male*. Philadelphia: Saunders, 1948.

Kinsey, A. C., Pomeroy, W. B., Martin, C. E., and Gebhard, P. H. *Sexual behavior in the human female*. Philadelphia: Saunders, 1953.

Kirkendall, L. A. Sex drive. In A. Ellis and A. Abarbanel (Eds.), *The encyclopedia of sexual behavior* (Vol. 2). New York: Hawthorn Books, 1961.

Kirkendall, L. A. The importance of touch. *Sexology Today*, March 1980, pp. 10–15.

Kirkendall, L. A., and Libby, R. W. Sex and interpersonal relationships. In C. B. Broderick and J. Bernard (Eds.), *The individual, sex, and society*. Baltimore: Johns Hopkins University Press, 1969.

Klein, T. A. Rhythm method of contraception. *Medical Aspects of Human Sexuality*, January 1982, pp. 113–117.

Knox, G. E., Reynolds, D. W., and Alford, C., Jr. Perinatal infections caused by rubella, hepatitis B, cytomegalovirus, and herpes simplex. In E. J. Quilligan and N. Kretchmer (Eds.), *Fetal and maternal medicine*. New York: Wiley, 1980.

Kollias, K., and Tucker, J. Interview: Women and rape. *Medical Aspects of Human Sexuality*, May 1974, pp. 183–197.

Kolodny, R. C., Masters, W. H., Hendryx, B. S., and Toro, G. Plasma testosterone and semen analysis in male homosexuals. *New England Journal of Medicine*, 1971, 285, 1170–1174.

Kolodny, R. C., Masters, W. H., Kolodner, R. M., and Toro, G. Depression of plasma testosterone levels after chronic intensive marihuana use. *New England Journal of Medicine*, 1974, 290, 872–874.

Kronhausen, P., and Kronhausen, E. *The sexually responsive woman*. New York: Ballantine, 1965.

Krueger, D. W. Men who wear women's clothes. *Medical Aspects of Human Sexuality*, October 1980, pp. 16–63.

Labrum, A. H. Menopausal symptoms: Distinguishing psychogenic from physiological. *Medical Aspects of Human Sexuality*, February 1980, pp. 75–76.

Ladas, A. K., Whipple, B., and Perry, J. D. *The G spot and other recent discoveries about human sexuality*. New York: Holt, Rinehart & Winston, 1982.

Landau, R. L. Gonads: What you should know about estrogens. *Journal of the American Medical Association*, 1979, 241, 47–51.

Langfeldt, T. Childhood masturbation. In L. L. Constantine and F. M. Martinson (Eds.), *Children and sex: New findings, new perspectives*. Boston: Little, Brown, 1981. (a)

Langfeldt, T. Processes in sexual development. In L. L. Constantine and F. M. Martinson (Eds.), *Children and Sex: New findings, new perspectives*. Boston: Little, Brown, 1981. (b)

Larsen, K. S., Reed, M., and Hossman, S. Attitudes of heterosexuals toward homosexuality: A Likert-type scale and construct validity. *Journal of Sex Research*, 1980, 16, 245–257.

Laury, G. V. Sex in men over forty. *Medical Aspects of Human Sexuality*, February 1980, pp. 65–71.

Leboyer, F. *Birth without violence*. New York: Alfred A. Knopf, 1975.

Lederer, W. J., and Jackson, D. D. *The mirages of marriage*. New York: W. W. Norton, 1968.

Ledger, W. J. Bacterial infections during pregnancy. In E. J. Quilligan and N. Kretchmer (Eds.), *Fetal and maternal medicine*. New York: Wiley, 1980.

Lehrman, N. *Masters and Johnson explained*. Chicago: Playboy Press, 1970.

Levin, R. J. The Redbook report on premarital and extramarital sex. *Redbook*, October 1975, pp. 38–44, 190.

Levin, R. J., and Levin, A. A. Redbook report: Sexual pleasure. *Redbook*, September 1975, pp. 51–58.

Levine, M. I. Sex education in the public elementary and high school curriculum. In D. L. Taylor (Ed.), *Human sexual development*. Philadelphia: Davis, 1970.

Lewis, H. R., and Lewis, M. E. Anal sex. *Sexology Today*, March 1980, pp. 32–34. (a)

Lewis, H. R., and Lewis, M. E. Vasectomy. *Sexology Today*, April 1980, pp. 52–54. (b)

Lloyd, R. *For money or love: Boy prostitution in America*. New York: Vanguard, 1976.

Luffman, D., and Parcel, G. S. Adaptation of an instrument to measure premarital sexual permissiveness attitudes in young adolescents. *Journal of Sex Education and Therapy*, 1979, 6, 21–24.

Luttge, W. G. The role of gonadal hormones in the sexual behavior of the rhesus monkey and human: A literature survey. *Archives of Sexual Behavior*, 1971, 1, 61–88.

Lyon, P., and Rosen, D. H. Lesbian sex techniques. *Medical Aspects of Human Sexuality*, September 1974, p. 183.

Macdonald, A. P. Research on sexual orientation: A bridge that touches both shores, but doesn't meet in the middle. *Journal of Sex Education and Therapy*, 1982, 8, 9–13.

MacDougald, D., Jr. Aphrodisiacs and anaphrodisiacs. In A. Ellis and A. Arbarbanel (Eds.), *The encyclopedia of sexual behavior* (Vol. 1). New York: Hawthorn Books, 1961.

Mace, D. R. The physician and marital sexual problems. *Medical Aspects of Human Sexuality*, February 1971, pp. 50–62. (a)

Mace, D. R. Sex and marital enrichment. In H. A. Otto (Ed.), *The new sexuality*. Palo Alto: Science & Behavior, 1971. (b)

Mace, D. R. Emphasizing the positive in marriage. *Medical Aspects of Human Sexuality*, July 1980, pp. 32–43.

Mahoney, E. R. Religiosity and sexual behavior among heterosexual college students. *Journal of Sex Research*, 1980, 16, 97–113.

Malatesta, V. J., Pollack, R. H., Crotty, T. D., and Peacock, L. J. Acute alcohol intoxication and female orgasmic response. *Journal of Sex Research*, 1982, 18, 1–17.

Malcolm, A. H. Sex goes to college. *Today's Health*, April 1971, pp. 26–29.

Marchant, D. J. Fundamentals of diagnosing breast disease. *Medical Aspects of Human Sexuality*, July 1980, pp. 29–30.

Marmor, J. (Ed.). *Sexual inversion*. New York: Basic Books, 1965.

Marmor, J., Finkle, A. L., Lazarus, A. A., Schumacher, S., Auerbach, A., Money, J., and Morris, N. Viewpoints: Why are some orgasms better than others? *Medical Aspects of Human Sexuality*, March 1971, pp. 12–23.

Martin, P. L. Sexual desire and response after oophorectomy. *Medical Aspects of Human Sexuality*, July 1980, pp. 115–116.

Martinson, F. M. Childhood sexuality. In B. B. Wolman and J. Money (Eds.), *Handbook of human sexuality*. Englewood Cliffs, N.J.: Prentice-Hall, 1980.

Martinson, F. M. Eroticism in infancy and childhood. In L. L. Constantine and F. M. Martinson (Eds.), *Children and sex: New findings, new perspectives*. Boston: Little, Brown, 1981. (a)

Martinson, F. M. Preadolescent sexuality: Latent or manifest? In L. L. Constantine and F. M. Martinson (Eds.), *Children and sex: New findings, new perspectives*. Boston: Little, Brown, 1981. (b)

Masters, W. H., and Johnson, V. E. *Human sexual response*. Boston: Little, Brown, 1966.

Masters, W. H., and Johnson, V. E. Major questions in human sexual response. A lecture presented to the Harris County Medical Society, Houston, March 1967.

Masters, W. H., and Johnson, V. E. *Human sexual inadequacy*. Boston: Little, Brown, 1970.

Masters, W. H., and Johnson, V. E. Sexual values and sexual function. A paper delivered at the fortieth anniversary meeting of the Marriage Council of Philadelphia, Philadelphia, December 1971.

Masters, W. H., and Johnson, V. E. *The pleasure bond: A new look at sexuality and commitment*. Boston: Little, Brown, 1975.

Masters, W. H., and Johnson, V. E. *Homosexuality in perspective*. Boston: Little, Brown, 1979.

Maultsby, M. C., Jr. *Help yourself to happiness*. Boston: Marlborough House, 1975.

May, R. *Love and will.* New York: W. W. Norton, 1969.

Mazur, R. Men's sexual health: A radical approach. *Sexology Today,* October 1980, pp. 44–49.

Mazur, T., and Money, J. Prenatal influences and subsequent sexuality. In B. B. Wolman and J. Money (Eds.), *Handbook of human sexuality.* Englewood Cliffs, N.J.: Prentice-Hall, 1980.

McCaghy, C. H. Child molesting. *Sexual Behavior,* August 1971, pp. 16–24.

McCarthy, B. W. Strategies and techniques for the treatment of ejaculatory inhibition. *Journal of Sex Education and Therapy,* 1981, 7, 20–23.

McCarthy, B. W., Ryan, M., and Johnson, F. *Sexual awareness.* San Francisco: Boyd & Fraser, 1975.

McCary, J. L. *An introduction to sexology, a neglected subject.* Houston: Pierre St. Le Macs, 1966.

McCary, J. L. Nymphomania: A case history. *Medical Aspects of Human Sexuality,* November 1972, pp. 192–202.

McCary, J. L. Sexual advantages of middle-aged men. *Medical Aspects of Human Sexuality,* December 1973, pp. 139–153.

McCary, J. L. *Freedom and growth in marriage.* Santa Barbara, Calif.: Wiley, 1975.

McCary, J. L. *Freedom and growth in marriage* (2nd ed.). New York: Wiley, 1980.

McCary, S. P. The interrelationship between relevant sex variables and individuals' reported ages and sources of information for learning and experiencing sexual concepts. Doctoral dissertation, University of Houston, 1976.

McCary, S. P. Ages and sources of information for learning about and experiencing sexual concepts as reported by forty-three university students. *Journal of Sex Education and Therapy,* 1978, 4, 50–53.

McCormack, W. M. Sexually transmitted urethritis in men. *Medical Aspects of Human Sexuality,* November 1976, pp. 124–129.

McGuire, T. F., and Steinhilber, R. M. Frigidity, the primary female sexual dysfunction. *Medical Aspects of Human Sexuality,* October 1970, pp. 108–123.

Meissner, W. W. Psychoanalysis and sexual disorders. In B. B. Wolman and J. Money (Eds.), *Handbook of human sexuality.* Englewood Cliffs, N.J.: Prentice-Hall, 1980.

Menninger, K. A., and Menninger, J. L. *Love against hate* (reprint). New York: Harcourt, 1959.

Mestman, J. H. Thyroid and parathyroid diseases in pregnancy. In E. J. Quilligan and N. Kretchmer (Eds.), *Fetal and maternal medicine.* New York: Wiley, 1980.

Meyer-Bahlburg, F. L. Sexuality in early adolescence. In B. B. Wolman and J. Money (Eds.), *Handbook of human sexuality.* Englewood Cliffs, N.J.: Prentice-Hall, 1980.

Money, J. *Sex errors of the body.* Baltimore: Johns Hopkins University Press, 1968.

Money, J. Clitoral size and erotic sensation. *Medical Aspects of Human Sexuality,* March 1970, p. 95.

Money, J. The need for sex rehearsal play. *Sexology Today,* May 1980, pp. 21–24. (a)

Money, J. *Love and love sickness: The science of sex, gender difference, and pairbonding.* Baltimore: Johns Hopkins University Press, 1980. (b)

Money, J. Paraphilia and abuse-martyrdom: Exhibitionism as a paradigm for reciprocal couple counseling combined with antiandrogen. *Journal of Sex and Marital Therapy,* 1981, 1, 115–123.

Money, J., and Bennett, R. G. Post adolescent paraphilic sex offenders: Antiandrogenic and counseling therapy follow-up. *International Journal of Mental Health,* 1981, 10(203), 122–123.

Money, J., and Bohmer, C. Prison sexuality: Two personal accounts of masturbation, homosexuality, and rape. *Journal of Sex Research,* 1980, 16, 258–266.

Money, J., and Ehrhardt, A. A. *Man and woman, boy and girl: The differentiation and dimorphism of gender identity from conception to maturity.* Baltimore: Johns Hopkins University Press, 1972.

Money, J., and Yankowitz, R. The sympathetic-inhibiting effects of the drug Ismelin on human male eroticism, with a note on Mellaril. *Journal of Sex Research,* 1967, 3, 69–82.

Moore, S. L. My most unusual sexual case: Satyriasis. *Medical Aspects of Human Sexuality*, May 1980, pp. 110–111.

Mudd, E. H. The couple as a unit: Sexual, social, and behavioral considerations to reproductive barriers. *Journal of Marital and Family Therapy*, 1980, 6, 23–28.

Murdock, G. P. *Our primitive contemporaries.* New York: Macmillan, 1934.

Murray, L. *Childhood sexuality.* Washington, D.C.: American Association of Sex Educators, Counselors and Therapists, 1982.

Murstein, B. I. *Love, sex, and marriage through the ages.* New York: Springer, 1974.

National Center for Health Statistics. *Age at menarche* (DHEW Series 11, No. 133). Washington, D.C.: U.S. Government Printing Office, 1974.

National Institute of Allergy and Infectious Diseases. *Sexually transmitted diseases* (DHEW Publication No. [NIH] 76-909). Washington, D.C.: U.S. Government Printing Office, 1976.

Neiger, S. Sex positions. *Sexology*, June 1968, pp. 730–733.

Nelson, J. A. The impact of incest: Factors in self-evaluation. In L. L. Constantine and F. M. Martinson (Eds.), *Children and sex: New findings, new perspectives.* Boston: Little, Brown, 1981.

Netter, F. H. *Reproductive system.* Summit, N.J.: CIBA Pharmaceutical Products, 1961.

Neu, C., and DiMascio, A. Variations in the menstrual cycle. *Medical Aspects of Human Sexuality*, February 1974, pp. 164–180.

Neubardt, S. *Contraception.* New York: Pocket Books, 1968.

Ogren, D. J. Sexual guilt, behavior, attitudes, and information. Doctoral dissertation, University of Houston, 1974.

Oill, P. A., and Guze, L. B. Diagnosis and treatment of anorectal gonorrhea. *Medical Aspects of Human Sexuality*, June 1980, pp. 91–92.

One million Americans chose sterilization in 1980. *Sexuality Today*, 1981, 4(52), 1.

Oriel, J. D. Chlamydial infections. *Medical Aspects of Human Sexuality*, March 1980, p. 137.

Ovesey, L., and Meyers, H. Retarded ejaculation. *Medical Aspects of Human Sexuality*, November 1970, pp. 98–119.

Pauly, I. B., and Goldstein, S. G. Prevalence of significant sexual problems in medical practice. *Medical Aspects of Human Sexuality*, November 1970, pp. 48–63.

Pepitone-Rockwell, F. Counseling women to be less vulnerable to rape. *Medical Aspects of Human Sexuality*, January 1980, pp. 145–146.

Peplau, L. A. What homosexuals want in relationships. *Psychology Today*, 1981, 15, 28–38.

Pepmiller, E. G. How the handicapped make love. *Sexology Today*, September 1980, pp. 30–34.

Piemme, T. E. Factors contributing to VD epidemic. *Medical Aspects of Human Sexuality*, August 1974, p. 117.

Pietropinto, A. P. Frequency of coitus after twenty years of marriage. *Medical Aspects of Human Sexuality*, September 1980, p. 5.

Pomeroy, W. B. Parents and homosexuality: I. *Sexology*, March 1966, pp. 508–511. (a)

Pomeroy, W. B. Parents and homosexuality: II. *Sexology*, April 1966, pp. 588–590. (b)

Poulson, D. Hot tubs and reduced sperm counts. *Medical Aspects of Human Sexuality*, September 1980, p. 121.

Powell, D. Building up your "hidden" sex muscle: The ultimate male orgasm. *Sexology Today*, November 1981, pp. 65–68.

Primeau, C. *Intercorrelations of sex variables among a selected group of psychologists.* Doctoral dissertation, University of Houston, 1977.

Pritchard, J. A., and MacDonald, P. C. *Williams obstetrics* (16th ed.). New York: Appleton-Century-Crofts, 1980.

Quinn, R. W. Epidemiology of gonorrhea. *Southern Medical Bulletin*, 1971, 59(2), 7–12.

Raboch, J. Will hormones increase your sex power? *Sexology*, May 1970, pp. 9–12.

Rada, R. T. Alcohol and rape. ·*Medical Aspects of Human Sexuality*, March 1975, pp. 48–60.

Ramey, E. Men's cycles (they have them too, you know). *Ms.*, Spring 1972, pp. 8–14.

Reassessing the Pill's risks. *Time*, June 30, 1980.

Reiss, I. L. Sexual codes in teen-age culture. *The Annals*, November 1961, pp. 53–62.

Reiss, I. L. The influence of contraceptive knowledge on premarital sexuality. *Medical Aspects of Human Sexuality*, February 1970, pp. 71–86.

Reiss, I. L. Heterosexual relationships. In R. Green (Ed.), *Human sexuality: A health practitioner's text*. Baltimore: Williams & Wilkins, 1974.

Resick, P. A., Calhoun, K. S., Atkeson, B. M., and Ellis, E. M. Social adjustment in victims of sexual assault. *Journal of Consulting and Clinical Psychology*, 1981, 49, 705–712.

Reyner, F. C. Venereal factor in cervical cancer. *Medical Aspects of Human Sexuality*, August 1975, p. 77.

Reyniak, J. V. Changes in breast size during menstrual cycle. *Medical Aspects of Human Sexuality*, June 1976, pp. 81, 84.

Robertson, W. B. Maternal-infant nutrition. In E. J. Quilligan and N. Kretchmer (Eds.), *Fetal and maternal medicine*. New York: Wiley, 1980.

Roen, P. R. Painful testes. *Medical Aspects of Human Sexuality*, December 1981, pp. 60w–60x.

Rosen, H. S. *A survey of the sexual attitudes and behavior of mate-swappers in Houston, Texas*. Master's thesis, University of Houston, 1971.

Rosen, L. R. Enjoying sex during pregnancy. *Sexology Today*, March 1980, pp. 50–53.

Rubin, I. The new Kinsey report. *Sexology*, February 1966, pp. 443–446.

Rubin, I. The prostitute and her customer. *Sexology*, June 1969, pp. 785–787. (a)

Rubin, I. New sex findings. *Sexology*, November 1969, pp. 65–66. (b)

Rubinson, L., Ory, J. C., and Marmata, J. N. Differentiation between actual and perceived sexual behaviors amongst male and female college students. *Journal of Sex Education and Therapy*, 1981, 7, 33–36.

Ruff, C. F., Templer, D. I., and Ayers, J. L. The intelligence of rapists. *Archives of Sexual Behavior*, 1976, 5, 327–329.

Russell, D.E.H. Pornography and violence: What does the new research say? In L. Lederer (Ed.), *Take back the night: Women on pornography*. New York: Morrow, 1980.

Sagarin, E. Prison homosexuality and its effect on post-prison sexual behavior. *Psychiatry*, 1976, 39, 245–257.

Saghir, M. T., and Robins, E. *Male and female homosexuality: A comprehensive investigation*. Baltimore: Williams & Wilkins, 1973.

Sandberg, E. C. Psychological aspects of contraception. In B. J. Sadock et al. (Eds.), *The sexual experience*. Baltimore: Williams & Wilkins, 1976.

Sandler, J., Myerson, M., and Kinder, B. N. *Human sexuality: Current perspectives*. Tampa, Fla.: Mariner, 1980.

Sarver, J. M. and Murry, M. D. Knowledge of human sexuality among happily and unhappily married couples. *Journal of Sex Education and Therapy*, 1981, 7, 23–25.

Schneidman, H. Shaving pubic hair unnecessary for pediculosis pubis. *Medical Aspects of Human Sexuality*, August 1980, pp. 6–11.

Schwartz, M. F., Kolodny, R. C., and Masters, W. H. Plasma testosterone levels of sexually functional and dysfunctional men. *Archives of Sexual Behavior*, 1980, 9, 355–365.

Scott, M. D. Turner's syndrome. *Medical Aspects of Human Sexuality*, September 1980, pp. 87–88.

Sebastian, J. A. Cervical cancer a sexually transmitted disease. *Medical Aspects of Human Sexuality*, October 1980, pp. 75–124.

Shah, F., and Zelnik, M. Sexuality in adolescence. In B. B. Wolman and J. Money (Eds.), *Handbook of human sexuality*. Englewood Cliffs, N.J.: Prentice-Hall, 1980.

Shearer, L. From man to woman. *Parade's Special Intelligence Report (Houston Post)*, November 8, 1981, pp. 16–17.

Shearer, M. R., and Shearer, M. L. Sex, frankly speaking. *Houston Post*, May 20, 1983.

Silny, A. J. Sexuality and aging. In B. B. Wolman and J. Money (Eds.), *Handbook of human sexuality*. Englewood Cliffs, N.J.: Prentice-Hall, 1980.

Simkins, L., and Rinck, C. Male and female sexual vocabulary in different intrapersonal contexts. *Journal of Sex Research*, 1982, *18*, 160–172.

Slovenko, R. Statutory rape. *Medical Aspects of Human Sexuality*, March 1971, pp. 155–167.

Smartt, W. H., and Lighter, A. G. The gonorrhea epidemic and its control. *Medical Aspects of Human Sexuality*, January 1971, pp. 96–115.

Smith, C. G. Effects of marijuana on male and female reproductive systems. *Medical Aspects of Human Sexuality*, April 1980, pp. 10–15.

Smith, L. Religion's response to the new sexuality. *SIECUS Report*, November 1975, *1*, 14–15.

Solnick, R. L., and Birren, J. E. Age and male erectile responsiveness. *Archives of Sexual Behavior*, 1977, 6, 1–9.

Sonenschein, D. The ethnography of male homosexual relationships. *Journal of Sex Research*, 1968, 4, 69–83.

Sontag, S. The double standard of aging. In S. Gordon and R. W. Libby (Eds.), *Sexuality today and tomorrow: Contemporary issues in human sexuality*. N. Scituate, Mass.: Duxbury Press, 1976.

Sorenson, R. C. *Adolescent sexuality in contemporary America*. New York: World, 1973.

Speidel, J. J. Knowledge of contraceptive techniques among a hospital population of low socio-economic status. *Journal of Sex Research*, 1970, 284–306.

Steen, E. B., and Price, J. H. *Human sex and sexuality*. New York: Wiley, 1977.

Steinem, G. Erotica and pornography: A clear and present difference. In L. Lederer

(Ed.), *Take back the night: Women and pornography*. New York: Morrow, 1980.

Steinhart, J. What women are learning about vibrators. *Sexology Today*, April 1980, pp. 17–21.

Study cites herpes drug effectiveness. *Houston Post*, June 3, 1982.

Study finds sixty percent of gay men get sexually transmitted disease. *Sexuality Today*, 1981, 4(48).

Sullivan, W. Boys and girls are now maturing earlier. *New York Times*, January 24, 1971.

Supreme Court agrees Congress can ban most welfare abortions. *Houston Post*, July 1, 1980.

Swartz, D. P. Vaginal odors. *Medical Aspects of Human Sexuality*, October 1981, pp. 96I–96M.

Symonds, C. L., Mendoza, M. J., and Harrell, W. C. Forbidden sex behavior among kin: A study of self-selected respondents. In L. L. Constantine & F. M. Martinsen (Eds.), *Children and sex: New findings, new perspectives*. Boston: Little, Brown, 1981.

Syphilis trends in U.S.—Increase of 33 percent. *Sexuality Today*, 1981, 4(50), 2.

Tannahill, R. *Sex in history*. New York: Stein & Day, 1980.

Tanner, J. M. Growth and endocrinology of the adolescent. In L. Gardner (Ed.), *Endocrine and genetic diseases of childhood*. Philadelphia: Saunders, 1969.

Terman, L. M. *Psychological factors in marital happiness*. New York: McGraw, 1938.

Thornburg, H. D. Age and first sources of sex information as reported by 88 college women. *Journal of School Health*, 1970, *40*, 156–158.

Thorpe, L. P., Katz, B., and Lewis, R. T. *The psychology of abnormal behavior*. New York: Ronald, 1961.

Tietze, C. Fertility while breast feeding. *Medical Aspects of Human Sexuality*, November 1970, p. 90.

Tietze, C., Bongaarts, J., and Schearer, B. Mortality associated with the control of fertility. *Family Planning Perspectives*, 1976, *8*, 6–13.

Tietze, C., and Lewit, S. Joint program for the study of abortion (JPSA): Early medical complications of legal abortion. *Studies in Family Planning*, 1972, 3, 97–122.

Townley, J. Prostitution: Should it be legalized? *Sexology Today*, May 1980, pp. 40–45.

Toxic shock illness cases rise. *Houston Post*, August 29, 1980.

Unger, K. W. Medical problems caused by homosexual relations. *Medical Aspects of Human Sexuality*, February 1975, p. 152.

U.S. Bureau of the Census. Trends in child-spacing: June 1975. *Current Population Reports*, February 1978, Series P-20 (315).

U.S. Department of Health and Human Services, Public Health Service. *Herpes genital infection factsheet*. Atlanta: Center for Disease Control, 1982. (a)

U.S. Department of Health and Human Services, Public Health Service. *Sexually transmitted disease statistical letter 1980*. Atlanta: Center for Disease Control, 1982. (b)

U.S. Department of Health and Human Services, Public Health Service. Prevention of acquired immune deficiency syndrome (AIDS): Report of interagency recommendations. *Morbidity and mortality weekly report*, 1983, 32(8), 101–103.

Van Den Haag, E. Love or marriage? In M. E. Lasswell & T. E. Lasswell (Eds.), *Love, marriage, family: A developmental approach*. Glenview, Ill.: Scott, 1973.

Van Emde Boas, C. Ten commandments for parents providing sex education. *Journal of Sex Education and Therapy*, 1980, 6, 19.

Vaughan, V. C., and McKay, R. J. (Eds.). *Nelson textbook of pediatrics* (10th ed.). Philadelphia: Saunders, 1975.

Vetri, D. The legal arena. Progress for gay civil rights. *Journal of Homosexuality*, 1980, 5, 25–34.

Wabrek, A. J., and Wabrek, C. J. Vaginismus. *Journal of Sex Education and Therapy*, 1976, 2(1), 21–24.

Weaver, R. G. Scrotum and testes. *Medical Aspects of Human Sexuality*, October 1970, pp. 124–143.

Weinberg, J. Sexuality in later life. *Medical Aspects of Human Sexuality*, April 1971, pp. 216–227.

Weinberg, M. S. Nudists. *Sexual Behavior*, August 1971, pp. 51–55.

Weinberg, M. S., and Williams, C. J. Male homosexuals: Their problems and adaptations. In M. S. Weinberg (Ed.), *Sex research: Studies from the Kinsey Institute*. New York: Oxford University Press, 1976.

Westoff, L. A., and Westoff, C. F. *From now to zero: Fertility, contraception, and abortion in America*. Boston: Little, Brown, 1971.

Whitam, F. L. Childhood indicators of male homosexuality. *Archives of Sexual Behavior*, 1977, 6, 89–96.

Wiener, D. N. Sexual problems in clinical experience. In C. B. Broderick and J. Bernard (Eds.), *The individual, sex, and society*. Baltimore: Johns Hopkins University Press, 1969.

Wilcox, D., and Hager, R. Toward realistic expectations for orgasmic response in women. *Journal of Sex Research*, 1980, 16, 162–179.

Williams, J. H. Sexuality in marriage. In B. B. Wolman and J. Money (Eds.), *Handbook of human sexuality*. Englewood Cliffs, N.J.: Prentice-Hall, 1980.

Willscher, M. K. Reversing vasectomy. *Medical Aspects of Human Sexuality*, August 1980, p. 6.

Wise, T. N., and Meyer, J. K. Transvestism: Previous findings and new areas for inquiry. *Journal of Sex and Marital Therapy*, 1980, 6, 116–128.

Witkin, M. H. Procedures to enhance female coital response. *Medical Aspects of Human Sexuality*, October 1980, pp. 87–88.

Wolchik, S. A., Beggs, V. E., Wineze, J. P., Sakhelm, D. K., Barlow, D. H., and Mavissakalian, M. The effect of emotional arousal on subsequent sexual arousal in men. *Journal of Abnormal Psychology*, 1980, 89, 595–598.

Worley, R. J. Significance of thirty-five-day menstrual cycles. *Medical Aspects of Human Sexuality*, August 1980, p. 11.

Wright, M. R., and McCary, J. L. Positive effects of sex education on emotional patterns of behavior. *Journal of Sex Research*, 1969, *5*, 162–169.

Wyatt, J., and Stewart-Newman, C. The educationally oriented adult: Attitudes toward sex education. *Journal of Sex Education and Therapy*, 1982, *8*, 22–24.

Zastrow, C. H. Self talk: A new theory to understanding and treating sexual problems. *Journal of Sex Education and Therapy*, 1979, *6*, 51–57.

Zelnik, M., and Kantner, J. F. Sexual and contraceptive experience of young unmarried women in the United States, 1976 and 1971. *Family Planning Perspectives*, 1977, *9*, 55–71.

Zinsser, H. H. Sex and surgical procedures in the male. In B. J. Sadock et al. (Eds.), *The sexual experience*. Baltimore: Williams & Wilkins, 1976.

INDEX

Abnormalities, sexual. *See* Variance, sexual
Abortion
  induced, **98**
  socio-legal aspects of, 98–102
  spontaneous, **98**
Abstinence, sexual, 94, 107
  periodic, 108
Adjustment, marital. *See* Marital
    adjustment
Adolescence, attitudinal formation in,
    181–183, 200–202
  sexual activity during, 183–184
Adrenal glands, 30
Adultery. *See also* Mate-swapping
  attitudes toward, 186, 188, 209
  incidence and frequency, 208–210
  and romantic love, 123
Agglutination test for pregnancy, 74
Aging process
  and frequency of marital coitus, 186,
    197
  and impotence, 269–273
  and sex drive, 186–189, 202
  and sexuality, 44–45, 62–64, 126,
    176–189
Alcohol
  as alleged aphrodisiac, 151
  damaging effects on the unborn child,
    75–76
  effect of, on sexual performance, 154
  role of, in impotence, 151, 268, 270
  role of, in rape, 239
Amniocentesis, 74
Amphetamines, as a sexual stimulant, 152
Amnion, 79
Amniotic fluid, 79, 102
Amyl nitrite, 152
Analism, sexual (anal intercourse), 144,
    252
Anaphrodisiacs, **150–155**
Androgen
  and hermaphroditism, 307–308
  as an aphrodiasiac, 153
  deprivation, 26, 153
  excess androgen, 31
  in embryonic development, **26–27**
Animals
  humans crossbreeding with, 85
  parthenogenesis in, 85
  sexual contact with, 227
Anxiety, sex-related, 4, 8, 153, 165, 171,
    176, 184, 199, 264, 270, 274
Aphrodisiacs, 32, **150–153**
Areolae. *See* Breasts

Artificial insemination, 73
AASECT (American Association of Sex Ed-
    ucators, Counselors and Therapists),
    16, 280
Attitudes, sexual, 4–18, 194–202,
    254–256
  vs. behavior, 4, 14–16, 198
  cultural influences on, 5, 7–9, 194, 200,
    255
  differences between sexes in, 160, 255
  discrepancy, parental experience vs.
    teaching, 5–7, 11, 14–16, 201–202
  in Greek culture, 7–8, 251
  shifts in, 7–8, 218
Autosomes. *See* Chromosomes

Baby. *See* Fetus
"Baby blues." *See* "Postpartum blues"
"Band-Aid operation," 95
Barrenness. *See* Sterility
Bartholin's glands, 58, 165
Behavior, sexual, 4–9, 202–211
  criteria for acceptable, 9, 16, 176, 185,
    189, 207, 218–219, 254–256
  cultural differences in, 7–9, 176, 194,
    251, 254–255
  and love, 127–128
Bestiality, 227
"Billings" method of contraception, 108
Birth, 80–82. *See also* Childbirth
  date, predicting, 80
  defects, 74, 75–76
  fetal presentations, 81
Birth control, 6, 91–111. *See also* Abor-
    tion; Abstinence; Contraception;
    Sterilization
  calculating success-failure rates, 102
  in premarital relations, 6
Birth control pills, 103–106, 109–110
  hazards of, 105
  for men, 109
  "morning-after," 109
Birthmark, 84
Bisexuality, 185, 248, 258–259
Bladder, disorders in, 303
Blood pressure, in sexual response, 166,
    168, 170
Breast-feeding. *See* Lactation
Breasts
  changes in, 60, 83
  enlarged male, 306
  malignancy in, 300
  in sexual response, 44, 165, 167

Breasts (*continued*)
  stimulation in foreplay, 142
  supernumerary, 305
Breech birth, 82

Caesarean section, 82
Cancer
  breast, 300
  cervical, 299–300
  penile, 42, 299
  and the Pill, 109
  prostatic, 300
  testicular, 300–302
Cantharides, 152
Carcinoma. *See* Cancer
Casanova, 93
Castration, 97
  fear of, 219
  as sterilization, 97
Celibacy. *See* Abstinence
Cell division. *See* Meiosis; Mitosis
Censorship, 228, 231
Cervix
  in abortion, 101–102
  cancer in, 299–300
  in childbirth, 80
  description and function, 51(fig.),
    53–54
  erosion of, 305
  in pregnancy, 74
  in sexual response, 40, 142, 278
Chancre, **292**
Change of life. *See* Menopause
Chastity. *See* Virginity
Childbirth, 80–82
  age factor, 72
  "natural," 83–84
Child molestation, 225–227, 238
Children
  unwanted, 92
  VD infection of, 76
Christian-Judeo ethic, 7–8
Chromosomes
  anomalies of, 306
  autosomal (nonsex), 22
  in fertilization, 50, 70
  sex-determining (X and Y), 23, 70
  in spermatogenesis, 36–38
  supernumerary, 306
Circumcision, **41–42**
  and cancer, 42, 299
  effect of, on ejaculation, 271
Climacteric, in females. *See* Menopause

Climacteric, in males, **45**
Climax. *See* Orgasm
Clitoris
  in coitus, 145, 148, 162, 164, 166, 170
  description and function, 57–58
  embryonic development, **26**
  in masturbation, 139–140
  in sex play, 142, 143
  in sexual response, 57–58, 164, 166,
    170
  surgical removal of, 140
Cloning, 71
Cocaine, as a sexual stimulant, 152
Coitus. *See* Intercourse, sexual
Coitus interruptus, 108, 272
Colostrum, 83
Conception, 70–74. *See also* Fertilization;
    Pregnancy
  age factor and, 63, 72
  factors against, 72
  optimal time for, 72
  without prior intercourse, 85–86
  ratio, male-female, relative to sperm
    count, **44**
  during "safe" period, 52
  unfavorable time for, 108
Conceptus, **52**, 77
Condom, 93, 107, 279
  as prophylactic, 289–290
Congenital syphilis, 76, **294**
Contraception, 94, 102–111
  defined, **94**
  future, 109–110
  hot-bath technique, 36
  irritants in (chemical), 106–107
  and premarital intercourse, 6
  and VD, 93, 107, 290
Copulation. *See* Intercourse, sexual
Corona, penile, 40–41, 41(fig.), 167
Corpus luteum, **61**
Cortex of brain, and sexual behavior, 22
Couvade, 85
Cowper's glands, 38–39, 39(fig.), 167
Crab lice, 302
Cramps, and the IUD, 107
  menstrual, 53–60. *See also*
    Menstruation
Crime, sex. *See* Offense, sex
Crossbreeding, human-infrahuman, 85
Cross-dressing, 222
Courtship, 119–120, 198
Cunnilingus, **143**, 184, 205, 252. *See also*
    Oral-genital contact
  and VD infection, 295

Curettage (curettement). *See* Dilatation and curettage
Cycle, menstrual. *See* Menstruation
Cystitis, 303
Cysts, 278
Cytoplasm, **50**

D & C (dilatation and curettage), 101–102
Death, maternal, 106
Depressants, sexual. *See* Anaphrodisiacs
Dermatoses, genital, 302
Deviation, sexual. *See* Variance
Diaphragm, 103, 104(fig.), 279
    and the G Spot, 54
Dilatation and curettage. *See* D & C
Disease, venereal. *See* Sexually transmitted disease (STD); Venereal disease
"Doctrine of signatures," **151**
"Don Juanism," 236
Double standard, 9, 12, 171, 195, 198, 238
Douching
    to avoid VD, 290
    as contraceptive, 103, 107, 108
    ill effects of, 279, 302
Down's syndrome, 74
Drive, sex. *See* Sex, drive
Ductless glands, **22**
Dysfunction, sexual, 126, 186, 262–283
    female, 160, 194, 273–279
    male, 268–273
    therapy for, 137, 265, 280
Dysmenorrhea, **31**, 60
Dyspareunia, 278, 279

Ectoderm, 77
Ectopic endometrium, 61
Ectopic pregnancy (tubal pregnancy), 77
Education, sex, 4–16
    faulty, 6, 10, 208, 267
    and illegitimacy, 5, 6
    and premarital pregnancy, 5
    sources of, 9–16
    and VD, 5–6
Educational level
    and abortion, 100
    correlated with sexual attitudes, 196, 198, 207
    correlated with sexual behavior, 144, 205, 206, 209
    correlated with sexual dysfunction, 278
    and use of contraception, 102, 200
Egg. *See* Ovum
Ejaculate, 38, 44
Ejaculation, **44**, 160, 169. *See also* Orgasm
    alleged female, 54, 160
    control of, 44–45, 137, 169
    first, 30, 203

frequency of, and sperm count, 72
    painful, 278
    premature, 137, 271–272
    pubescence, 30
    retarded, 272–273
    "weakening" effect of, 38
Ejaculatory ducts, 39(fig.), 43, 169
Ejaculatory fluid. *See* Semen; Seminal fluid
Embryo
    abortion of, 100–102
    embryonic period, 77
    feminized male, 26
    male-female differentiation, 22–27
    masculinized female, 27
Emission, nocturnal. *See* Nocturnal emission
Endocrine glands, description and function, **22**–38. *See also* Adrenal glands; Corpus luteum; Ovaries; Pituitary gland; Testes
Endoderm, 77
Endometriosis, **61**, 305
Endometrium, 59, 61, 305
    ectopic, 61
    "engagement ovaries," 305
Epididymis, 37(fig.), **38**
Epididymitis, 291, **303**
Episiotomy, 278
Erection, clitoral, 57–64
Erection, penile, 42–45, 152, 165, 170. *See also* Penis
    in aging process, 44–45, 269
    failure, 268–271
    loss of, 170
    morning and nocturnal, 44, 269
    in older men, 45
    painful, 278
    physiology of, 42–43, 165
    in puberty, 29–30
Erogenous zones, **139**
Estrogen
    as an anaphrodisiac, 155
    functions of, 30–32
    in menstrual cycle, 60–61
    in the Pill, 104–105
    therapy, 62
Ethics
    changes in, 195–199
    code of, 8, 201–202
    differing sexual, 7–9, 198, 218
    Judeo-Christian, 7–8, 16
Exhibitionism, 220, 221
    pseudoexhibitionism, 221
Extramarital coitus. *See* Adultery

Fallopian tubes
    abnormalities in, 304
    description and function, 52(fig.), 53, 77
    sterilization via, 94–96
False pregnancy, 85

Fantasy, sexual, 134, 137–139
Fellatio, **143**, 184, 205, 237. *See also* Oral-
   genital contact
   and herpes infection, 295
Fertility
   duration of, in women, 63–72
   maximum, in men, 72
   reduced, in men, 72
   after vasectomy, 97
Fertilization, 70–73. *See also* Conception;
   Ovum; Pregnancy; Sperm
   without ejaculation, 39
   without penile penetration, 85–86
   site of, 52, 77
Fetishism, **231–232**
Fetus
   development of, 77, 78(fig.), 79
   identifying sex of, 74
   and "marking" myth, 84
Flagyl, 298
Foam, contraceptive, 107, 108
Follicles, ovarian, 50, 60–61. *See also*
   Graafian follicle
Foreplay. *See* Sex, foreplay
Foreskin. *See* Prepuce, penile
Frenum, 40, 41(fig.), 143
Frigidity. *See* Dysfunction, female

Gametes. *See* Ovum; Sperm
Gender identity, 176, 177–178, 224–225
General paresis, 292, 295
Genes, **70**
Genitalia
   differentiation of, male-female, **22**–27
   prenatal development of, 23–27
   pubescent changes in, female, 27–29
   pubescent changes in, male, 29–30
German measles, 76, 100
Germ cells. *See* Ovum; Sperm
Gestation. *See* Pregnancy
Gigolo, 237
Glands, sex. *See* Ovaries; Testes
Glans, clitoral, 57–58
   in masturbation, 139, 140
   in sexual response, 164, 166, 170
Glans, penile, **40**, 41(fig.)
   disorders in, 278
   in masturbation, 139
   in sexual response, 166
Gonadotropic hormones, 30–32, 50
Gonads. *See* Genitalia; Ovaries; Testes
Gonorrhea, 288, 290–291
   incidence of, 289
   risk to the unborn child, 76
Graafian follicle, **61**
"Group sex," 180
   fantasies about, 142
Guilt, sexually oriented, 4, 8, 9, 18, 178,
   183, 184, 199, 219

Hair, pubic, 57
   onset of growth of, 27, 30
Heart rate in sexual response, 166, 168,
   170
Hermaphroditism, **27**, 306–308
Herpes, 294–296
   risk to the unborn child, 76
Homosexual, Homosexuality, 244–261.
   See also Lesbianism
   appearance and behavior, 252–253
   attitudes toward, 185, 254–256
   conflict, 255–270
   experiences in childhood and adoles-
      cence, 180, 183, 257–258
   and impotence, 270
   incidence and frequency, 246–249
   theories regarding, 249–252
   in transsexualism, 223
   in transvestism, 222
   and VD, 296–297
"Honeymoon cystitis," 303
Hood, clitoral, 26, 57, 166
Hormones, Hormonal, **22**. *See also* Androgen; Estrogen; Gonadotropic hormones; Progesterone; Testosterone
   as anaphrodisiacs, 155
   in birth control pills, 104–105
   cyclic changes in, 59–62
   deprivation, 26, 40
   in homosexuality, 251–252
   imbalance, 32–33, 60, 251–252
   influence on prenatal development,
      26–27
   in lactation, 83
   male and female groups, 30–32
   in pregnancy, 31
   in puberty, 30–32
   therapy, 62, 106, 155, 223
Hot flashes, 63
Hunt, M., 196–197
Huntington's chorea, 92
Hustlers, 237
Hymen, 55–57
   abnormalities of, 57, 304
   as proof of virginity, 55
   rupture of, 55, 278
   and "virgin birth," 85–86
Hypothalamus, **22**
Hysterectomy, **95**
Hysterotomy, **102**

Illegitimacy, 5
Implantation of ovum, 31, 50, 61, 77
   prevention of, 106
Impotence, 8, 126, 268–271
   after castration, 97
   causes of, 269–271
   emotional causality, **43**
Impregnation. *See* Conception;
   Fertilization

Inadequacy, sexual. *See* Dysfunction
Incest, 232–233
Infertility. *See* Sterility
Insemination, artificial, 73
Intercourse, sexual
    alternatives to, 9, 13
    anal, 144, 252
    boredom in, 137, 171
    delaying orgasm in, 137, 171
    extramarital. *See* Adultery
    getting "hung up" in, 41
    incidence and frequency of, marital,
        186, 197, 207–208
    interfemoral, **144**, 252
    learning factor in, 137
    during menstruation, 61
    and older people, 63, 186–189
    pain in, 278
    positions in, 144–150
    postmarital, 188, 210–211
    during pregnancy, 75
    preliminaries to, 126, 141–144
    premarital. *See* Premarital coitus
Interfemoral intercourse, **144**, 252
Intimacy, emotional, 116–128
    avoidance of, 118–119
    in courtship, 119–120
    maintaining love and intimacy, 124–126
Intromission, 137
Ismelin, 155
IUD (Intrauterine contraceptive device),
    104(fig.), 106–107
"Jock itch," 302
Johnson, Virginia E. *See* Masters and
        Johnson
Judeo-Christian ethic, 7–8, 16

Kaplan, Helen, 265, 268, 273, 279
Karyotype, **306**
Kinsey research, 5, 196–197, 246–247
Klinefelter's syndrome, 306

Labia majora, 57, 58
    disorders in, 298
    prenatal development, 23–26
    pubescent changes, 28
    in sexual response, 163, 169
Labia minora, **26**, 57, 58
    disorders and infections of, 292, 298
    prenatal development, 23–26
    pubescent changes, 28
    in sexual response, 40, 143, 163, 166,
        169
Labor. *See* Childbirth
Lactation, 83
    menstruation during, 83
    role of hormones in, 31
    use of Pill during, 105
Lamaze method, 83–84

Laparoscopic sterilization, 95
Leboyer method, 84
Lesbianism. *See also* Homosexuality
    incidence and frequency, 248
    in prison population, 249
Leukorrhea, 297–298
Love
    the many aspects of, 120–126
    and sexual interaction, 127–128, 171
Lymph-gland infection (VD), 292

Mace, David, 277
Maidenhead. *See* Hymen
Major lips. *See* Labia majora
Mammary glands, 31
Marijuana, and fertility, 72
    as a sexual stimulant, 152
Marital adjustment
    and communication, 125
    and love, 123–124
    and sex education, 7
    and sexual adjustment, 124–126,
        185–186, 207
    and sexual inadequacy, 270
"Marking" offspring, 84
Marriage
    monotony in, 123, 186, 188, 207, 209
    unrealistic expectations of, 123
Masochism, 219
Mastectomy, 300
Masters (William H.) and Johnson (Vir-
        ginia E.), 5, 58, 161, 251–252, 265,
        273
Masturbation, **139–141**, 203–204
    attitudes toward, 9, 140, 183
    and exhibitionism, 220
    "excessive," 141
    fallacies concerning, 140, 141
    incidence and frequency, 139, 177,
        180–181, 183, 189
    among men, 139
    mutual, 75, 141
    among women, 58, 139, 161
Mate-swapping, 223–224
Maternal death, 106
Meiosis, **38**, 50
Menarche, **27**
Menopause, **29**, 63–64, 188
    sex activity following, 63, 188
Menstrual extraction (abortion), 100–101
Menstruation
    beginning of (menarche), 27–28
    and birth control pills, 104, 105
    and lactation, 83
    coitus during, 61
    description and cycle, 58–62
    difficulties during, 60
    hormonal influence on, 30, 59–61
    at menopause, 63
    negativism toward, 62

Menstruation (*continued*)
  regulation of, 106
  related to toxic shock syndrome, 60
  and rhythm method, 108
  and vaginal infections, 298
  vicarious, 61
Mesoderm, 77
Minipills, 105
Minor lips. *See* Labia minora
Miscarriage, 75, 98
"Missionary position," 9, 145
Mitosis, 38, 70
Mongolism. *See* Down's syndrome
Moniliasis (monilia), 298–299
Monorchism, **304**
Mosaic law, 7
Mons pubis. *See* Mons veneris
Mons veneris, 26, 57
Myotonia (muscle tension), in sexual re-
    sponse, **163**, 166
Müllerian ducts, **23**, 304

"Natural childbirth," 83–84
Neurosyphilis, 294
Nipples
  as erogenous zones, 142
  in sexual response, 165, 167, 170
  supernumerary, 305
Nocturnal emission, 30, 183, 204
Nocturnal orgasm, female, 204
Nonvenereal diseases, 297–303
Nudism, 221
Nymphomania, **234–235**

Obscenity, **227**
Offense, sex
  against children, 225–227
  and pornography, 228
Older age and sex. *See* Aging process
Oocyte, 50, 52
Oogenesis, 50
Oophorectomy, **95**
Oral contraception. *See* Birth control pills
Oral-genital contact, 9, 143–144, 184,
    205. *See also* Cunnilingus; Fellatio
Oralism, sexual. *See* Oral-genital contact
Orgasm, 158–159, **160–172**
  blocks against, 160, 171, 276
  capacity, 137, 142, 161, 169, 171,
    203–204, 208
  clitoral vs. vaginal, 162, 277
  delaying, 137, 171, 271
  excitement phase, **162–166**
  female, 162, 166
  female dysfunction in, 273–277
  importance of, 160, 171, 264
  and length of, 160, 168
  intromission, **137**
  male capacity, 142, 171

male dysfunction in premature ejacula-
    tion, 271
male dysfunction in retarded ejaculation,
    272
  in marital adjustment, 160
  during menstruation, 61
  multiple, 142, 161, 169, 171, 202, 208
  nocturnal. *See* Nocturnal emission
  orgasmic phase, **168–169**
  pain during, 278
  plateau phase, **166–168**
  refractory period, **169**
  resolution phase, **169–170**
  simultaneous, 170–172
  statistics regarding, 202
Orgasmic platform, 166, 168, 170
Ova. *See* Ovum
Ovaries, Ovarian
  congested, 305
  description and function of, 50–53
  follicles. *See* Follicles, ovarian
  surgical removal of (oophorectomy), **95**
"Oversexed." *See* Nymphomania; Satyriasis
Ovulation, 30, 50, 61
  inhibition of, 104, 105
  initial, 27
  an menopause, 63
  temperature change at, 108
Ovum, 23, 50
  fertilization of, 70–72
  after fertilization. *See* Implantation of
    ovum
Oysters, alleged aphrodisiac, 151

Pap smear test, 299
Paraphilia, **218**
Paresis, 292, 294
Parthenogenesis, 85
Parturition. *See* Birth; Childbirth
Pediculosis pubis, 302
Pedophilia, **225–227**
"Peeping Tom," 221
Pelvic Inflammatory Disease (PID), 291
Penetration, penile. *See* Intercourse, sexual;
    Penis
Penicillin, in VD treatment, 291, 292
Penis. *See also* Erection, penile
  cancer of, 42, 299
  description and development, 23, 30,
    39–45
  disorders in, 299
  in foreplay, 143
  in sexual response, 39–40, 160–165,
    166, 169, 170
  size, 39–40
  stimulation of, 139, 143
  "trapped" in coition, 41
  VD infection of, 292, 296
Penis captivus, 41
Period. *See* Menstruation

Perspiratory reaction, coital, **170**
Perversion, sexual. *See* Variance
Petting, 62, 141, 201–202, 204, 252. *See also* Sex, foreplay
    marital, 188, 205
    premarital, 141, 183, 202, 205
Phallus. *See* Penis
Pill, The. *See* Birth control pills
Pinta, 297
Pituitary gland, **22**, 30, 83, 252
PKU (Phenylketonuria), 74
Placenta, 79–80, 82
Pleasuring, 267
Polar body, **50**
Population control, 92
Pornography, 227–231
    effect of, on children, 228
    legal aspects of, 227
    as link to sex crime, 228, 229
    patrons and sources of, 230, 231
    President's Commission on, 228, 229, 230
Positions
    birth, 82
    coital, 144–150
"Postpartum blues," 82
Potassium nitrate, 155
Potency, 40, 267, 268. *See also* Impotence
Precoital fluid, 39
Pregnancy, 73–77. *See also* Conception; Fertilization
    activities during, 74–75
    coitus during, 75
    duration of, 80
    false, 85
    hormonal maintenance of, 30–31
    without intercourse, 85–86
    premarital, 5, 6, 9, 10, 183. *See also* Illegitimacy
    prevention. *See* Abortion; Abstinence, sexual; Contraception; Sterilization
    signs of, 74
    spacing of, 92
    spontaneous termination of (percentages), 98
    tests, 74
Premarital coitus
    attitudes toward, 5–16, 141, 194, 195–199, 202
    and contraception, 6
    deterrents to, 10
    incidence and frequency, 5, 205–207
    with prostitutes, 206, 236
Premarital pregnancy. *See* Illegitimacy
Premature ejaculation, 137, **267**, 271–272
Prenatal development, of the male and female genitalia, 22–27, 77–80
Prepuce
    clitoral, 26, 56(fig.), 57
    penile, 26, **41**, 42(fig.), 271
President's Commission on Obscenity and Pornography, 228, 229, 230

Primary sexual characteristics. *See* Genitalia
Progesterone (progestin)
    in birth control pills, 105
    in fertilization, 50
    functions of, **31**
    in menstrual cycle, 31, 60
Promiscuity, 236
    homosexual, 253
    and sex education, 5–6, 10
    and STD, 289, 296
Prostate gland
    description and function of, 38, 39(fig.)
    disorders in, 272, 278, 300, 303
    in sexual response, 38, 160, 169
Prostatic fluid, 38
Prostatitis, 303
Prostitution, 236–238
    legal aspects of, 237
    and premarital sexual behavior, 206, 236
Pseudocyesis, 85
Pseudoexhibitionism, 221
Puberty (Pubescence), 27–30, 180, 181, 183
    in boys, 29–30
    in girls, 27–28, 58
    use of Pill during, 105
Pubic hair, 27, 30, 57

Rape, 238–240
    legal aspects of, 239–240
    male homosexual, 238
    and "morning-after" pill, 109
    and pornography, 228–229
    prevention, 239
    statutory, **238**
    trauma of, 240, 278
Reduction division (cellular), 38, 50
Religious belief
    and abortion, 98
    influence on diverse forms of sexual behavior, 9, 204, 205, 233
    influence on sexual attitudes, 7–9, 199–200, 255
    of sex offenders, 233
    and sexual functioning, 270
Reproduction. *See also* Fertilization
    asexual, 85
    organs and systems. *See* Genitalia
Respiration, in sexual response, 170
Revolution, sexual, 196, 198
Rhythm method, 108
"Rubbers." *See* Condom

Sadism, 219
"Safe" period (birth control), 108
    impregnation during, 52, 108
    rhythm method, 108
    temperature method, 108

Saline abortion, 102
Salpingectomy
    partial, 94
    total, 96
Salpingitis, 291
Saltpeter, 153
Sanger, Margaret, 92, 110
Satyriasis, 234–236
Scabies, **302**
Scopophilia, 221
Scrotum:
    development and function of, 25, 30,
        36–37(fig.)
    disorders and infections of, 303, 304
    in sexual response, 143, 165, 167, 170
    in vasectomy, 96
Secondary sexual characteristics, 27–30,
    31, 97
Self-stimulation. *See* Masturbation
Semen, **38**
    description of, 38–39
Seminal fluid, 38–39, 169
    after vasectomy, 96
Seminal vesicles, 38, 39(fig.)
    in sexual response, 169
Seminiferous tubules, 36, 37(fig.)
Sensate focus, 267
Sex, Sexual
    abnormalities. *See* Variance; Venereal
        disease
    adjustment in marriage. *See* Marital
        adjustment
    "appeal," 200
    arousal, 135–144
    attitudes. *See* Attitudes, sexual
    determination, at conception, 22
    drive, and aging, 63, 64
    drive, after sterilization, 96, 97
    drive, differences in, 188, 200, 202–203
    drive, female, 63, 134, 188, 202–203
    drive, male, 45, 200, 202
    drive, misdirected, 5
    drive, peaks (male-female), 188, 202
    drive, and race, 199
    drive, after sterilization, 97
    dysfunction. *See* Dysfunction, sexual;
        Education, sex
    ethics, 7–9, 14–18, 195–199
    fantasy, 134, 137–139
    flush, **45**, 166, 169, 170
    foreplay, 141–143, 188, 252
    glands. *See* Ovaries; Testes; Hormones
    ignorance, 4–7
    inadequacy. *See* Dysfunction, sexual
    intercourse. *See* Intercourse, sexual
    "moron," 273
    offenders. *See* Offenders, sex
    and older people. *See* Aging process
    oral-genital. *See* Oral-genital contact
    primal, 27, 143–144, 184–205, 252
    reassignment surgery, 223
    response cycle, 162, 168

revolution, 196, 198
role inversion. *See* Transsexualism
secondary characteristics, 27–30, 32, 58
stimuli, 126. *See also* Aphrodisiacs
therapy, 137
unresponsiveness, 275–276
Sexually transmitted disease (STD),
    288–299. *See also* Venereal disease
    and ignorance, 6
    and pregnancy, 76
    and birth control, 107
Shaft, penile, 40, 41
"Signatures, doctrine of," **151**
Skin disorders. *See* Dermatoses
Smegma, **42**, 58
Somatic cells, 70
Spanish Fly, 152
Sperm, **36**, 38
    count, per ejaculation, 23, 44
    count, reduced, 72
    maturation of, 31
    migration, 85
    production of, onset, 30, 38
    after vasectomy, 97
    X- and Y-bearing, differences in, 71(fig.)
Spermatocyte, 38
Spermatogenesis (sperm production), 36,
    38, 252
Spermatogonia, 36
Spermatozoa. *See* Sperm
Sterility
    disorders causing, 72
    temporary, in men, 72
Sterilization, 94–97
    for men, 96–97
    for women, 94–96
"Stone ache," 305
Suction abortion, 101
"Sweating" process, vaginal, 55,
    163–165(fig.)
Swinging, 186, 233–234
Syphilis, 288, 291–**294**
    congenital, 76, 294
    nonvenereal, 297

Techniques, sexual, 135–144
Temperature method of birth control, 108
Testes, Testicles
    animal, as aphrodisiac, 32, 51
    congested, 165, 167
    development and function of, 23,
        36–38, 37(fig.)
    disorders and infection of, 291, 303
    hormonal production in, 31
    one only, 36, 304
    in sexual response, 143, 165, 167, 170
    surgical removal of. *See* Castration
    undescended, 36, 304
Testosterone
    function of, 31
    in homosexuals, 251

Tinea crusis, 302
Transsexualism, 223–225
Transvestism, 222
Treponema pallidum, 292
Trichomoniasis, 298
Tubal ligation, 94, 95(fig.)
Tumescence. *See* Erection, penile
Turner's symdrome, 306
"Tying of tubes." *See* Tubal ligation; Vasectomy
Tyson's glands, 42

Umbilical cord, 82
Urethra
    disorders in, 290
    in prenatal development, 26
    in sexual response, 54, 139, 165, 169
Urethral bulb, 169
Urethritis, 290
Urination
    pain or difficulty, female, 290, 296
    pain or difficulty, male, 290
Uterus, Uterine, 52–53
    abnormal bleeding from, 304
    contractions, in orgasm, 53, 166
    cramping, 60. *See also* Menstruation
    displacement of, 305
    fetal attachment to. *See* Implantation
    in labor, 80
    in pregnancy, childbirth, 53, 80
    in sexual response, 61, 164, 165
    tubes. *See* Fallopian tubes

Vacuum curettage, 101
Vagina, Vaginal
    anomalies in, 304
    description and function of, 54–55
    disorders and infections of, 278, 291, 297–299
    lubrication, 55, 163–165(fig.)
    painful contractions of, 277
    prenatal development of, 23
    in sexual response, 55, 139–140, 163–164, 166, 168, 170
Vaginismus, 57, 277
Vaginitis, 302–303
Van Emde Boas, 16
Variance, sexual, 216–243
    viewpoints toward, 7–9, 128, 185, 203–204, 218–219
Vas deferens, Vas, 37(fig.), 38, 96–97, 169

sterilization via, 96–97
Vasectomy, 96–97
Vasocongestion, **163**, 164, 165, 167, 169–170
Vas sclerosing, **97**
VD. *See* Venereal disease
Venereal disease, 289–297. *See also* Sexually transmitted disease
    condom as preventive in, 290
    sex education, correlated with, 6
    teenage victims of, 183, 289
Vestibule, 24(fig.), 26, 54, 298
Vibrator, in sexual arousal, 140
Vicarious menstruation, 61
Virgin birth, 85–86
Virginity
    attitudes toward, 8, 9, 55, 238
    chastity and carcinoma, 299
    hymen as proof of, 55
    purity equated with, 8
Voice-change, in males, 30–31
    after castration, 97
Voyeurism, **221**
Vulva
    description of, 26, 54
    disorders and infections of, 291, 296, 298–299
    in sexual response, 57–58, 143, 160, 171
    surgical removal of, 58

Wassermann test, 292
"Wet dreams." *See* Nocturnal emission
Wife-swapping. *See* Mate-swapping
Withdrawal. *See* Coitus interruptus
Wolffian ducts, 23
Womb. *See* Uterus

X chromosome, anomalies, 306
    in fertilization, 23, 70

Y chromosome, anomalies, 306
    in fertilization, 23, 70
Yohimbine, 152
Youth
    alleged moral decay among, 5, 10
    attitudinal formation in, 127, 180–183

Zygote, 77